RIVER OF FIRE

RIVER OF FIRE

THE CLYDEBANK BLITZ

John MacLeod

BIRLINN

First published in 2010 by
Birlinn Limited
West Newington House
10 Newington Road
Edinburgh
EH9 1QS

www.birlinn.co.uk

ISBN: 978 1 84341 049 2

940·5341432

British Library Cataloguing-in-Publication Data
A catalogue record for this book is available from the British Library

Typeset by Iolaire Typesetting, Newtonmore
Printed and bound by MPG Books Ltd, Bodmin

For

Mrs Agnes I. Kinnis

Clydeside evacuee of the Second World War

Teacher of Primary 1B at Scotstoun Primary School
1971–72
where she taught me my letters
and
Teacher of Primary 7B at Jordanhill College School
1977–78
where she taught me to fly

CONTENTS

LIST OF ILLUSTRATIONS

PREFACE

The Clydebank Blitz, and what Glasgow and the towns of the Clyde coast endured during the Second World War, has fascinated me since I was a dislocated Highland child – a son of the Free Church manse – growing through the 1970s in the western reaches of Glasgow from infant to adolescent.

When I began school, at Scotstoun, in April 1971, the war itself had ended only a quarter-century before and was still very close to us, in a way hard for my generation's children to appreciate. We now see most keen interest in these things, from the battle for national survival through the darkness of the Third Reich to the hardships and simple, doughty values and good humour of the Home Front, as those who personally endured those years and witnessed those realities, especially as adult experience, quietly slip from us with each passing year.

And we must never forget what we, as a nation and indeed as a civilisation, owe to those men and women – and indeed to many who were then but boys and girls – in a war of unparalleled savagery. This war the criminal state of Nazi Germany had criminally launched; this war she very nearly and criminally won; and this war she lost only after untold atrocities and a cold-blooded endeavour in genocide that will flame to the end of this world in the annals of infamy.

I am grateful to Hugh Andrew, Andrew Simmons and all the resourceful and unfailingly cheerful staff at Birlinn for giving me the opportunity to write this book. And I especially wish to thank Provost Denis Agnew, Mrs Joan Baird, Mrs Susan Holmes, Mr Hector Kearns, Mr John McNeill JP and Mrs Helen McNeill, the Reverend Peggy Roberts and all friends in Clydebank, all those who have gladly taken time to speak to me or to write with details of their own recollections or their family experience, and the staff and resources of West Dunbartonshire Council for their invaluable help in illustrating this book. I also deeply appreciate the kindness of Mr Billy Kay, a distinguished broadcaster, sage and scholar of Scottish life and culture, for supplying a recording of his important 1981 Radio Scotland oral history of the Clydebank Blitz, the best documentary on that experience which will ever be broadcast. And – I write this with deepest sadness – my gratitude, too, to the late Reverend Donald MacLean, for many years Free Presbyterian minister of Glasgow, who spoke to me a few weeks before his lamented death on 13 August 2010: though ninety-five years old, he was as sharp, buoyant and splendid as ever.

I am also indebted to the good people of Carradale, Argyll and Bute, and particularly to Mrs April Simpson – first cousin of James MacKinven, the last of his near kin and who knew him well – for entrusting me with a complete copy of his surviving papers and photograph, as well as poems previously unpublished and in his memory by Naomi Mitchison and Joan Adeney Easdale. A fine photograph of Jim and his father was kindly supplied by Miss Christine Ritchie. I am most grateful for all their help generally in Carradale to Mr Martin and Mrs Chris Mears. I have not made much of James MacKinven – he was not from Clydebank, nor did he die there – but he is worth memorialising, both from the waste of real talent and from the solemnity of being in the wrong place at the wrong time.

I must also with great gratitude again acknowledge the time and sacrifice again of Dr Robert Dickie FRCGP DRCOG; and on this occasion of Mr Bill Heaney, a great son of Dunbartonshire and one of the most respected journalists in Scotland – as well as a senior pillar of the Labour movement and sometime high counsel to Scotland's second First Minister, the Rt Hon. Henry McLeish MP, MSP – for taking the time and trouble to read, in early drafts, these chapters. Dr Dickie and Mr Heaney sacrificed much of their scant leisure time to this chore and made very many helpful suggestions, as well as pointing out egregious errors, occasional blunders in the congruity of my English, the odd lapse of taste or judgement and still odder moments of entire opacity. I also appreciated the encouragement of Mr Andrew Murray, Tolsta, at a difficult point in the project in March 2010.

Responsibility for any mistakes in this work, nevertheless, is mine and mine alone. Anyone who wishes to correct me on a given point, or to supply further material or anecdote for a future edition, is most welcome to contact me at the address below.

While I have taken time to detail in some measure what was endured by the people of Glasgow and other communities – especially Cardross, Dumbarton, Paisley and Port Glasgow and in particular Greenock – under the assault of the Luftwaffe in the spring of 1941, this book is unashamedly centred on Clydebank, the people of Clydebank, and what befell them as a social and human experience in the Blitz. It is neither a military history nor a detailed and technical account of what the German air force – whose inept leadership did more than any other talon of the Nazi state to lose Hitler the war, admittedly with much fatuous meddling from the Führer himself – actually did in the skies over central Scotland. Much new, interesting documentation from the contemporary Luftwaffe perspective has emerged in recent years, but it is for other writers to explore and emphatically for such as can fluently read German.

I have devoted much time in the early pages of the book to describing the rise of Clydebank and both the human character and the physical environment of the town, which was effectively destroyed for ever in March 1941. I have besides also devoted some space to the rise of the Scottish Labour movement with which the town, and wider Clydeside, is so associated, and which had some bearing on her preparations for an aerial assault and, perhaps still more, why there has been so little recognition of her ordeal in a wider Britain. It is important to me that this remarkable community – which I have long loved – is not cast as a mere victim; and that people should know much of that town, that order and its values largely obliterated in March 1941. The values endure: the townscape and its 1941 community were lost to Scotland for always.

But I have also, in the penultimate chapter, demonstrated quietly how two great German cities – as Air Marshall Arthur 'Bomber' Harris pitilessly put it – having helped to sow the wind, would reap (and that tenfold) the whirlwind of terror bombing; and touched at various points in the text on what was endured, in particular, by the people of London.

Even in a new and self-consciously progressive century, ordinary men and women – regardless of politics, creed or colour – have still died, by the thousand and by means of still more terrible technologies, from vainglory and vengeance in the air. And, even in Britain and in America, we have still not cured ourselves of rulers – as the past decade dreadfully attests – possessed by that 'Jupiter complex' and who exult in dispensing it. If a future government be tempted again to hurl casual, politically cheap death from the skies, it is important to remember how once it was visited – well within living memory – over Scotland and especially over the coasts of Clyde; and how blood might, in providence, be again visited upon our streets, and upon us and upon our children.

John MacLeod,
'Drover's Rest',
Maryhill,
Isle of Lewis,
September 2010
jm.macleod@btinternet.com

I

THE JOYS OF THE TOWN

Come, let us remember
The joys of the town,
Gay cars and bright buses
That go up and down.
Shop windows and playgrounds
And swings in the park,
And street lamps that twinkle
In rows after dark.

And let us remember
The chorus that swells,
From hooters and hammers
And whistles and bells;
From fierce-panting engines
And clear-striking clocks,
And sirens of vessels
Afloat in the docks.

Come, let us now lift up
our voices in praise,
And to the Creator
A thanksgiving raise,
For towns with their buildings
Of stone, steel and wood,
For people who love them
And work for their good.

We thank thee, O God,
For the numberless things,
And friends and adventures
Which every day brings;
O, may we not rest
Until all that we see
In towns and in cities
Is pleasing to Thee.

Doris M Gill, 1940. This children's hymn was still widely sung, in the sugary 'Moderate' tradition of the Church of Scotland, in Glasgow schools in my own childhood. They have their own bland truth – the things that, in a lost Scotland, entranced boys and girls – but such regular morning worship is no longer a feature of our non-denominational state schools.

1

A GRIEF INTERRED

If you did not know what had happened here, almost 70 years ago, you would all but cringe from the ugly jumble of buildings as the train whines into the station. You have the impression of rather too many buildings, and bits of buildings, and a jumble of styles – most concrete, block, brick and stucco – and the impact is all the more immediate from this high-level station, giving you the sense of chaotic roofscape. You are struck at once by how everything seems slightly too close together; and by a short blunt stretch of tenement, indubitably pre-Great War and in good red sandstone, that seems at once noble and interrupted, as if but all that was ever completed, or but the remnant of something destroyed.

Things look better down on the street. Now the place seems less claustrophobic than cosy, less tired than experienced. You can imagine friendship here: wifies meeting with bags of shopping; talk of stair-washing; cheerful conversations bellowed from one window to the next. But you have already spotted the ranked taxis, and advance to the diesel-rattling cab at the front. The driver is thickset, getting on in years. He seems thrown when you ask for the memorial, and for the cemetery – not the new one, you assert; the old one – and it is as if he did not know where it is.

It is a grey day in mid January. Heavy and unwonted snows over the festive season have not long receded. We chug uphill, by the Clyde Shopping Centre, by angular post-war schools, by acres of modern public housing. We join the main road – the A82, that remarkable highway from central Glasgow to Inverness – on that sweep of it, from Knightswood to the Vale of Leven, where everyone knows it as the Boulevard and which still has a curved, dualled and unmistakably 1930s' charm.

We are well on it before two burial grounds are in sight. The one north of the road is sprawling, manicured, modern, announced by the angular shrine of the local crematorium. The one you want looms to your left. It is walled, thick with trees, mysterious. There are great iron gates on an inward sweep of wall and a sombre lodge. Though, still on the main road, you look hard as the driver pauses, hesitates, demands again if you are sure, and then turns in, there is no signage for the memorial or any indication to draw the interest of those who remember what happened to this community, one moonbright night in March, when the Germans came.

Unexpectedly, the taxi-driver bowls right in to the cemetery, and goes bumping up a central avenue, looking oddly about him. If he be indeed local, he seems abysmally uninformed. He also seems suspicious, though his mood lightens when you settle the fare in hard cash. No, he does not know where the monument is; no, he cannot wait; and, no, he has no radio to send another cab to retrieve you later – but, yes, the nearest railway station is just down by . . . In fact, he can scarcely wait to be gone, and it is weeks later before it dawns on you that these days, in a very different society and especially around such an urban sprawl as Greater Glasgow – with a mildly deserved reputation for drugs, violence and organised crime – those who operate cars for hire do not like being taken to odd, out of the way places by strange men from out of town.

The cemetery is huge, thoughtful and faintly oppressive, with great Victorian headstones in abiding memorial to this businessman and that good, respectable civic functionary most conscious of his goodness and his respectability. There is much evergreen shrubbery, and tall trees with dark birds croaking in them and crawling ivy. You cannot see what you seek. You pad back down to the lodge to enquire, but there is no life to be seen – just traffic hurtling tirelessly along the Boulevard, a scent of salt and industry as the river beyond kisses the sea and the steady trundle of tyres over the high bridge to Erskine.

Finally you find it by entire accident, retracing your steps and taking the first left turn. It is smaller than it appears in photographs, and oddly understated, despite the sombre gilded inscription and the old burgh arms and the carved stone wreaths, and its purpose – to honour many unnamed, unclaimed dead below it; anonymous bodies and bits of bodies – seems distinctly compromised by a big new plaque, flat on the ground before it and remorselessly listing name after name of folk already, for the most part, in known and memorialised places of rest.

In truth, the monument stands at the head of but one great grave, stretching down the brae in a patchy trail of forlorn and lesser headstones. Some commemorate entire families. Most honour individuals; some, a married couple. Some are so obscured by tangled ivy you have to pull it back to read faded, forgotten words. One warden killed in the line of duty that night, Albert Bowman, is but honoured by a patch of inscribed concrete, embedded in the ground. Again and again you see the same date; read the same mantra: 'Killed By Enemy Action'. But scarcely any of these stones seems to be maintained. Most, you suspect, are no longer visited. You have to be well in your seventies to have any memory of someone who lies here; you would have still to live here, or not far away, to be able regularly to come by and stand amidst these trees and by the scent of estuary, and remember your loved one – and so very many people, entire families and streets of families, had to leave this place, after that night the bombers came.

The walk to the station, though scarcely five minutes, is not easy. There are no pavements, the traffic is most rapid and you need your wits about you safely to negotiate a slip road. When you reach it, there is a protracted wait for a westbound train. When it comes, the compartment jostles with kindly older people, a happy toddler and its doting teenage parents. You have to change several stops later, by which time the schools are out and black-clad teenagers jostle the platform, in the timeless noise of liberated scholars and in the half-recalled exuberance of the west-coast accent – at once, at least in these ears, both redolent of childhood and a remorseless, daily, Teuchter-baiting oppression – but as you catch a new train and chug westwards again, amidst trees and soon by the wintry shimmer of the sea, you leave in moments industrial Scotland behind.

You alight again. It is many years since you stood in this village and were told the story behind that gaunt tower ('It was bombed in the war,' said Bill Davis casually, 'by the Germans . . .', when you were 11, a midge-lurking night that remote summer of 1977, and fishing with him in the burn by Burnside Cottage), and you have to follow a gaggle of youngsters off the train and into the nearest newsagent and await your turn before you can charm directions at the till.

It lies at the east of the village, beyond an inn and a golf course and across that same stream of the moist July evening scooping for eels, trout and sticklebacks; and when you first glimpse it – tall and stately, in an elevated country churchyard; it looks intact and still at least a weekly haunt for worship of the Most High – it is hard at first to credit that Hitler ever bothered, so remote are you here from the machinery of war and the inviting target of a great city. Not indeed, one supposes, that he meant this assault on one quiet, parochial endeavour for salvation and grace.

But the clouds shift as you approach, and the rays of the setting sun gain momentary brilliance, and you see there *is* just the tower of an old parish church, and the shattered remnants of not much else beyond.

Only one gate now hangs where once there were two. You clamber mossy steps. It is very peaceful. That great Gothic tower – as a plaque attests, though it does not explain what happened here, that night the aeroplanes came – has long been made safe. But the mass of the building has gone; the whole levelled to sill height and left as a memorial to one night of horror in a place of quiet decency.

You might not know, but you would see this gaunt ruin of a church and wonder; and look over the road, and ask yourself why you saw nothing but modern houses. And then something would strike you in this graveyard itself. A heap of broken monument, and smaller bits of monument, piled in the corner. A table-tomb buckled half out of the ground, as if by some fantastic force – but long ago, to judge by the lichen. And the stones still standing in serried rows – but askew, tilted, or leaning just a little backwards – and then see that there are bits missing, an urn vaporised here and some bauble of granite lost there.

And then, with chill horror – as you reach the right angle – you see lumps gouged out of the very faces of tombstones, as if machine-gunned from the air, or blasted all at once and with enormous power from just behind you and to your right, from the very church itself in an instant of apocalypse.

Almost on cue, a siren wails. Or a whistle, rather, rising and industrial, with all the more power and poignancy over water. Your head says that it is only the shipyard whistle – we scarcely speak, in the twenty-first century, of shipyards in the plural now – from Port Glasgow. But you remember other shipyard whistles, as you walked from school; and that still eerier sound, on documentaries watched in boyhood, those programmes about the war everyone grown up seemed to remember and no one seemed eager to discuss.

And were you not aware – and had you never heard – of Clydebank, and Clydeside, and Cardross, and the war, and the Germans, and the bombers – you would still know that, many years ago, something terrible had been done here. You might wonder what had been wrought, and why. You might wonder if anyone had survived.

On a fine moonlit evening on Thursday 13 March 1941, just after 9 p.m., the first of 236 German bombers converged on Clydeside. The operation had been planned for weeks. That morning, as local intelligence already knew, the Luftwaffe had sent some weather-reconnaissance missions over central Scotland: for most of the day, silent, unseen, Luftwaffe radio-navigation beams had locked on Clydebank and, in particular, the vital operations of the war effort against the Third Reich – shipyards, factories, oil storage depots, this base and that plant.

The aircraft – most were Junkers 88s and Heinkel 111s – had taken off from airfields by Hitler's 'Atlantic Wall', on the western shores of occupied Europe – from bases in northern France, Holland, Germany proper and (in the final wave of assault) Norway and Denmark. As sirens began to howl, they crossed the British coast by Northumbria, or headed in over Aberdeenshire. Some navigated by the Clyde Valley; others, from the north, first located Loch Lomond, and then steered themselves to their field of duty by the Vale of Leven. By ten past nine, over the western suburbs of Glasgow, over Dumbarton and Drumchapel and – especially – over the densely housed and most productive little town of Clydebank, the bombs had begun to fall. And the next night, it happened all over again.

This was not the only Luftwaffe mission over Britain on 13 March. That night also saw determined attacks on Liverpool, Birkenhead and Hull, with heavy fatalities. Nor was it the first bombing of Scotland: the war had already seen attacks, most sporadic and some even by lone aircraft, since almost the first weekend of the war. The very first death of a British civilian by enemy action was at Bridge of Wraith, Orkney. The very first bombs to fall in the west of Scotland – on 11 July 1940 – had been by Salen on the Isle of Mull. Thereafter, vague and apparently ill-thought attacks had killed by the ones and twos and little groups, in Greenock and Yoker, Partick and Gourock, Scotstoun and Campbeltown. There had even been two lamentably unsuccessful raids on the vital British Aluminium works by Fort William – the last only that morning.

But this was of a whole new order for Scotland. This – and in particular for

Clydebank – was pitiless, saturation bombing. It was of such ferocity that the explosions could be heard clearly at Bridge of Allan in Stirlingshire; of such frenzy that the glow in the night sky could be clearly seen from rural Aberdeenshire, from the Inner Hebrides, from the coast of Northern Ireland and even from RAF aircraft circling over Dyce, only a few miles from the centre of Aberdeen on the other side of the country. And it was so terrifying that, even today, nearly 70 years later, there are still hundreds of survivors, all over Scotland and indeed across the world – many then very small children – haunted by the experience, prone to flashbacks and nightmares and bouts of depression, who can still eerily mimic the strange, throbbing, coming-and-going rumble of Nazi planes.

The wider damage and bloodshed was such – in Glasgow alone, on 13 and 14 March, 647 people were killed – that it is too easy to lose focus on Clydebank itself.

The town was all but destroyed. From one geographically small community, 528 people were dead; 617 seriously injured. Hundreds – perhaps thousands – more were superficially hurt and cut. Of some 12,000 dwellings – including tenement blocks as well as villas and semi-detached homes – only 7 were left entirely undamaged. Four thousand homes were completely destroyed: 4,500 would be uninhabitable for months.

The Luftwaffe besides flattened or substantially wrecked nine local schools. The bombs hit churches without respect of denomination – Roman Catholic and Episcopalian, Kirk and Free Presbyterian – though the loss of schools and places of worship was, for the duration of the war at least, academic, with at least 35,000 people homeless and almost fantastic dislocation. The morning of 14 March saw thousands and thousands of dazed, filthy, bloodied survivors shambling along Dumbarton Road into Glasgow and, by the night of Saturday 15 March – as official records would eventually reveal – it was reckoned the near-fabulous total of over 40,000 people had left the town, amidst much chaos. Meanwhile, as buried survivors were yet extricated – often at great peril to the workers involved – something irredeemably squalid lingers from accounts of the official mass burial of Clydebank Blitz victims. The authorities did not supply even cardboard coffins, so that bodies were lowered into wet Dunbartonshire earth in the indignity of bed sheets and kitchen string; almost as soon as the interment had actually begun, the official party of politicians, bureaucrats and clergy hastened quickly away.

There is still a place called Clydebank, and many who survived March 1941 still live there. But thousands who fled never returned; and, of those who did, many only after months or years, and to different streets, and to wholly new streets. Even today – it is in the direct flight-path to Glasgow Airport – the physical destruction of the old Clydebank is obvious at a glance from the air. The specific human community, the one that had retired for the evening on Thursday 13 March 1941, was smashed beyond recovery in a single night.

Clydebank grieved for herself, and she grieves still. Though determined German bombing would continue into May 1941 – Glasgow, Port Glasgow,

Paisley, Greenock, Dumbarton, assorted towns on the Ayrshire coast and even (and with considerable destruction) the quiet village of Cardross, a few miles east of Helensburgh – the savagery of that raid on Clydebank was never in Scotland repeated. The whole campaign remains Scotland's greatest human disaster in modern history. And it is rightly known – both in all and in the particular focus of those two nights of terror – as the Clydebank Blitz.

What befell Clydeside generally in those dark days of the Second World War is a tale of almost unbelievable horror – a child's hand found in a gutter; a lady's smart laced boots later recovered, with her feet still inside them; the elderly workman who returned, after a fraught night shift, to find all but a handful of his huge family, through four generations, had been obliterated – of profound humanity, at both its most heroic and its meanest; and of history itself, as the Second World War and all it entailed recedes further and further into living memory.

For my generation – born in the late 1960s, at the tail end of the post-war baby boom – we readily overlook how, in our own adult life, the Second World War has retreated into true history from a recent and still defining collective national experience.

At the age of 84, our present Queen is the last head of state or government (save, arguably, Pope Benedict XVI, who was briefly forced as a youth into German uniform) actually to have served in the Second World War. Yet, from 1935 to 1993, an unbroken succession of American presidents had fought. As recently as 1996, a 73-year-old veteran, Bob Dole, was a candidate for the Oval Office, and – though she did not herself toil in any capacity – Margaret Thatcher dominated Britain throughout the 1980s with attitudes forged by the crucible of war.

Early in 2010, you have to be at least 82 lawfully to have seen active service for Britain in the Second World War and practically 70 to have even the dimmest memory of its end.

Yet, in my own schooldays, classmates included the small sons of 40-something veterans. We were taught by men who had actually fought; by women who had lived through the rigours of rationing and the wider perils and indignities of the 'Home Front'. Their presence lent a heavy emotion to the annual little Service of Remembrance, when the Head Boy and Head Girl trooped forth from a silent assembly to lay a wreath of poppies below the bronze plaque, at the school portals, to the honoured Jordanhill dead.

But they were people of a quiet, disciplined otherness, in a Scottish state-school environment that, even under the Callaghan government, was – at least in one Glasgow academy – then still largely unchanged from the 1940s: strict uniform codes, learning by rote, daily morning worship and corporal punishment. Bright, be-gowned and remote, their values – duty, deference, good manners, social order, a conforming middle-class Christianity and entire disdain for the 'frivolous' – were already besieged by 1980, even as we continued to line up of a morning with our hymn books, or strip to our waists for boot-camp PE, or rehearse obediently for that summer's outing in Gilbert and Sullivan.

We ourselves were really rather bored with the war – especially when those involved, like Mr Forsyth next door – serene, worldly, an architect, who once let slip he had served with Bomber Command – were so loath to talk about it. And, though we knew vaguely that Mr Graveson – a gentle Modern Languages teacher who could barely control his class – had gone through something awful nearly 40 years before, we continued to rib him regardless. (He died, suddenly and in harness, in 1984. Decades on, in dreadful regret, I learned that after some fraught mission or other – a POW break-out, or a Special Operations Executive exercise – he had been captured and tortured by the Gestapo.)

We quite forget that the troubled years of the Heath premiership – strikes, protests, sit-ins, the resurgent 'Troubles' of Northern Ireland, power cuts and the infamous 'three-day week' and 'oil shock' and rampant inflation and the specific threat of petrol-rationing – were, historically, nearer the Second World War than the Falklands conflict is to us now; which is why, in abiding folk-memory of hardship and deference, people then so meekly put up with it all.

And the folk-memory of Hitler's war – the perils of appeasing empires of evil; our woeful unpreparedness for the conflict in 1939 – remained potent in British politics until very late in the twentieth century. Mrs Thatcher and her Conservative government were twice re-elected, despite their contentious agenda and her highly abrasive and confrontational style, because the Labour Party twice and stubbornly went to the polls on a policy of unilateral nuclear disarmament. The stance, however high-minded, so alarmed the British public that hundreds of thousands of voters went against their own economic interests to keep Labour firmly out of government, as Conservative campaign materials – with their evocation of Churchill and the Battle of Britain – rather gave the impression that the Tories, if not quite Thatcher herself, had won the war single-handed.

We forget so much; or make assumptions – from our own understanding of the Second World War, or subsequent decades, today – about similar attitudes in the recent past. But for ordinary British people, the Second World War did not end overnight and in bright and shining peace. Austerity continued for years afterwards – partly because we struggled to pay off horrendous national debt; partly on account of the loss of so much shipping. Rationing would linger until 1954; 'National Service' – compulsory, two-year military con-scription for most young men – would endure, like hanging, into the 1960s. Britain still fought in the 1950s – in Korea; in Malaysia; in assorted and minor duties of global *gendarmerie* – and, through decades, we maintained a huge army on the Rhine for, of course, the ongoing burden of the 'Cold War' against the Soviet Union. Our air raid warning network would stay opera-tional into the 1990s – sirens adorned the already obsolete Edinburgh police boxes when I was a student – and, as West Germany was a NATO ally and the front-line against the Warsaw Pact, there was little enthusiasm for anti-German sentiment. ('We're quite pally with the Germans now,' my mother once crisply told us, driving us to school around 1976, up Southbrae Drive with its view of the cranes in nodding homage over the Clyde.)

In Scotland, the political impact had been almost immediate. In 1945, Willie Gallagher – incumbent Communist MP – was returned by a country mile for West Fife. In 1950, he was ousted by Labour's Willie Hamilton. (Ironically, Hamilton – by later standards a moderate, sober and socially conservative Labour MP – was by the 1980s a national hate figure, for his unabashed and vocal contempt for the Royal Family.) Communism remained a potent force in the trade unions and never quite lost an electoral toe-hold – Fife still has a Communist local councillor; even in the 1970s, it retained clout in Clydebank, perhaps another reason why its 1941 ordeal has so little national resonance.

And Second World War archaeology, so to speak, is extensive. On the perimeter of most Scottish towns – especially near the coast, or on prominences in the landscape – hundreds of decaying concrete installations are still to be found: gun emplacements, pill-boxes, watch-points and so on. In almost every street of pre-Great War bourgeois housing – Stornoway is a notable exception, distance rendering the freight uneconomic – the nubbles of severed iron can still be seen on low garden walls, where railings were cut down by the mile to be smelted into tanks, guns and so on for the 'war effort'. (But little of it actually was: most of Edinburgh's lovely wrought iron was finally dumped in the Forth, and by great public buildings, like the Palace of Holyrood House, the railings were oddly unmolested.)

And surprisingly few corners of the Scottish coast escaped some Nazi attention. The very first daylight bombing raid of the war on mainland Britain – on 1 July 1940 – was on Wick: 15 were killed, 8 of them children, and a local minister stared in horror as his little girl ran to the manse for her life, as machine-gun bullets tore up the street around her. On their way home from Clydebank in March 1941, another German aircrew emptied their last bombs behind the village of Arnol, on the west side of Lewis. One exploding 'Luftmine' did minor damage to what from 1964 became the conserved island 'black house', now in the care of Historic Scotland. Three other bombs left craters almost 40 feet across; more simply vanished into deepest peat, where they lie undetonated still. And, even today, an unearthed, unexploded bomb can cause Clydeside alarm, the evacuation of houses and a news item on *Reporting Scotland*.

Other social consequences are oddly forgotten. The war lasted six years, with enormous movement of people, great dislocation, whole new opportunities and extraordinary temptations. Far from home, family, church and community and former restraints, people did things they would not normally have done; meanwhile, children attained adulthood scarcely seeing their fathers or even their mothers and often schooled but fitfully by elderly, failing teachers, recalled hastily to service and in temporary and ill-suited facilities. (Across Scotland, and especially in the major cities, the best school buildings were commandeered for all sorts of military purposes.)

In the years after the war, marital breakdown, inadequate contraception, homosexuality, prostitution, and a shockwave of juvenile crime and widespread gang warfare became the stuff of hysterical discussion; far into the

1950s – like many other rural locales – childless Hebridean couples could readily secure unwanted infants for adoption after procedures we would now deem most cursory.

It is still fashionable, especially in Evangelical circles, to bewail the 1960s as the time when Britain definitively sank into an enduring Sodom and Gomorrah. But that is both to contrast it in righteous retrospect with the social backlash of the 1950s (when women retreated to the kitchen as headlines screamed with exemplary hangings, smothered infants or the latest homosexual show-trial) and to obscure the reality: that much of the 'permissive society' legislation of the late 1960s was but an honest if defeatist response to the moral collapse of the early 1940s and the Second World War. What society had largely ceased to regard as sinful could not indefinitely be regarded as criminal, but few, even today, care to admit that our Finest Hour did much to accelerate a post-Christian and much less cohesive society.

Our ethical view of the war has also changed more than we grasp. For one, too many now assess Allied commanders and Allied strategy with the righteous, armchair philosophy of those who have never lived in total war, never been bombed, never been shot at, or subsisted on scanty rations in a country fighting for its very life.

President Truman, for instance, is execrated for his decision in August 1945 to use atomic weapons – despite ample evidence that a sizeable faction of what by then passed for Japanese government vowed to fight on even after Hiroshima; that fanatical troops stormed the palace to stop him even as Emperor Hirohito broadcast the decision to surrender; that the war would otherwise have endured for at least a year; and at the cost of at least 100,000 Allied lives, to say nothing of Japanese ones.

And Air-Marshal Arthur 'Bomber' Harris and his forces (to say nothing, later, of American comrades in the endeavour) are likewise vilified for the 'saturation bombing' of German towns and cities, with untold loss of life: at Hamburg, alone, in July 1943, some 40,000 people – and perhaps many more – were killed; figures for the notorious raid on Dresden, in March 1945, range from just 25,000 to over 150,000.

Some even assert that Harris and his aircrews should be regarded as no more than war criminals, blithely unloading fire and death on helpless people. They forget how Britain found herself, after her best efforts to prevent it, waging a desperate war against an evil dictatorship; that, from June 1940, bombing of German war production (and, of necessity, German cities) was practically her only effective means of fighting back; that Britain did not start the terror-bombing; that public opinion made it politically essential; that subsequent alliance with Soviet Russia forced it diplomatically; and that the Germans were far from 'defenceless' until at least December 1944. And there is no moral equivalence between young men flying hundreds of miles into hostile territory, enduring flak and fighters, storm and fog to offload bombs and then, exhausted and like as not damaged, flying home again over enemy-occupied land and the chill North Sea . . . and well-fed guards far from any front line cramming naked men, women and children into gas chambers.

Of Britain's entire war losses – the total of men killed in action – a full 25 per cent had flown and died with Bomber Command: no special Bomber Command campaign-medal was ever struck, and of all the commanders-in-chief by war's end, Harris alone never received a peerage – though it is not clear whether it was spitefully denied him, or if he himself repudiated the suggestion after the insult to his men.

There are legitimate concerns, not entirely from complacent hindsight, about some aspects of British or Allied conduct in the war. Leopold, king of the Belgians, was scapegoated for the Dunkirk disaster, which was in no way his fault. The destruction in 1940 of much of the French fleet, by British ships, in Oran remains contentious. The Americans fought their entire campaign with racially segregated forces – not that one would know it, from such deft rewriting of history as is evident in, for instance, films like *The Dirty Dozen* or, more recently, *Pearl Harbor*. The Nuremberg trials were in many respects a monstrous example of 'victor's justice' – such as the presence of Soviet judges on the bench (despite her part in 1939, and such atrocities as the Katyn massacre), the express denial of the *tu quoque* defence and the imprisonment (and, for the hapless Jodl and Keitel, indeed execution) of honourable German generals. And, even in the summer of 2009, our treatment of surviving Gurkha veterans could embarrass a British government.

And we are also overapt to emphasise our part in the Second World War as a conscious moral crusade against Nazi terror and, in particular, Hitler's persecution of the Jews. A Scottish teenager today, studying his Higher History, would almost certainly cite this as a major war aim. It is difficult to explain that, in 1939, anti-Semitism was still significant in, at least, English life: Jews were widely denied membership in golf clubs, for instance. From the crisis of June 1940 many German Jewish refugees were, like all other 'enemy aliens', rounded up and interned for the duration; so many were lost at sea (most infamously in the *Arandora Star*, torpedoed by a U-boat off Ireland on 2 July 1940) to German torpedoes that the policy was shamefacedly abandoned.

It is also widely forgotten that even in the 1970s the 'Final Solution' had little place in British consciousness; indeed, the modern use of the term, 'Holocaust', dates only from an American-made 1978 TV mini-series of that name.

Indeed, the 'Final Solution', not least from the exigencies of the Cold War, was rapidly downplayed in the West after Nuremberg. General Jodl might have swung; but Wernher von Braun – who had used Jewish slave-labour for the V2 rocket programme – was bundled to America in all his expertise, became an honoured citizen and helped put man on the Moon. Very few who actually served as guards in Auschwitz, for instance, were ever even brought to trial, far less punished. Many who had done very nicely, thank you, from the manufacture of plant for Nazi death camps ended up as honoured West German industrialists. Only in the 1990s did determined prosecution of Nazi war criminals resume with significant vigour, and by then, inevitably, they were scant, elderly and had been mostly junior functionaries. (At the time of writing, the trial of 89-year-old John Demjanjuk – a Ukrainian who spent many years as a naturalised US citizen and most of the last two decades as the accused in some war crimes court or other – proceeds in Germany, on 27,900 counts of acting as accessory to murder and on the charge, yet definitively to be established, that he served as a guard at the Sobibor death camp.)

In Glasgow, over 30 years ago, the war was both still rather recent, rather raw and not so far beyond present normality. Many homes still boasted Anderson shelters as garden sheds. On some lamp-posts, the faded white lines – from days of blackout, when a touch of bright paint lent some visibility for cars and pedestrians – could yet be discerned. To this day, odd cracks and damage to walls, kerbs and so on can be seen in these western suburbs of Glasgow: in the 1970s, there were still mysterious gaps – a blaes football pitch between rows of Edwardian semis; or an incongruously modern building as an erratic amidst much older houses. We knew there had been bombs. We knew even – Mr Forsyth, whose semi-detached abutted our semi-detached, could point out the superficial damage to our own manse – that one had fallen very near by. When the new Clyde Shopping Centre opened at Clydebank – at a time when there were very few retail parks, as we now call them, and this one was deemed the last word in modernity – my mother frequently took us to it, and in a mural by local schoolchildren by the landscaped reach of the Forth and Clyde Canal that runs through the park, a German bomber featured on one fiery panel. It had the remote, faintly terrible air of a dragon, say, in some stained-glass window. But, as far as daily life went, the horror of March 1941 was very much a grief interred.

One or two incidents in those years did bring the Clydebank Blitz very close. Shortly after New Year 1977 – several months before my eleventh birthday – I was tripping down the stairs when the house and floor shook beneath me, as the district resounded to a mighty, distant explosion. The force was such that I almost lost my footing. My father burst from his study, looking alarmed, grim. A minute or two later, pausing only to don jacket and clerical collar – and refusing on any account to take myself – he was in the car, heading west over Anniesland Road and Kingsway. (He had immediately suspected – understandable, in the context of the time – an IRA atrocity, and that pastoral help might be needed.)

But most neighbours had other thoughts. They came out and stood in their gardens, talking quietly, glancing at the sky certain that, with perhaps terrible consequence, some long-buried German bomb had gone off. In fact, there were no casualties, and the event – if spectacular – was prosaic. Two small boys had flung up a crude gang-hut beside a whisky-bond in Yoker, lit a fire and then headed home for their 'piece'. The fire had spread and the piled casks of spirits had gone up – with the warehouse – in one resounding bang, with neither loss of life nor injury. The company subsequently sued the boys' parents; but the courts at length, several years down the line, refused finally to uphold the action.

A year or two after that, Scotstoun Primary School – where I had begun my
education in 1971, climbing socially three years later after determined parental
agitation – was put in almost comical alarm by two other little Glasgow lads. A
local woman with more imagination than sense had found a small unexploded
bomb – probably a German 'Thermite' incendiary and, over 30 years on, quite
harmless – and propped it up as an adornment in her rockery. Weeks or
months later, the passing pair could not resist. They entered her garden, made
off with their prize and bore it proudly into the school premises, where they
were confronted by an appalled mistress. 'Look what we found, Miss. We
think it's a bomb . . .'

But one thing – vague, nagging, dimly sensed – puzzled me as I grew towards
the next decade. Of late – especially as political and economic conditions have
begun eerily to remind us of them – it has become much less fashionable to
mock the Britain of the 1970s. It was certainly a gentler time, marked by much
more honest politics, unemployment that was by historic standards really quite
low, the dawn of modern conservation and environmental concerns, and quiet
improvement in race relations. Many more of us lived within walking distance
of work, shops and amenities, and most mothers did not then work, so that
few of us headed home at the end of a school day to an empty house and
newspapers could still moralise about hapless 'latch-key kids.'

But there was steady, at times rapid, inflation. Industrial relations were
always fraught and occasionally – especially at the end of the Heath or
Callaghan administrations – frightful. Winters were much colder, life much
drabber, our diet – for instance – much duller and our lifestyles far more
modest. There seemed always to be fearful awareness of prices and grown-ups
constantly fretted about money. Glasgow itself was still a drab city, oozing
neglect and decay. We were aware of the war. When Viscount Montgomery –
one of its last great commanders – died in April 1976 we watched his funeral,
live on television, with worshipful commentary. But we knew too as small
boys that the Germans, the French and even the Italians – those we had
vanquished – made, really, much better cars. We were assured that, whatever
the SNP might say, Scotland was too wee, too poor ever to govern herself. Yet
Britain unbroken seemed a land lost and stumbling.

It was still more evident, of course, to adults, especially those able for
themselves to see how now fared the lands we had occupied in 1945 – as John
Mackintosh, a highly regarded and gossipy Scots academic and, until his sadly
early death in 1978, a Labour MP, once related pawkily to David Steel, then
the new leader of the Liberal Party. Mackintosh was a convinced European
and

. . . loved to tell the tale – suitably embroidered – of how on the same day he had
addressed trade-union meetings in Frankfurt and Glasgow on the same theme of
brotherhood in Europe. In Frankfurt he had been met by a chauffeur-driven car
and taken to the union headquarters, where the glass doors had automatically
slid open, and he gave his talk in a warm, carpeted lecture room, complete with

visual aids. Catching a direct flight to Glasgow, he had to take a bus ride from the airport, make his way to the Keir Hardie Hall, climb the stone stairs with chipped dark-brown wall paint and settle in a room with rickety wooden chairs and a bare light bulb. At the end of his persuasive address, a voice said: 'But John, ye dinna understand. We're no goin' tae be dragged doon to their standards.'

Britain – Glasgow – certainly bore, in the 1970s, visible and human evidence of a country that had fought a world war. But everything suggested, even to a small boy, that by every sensible measure, she had actually lost it. As, indeed – soberly considered – we had.

There is an abiding British mythology of the Second World War, as sketched with cruel accuracy by such recent writers as Gordon Corrigan. We had sleepwalked to near-disaster through the 1920s and 1930s thanks to yellow-livered men like Neville Chamberlain, who had cut and cut again our armed forces despite repeated, brave warnings from the marginalised Winston Churchill, the Labour opposition and even the far-sighted Communists. Nevertheless, in 1939 we went heroically to war with the noble purpose of saving the world from Nazi tyranny and to make the world safe for democracy. We were let down by the French and Belgians – after all, they were foreigners – and driven back to the beaches of Dunkirk, as Parliament came to its senses and threw out the useless Chamberlain, replacing him with the great and universally respected Winston Churchill.

Though the British Expeditionary Force had no chance against an overwhelming host of German tanks and troops – who had invented a fiendishly clever new sort of warfare – there was a miracle: most of our troops were heroically rescued and borne home to fight again by lots of brave little boats. There followed the Battle of Britain, when we stood calmly shoulder to shoulder under a rain of bombs as jolly public-school types blew the Luftwaffe out of the Home Counties skies. Meanwhile, Mr Churchill – who knew much more about how to fight a war than the professionals – winnowed out a succession of hopeless commanders until he found the great Montgomery, whose victory at El Alamein was the turning-point in the war. After two years of Britain fighting all alone against tyranny, America joined us – they could see which way the wind was blowing – and, under Churchill's leadership, we returned in power and might to Europe, marching remorselessly into Germany as evil Bolshevik Russia moved in from the east, taking full advantage of the situation. The First World War had been an incompetent bloodbath, ending in a pointless score-draw after hopeless mismanagement. The Second World War was a grand endeavour, fought with unfaltering national morale and conducted with steady competence against a demonic dictatorship, and indeed our finest hour.

None of those assumptions is true. Britain could not have honourably stayed out of the Great War – in term of our treaty obligations, our national interest (which can at no time allow the ports on the opposite side of the

Channel to fall into the hands of a hostile power) and the highly unpleasant character of the Kaiser's Germany. British casualties, though appalling – for the entire war we faced the concentrated fighting force of the enemy on one bloody front – were not nearly as high as many imagine: there was no 'lost generation', most who fought survived, and our fatalities were proportionately lower than those of France or Germany. The war was supported from start to finish by the vast majority of the British people and ended with an entire and emphatic Allied victory, led by British generals in one of our greatest national achievements. It was many years after the Armistice of November 1918 – after the economic travails of the inter-war decades and the re-match in 1939 – before widespread questioning of the Great War effort began and the real damage has been since the early 1960s, largely by the endeavours of untold English teachers.

Britain ended that conflict with the finest army and the greatest navy in the world and had herself invented – in tactics which quite turned the tide from July 1918 – what the world would, from 1940, dub 'blitzkrieg': rapidly moving forces; the use of concentrated armour – tanks; and immediate tactical support from the air. She then rapidly forgot them, leaving the lessons to be absorbed by the Germans – notably Heinz Guderian, who by the late 1930s was the world's expert on armoured battle. Britain then cut and cut and cut again her defence spending – with the enthusiastic support of Winston Churchill, Chancellor of the Exchequer from 1925 to 1929 – and naively signed the Treaty of Washington in 1922, a deal cooked up by the Americans by which Britain threw away her huge naval advantage. There was even talk of abolishing the Royal Air Force.

Neville Chamberlain was a decent man haunted, like many others, by memories of Flanders. Despite David Lloyd George's spiteful jibe that he 'would make a good Lord Mayor of Birmingham in a lean year', Chamberlain from 1934 – by which time he was chancellor in a Tory-dominated 'National Government' – pushed harder than anyone else for serious rearmament. (So, by this point and vocally, did Winston Churchill, a largely isolated back-bencher who once and twice squandered regained credibility on fatuous sideshows, from romantic support for the wretched King Edward VIII to his hysterical opposition to any Indian self-government.)

That did not make Chamberlain a good prime minister. He succeeded Stanley Baldwin, unopposed and by general acclaim – which never, as attested again in 1955 and 2007, seems to produce men actually up to the job – shortly after the Coronation in 1937 and only two years shy of his seventieth birthday. He insisted on being, for all practical purposes, his own foreign secretary – provoking the resignation of the official one, the young Anthony Eden, in 1938 – and he lacked the judgement for it. Chamberlain seems genuinely to have believed he could do honest business with Adolf Hitler. He failed (though it was probably too late) to launch the one initiative that could have given the Third Reich hard second thoughts about launching a war: triangular diplomacy with the Soviet Union. And the deal finally cut at Munich in the autumn of 1938 – selling Czechoslovakia down the river – was of matchless moral squalor, not only sacrificing the right for the expedient but, by granting the Sudetenland to Germany, stripping her of her best natural defences. (Those who vaunt 'plucky little Poland' should remember that she too moved quickly to extort territorial gains from the beleaguered Czechs.)

But Chamberlain had started from a bad place. Britain had not even begun to think of rearming until 1930 and not in any seriousness till 1934. Baldwin – who bears much more of the blame for the Second World War than is widely realised – passed up the best chance to stop Hitler in his tracks, when the Führer audaciously reoccupied the Rhineland in 1936. ('I do hope you will not trouble me with foreign affairs just now,' he querulously minuted Eden.) Britain was simply not in a position to fight that autumn. Chamberlain's parliamentary private secretary at Munich, the Scottish Unionist MP for Lanark, was Alex Dunglass, heir to the Earl of Home, who himself many years later would briefly serve as prime minister. 'The one excuse I would make for Munich,' Home told me bleakly in 1990, 'is that it bought us a year.' He remembered Hitler and his odd, ape-like gait – arms swinging in unison as he walked – with a shudder: 'the most loathsome, obnoxious, and disgusting man I ever met'. Chamberlain's feeble twelve-month advantage was indeed tenuous; but it made all the difference.

There were other realities today conveniently forgotten. Though several American presidents have not hesitated since to reference the Munich sell-out as some sort of awful warning – from John F. Kennedy to George W. Bush – the president of the day, Franklin D. Roosevelt, telegraphed hearty congratulations to Chamberlain and remained firmly at the helm of an utterly 'Isolationist' policy, vociferously supported even by his Republican opponents. There was no American support for Britain and France. There were real British concerns about French readiness for war – as events would prove. The policy of appeasement was supported by most of the House of Commons, including the Labour Party – who had an openly pacifist leader, George Lansbury, until 1936; as late as 1937 three Labour-controlled Scottish local authorities (including Clydebank) refused to have any truck with government-directed precautions against air raids. And though the Communist Party – small but influential – initially hailed Britain's entry into the war against Fascism, within a month it dramatically reversed its position – on orders from Moscow.

Until almost the eve of war, there was simply no public support for rearmament. Britain was war-weary, battered by unemployment, social unrest and 'the slump,' as it was generally described. The public are always reluctant to pay for tanks and guns and soldiers' boots at the cost of roads, schools and hospitals. At a time of painful political realignment, with the Liberals in steady decline and periods of minority or coalition government, any party proposing vigorous defence-spending would have been clobbered at the polls. At a parliamentary by-election in East Fulham, in October 1933 and on a platform of explicit pacifism, one candidate overthrew a 14,000 Conservative majority, winning the seat for Labour by some 4,000 votes. Battered over the head by churchmen, pacifists, outraged veterans, the pretentious Peace League and all manner of anti-war and disarmament propaganda – to say nothing of an ongoing economic crisis so serious King George V had in 1931 forced the major parties together into the National Government – our rulers had, really, very little room for manoeuvre.

There was more regard, too, for Germany – and even her new Nazi regime – than many remember. It is to a degree understandable. Since the Glorious Revolution, Protestant Britain had been in natural (and usually anti-French) alliance with assorted German states; and every heir-apparent to the throne, from the death of Queen Anne to our present Queen even in 1947, took in marriage some princess or princeling of German birth or substantially German descent. The English themselves are largely of Saxon stock. There was quiet but widespread sympathy, in the 1930s, with German aspirations, many of which seemed legitimate or at least understandable. As the British economy toiled, Hitler's apparent success in restoring German industry attracted genuine interest: Lloyd George and (a year or two after the Abdication) the Duke of Windsor went on jolly German jaunts, and even Churchill praised what the Führer had done. The Nazi regime, after all, did not threaten big business or vested private interests – unlike perfidious Bolshevism – and (particularly against the record of France and Russia) the harassment of the Jews did not become international scandal until the *Kristallnacht* pogrom of 1938. (The state-sanctioned, industrial murder of Jews would not begin until 1942.)

Other cherished fables of the Second World War can quickly be demolished. Britain did not go to war to save Poland, far less to save democracy. Nothing could be done in time for Poland and democracy, in 1939, was a rare commodity anywhere on the planet beyond Britain, her dominions and the United States. Britain went to war because she deemed it in her own interests to do so and could not, in 1939 any more than in 1914 or at any time in modern history, allow a single power to rule all Europe. The British and French were not vastly outnumbered by German forces in the Battle of France. They were routed, with embarrassing ease, by greatly inferior forces with better tactics, better (if often over-engineered and complicated) armour and far better generals. 'Little ships' did not bear home the British Expeditionary Force; they acted as tenders in the shallow waters off the Dunkirk beaches, ferrying men out to the substantial vessels that did.

A negotiated peace, besides, after the rout in France, was for several days a very serious possibility – more weighed than those involved, including Churchill himself, afterwards ever cared to admit. General Conservative knowledge that R.A. Butler, a mid-ranking minister and vocal pre-war 'appeaser', had been involved in tentative discussions (through the neutral Swedish Embassy) was the real reason he never became prime minister. Some revisionist biographers of Churchill, and others, have suggested a deal with Nazi Germany in 1940 might have been the wisest outcome. The morality of this apart, the outcome of such an end to war in the West would have been unthinkable. We would either have ended up with a Nazi German empire in entire control of the Continent – including all the tracts of the western USSR worth having and, by the end of the decade, with atomic weapons – or, on another and by no means incredible alternative, a Soviet Communist empire right to the English Channel and it, too, with atomic weapons.

Men from all classes and backgrounds and with all sorts of accents – including Scottish, Irish, American and a large number of brilliant Poles – fought the Battle of Britain; we won because we had better fighter-planes and we were fighting over our own territory, but chiefly because Germany changed tactics just as she was steadily winning it. She abandoned the true military necessity – the entire destruction of the Royal Air Force, its facilities, its radar-installations, its pilots – to start the terror-bombing of London.

Churchill is a colossal figure and an indisputably great man, of such abiding stature that it is difficult to write even the most intelligent criticism without feeling faintly cheap. As the inspiring figure who put fire in Britain's belly and who, in Kennedy's words, 'mobilised the English language and sent it into battle', his contribution to the national effort and the final, entire destruction of the Third Reich is incalculable. But many aspects of his detailed record as a wartime prime minister – he assumed the defence brief as well as the premiership – do not stand up to close scrutiny. Many wild ideas and blind alleys cost time, money and lives. (Of his record – from 1951 to 1955 – as a peacetime premier, the less said the better.)

At times moody and vindictive, Churchill sacked, marginalised and in one or two instances practically destroyed a succession of commanders whose real crime was their refusal to let him micro-manage matters and realities he knew nothing about. One of the very few generals who did keep on his right side – Montgomery – is a vastly overrated figure, a cocky little man who stole the thunder of his much more substantial predecessor – Claude Auchinleck – in the triumph of El Alamein, which may indeed be the largest battle ever fought on land, but was of no great bearing on the final result of the war. The one battle Montgomery did conceive, plan and execute entirely of his own making – Operation Market Garden, a bid in late 1944 to bring the war to an early end by a swing through Holland – was, from the first disintegrating gliders to the fiasco of Arnhem, an unmitigated disaster. Churchill should firmly be cleared of one charge often laid at his door – though he drank frequently, he was emphatically not an alcoholic; and on one critical matter, the sinister Soviet ambitions for post-war Europe, he was dismally right when President Roosevelt was pig-headedly wrong.

What is much more telling is what we forget. The popular, British lay analysis of the war almost invariably overlooks the three fields in which the country's effort was crucial: the Royal Navy and that generally overlooked Cinderella, the Merchant Navy, and the war at sea; the efforts of Bomber Command; and our formidable Intelligence, whose achievements (both in the rapid annihilation of the German spy network in Britain, and the breaking of the Enigma code) were vital.

But we forget Clausewitz's first maxim of war: it is won by concentrating your maximum force against the maximum force of the enemy, and by that measure the Second World War was won – on the bloodied and frightful fields of Eastern Europe – by the Soviet Union. Her collusion with Hitler in launching the Second World War is beyond dispute. The depravity of her own regime is beyond defence. But from June 1941 – Hitler was forced to postpone his assault on Russia by five fateful weeks; otherwise, it might well have succeeded – the main fight of attrition, fought without quarter and with untold outrages on both sides, was waged on land against Germany by the Russian people. At least 20 million of them died in what is still remembered as the Great War For The Motherland – a hundred times Britain's entire losses in every theatre of the Second World War. Even at the height of the war in the west – in June and July 1944 – the Third Reich could at no time devote more than 25 per cent of her soldiers to fending off the efforts of Britain and America, so entangled was she by the Red Army on her second front. The collapse of 'Army Group Centre' in June 1944 – when the German lines finally, fatally, broke in the East – is at least as important as D-Day, though few in Britain have ever heard of it.

But Britain had long since lost the battle, in June 1940. By early 1942 she had in a real sense lost the war – to America, whose incredible industrial resources, brought safely over the seas by the endeavours of the Royal Navy and borne in vast quantities, by the grim Arctic Convoys, not least to the Soviet Union – finally turned the tide.

Within months, we were effectively under American occupation; and American forces remain in Britain still. 'The strategic defeat of the British Empire by the USA,' writes Peter Hitchens, 'though one of the central events of the last century, is seldom if ever acknowledged as such. To do so would be too painful, and would upset our principal foreign alliance.' There were immediate consequences. All British assets overseas were handed to America; and almost all British gold; and the policy of 'Imperial Preference' – a tariff on goods imported to Britain from outwith the Commonwealth – was perforce abandoned. We handed over besides, and without demur, everything we had accomplished in the field of atomic research, in which by 1941 (not least with some helpful German refugees) Britain led the world – and with no undertaking the results of any further discoveries would be shared. The Empire would be quietly, and not least at American behest, dismantled at steady speed in the years of peace.

But it is time, now, to consider the Scotland of 70 years ago and to meet the people of Clydebank.

2

THE RISINGEST BURGH IN SCOTLAND

In 1870, there was no such place as Clydebank. By 1941, it had been a bustling burgh for over half a century, and a community of notionally 42,000 people. (In fact, a decade after the last census and abuzz with war industry, it harboured many more.)

What is now densely housed and largely post-industrial sprawl was in 1870 so much farmland in Dunbartonshire: a few hamlets and larger villages, like Dalmuir and Duntocher, Faifley and Hardgate and Old Kilpatrick, and some dusty, even desultory industry. There were minor mines for coal, whinstone and limestone; the odd cotton-mill and some little yards for building little ships. Clydebank is, effectively, a new town, with a hastily adopted new name, and born in rather a hurry, when the rapidly growing Glasgow economy led to irresistible demand for additional docking space along the city's quaysides. Pressed to create more ship quays, the Clyde Navigation Trustees resorted to ruthless use of their statutory powers for compulsory purchase and demanded (and duly recovered) the land occupied by the 'Clyde Bank Iron Shipyard' at Govan, where the Trust would subsequently build Princes Dock. Its owners, the eponymous brothers of J. & G. Thomson Ltd, had hastily to acquire new territory, and the pair soon agreed terms with Miss Hamilton of Cochno for a suitable chunk of her Dunbartonshire estates.

This was appropriately flat land on the 'West Barns o' Clyde', on the north side of the river a little west of Yoker, and ideal for their purposes. For one, the main road west from Glasgow ran through it. For another, so did the Forth and Clyde Canal. And – right opposite the site of the new yard – the River Cart flowed into the Clyde from Paisley. This may not have been of great significance in 1870. By the Second World War – when the men of Clydebank had built the behemoth that was the most famous ship in the world, and had almost completed one still bigger – the handy junction of waters meant a great deal, allowing the launch of much larger vessels than would otherwise have been possible so far upriver.

On 1 May 1871, a local gentlewoman and minor laird, Miss Grace Hamilton, ceremoniously cut the first sod at West Barns for the new shipyard. The lack of an immediate workforce – or people in any number, period – was not at first thought a problem; the company could convoy labour daily from the city by paddle steamer. But it was far from ideal, and soon J. & G. Thomson built a few tenements. Completed in 1872, and hard by the shipyard gates, the sweep of housing comprised 126 little flats, each with two rooms and a kitchen, and was officially named Clydebank Terrace. Everyone, though, informally dubbed the street 'Thomson's Buildings': remarkably, the flats would largely survive the Blitz, only to succumb to witless town planning (and the wrecker's ball) in 1978. And the rapidly expanding community around the yard was to many 'Tamson's Town'.

By 1875, a private housing scheme for a shipyard in Nowheresville was already a community, with yet more houses, and a school, and a large shed quickly dubbed the 'Tarry Kirk', for it served not only as a workers' canteen and community hall but hosted church services. Proper churches (Established, Free, Roman Catholic and so on) were soon rising for the care of souls, and sanctioned as charges, and settled with clergy. There were soon more schools. The place grew remorselessly. Other companies set up shop. By 1880, at least 2,000 men were living there; by the end of 1882, the town even had a train link – the Glasgow, Yoker and Clydebank Railway, on a spur from Hyndland station by Jordanhill, Scotstounhill, Garscadden and Yoker. By the end of 1896, three railways would serve Clydebank, with five tracks. From 1903, there was also a busy tramcar network

Between 1882 and 1884, the Singer Manufacturing Company built an enormous new factory at Kilbowie, just half a mile inland from the Clyde Bank yard. Yet more workers (and their families) flocked to the area, for the Singer plant alone employed a vast workforce; by 1911, no fewer than 11,000 people would be turning out sewing machines for the Empire. The concern's stolid 190-foot tower – augmented during further expansion of the plant between 1905 and 1906 – became a prized landmark, for the great four-faced clock that adorned it was bigger than its Westminster kinsman and almost certainly the largest in the world. At its apogee from 1906, each clock face was 26 feet in diameter; each minute hand was over 15 feet long and, at its broadest, 18 inches wide. The hour hand was 8 feet 6 inches long. Every one of the numerals was 3 feet 6 inches high; the letters of SINGER, above each face on each side, were 13 feet high and 1 foot wide. It was raised for the glory of Singer's, this tower and timepiece; but it became the glory of Clydebank.

Singer's even won their own station on the extended railway line. And in 1886, the people of this pioneering and extraordinarily young community formally petitioned for local autonomy, as they now qualified as a 'populous place'. It was granted, and the new town became an official 'police burgh' on 18 November. There was a determined (and arguably wiser) bid to call this new entity Kilbowie; but the new burgh's very first Provost was James Rodger Thomson of the eponymous shipyard, and he had his way. The company town, begotten by the Clyde Bank Ship Yard, became for ever Clydebank.

Thomson, a pompous, genial paternalist, was one of three Big Men in the 'risingest burgh', if the weakest as a money-man: in 1899, he lost control of his business. Robert McAlpine, his builder, founded a huge company and duly bought himself a knighthood – nay, a baronetcy; and his empire endures to this day. 'Concrete Bob' had lived the Scottish industrial dream. Born in Newarthill in Lanarkshire, in 1847, he had left school when but ten – to work down a coal-mine. McAlpine turned from that choking, dangerous trade to become an apprentice bricklayer and, by graft and brains and ruthlessness, became great. He built much of Clydebank, from shipyard-workers' housing to the curious flat-roofed tenements at Radnor Park (which have a notable part in our story) to the great new Singer's complex. He built besides much of Glasgow's subway tunnelling, undertook contracts in Europe and was a noted pioneer of labour-saving machinery and concrete construction. His hapless son and namesake, always in his shadow, finally inherited the old ogre's fortune and baronetcy in 1934 – and died within the fortnight.

And there was William Beardmore, a London lad and son of a London engineer, born in 1856 and who came to Glasgow as a child of five in 1861; his engineer father co-founded the enormous Parkhead Forge. Well schooled and – shrewdly – apprenticed into the family trade at 15 rather than sent off for the life of an Oxbridge drone, William rose through the clan ranks and became head of the business at 30. It was soon a limited company – William Beardmore & Co. – and he moved into shipbuilding and armaments, buying several Clyde yards and assorted torpedo and munitions plants. In 1900, Beardmore moved on Clydebank – expressly, Dalmuir, its undeveloped western end – and there William Beardmore & Co. rose as one of the biggest and most advanced shipyards in the world, building liners, warships, and – among many notable vessels – the 'dreadnought' HMS *Ramillies* and, in 1916, the huge HMS *Argus*, the first through-deck aircraft-carrier in the world.

William won the usual fruits. He turned his handsome inheritance into a prodigious one; he bought his Highland estate (at Strathnairn, where he died in 1936); he collected his baronetcy in 1914 and his peerage six years later. He sponsored the 1907 Shackleton expedition to Antarctica, and a glacier was wisely named after him. Beardmore had (or affected to have) a social conscience, for – among many great bodies whose boards he adorned – he served as chairman of the Industrial Welfare Society.

A young, radically minded employee, David Kirkwood – of whom we shall hear much more – never quite got over his awe of this formidable Victorian patriarch. Beardmore was summoned once, in front of Kirkwood, when a wretched craftsman, cutting a great crank, made some elementary mistake, miscalculating the job by 1,000th of an inch and wasting £1,000-worth of materials – a huge sum in Edwardian times, when if you had £150 a year you could afford a maid. The great man ambled down, puffing a goodly cigar. He wordlessly beheld the useless crank. Then he turned to the manager. 'Can we make another?' 'Yes, sir.' 'Then get the thing done.' And away Beardmore swept in his mercy – 'a very god', Kirkwood would memorialise, 'To err is human, to forgive divine.' Repeating this story, T.C. Smout adds, 'Autocracy, when clothed in visible, if occasional, benevolence and mercy, could get away with a great deal.'

Such emperors ruled the young Clydebank. Dozens and dozens more owned it; for such housing as was not built expressly by companies for their workers was leased privately – poor and rickety as it might be – from a host of little bourgeois landlords, most in Glasgow, most of the stock managed by cold-eyed factors. Both business barons and these Rachmans had a vested interest in a biddable, insecure, economically powerless working class. And their power and fortune depended on maintaining this pleasant order in housing provision for their social inferiors. For decades, then, they would wage war against any provision of public housing.

A 'Citizens' Union' in Glasgow was ruthlessly formed to win municipal elections and bring down a lord provost who dared plan to erect affordable working-class homes on the rates. Factors and petty landlords and builders took care to pack councils and their committees. They salved conscience, as Smout darkly outlines, by three cherished tenets: that only the 'undeserving' poor were homeless (by dint of booze, shiftlessness and immorality); that any interference in an untrammelled free market was a moral outrage; and that philanthropy and charitable endeavour (carefully dosed, lest thrift die out) could cope with the losers in this society. It would take one world war to shake this hegemony; another to overturn it. It has not yet been slain; and it is remorselessly returning.

Clydebank grew and grew. It would soon absorb Kilbowie, Dalmuir, Hard-gate and Old Kilpatrick, whose history can be traced to the eleventh century and which, whether or not it is indeed the birthplace of Ireland's saint, in 1314 sent a contingent of fighting men to Bannockburn. The local government map toiled to keep up. It was 1906 before the burgh boundaries were expanded to include Radnor Park, halfway up the great brae of Kilbowie Road and dominated by McAlpine's great flat-roofed tenements, rising to the north of Singer Station and overwhelmingly the dwellings of Singer employees; in fateful detail, their leads were sealed thickly with bitumen, against the warm and frequent western rain. Some well-travelled sailor, in the mists of Clyde-bank folklore, remarked how much these new terraces reminded him of Jerusalem; and the flats were soon universally known as the 'Holy City'.

To the west, Dalmuir already boasted the Clyde Navigation Trust work-shops (developed in 1860, though they would close in 1907); William Beard-more had opened his own major shipyard in 1905, and John Brown and Co. had bought out Thomson's in 1899. It was these great concerns – with Singer's – who dominated the local economy, not only employing men (and women, especially in cabinet and polishing work) by the thousand, but serving as a magnet to a host of smaller businesses, not least builders. After Thomson's initial beneficence, the construction of urgently-needed housing fell to rising entrepreneurs like J.W. Anderson, Leslie Kirk and, of course, 'Concrete Bob'. The burgh boundaries would have to be extended again – in 1925 and 1937; and twice more after the war, Clydebank finally fixing her skirts on District Council incarnation in 1975.

In 1892, the Burgh of Clydebank adopted an engaging coat of arms – over the motto *Laboria et Scientia*, 'By Work and Knowledge' – when that year's Burgh Police (Scotland) Act made a 'common seal' legally obligatory. Though mocked by one authority as a 'fine healthy specimen of home-made heraldry', and with the usual touches of grandiloquence – the shield topped by a 'mural crown' and cut by the Lennox Cross – there was imaginative detail: a stag's head in the 'dexter fess' position from the personal arms of James Rodger Thomson, who owned the shipyard (and assumed his throne as first Provost); a lion rampant at 'sinister fess' from those of a local laird, Alexander Dunn Pattison of Dalmuir; a 'garb' or wheat-sheaf as crest, in genuflection to surviving farmland and, most engagingly, a modern battleship at base and a wee sewing-machine at chief. It was only in 1932, though, after heavy pressure, that all this was formally 'matriculated', with little alteration, by the office of the Lord Lyon King of Arms.

Clydebank's secure and remarkably rapid rise speaks much for her people. It owes something besides to the conscious paternalism of great employers, however cynical. Singer's went far to provide social and leisure facilities for its gargantuan workforce. The town's library was bankrolled by Andrew Carnegie himself, the Dunfermline-born American steel magnate; though the Burgh had to furnish the land and fund its subsequent operation. The handsome building, on Dumbarton Road by the Town Hall, was opened on 1 October 1913, boasting lending and reference areas, a newspaper room, a magazine room, a student's room and a residence for the librarian himself: in the basement, there was a staffroom and even a bookshop. Such beneficence, of course, should be set in its context. The princes of Clydebank industry, from the Thomson brothers to William Beardmore and Singer's American bosses, had not made millions by being kind. Of blithely cavalier attitude to health and safety, they hired and fired and paid off as cash flow dictated. Yet even Beardmore was an earthy, practical character held in some grudging esteem. It was 'middle management' – the bowler-hatted foremen, humbly born, smart but often spiteful; or the factors who controlled most housing – who became the abiding focus of hatred in a town which, by 1914, already had a name for radical agitation and fraught industrial relations.

There is a distinct Clydebank humour. Decades after the Blitz, the aghast headmaster of Clydebank High School burst into the staffroom, where young teachers were bawling out some football anthem: 'Gentlemen, you are professionals!' One thought (though had more sense than innocently to say it), 'Really? I didn't think our singing was that good.' A friend, Jack House related in 1969, 'voyaged in a cargo ship which sailed from the Clyde to Finland. The chief engineer was a Clydebank man, and he had taken his young son with him as a cabin boy. One day they went to see a famous waterfall in a Finnish lake. My friend was captured by its beauty and turned to the cabin boy, who was standing beside him looking at the scene, and said, "Have you ever seen anything so wonderful?" "Aye, not bad," said the boy, "but have you ever seen Clydebank Public Park?"'

Yet Clydebank, like Paisley across the river, has long feared for enduring independence. The 'Bankies' are not Glaswegians and dread collapse into the city bounds. It is no idle threat: Partick and Govan were independent burghs as recently as 1912. My own Glasgow streets in the 1970s – the avenues of Scotstoun, Jordanhill and Knightswood – had even in 1914 been part of Renfrewshire: to this day, carved proclamation on the southern wall of Scotstoun Primary School, completed in 1905, lays its glory at the feet of the 'Renfrew Landward School Board'. Clydebank Burgh itself profited from the demise of Yoker in 1925, acquiring much of her territory and pushing her eastern boundary towards the cobbled slip of the Yoker–Renfrew ferry. Yoker, by the way – *An t-Iochdar*, a 'low-lying place' – is a Gaelic name; and many others around Clydebank, like Dalmuir and Dalreoch and Drum-chapel, remind us how long that language endured on the northern reaches of Clyde; it was spoken on the Dunbartonshire banks of Loch Lomond and Loch Long even at the turn of last century. The 'risingest burgh' besides attracted hundreds of Highland migrants, with Gaelic services regularly held in the town by 1893 and right till March 1941.

But central to Clydebank's story is an industry: the building of ships; the politics forged by united, assertive people in a new economic order; and the river that is still substantially defined for the world by hammers and rivets, ships and socialism.

Glasgow made the Clyde; but the Clyde made Glasgow. Though respected and rich, this was until the Industrial Revolution a tiny city, smaller than modern Perth, her former bounds now lost in the sprawl of today. Glasgow's first prestige was ecclesiastical. The bishopric was settled by the eleventh century – under the patronage of King David I – and soon became one of the grandest in Scotland; the city's cathedral (now properly, as a Presbyterian place of worship, its high kirk) can be confidently dated to 1197, incorporates probably some of an earlier twelfth-century structure and may occupy the site of a church founded by Kentigern ('St Mungo') in the seventh century. Glasgow was elevated to an archdiocese in 1492 and had already been raised to the status of royal burgh by a charter from King William the Lion in 1178. Even after the Reformation, Glasgow hosted an important General Assembly, in 1638, when the Kirk doughtily reasserted its Presbyterial order against plans for a restored episcopacy by King Charles I.

The city was still more important as an academic centre: founded in 1451, by a papal bull from Pope Nicholas V, her university is the fourth-oldest in the English-speaking world and, in Scotland, younger only than St Andrews. It was a noted centre of the Scottish Enlightenment and, though it has never acquired the snob cachet of, say, Edinburgh, is by any fair judgement the strongest centre of tertiary education in Scotland, still offering both a complete range of professional departments, from architecture through dentistry, to a host of academic courses. Alumni include two prime ministers, six Nobel laureates, and some globally celebrated inventors and scientists – Lord Kelvin,

John Lister (pioneer of asepsis in surgery), John Logie Baird (a son of Dunbartonshire), John Boyd-Orr and two eighteenth-century gentlemen whose impact on nineteenth-century Scotland – and Clydebank – was epochal: Adam Smith, father of economics, and James Watt, who did not invent the steam engine, but devised the first that worked properly and that drove the Industrial Revolution.

In the early eighteenth century, this centre of sermons and learning was a neat, attractive place. That cynical Englishman, Daniel Defoe, paid a visit and opined, with only the faintest meow, that this 'was the cleanest and beautifullest, and best built city in Britain, London only excepted'. At that time, certainly, Edinburgh (which Defoe loathed) was a fetid, medieval tip. Nevertheless the capital still led Scotland: a growing centre for the very new business of banking (for which Scots had a natural flair), the centre of Scots law and the wider Lothian base for most of the hard-headed leaders of the Kirk.

Though Glasgow still only boasted some 13,000 people, the 1707 Union opened up priceless trade opportunities. She was favoured by geography for European commerce with America: lucrative business in sugar, in cotton and especially in tobacco. As early as 1718, the first Glasgow mercantile ship crossed the Atlantic. In 1724, 4,192,576 lb of the weed was landed on the estuarial Clyde: some 3,000,000 was then exported, most to France. By 1735, there were 67 Clyde ships serving untold smokers. By the time of the American War of Independence, there were 386 – with a combined capacity of 22,892 tons – and what was now a booming commercial city controlled more than half the British tobacco industry, as new streets west of the original medieval city arose with names in celebration of Whig politics and New World opportunity – Hanover Street and Frederick Street and Brunswick Street; Plantation, and Virginia Street and Jamaica Street. In 1710, according to parish records, there were but 129 weddings in the city, and 470 baptisms; in 1790 (as the city shrugged off the late American reverse) there were 480 marriages, and 1,449 infants were that year sprinkled. This was a boom-town, and a very young one.

But there was one infuriating problem: the Clyde itself was not navigable beyond the Erskine narrows to the heart of the city. The river, swift, serene and shallow, was probably much like the River Ness through the Highland capital today; readily waded, spates apart, and generally but two or three feet deep. The 'tobacco lords' first fretted as Greenock, a venerable deep-water port by the open Firth, took full advantage; then invested heavily in their own new harbour-town a little to the east, Port Glasgow.

Much effort, time and money was vested in curing this bottleneck, against seemingly intractable problems of landscape and geology; apart from the frustrations of the Clyde herself, the Port Glasgow facilities kept silting up. Though it would be 1880 before the modern maritime thoroughfare to the very heart of the city was complete, the breakthrough came in 1768, when the city fathers hired a hard-nosed English engineer and consultant, John Golborne. They had wisely dismissed such earnest suggestions as vast waterproof bags (for ships to tow tobacco behind them as, much shallower in draught, they waded upriver) or a 'training wall' at the Broomielaw, to speed up the current and scour the bed).

The Broomielaw proposal – from a Dr Wark – was the germ of a good idea, but it was Golborne, from Chester, who executed a great scheme and to whom history has granted the laurels. Golborne had not come to Glasgow, in September 1768, to discuss the Clyde at all: the magistrates had, rather, sought his wisdom on the building of a ship-canal across central Scotland. Once he was in town, though, it was too good an opportunity to miss. Golborne, for no mean gold, duly made full inspection of harbour works and the larger river and estuary, and on 30 November he met the Glasgow's rulers with a hard plan.

The Port Glasgow difficulty was easily fixed: at Golborne's suggestion, a stream was diverted through the mud-swamped harbour basin and together with some new quayage this would keep it clear thereafter. (The works were duly executed in 1772, and proved him right.) But he had paid most attention to the river proper. The Clyde, he intoned, was 'at present in a state of nature, and for want of due attention the channel has been suffered to expand too much.' The banks, after all, were softer than the bed, and it was far easier for the enthusiastic weight of waters to erode on either side than to carve new depth below. In detail, Golborne observed, from the deep water at Port Glasgow to the Dumbuck shoal, near Erskine, the channel was nowhere less than 12 feet deep. At those shoals, though, and as a consequence of the rock and underwater terrain – 'the first and grand obstacle to navigation' – the outflowing river fell in two separate and much shallower channels, neither deeper than a yard. Still further upstream, deep water was again to be found in one busy channel, by Dunglass Castle at Bowling; but problems resumed at the Kilpatrick sands, and deep water beyond that stopped emphatically at News-hot Isle. Once more the current divided, and beyond this point to Glasgow itself the Clyde was not realistically navigable; in many places and in most conditions only a foot in bubbling depth.

Golborne's solution, if orotundly phrased, was sound. 'I shall proceed on these principles of assisting nature when she cannot do her own work, by removing the stones and hard gravel from the bottom of the river where it is shallow, and by contracting the channel where it is worn too wide . . .' Simply put, amidst as much dredging as was practicable the channel had to be narrowed, so that the water would flow much faster. He would build jetties and dykes – 'groynes' – from either side; as for the Dumbuck shoal, one of the two channels should be blocked entirely, so that 'the reflowing current would then act with greater force, and grind down a deep and capacious channel, and this must be obvious to any intelligent person.' From Dumbuck onwards, more dykes were to be built, all the way up to Glasgow, in pairs from either bank and to 'half-tide' height' – low-water level.

'By these means, easy and simple in themselves, without laying a restraint in nature, I humbly conceive that the River Clyde may be deepened so as to have

4 feet, or perhaps 5 feet depth up to the Broomielaw.' The principle was sound. Execution was tricky, and victory took time, though no one could fault the Glasgow magistrates for want of alacrity: the Second Act for the Improvement of the Clyde Navigation was done and dusted by 9 January 1770. Such mighty engineering works, of course, would not cheaply be wrought, so the city fathers proposed in detail the passage-charge and harbour dues they would levy (per ton of cargo borne or unloaded) and, well aware most of the work would not actually be done within the city bounds, and 'in consideration of the great labour they must be at and of the risk their common stock must run, in improving the navigation' they proposed what would become the Clyde Navigation Trust: a single body with responsibility for the whole river and in undisputed control of its life.

So the Herculean toil began. Jetties of rubble were duly built; sandbanks and shoals were dredged. The river was narrowed; the scour increased. On Golborne's advice, the spoil brought ashore by dredgers was dumped between these groynes, and planted with 'willows or other shrubs for the safety or preservation of the banks, and for preventing the same from being hurt or carried away by the river'. A young, Greenock-born engineer, James Watt, had already completed his report on Dumbuck, near Dumbarton. The jetty duly constructed at Longhaugh Point – to block the southern channel – proved insufficient, so a 'training wall' called the Lang Dyke was in 1773 built on the Dumbuck shoal itself to preclude the flow of water into the forbidden way. The remains of the Lang Dyke can still clearly be seen today, as well as several Golborne jetties.

In all – without, until well into the nineteenth century, readily manoeuvred ships or much powered machinery – the works took decades. Hundreds of these groynes would be built; tens of thousands of tons of mud, sand and gravel excavated. Sometimes the improved flow soon and speedily deepened the way; sometimes additional dredging had to be done – and, in fact, dredging has never since been ceased, though operations far up the river were in recent years much reduced and, since the completion of the Pacific Quay bridge in 2007, ceased beyond Govan. It would be the 1850s before new technology allowed really good dredging and a huge volcanic plug – the Elderslie Rock – was not finally beaten, with explosives and all other possible means, until the 1880s. From that day, great ships could sail to the very city centre – and, by then, Glasgow was a capital for iron and steel. Glasgow had made the Clyde; the Clyde now confirmed Glasgow, and much else on its newly engineered banks, the world's first factory of shipping.

Long before Golborne's labours bore fruit, though, tobacco had gone; American war, and triumphant revolution, fast killed the trade between 1775 and 1777. But, if Glasgow merchants had momentarily lost their income, they held prodigious capital. They now focused on the West Indian commerce and besides, with useful credit facilities from the Edinburgh banks, began rapidly to develop Glasgow and the Clyde valley generally for the whole new industry of cotton. Textiles (in linen and woollens) were long and lucratively established in western Scotland. New machinery – the spinning-jenny, the powered mill, the 'mule' – opened up new possibilities, especially in an area already equipped with relevant skills, much money and abundant water-power. From 1792 – though it took time to take hold – there was also the might of steam.

Born at Greenock in 1719, of staunchly Presbyterian and Covenanting stock, James Watt was a clever, cautious young man who had been schooled largely by his mother, was clever with his hands and exceptionally good at maths. He had hoped to follow his father into the specialised trade of making mathe-matical instruments, but young Watt – who studied the business in London for a year – had not served the required seven-year apprenticeship in Scotland under the Glasgow Guild of Hammermen, who operated a mighty closed shop. Though no one else in Scotland made compasses, protractors, squares and so on, with bleak spite they denied Watt membership and closed that calling.

He was saved by three professors of Glasgow University, who encouraged him in 1758 to set up a little workshop within their precincts. Four years later a friend drew his attention to the almost wholly untapped possibilities of steam power, and Watt began to explore the field. Though experimental steam-driven devices – as diverting little novelties – had been around for two centuries, only in 1698 had a machine of any practical application – a water pump, developed in 1698 by Thomas Savery – appeared. It was weak, huffy and wheezing, though in 1712 Thomas Newcomen had popped up with a slightly better 'atmospheric' design, which could drain mine-workings of flood water at greater depth. The University of Glasgow had a model of the Newcomen engine and – though it was away for repairs when Watt first grew curious – he soon had his hands on it, completing the overhaul in 1763.

Watt was sure this cumbersome slow machine could be bettered. He quickly grasped that four-fifths of the thermal energy in the steam was wasted in heating the cylinder, where the steam was condensed by the direct injection of cold water. He added a separate condensing-chamber and tweaked the plant besides to keep the cylinder itself as hot as the steam. Those were huge breakthroughs. In 1765 he completed a working model. It took 11 years, though, before the Watt engine could be developed commercially. For one, the process of securing a patent (which then required an Act of Parliament) was tedious; for another, the skilled iron-workers of the day were heat-it-and-bash-it blacksmiths, hardly the craftsmen Watt's tightly calibrated design needed.

By the end of 1776 – in partnership with Matthew Boulton and with precision-boring techniques lifted directly from cannon-making – Watt was in business; his design, which burned only a quarter of the coal consumed by Newcomen's beast, in fast demand for mine-pumping operations. At Boulton's suggestion – and circumventing yet more patent difficulties by using 'sun and planet' gear rather than a simple crank – the Watt engine could soon operate with rotational power rather than just a nodding, 'reciprocal' movement.

Later, the Greenock boffin made other improvements: a 'double-acting' mechanism, the 'compound' operation of two or more engines in one unit; a steam-pressure indicator, a throttle-valve and a 'centrifugal governor'. Watt was especially proud of his 'parallel motion' linkage, patented in 1784 and which linked the arcing movement of the rocking-beam to the straight-line work of cylinder-rod and piston.

Watt's new engine had enormous impact. It burnt far less coal. It worked much better. Its rotary motion made it suitable for powering factory machinery, which meant that mills and plants now sprouting everywhere could finally be sited away from rivers, greatly accelerating what we now know as the Industrial Revolution. It made James Watt's fortune. But it was far from perfect. Like Newcomen's design, it was still an 'atmospheric' engine: the piston driven not by the expanding steam, but the vacuum steam made as it condensed. Actually – as his later tweaks, all evidently safety-related, attest – Watt had an absolute horror of high-pressure steam, partly because of the problem of leaks but largely on humanitarian grounds, for he dreaded catastrophic explosion. All his engines worked on majestically low pressure and, until someone took steam power in a bolder direction, it was fit only for ponderous operations rather than the 'prime mover' needs of a new age.

Cornwall – with its rich but flood-prone tin-mines – proved a fat market for Watt and Boulton; and at century's end a clever son of the county, Richard Trevithick, finally braved the full potential of steam. Still not 30, and the son of a highly respected 'mining captain', Trevithick had became an engineering consultant when only 19. He was at first eager to find some alteration that would save the business the burden of royalties for Watt's patented condenser. He was not the first to grasp the potential of steam (as opposed to atmospheric) pressure, or that a safe engine on that principle was now doable; but he was the first in Britain actually to build a practical high-pressure engine, in 1799. He used a double-acting cylinder, a four-way valve and a rotator crank; and the used steam was vented straight into the atmosphere, with no need for a condenser at all. Though still rather primitive, the much more powerful technology had immediate possibilities: less than two years later, in 1801, Trevithick had built the 'Puffing Devil' – the very first steam vehicle – which on Christmas Eve chugged triumphantly from Camborne to Beacon with a few nervous passengers.

It was the rising engineers of the coal country in north-east England – clever Geordies, of which George and Robert Stephenson are the most famous – who exploited Trevithick's achievement in railway locomotion. (Trevithick's cumbersome road vehicles were slow, uncomfortable and costly to run; and the explosion of one of his stationary high-pressure engines in 1803, at Greenwich, killing four people, was a public-relations disaster naturally exploited by Watt and Boulton.) But it fell to the Scots – and the Clyde – to develop the maritime potential of high-pressure steam.

Work on a Forth and Clyde Canal had begun in 1768, even as Golborne hatched his plans for improvement of the river, and the 'navigation' – from

Bowling to Bo'ness, in conjunction with the new Union Canal from Edinburgh
– was completed in 1790. Early in the new century, Thomas, Lord Dundas –
scion of a mighty, sleekit Scottish dynasty and governor of the new canal –
sanctioned the trial of a little steam-powered ship, named in honour of his
daughter and to a design by William Symington, a 33-year-old engineer from
Leadhills in Lanarkshire.

This canal endeavour was the first practical British proof of the usefulness of
steam-driven shipping. As early as 1788, the young Symington had shown that
a steam engine could work on a boat: friends joined him for a brief, very slow
cruise round the local Dalswinton Loch on 14 October, though details of that
'success' are most vague. Symington had at least proved a steam engine could
be lit on a boat without promptly burning it to the waterline, but later legend
that Robert Burns was among his passengers can firmly be discounted; it is
mentioned nowhere in the bard's verse, correspondence or papers, not even in
a letter he wrote that very evening.

Experiments with one prototype on the River Carron, near Falkirk, in 1801
had been more encouraging. Symington's new boat, however, used a single
midline crank-driven paddle wheel powered by a low-pressure horizontal
engine. Naturally, he named her to flatter his patron's daughter – the *Charlotte
Dundas* – and on 4 January she bore Lord Dundas and a little party on a splashy
wee canal voyage. Symington later effected some improvements, and in March,
and in the teeth of a strong breeze, the *Charlotte Dundas* triumphantly towed
two 70-ton barges almost 20 miles along the Forth and Clyde Canal to Glasgow,
taking – in what was still emphatically the age of the horse – a mere 9 hours. It
seems incredible the possibilities of Symington's invention were not seized. But
the Canal Board saw only the perils of erosion to the banks from the wash of
such a vessel. The Duke of Bridgewater, who liked the notion of steam-powered
tugs on his important canal and had hired Symington to build him half a dozen,
most thoughtlessly and suddenly died. Symington was never even reimbursed
by Lord Dundas or anyone else for all he had spent on his sturdy pioneer, which
was soon abandoned in a Bainsford backwater. The duke's demise denied him
almost certain fortune, and poor Symington 'sought consolation in the bottle',
Andrew McQueen sadly records, 'and although he lived many years longer it
was only to see others reap where he had sown, and at his death, in 1831, he was
in very straitened circumstances.' In 1861, with blithe unawareness of her
significance, what remained of the *Charlotte Dundas* was demolished for scrap.
We have still scant respect for historic ships.

It fell to Dunbartonshire, and Henry Bell – in the teeth of pig-headed disdain
– to show what could be done. Bell was actually a Lothian man, born at
Torphichen in 1767, and his people were what we would now call civil
engineers. They laboured in rock, not metal; and built bridges and mills and
harbours, not machines; and when Henry had completed his studies at the
parish school he was in 1780 apprenticed to a stonemason. Three years on, he
began another apprenticeship, with his uncle – a millwright – but the youth
was already brewing an interest in boats.

Bell is an engaging character because, in contrast to so many of the self-made architects of the Industrial Revolution, he was really rather a duffer. Though he had vision and passion, his lofty disdain for detail and great manual clumsiness were not the stuff of a born inventor. He could not even settle on a steady trade. When he returned to Scotland in 1790, after some vague work in London, it was as a house-carpenter in Glasgow, and a bad one. He had ambitions to become a civil engineer, and joined the city's Corporation of Wrights in 1797, but got nowhere: he had neither the capital, the skill nor the discipline. A bewildered contemporary would conclude that Bell

> had many of the features of the enthusiastic projector; never calculated means to ends, or looked much farther than the first stages or movements of any scheme. His mind was a chaos of extraordinary projects, the most of which, from his want of accurate scientific calculation, he never could carry into practice. Owing to an imperfection in even his mechanical skill, he scarcely ever made one part of a model suit the rest, so that many designs, after a great deal of pains and expense, were successively abandoned. He was, in short, the hero of a thousand blunders and one success.

Bell was inept and pompous; but he needed only to be lucky once. He claimed, in later memoirs, to have been enchanted by marine steam as early as 1800, and that he had written Lord Melville and the Admiralty that year to 'show his lordship and the other members of the Admiralty, the practicability and great utility of applying steam to the propelling of vessels against winds and tides, and every obstruction on rivers and seas, where there was depth of water'. They ignored him. He pressed again in 1803, with no further success, though – and we have only Bell's word for this – Lord Nelson himself supposedly protested that 'if you do not adopt Mr Bell's scheme, other nations will, and in the end vex every vein of this empire. It will succeed . . . and you should encourage Mr Bell.'

The unwanted pioneer then touched up his prospectus and sent it all over the world – he claimed – to European capitals and even across the Atlantic. 'The Americans,' he writes grandly, 'were the first to put my plan into practice . . .' Certainly steamboats appeared on the great rivers of the United States from 1807, and an 1822 Report from the House of Commons flatly asserted that Robert Fulton, pioneer of American steam, had been generously fed information and even a model by Henry Bell. This is most improbable. Fulton was a much abler man than Bell: there had been steamboat trials in America as early as 1786, and Bell's astute dating of his own averred genius to 1800 was probably a sour bid to spite both Fulton and Symington.

In 1808, Henry Bell removed to Helensburgh, on the north shore of the Firth of Clyde by the mouth of the Gareloch, and took charge of the Baths Hotel. Mrs Bell, though, seems to have done most of the work, as the genius schemed away 'without much regard to the ordinary affairs of the world.' He was eager to drum up trade and had an instinct for advertising and self-promotion. In

1812, he ordered a boat. There had been an exciting comet in 1811; and so the *Comet* his craft became. He ordered the 30-ton timber-hulled ship from Messrs John Wood & Co. of Port Glasgow, just across the Firth; and he had a 3-horsepower engine and a boiler manufactured in Glasgow. On the principle, one supposes, that a horse on four legs is faster than a man on two, he also insisted that his pride and joy have four paddle wheels – two on each side. But what really made Henry Bell's fame, if not quite his fortune, was an advertisement in every newspaper he could think of.

Steam Passage-boat, THE COMET, *between Glasgow, Greenock and Helensburgh, for passengers only.*

THE Subscriber having, at much expense, fitted up a handsome vessel to ply upon the Clyde, between Glasgow and Greenock—to sail by the power of wind, air, and steam—he intends that the vessel shall leave the Broomielaw on Tuesdays, Thursdays, and Saturdays, about midday, or at such hour thereafter as may answer from the state of the tide—and to leave Greenock on Mondays, Wednesdays, and Fridays in the morning, to suit the tide. The elegance, comfort, safety, and speed of this vessel require only to be proved, to meet the approbation of the public; and the proprietor is determined to do everything in his power to merit public encouragement.

The terms are for the present fixed at 4s. for the best cabin, and 3s. the second; but, beyond these rates, nothing is to be allowed to servants, or any other person employed about the vessel. The subscriber continues his establishment at Helensburgh Baths, the same as for years past, and a vessel will be in readiness to convey passengers in the COMET from Greenock to Helensburgh. Passengers by the COMET will receive information of the hours of sailing, by applying at Mr. Houston's Office, Broomielaw; or Mr. Thomas Blackney's, East Quay Head, Greenock.

HENRY BELL
Helensburgh, 5th August, 1812.

It was sensational. It was shameless. And it was a huge success, at least for Bell's place in history. The *Comet* sallied forth from Port Glasgow on 6 August 1812, paddled up to the Broomielaw and then paddled back down to Greenock at a daring five miles an hour against a headwind. William Orr, then a young lad of the town and later a redoubtable Clyde skipper himself, recalled decades later – with lovely Scots humour – the early arrivals of this dangerous new sort of boat. 'When she would be reported coming round Bailie Gammell's point, all of us children ran down the quay to see her blow up and see the sailors and passengers "fleein' in the air." We were not much disappointed at the time, as it was sure to happen soon.'

The *Comet* boasted a crew of eight, including (in typical Bell showmanship) a piper; her skipper was William MacKenzie, a Helensburgh schoolmaster, and one Robert Robertson was her engineer. It may not have been the first commercial steamboat venture in the world, but it was certainly the first seagoing one. Besides – casually, and of untold impact on his age and ours – Henry Bell and his *Comet* had invented the timetable. 'She was the first vessel moved by steam which successfully carried on a regular service in Europe,' Captain James Williamson would later observe in a seminal history of the Clyde steamers, 'thirteen years before the opening of the first public railway.'

A hopeless businessman, Bell never made any serious money. His pioneering efforts were simply copied – with much more success – by others; the larger and more powerful *Elizabeth*, for instance, was in direct competition from March 1813, and by 1818 there were dozens of bigger, better, quicker steamers chuffing around and up and down the Clyde. He tried the wee *Comet* on a brief new service on the Firth of Forth, from Grangemouth to Newhaven, and from September 1819 ran a West Highland run, to Oban and Fort William via the Crinan Canal. He rebuilt and lengthened his craft for this heroic venture – and sensibly removed one pair of wheels – but in December 1820, sailing south from Fort William, she was emphatically wrecked near the Crinan Canal, after being overwhelmed by storm and tide. Henry Bell, with characteristic good fortune, was aboard. He and everyone else scrambled to safety from her grounded fore-end, from which her machinery was shortly salvaged; but the after-part of the ship floated remorselessly away to the maelstrom of Corryvreckan, and was never seen again.

Bell, not easily discouraged, built a new and better ship, *Comet II*, which assumed this run in July 1821 and could make it in an impressive 26 hours. Long before railways into the glens and a century, indeed, before decent Highland roads, this route from the upper Clyde to the heart of the West Highlands was the most convenient, and it would be as late as 1969 (latterly from Gourock and with intervening buses from Ardrishaig or Tarbert Loch Fyne to Oban) before it finally ceased. The *Comet II*, however, sank after a disastrous collision off Gourock in October 1825, mowed down in the dark by the steamer *Ayr* off Gourock. Neither ship had bothered to display any lights, and the *Ayr* – admittedly badly damaged herself – did not pause to pick up the casualties. Of the 80 souls aboard, only 18 survived, including one young woman who, unconscious, was towed to shore by her faithful dog. *Comet II* was later salvaged and spent many more years as a sailing schooner; but Bell's career in merchant shipping was over. The embarrassment of the disaster apart, those who had heavily invested in the new venture – most of them Lochaber gentry – never recovered their money, and no one would trust him again.

The flawed visionary could but watch as his dream, much more deftly taken up by others, made them rich and the Clyde great. By the mid 1820s, the Bells were in humiliating poverty. But there was a happy ending. Moved by his fate, a local doctor and others organised a generous collection; and the Clyde Navigation Trustees besides made him an annual pension of £100, which, when Henry Bell died at Helensburgh in 1830, was continued to his widow.

Silly as he was, Bell's innovation had belatedly won them comfort; and a stately obelisk has long stood in his honour on the rock of Dunglass, two miles upriver from Dumbarton; with the exception of 1974 and the brief languishing of the *Waverley*, paddle wheels have beaten the Clyde every summer since 1812, and pound it still. In 1962, for the 150th anniversary of that historic voyage, a replica of the little *Comet* was built, and after some steaming about she was mounted as a permanent exhibit in Port Glasgow – as befits not only the pioneer of all motorised shipping, but of Clyde shipbuilding.

Her legacy was not just a global, commercial idea, but the launch of an immediate market on Glasgow's own doorstep. The Firth of Clyde has a vast coastline, bristling with communities in this bay to the south and east and up many meandering straits and sea lochs to the Highland north, to say nothing of Arran, Bute and the Cumbraes. The new seaways also presented, as Bell had cleverly grasped if ineptly executed, immediate tourist access to the wilder Highlands – now eagerly sought, as the Romantic movement burgeoned and the works of Scott and 'Ossian' sold by the thousand.

The little flyboats which had hitherto borne folk from Glasgow to Greenock, as one Victorian later recalled, were but 'a species of wherry-built nutshells' and the name was no doubt sarcastic: usual time on passage was 10 hours. And the 'conveyance of goods and passengers to places more remote than Greenock was a more ambitious ship, generally known by the name of "Packet", which, with a fair wind, could reach the Isle of Bute in three days, but, when adverse, thought it "not wonderful" to plough the billowy main for as many weeks!' Even allowing for dramatic licence, the wider Firth was now opened up in a whole new fashion, and ports and resorts now developed with startling speed. These early decades of Clyde steam have more than a hint of the Wild West – cut-throat competition; graft and dirty tricks; grim ground-ings and frightful explosions; booze-cruises and gambling and reckless races – but the clamour for newer, better, bigger, faster boats for Clyde and West Highland service alone continued until the Second World War. With deep-water access, links by canal (and, in due time, by rail), the established iron-foundries of Glasgow and greater Lanarkshire, an abundance of locally mined coal and, of course, many engineers and many more skilled tradesmen, shipyard after shipyard sprang to life.

'Alongside the river,' writes Alan J.S. Paterson, 'shipbuilding grew rapidly, spurred on by the development of iron ships and steam propulsion. There appeared famous yards – Tod & McGregor, at Partick; James & George Thomson, at Govan; Henderson, at Renfrew; Blackwood & Gordon, at Port Glasgow, and many others stretched along the coast from Rutherglen to Ayr – and in the heat of their competition was evolved the classic Clyde paddle steamer, designed and built for passenger service in the shallow waters of the Firth, usually good-looking, often very beautiful, and above all, speedy and maneuverable. Development of the type reached a high point . . . and some of the better known shipyards produced vessels which were intended primarily as advertisements for their builders.' From the early twentieth century, operators increasingly favoured a new sleek screw-ship – with steam turbines – for the most lucrative express long-distance runs, though paddlers retained the advantage for stop-start cruises with frequent calls, and only fell utterly from favour from the early 1950s.

By the 1860s, Clyde steamers were of such repute that furtive American agents – the country was now ablaze in Civil War – paid colossal sums for paddlers to 'run' the Union blockade of Confederate ports. By 1900, the Clyde built ships for an Empire and battleships for a Queen, as the gentry she enriched built stately holiday homes in the likes of Helensburgh, Kilcreggan, Innellan or Tighnabruaich; as the most privileged professionals could commute to the city from some pleasant seaside village; as the better-waged tradesmen and employees took annual 'Glasgow Fair' leave, every July, for the cheap and cheerful facilities of Rothesay or Dunoon; as even the less well-off might at least manage a day-trip 'doon the watter'.

By 1901, when the *King Edward* – the world's first commercial turbine-steamer, with five propellers – was launched by Wm Denny & Bros of Dumbarton, the advertising had won these yards global renown. The men of Clydeside turned out coastal, ocean-going and fighting ships of every description; 'Clyde-built' had entered the language for the highest standards of workmanship. The ships, for a start, were tough. The *King Edward* alone would sail for over 50 years, and serve in two world wars; the 1946 *Waverley* washes on, nearly 65 years later, with abiding élan. And they grew increasingly luxurious.

Most durable of all was the legendary *Glencoe*, built as the *Mary Jane* by Tod & McGregor and launched for Sir James Matheson, new laird of Lewis, in 1846, with a steeple engine driven by a single cylinder. Sir James sold her in 1851, and in 1857 she was acquired by David Hutcheson Ltd, already establishing itself as the main shipping company for the West Highlands and Hebrides: one of the directors was a young man called David MacBrayne. From 1879, it was his business, and his name: four years earlier, remodelled and lengthened a little, the *Mary Jane* had emerged from a refit as the *Glencoe*. But that ancient steeple engine was still driving her in 1931, when – in a clever publicity stunt – she sailed from Skye to Glasgow to pose for pictures, at the Broomielaw, with the latest MacBrayne ship, the new diesel-electric *Loch Fyne*, in her curvy art deco boxiness.

To the last, the tough old thing bore a sign in her steerage compartment, the only covered accommodation for the poorest travellers: 'This cabin has accommodation for 90 third-class passengers, when not occupied by sheep, cattle or other encumbrances.' The age behind such sentiment was already far gone when the 85-year-old paddler was finally broken up that autumn of 1931; her splendid, archaic engine was rapidly acquired by Glasgow's Kelvingrove Museum. For the time being, it was stored in the basement, awaiting mounting and display. By 1945, of necessity in a struggle when non-ferrous metals fast became precious, the machinery of the *Glencoe* had been long smelted for the war against Nazi Germany, and technology infinitely more awful prepared to obliterate Hiroshima.

But it was Thomson's of Clydebank who, on 11 April 1878, launched – for the sum of £28,000 – what remains still the most famous MacBrayne ship and perhaps the best-loved of all Clyde steamers, the *Columba*. She was a luxury ship for a flagship route – the daily run from Glasgow to Ardrishaig, part of the 'Royal Route' to Inverness by a succession of barges, paddlers and two canals, sanctioned by Queen Victoria herself on an 1847 jaunt, in the sort of publicity Hutcheson – and MacBrayne – could not have bought.

The *Columba* was built of steel – then still thought very daring for a ship – and, driven finally at 19 knots by stately oscillating engines, just about the fastest steamer of her day and indeed faster than any modern vessel in the Caledonian MacBrayne fleet. It would be well after the Second World War before any bigger craft saw service in the Clyde and as recently as 1993 (when a new Arran ferry, *Caledonian Isles*, began service) before any surpassed her 311-foot length. Yet this was a beautiful greyhound of a boat, with curved and ornamented bow, much lovingly carved and gilded decoration, especially on her paddle boxes; majestic tall, raked masts and funnels either side of her paddles, and – inside – facilities and décor becoming a vessel catering expressly for the gentry and which only sailed at the height of the season: not much over four months of the year. Her saloons extended the whole width of the hull – then most unusual. She had a smoking-room, a book stall, a fruit stall, a hairdressing salon (with mechanical brushes) and even an onboard post office. Though in several respects distinctly dated – MacBrayne was already 65 and betraying the conservatism that would finally ruin the family business – the old-fashioned oscillating engines were of the smoothest operation, a shrewd consideration on so long a run. But let a contemporary reporter relate the wonders of this Clydebank marvel:

Descending from the promenade deck – which is 220 feet long and the whole width of the vessel – two staircases lead aft to the saloon. Between these staircases is a well-lighted and comfortably furnished smoking-room, from the windows of which a good view is obtainable of the engines. Further aft, and on either side of the boat, are ladies' and gentlemen's lavatories, the mountings of the wash-hand basins being silver and everything else en-suite. The saloon is a magnificent apartment nearly eighty feet long, lofty, and lighted by continuous plate-glass windows hung with crimson drapery. The ceiling both of this and of the dining saloon below is artistically stenciled in light slate-blue upon a rich ground of ribbed gold, and being paneled with boldly mounted girders, also painted blue, has a wonderfully light and agreeable effect. The seats are placed at right angles to the windows, as in a Pullman car, and are upholstered in crimson silk velvet. From the stern windows a fine view is obtainable, and the saloon being adorned with several large mirrors, has an air of space even out of proportion with its undoubted roominess. But the dining saloon is the great feature of the *Columba*. Situated below the main saloon, and of the same dimensions, it is decorated in the most lavish and artistic manner. The panels are of polished wood – teak, maple, mahogany, and rosewood being the materials used. Some of the panels are painted to represent inlaying in pattern, and the capitals of the pillars and moulding of the cornice are heavily coated with gold. The pillars are of teak, the upper part being white, with gold flutings. Great taste has been shown in the choice of the carpets and the upholstery, the chairs being covered with a rich, old-fashioned, dark canary-coloured velvet. At the stern end of the saloon, advantage has been taken of the narrowing and shelving character of the boat above the helm to arrange a conservatory, a fine lot of rare plants being disposed in front of the mirror which closes in the view. Mr Turner, the steward, who now undertakes the purveying both of the *Iona* and *Columba*, has effected a revolution in the art of dining on board ship by the use of round instead of long, straight tables, and by serving dinners at all hours instead of at one stated time. By this means, a little party of tourists may dine at their own table without interference from others, and at any time they may choose. The steward's pantry and scullery, leading off the dining saloon, are fitted up with all the latest improvements, one of the most novel of which is a counter warmed by steam, on which there is room for ten or fifteen dishes . . . Of all the appointments of the dining saloon, however, the most noticeable is a series of painted glass panels each containing a motto, and a group of figures illustrative of the text. Both in treatment and in colour the style of the pictures is strictly conventional, after the medieval school, and the panels attract attention as much by the vigour and strength of the drawing as by the quaint and droll effect produced. An idea of the pictures may possibly be formed from one or two of the mottoes: 'Gude claes open a' doors'; 'A' the wit's no in ae pow', 'Fine feathers make fine birds', 'A low bush is better than nae bield', 'Marry for love and work for siller', 'Ane at a time is guid fishing', and so on. The panels are the work of Messrs W & J Keir, of St Vincent Street, who have also contributed a larger stained-glass window, illustrating 'The landing of St Columba on the island of Iona' . . . The saloon for steerage passengers is plainly though substantially furnished, and below is a refreshment bar, with semicircular counter, silver-plated rail, decanters and glasses all complete. Forward of this again is the fore-cabin very comfortably upholstered. Bath-rooms, pursers' cabins, and store-rooms are closely adjacent, and their fittings serve to show how thoroughly the demands both of passengers and officials have been anticipated . . .

The *Columba* would sail for nearly 60 years, a 'Society' ship, carrying some of the most famous folk in the country to their annual Highland sporting-grounds. She made her last journey in April 1936, to Dalmuir – at the other end of the town that built her – and there the men of Arnott, Young & Co. (Shipbreakers) Ltd converged with 'hammer, chisel and oxy-acetylene flame', as Hitler's troops repossessed the Rhineland.

Glasgow had made the Clyde – but with rapid and, in decades, frightful impact on land, air and water. Between yards and factories, steamers and freighters and, of course, thousands of tightly packed new homes – as the conurbation swelled, and swelled more – Clydeside burned, day and night, prodigious quantities of soft local coal.

The grey, filthy, smut-laden air is immediately evident in Victorian photographs. At the city's heart, it all but blocked out the sun; this perpetual gloom, combined with poor and often windowless housing, made the city notorious for childhood rickets: strong bone demands vitamin D, which the body cannot manufacture without sunlight. Even down firth, as more photographs attest, prodigious quantities of smoke poured from steamer funnels until the latter decades of the nineteenth century, when serious efforts began to mitigate the nuisance – though not before thousands of passengers had sustained damage to clothing from tiny glowing cinders, or had a day's outing ruined by smut in the eye. Consumption, with cheap Lanarkshire coal and still cheaper labour, was almost heroic: the *Columba* alone, with what even in 1878 was not – by the standards of the time – thermally efficient machinery, devoured 18 to 20 tons every day as she flew to Ardrishaig and back.

Until well after the Second World War – when the growth in motor emissions added another toxic dimension – conditions, especially in winter and during one of the Clyde's thick advection fogs, could be appalling. My father, then a young student at the university, could remember a 1958 smog in Partick so bad a clean shirt might have to be donned two or three times daily; one coughed or sneezed black stuff into a handkerchief; you could not, out of doors at night, even see your hand in front of your face in certain weather. He recalls nights when you felt your way home with your hands along a tenement wall, navigating a street; the frequent tinkle of glass, as the criminal took advantage of the conditions with some enterprising smash-and-grab. Such were conditions on Clydeside even half a century ago. The Clean Air Acts – and the steady demise thereafter of solid, even 'smokeless' fuel for domestic use in urban Scotland – won notable improvement by the late 1960s; but it is difficult for a younger generation to believe how black and gaunt and ugly practically every pre-war structure was, especially nearest the river and its industrial heart, until far into the 1970s when widespread and determined stone-cleaning began.

Now mercifully beyond living memory is just how foul the Clyde herself quickly became, to the point where – even as Clydebank began to rise – it was affecting steamboat trade. Salmon had still run the river as late as 1812. As early as 1841, the Glasgow, Paisley and Greenock Railway opened for business on its self-evident route, and from that point river traffic from the city centre to the Tail o' the Bank – by Greenock, where an estuary becomes beyond doubt the green and briny sea – started steadily to decline. The train was much faster (if, for most, less comfortable), but there was another marketing advantage: the upper Clyde was fast becoming an open sewer, thick with all the raw waste of what would soon be the fourth-largest city in Europe. By 1864, only the poorest passengers would tolerate passage, especially in high hot summer, through such conditions. By the 1880s, the major steamer lines concentrated on lucrative trade from the new railheads at Greenock, Gourock, Wemyss Bay and in time Largs, Craigendoran and Helensburgh.

'Permit me, through the columns of your valuable daily newspaper,' wailed 'An Englishman' in the correspondence columns of the *Glasgow Herald*, 'to call the attention of the authorities of Glasgow to the deplorable state of the river Clyde. It is nothing better than the foulest sewer of any large town in England [*sic*]; and it is only astonishing to me that the effluvia constantly emitted has not been the cause of some serious epidemic . . . You have a city of palaces, magnificent streets, well paved and kept thoroughly clean, but your main artery, which should be as pure as possible, is a continuous stream of reeking filth and noxious vapours . . .'

But nothing was done until a new century, by which time the bulk of up-river passenger traffic had been destroyed. The Clyde remained a dubious waterway into my own lifetime; and it would be 1977, by which time I had almost completed primary school, before the salmon that adorned the city arms again began to run upriver, from sea to hill.

And, beyond smoke and ordure, grime and stench, there was a dreadful human cost to all this progress. The Clyde had made Glasgow: they had, between them, wrought besides entire new forms of social misery. And long before March 1941, it had all at last driven those who had nothing to sell save their labour to leaders who could campaign effectively on labour's behalf. In turn – especially in this new Clydebank, proud to style herself 'the risingest burgh in Scotland' – it made this river and her shores a byword for unrest, for socialism, and, in the eyes of jumpy authority, potential and serious sedition.

3

SHOULDER TO SHOULDER

In 1866, a labour dispute – at a time when workers had few meaningful rights in law – finally saw shipyard owners impose, for six long months, a 'lock-out' of all workers who had dared join a trade union. One was a skilled ship's carpenter who had a decade earlier moved with his family to a burgeoning Glasgow. Money was so tight that in 1863, when his eldest son was only seven, little James had to be sent out to work; though his parents, exhausted as they all were of an evening in a single-room tenement apartment, insisted on giving him lessons and he could at least read, write and count.

James was now 10 and working as a roundsman – delivering hot fresh morning bread – for a prosperous, rather religious city baker; even as the lock-out continued and his parents sold everything they could. With their last mean sticks of furniture gone, James's weekly pay – 4s 6d – was their only income, for his mother was again with child and could not work either. Chill and hungry, his little brother fell sick; his father, now frantic, had no choice but to go to sea, leaving them all to fend as best they could until things improved.

One night, with the infant due and his brother fevered and girning, James had tended his family as best he could. He had had scarcely an hour's sleep, nor bite of food, when – late and flustered – he scampered to work. It was Hogmanay, it was still dark and freezing, and he was late. He was at once summoned by his boss.

> Outside the dining room door, a servant bade me wait, till 'Master has finished prayers.' (He was much noted for his piety.) At length the girl opened the door, and the sight of that room is fresh in my memory even as I write, nearly fifty years later. Round a great mahogany table sat the members of the family, with the father at the top. In front of him was a very wonderful coffee boiler in the great glass bowl of which the coffee was bubbling. The table was loaded with dainties. My master looked at me over his glasses and said, in quite a pleasant tone of voice, 'Boy, this is the second morning you have been late, and my customers will leave me if they are kept waiting for their hot breakfast rolls. I therefore dismiss you and, to make you more careful in the future, I have decided to fine you a week's wages. And now you may go.' That night the baby was born, and the sun rose on the 1st of January 1867 over a home in which there was neither fire nor food.

In July 1892, at the other end of the United Kingdom, James Keir Hardie – now long active in the cause of Britain's workers and who had established a

'Scottish Labour Party', was returned as a 'Labour' MP for West Ham South, the first ever elected.

He could not hold on at the 1895 general election, but – out of Parliament – immersed himself thereafter in efforts to co-ordinate trades-union and disparate socialist groups into one coherent body that would sponsor Parliamentary candidates. Late in February 1900, at a two-day conference, the 'Labour Representative Committee' – the modern Labour Party – was born: James Ramsay MacDonald, the illegitimate son of a poor Lossiemouth fishergirl, was elected secretary. At that year's election, two Labour MPs – including Hardie, for the Welsh fastness of Merthyr Tydfil – were elected. In 1906 – the Liberals had complacently extended a limited electoral pact – Labour won 29 seats; in 1910, 42. After the 1923 general election, with Labour as the second-largest party in a hung Parliament, King George V called MacDonald to the Palace and asked him to form a government.

'Red Clydeside' – in myth as much as reality – bears heavily on the terrible bombing of Clydebank and western Glasgow in March 1941. For one, unease about the mettle of working-class people heavily coloured civil defence planning once Britain began to rearm. For another, long distrust of established authority (to say nothing of high-minded but naive pacifism) undoubtedly made Labour-run local authorities in some localities – and Clydebank was one of them – loath to co-operate, and late in doing so. It is nevertheless unlikely that Germany deliberately held back from full-scale bombing of Clydeside in the hope that it would slide into one seething hotbed of revolution; more improbable still – though it is nevertheless insinuated, by Meg Henderson and others – that the government did not unduly exert itself in the aerial defence of the region in March 1941.

All this, of course, followed over half a century of increasingly effective working-class politics, as Scotland began belatedly to address the human cost of a new order. 'Economic and political factors combined to introduce the Industrial Revolution in the west of Scotland before it made much impact on the continent,' write Drummond and Bulloch, 'and appropriately, therefore, Scotland also made great contributions to the early scientific study of Political Economy.' A number of eminent eighteenth-century Scottish minds – like David Hume, the philosopher – might be better known for their thoughts in this field, were they not lost in the dust of such a colossus as Adam Smith. Born at Kirkcaldy in 1723, and educated at Glasgow and Oxford, Smith settled finally in Glasgow, in 1751, as professor first of logic and then of moral philosophy. The university had close ties to the city's commercial life; Smith was well placed to observe Glasgow's rapid and most prosperous growth, and many merchants came to his lectures, especially a series when, in his own complacent words, he 'examined those political regulations which are founded, not so much upon the principle of *justice*, but that of *expediency*'. In due time, in 1776, these lectures became a book whose influence is incalculable: Adam Smith's *Inquiry into the Nature and Causes of the Wealth of Nations*.

Smith was not a nice man. The catalogue of his magnificent library survives: fat with the classics, history, geography, and philosophers from Plato to Hutcheson, Hume and Reid. There is much poetry and no less than 69 volumes of Voltaire. But there is practically nothing on religion. Smith was not spiritually minded and had but the 'Moderate' high-mindedness of the Kirk in his day: 'that pure and rational religion, free from every mixture of absurdity, imposture, or fanaticism, such as wise men have, in all ages of the world, wished to see established'. In fact – if we may mischievously borrow a word from Smith's most famous twentieth-century acolytes – he only cared for faith as long as it was privatised: a field of contemplation and reassurance for the gentry, framing wider social control of the rabble.

The Wealth of Nations is one of the great tomes of the Enlightenment, founded on that same bland Deism immediately familiar and comforting to almost everyone who then ran the country: 'that men lived in an ordered universe', write Drummond and Bulloch, 'ruled by divine law for the ultimate good of all who permitted an impartial and benevolent Providence for the well being of all'. Smith's masterpiece on these happy premises extolled the right-eousness of individual enterprise, the benefits of competition and, above all, the need for entire freedom from any government interference, political intervention or legal restraint. It was read joyously by the Glasgow merchants, by new industrialists throughout Britain and men throughout Europe who – like William Pitt the Younger – headed governments, or hoped shortly to do so.

Few – even today, when the Smith analysis has recovered alarming standing on all sides of the Commons – look too closely at its soul. In practice 'he restricted moral considerations to private life and divorced them from business and social matters. Thus he helped to bring about a society prepared to function without interference either from ethical considerations of religion or social considerations of government. Religion was banished to a private sphere, where it would not have contact with business . . . Adam Smith's teachings heralded a century in which ruthlessness in industry and commerce could be, and often were, combined with evangelical devotion and private charity on a large scale.'

And in the west of Scotland, especially, fortunes were built at untold social cost as even churchmen like Thomas Chalmers stubbornly refused to subject the economics of Adam Smith to any intelligent Christian critique, thereby granting 'something like a divine sanction to the consequences of uninhibited free enterprise'. The rise, after the Disruption of 1843, of the new Free and United Presbyterian Churches – who for decades eclipsed the established Kirk in Scottish life – was another factor. Unlike her, they had no state or lairdly emoluments and were wholly dependent on the givings of their people. It was inevitable that commercially successful laymen won great place; that ministers dependent on their munificence were loath to search consciences as to how, precisely, they made their money.

It is difficult to exaggerate the change that swept Scotland in the decades after Smith's book. For one – thanks largely to improved agriculture, and the earlier introduction of the potato – there was a massive increase in population. In a pioneering census of 1755, it was estimated that the little country supported 1,265,380 people. In 1801, it was over 1,600,000 – and grew inexorably thereafter. The eighteenth century had seen Scotland transformed from a land of peasants to a much more stratified, mercantile society.

Besides – a development that has never really been reversed – enterprise and leadership in almost all fields shifted steadily from Edinburgh to Glasgow. And, as it grew harder for a poor man to improve his social position, he grew the more willing to move out of the parish – and increasingly to the city: Smith himself complained that farmers near town now had to pay better wages to keep their hands. Social cohesion declined. David Hume and the Edinburgh gentry generally had lived more or less on top of the Old Town slums; now, as its gracious Georgian streets took shape, the rich decamped rapidly to the New Town. Society grew more segregated. By the late nineteenth century, Glasgow's wealthiest, too, had largely abandoned the city centre for new suburban villas. Churches moved out of town after their best givers, leaving behind but patronising 'missions' for the lower orders. What we now call the 'knowledge economy' saw striking change, especially with increasing specialisation: by the mid nineteenth century it was no longer possible for an educated man to be equally at ease in all fields of study – with the consequence that the clergy ceased to be intellectual leaders and that, of necessity (and with only one twentieth-century exception), university principals ceased to be ordained ministers.

All the while, thousands poured into the cities. By 1861, over half the population lived in the central and industrial belt; a century later, it held four-fifths of the Scottish people – the most ill-balanced distribution of population in Europe; the exclusion of Aberdeen from this ready reckoning means the denudation of the countryside was even worse. The pressures – centred on the issue of 'patronage', on the right of heritors (landlords) to appoint a given minister to a parish whatever the wishes of the people – that finally blew the Established Church in twain in 1843 owed much to the increasing impossibility of doing her job in a new demographic reality. The historic geography of parish ministry was quite unequal to expanding conurbation, and Westminster refused to grant anything like the finance required; the more serious a neglect at a time when education, poor-relief and even important functions of local government were the Kirk's responsibility.

The Borders of course lost many inhabitants; but the tide of new oppression to the north and west drew far more attention to the exsanguination of the Highlands and Islands, whose population grew considerably until 1841 and whose overwhelming export was people. It was in these decades that Evangelicalism took firm hold of the western seaboard and the first indication of a burgeoning Highland community in Glasgow is the founding of a 'Gaelic chapel' at Ingram Street, in 1772. A second would open at Duke Street in 1798; Greenock boasted one from 1792. As recently as the 1980s, six Glasgow churches – of three Presbyterian denominations – still held weekly Gaelic services: as early as 1893, when the Free Presbyterian Church of Scotland was founded, a small Gaelic-speaking group of Free Church 'separatists' in Clydebank, a town scarcely two decades old, quickly joined it.

It would be almost the twentieth century – when a new West Highland fishing economy would ensure that a high proportion of Clydeside migrants were experienced seamen – before most Highlanders could hope for anything more in the city than unskilled labour (for men) and domestic service (for women); by the Great War, Clyde shipping was so thick with Gaelic-speaking crewmen that people joked of the 'Skye Navy'. For now, they were an alien group, further jamming the slums and the victims of much (and abiding) prejudice, not readily distinguished from a far more momentous immigration to Scotland.

Unskilled workers, observes T.C. Smout,

> saved little, accumulated little in their homes, led a domestic life fragmented by the treadmill of toiling for a subsistence, and tended to be comparatively illiterate. Their house was in a slum area, their food mainly potatoes and meal unless scrag-ends of meat had to be purchased for the man to keep up his strength during a navvying job. Their future was depressing, and pointed downwards to a pauper's grave as their physical energy gave out . . . In many cases the unskilled workers were recent Irish immigrants, in some, displaced Highlanders . . . additionally separated from the Lowland artisan, and from all other Scots, by ethnic and linguistic barriers, and the Catholic Irish by religious barriers as well. It was hard for them to identify across such a divide, and native Lowland Scots despised both the Highland 'teuchter' and the Irish 'paddy.'

The scale of immigration from Ireland was vast. By the census of 1841, Scotland already had 125,000 people of Irish birth; at the height of the appalling potato famine, the 'Great Hunger' of 1848, nearly a thousand arrived in Glasgow every week. Though sober scholarship has established that 'sectarianism' in Scotland is largely a myth, if one in the interests of both recent Labour politicians and the Roman Catholic hierarchy steadily to stoke – in fact, we absorbed and integrated the Irish with remarkably little trouble – it was of signal cultural moment. At the Revolution of 1689, there were scarcely 50,000 Roman Catholics in Scotland, most in those places that evaded the near-total tide of sixteenth-century Reformation (like Galloway, or in Aberdeenshire and Banffshire) or pockets of Gaeldom that had been subsequently won for Mother Church by Franciscan mission (like Barra, South Uist and the 'Rough Bounds' of Knoydart). By 1800, the Catholic population had actually declined to 30,000. The 1755 survey had identified only 265 in Edinburgh, three in Renfrewshire and just two in all Lanarkshire. As recently as 1781, every Roman Catholic Glasgow were served by one peripatetic priest, from Drummond Castle in Perthshire.

Sectarianism – and one should not make light of the spite that soon locked so many of Irish origin into a siege mentality – was not an instinctive Scottish response to immigration; it was imported with it. Most of the new arrivals came from Ulster; it is not widely realised that many were Episcopalians and vocal Ulster Protestants. Most of these, as Smout points out, were of Scottish descent and of Scottish surnames, typically a man who 'found it easier to integrate than the Catholic, and aggressively asserted his Orange and anti-papistical sentiments as a way of allying himself to the native Scots and dissociating himself from his fellow Irishmen. The Catholic Irish were thereby driven even more firmly into a ghetto mentality, and clung to the bosom of Mother Church to find some kind of comfort and support in a totally unwelcoming environment.'

To this day the whole question of Irish immigration and – closely related – the revival of the Roman Catholic Church as a major force in Scottish life is the stuff of abiding mythology. (It is conceivably true that, in Glasgow in 1795, there were only 39 Catholic Irish in town and 43 vociferously anti-Catholic clubs, but it is impossible to document.) In terms of official, political venom, Edinburgh has actually a much worse record than Glasgow: the city saw serious anti-Catholic rioting in 1779, and menacing scenes (and the election of explicitly anti-Catholic councillors) as recently as the 1930s. Though it is now fashionable to deplore the Reverend John White, a prominent Church of Scotland figure between the wars, for his leadership in the Kirk's very vocal stand against continued Irish migration, it should be remembered that what White feared has indeed come to pass: Scotland is no longer in any meaningful sense a Protestant country. But that is in large measure because Roman Catholic clergy did a much better job of holding on to their own working-class people – by their sacrificial endeavours in the slums, and with striking pastoral skill – than the Presbyterians. And the abiding profile of Roman Catholic leadership in Scotland is largely because her bishops and cardinals have not been afraid to make strong stands on moral issues, even highly emotive ones: not, in recent decades, a habit of the Kirk. Nor has it all been one sex-obsessed rant. In 2001, in practically his last public act, Cardinal Thomas Winning publicly condemned prejudice and violence against newly arrived 'asylum-seekers' in one of the poorest corners of Glasgow. Winning, born in the Wishaw of the 1920s as the son of an illegitimate and latterly unemployed labourer (and, of course, Roman Catholic) knew well what it was to be on the outside looking in.

Assorted, archived material of Victorian Scotland gives chilling glimpses of this ruthless, divided country. In July 1866 there was a frightful accident on the Clyde steamer *Vesta*. A drunk merrily tossed a heaving-line overboard, while a little girl was standing on its coiled mooring-warp; the rope caught in the paddle wheel and, before the appalled master had a chance to stop the engines, her foot was caught and literally torn off. She died several hours later, but the newspaper account of the accident felt obliged to add, 'The value of the rope is stated to be about £15.' A minister of one United Presbyterian congregation in Glasgow took a service for another, and at the last minute his wife threw on the first coat she had to hand – worn and shabby – and scurried out to hear him. At sermon's end an elder accosted her at the door and said, 'We were so pleased to have you tonight, but wouldn't you be more at home at the mission?' In 1887, an architect was happy to produce plans for what was still a daring innovation: a crematorium 'suited to the requirements of Glasgow. . . . On the high level a chapel for the very rich; the second or better class chapel being on the ground level; the third or working class chapel to the right; and a Chapel for the pauper class to the left of the receiving room or Mortuary . . .'

But modern nightmare at its most Dickensian can scarcely conceive of the conditions – abiding well into living memory – in which hundreds of thousands of ordinary Scots were forced to live. There was besides the exploitation of women and children in frightful sweatshop conditions; much cruelty, not least to animals; wholesale filth and pollution; child prostitution; the wholesale and almost heroic abuse of alcohol for desperate oblivion (by 1839, it was reliably calculated that the average Scot over 15 drank a pint of spirits a week – an annual *per capita* consumption of over 2 gallons for every man, woman and child in the land); the near-total absence of workers' rights – but we come back, time and again, to the central problem of housing.

In 1881, one observer, J.B. Russell, gave Glasgow's Park Parish Literary Institute some home truths about how most of the city's people lived. Of 511,520 inhabitants in all, 126,000 lived in 'single ends' – one-room tenement flats without piped water or sanitation – or the scarcely bigger 'room and kitchen' apartments. It was a city long noted for gross overcrowding – only Dundee saw similar conditions – but Russell did not pull his punches.

It is those small houses which produce the high death rate of Glasgow. It is those small houses which give to that death rate the striking characteristics of an enormous proportion of deaths in childhood, and of death from diseases of the lungs at all ages. Their exhausted air and poor and perverse feeding fill our streets with bandy-legged children. There you will find year after year a death rate of 38 per 1,000, while in the districts with larger houses it is only 16 or 17. Of all the children who die in Glasgow before they complete their fifth year, 32 per cent die in houses of one apartment; and not 2 per cent in houses of five apartments and upwards. There they die, and their little bodies are laid on a table or on the dresser, so as to be somewhat out of the way of their brothers and sisters, who play and sleep and eat in their ghastly company. From beginning to rapid-ending the lives of these children are short parts in a continuous tragedy. A large proportion enter life by the side-door of illegitimacy. One in every five of all who are born there never see the end of their first year. Of those who so prematurely die a third have never been seen in their sickness by any doctor. 'The tongue of the suckling child cleaveth to the roof of his mouth for thirst; the young children ask bread and no man breaketh it unto them.' Every year in Glasgow the deaths of from 60 to 70 children under five years of age are classified by the Registrar-General as due to accident or negligence; and it is wholly in these small houses that such deaths occur. Half of that number are overlaid by drunken mothers, others fall over windows and down stairs, are drowned in tubs and pails of water, scalded, or burned, or poisoned with whisky. I can only venture to lift a corner of the curtain which veils the life which is lived in these houses. It is impossible to show you more.

The 1861 census confirmed that 34 per cent of all Scottish houses had only one room; 37 per cent but two. One family in a hundred lived in homes without any windows. Such conditions 'made domestic life as it was known to the middle classes impossible', Smout observes. 'There was no privacy, no play space, no work space, no place to get out of the tensions of family life, to think, relax, or sulk. There was not even space to die.' A few of the lowest poor, observed an Edinburgh gynaecologist who assisted in a disturbing 1842 study, *Reports on the Sanitary Condition of the Labouring Population of Scotland*, 'have a bedstead, but by far the larger portion have none; these make up a kind of bed on floor with straw, on which a whole family are huddled together, some naked and the others in the same clothes they have worn during the day'.

City localities that, but decades earlier, had housed the gentry were now slums. Some of the worst housing in Europe surrounded the universities of Glasgow and Edinburgh, where folk lived in revolting conditions. 'Cooking and all the physical functions of humanity,' muse Drummond and Bulloch, 'went on incessantly among large families in "single ends" and created an unspeakable atmosphere. In the heat of summer the foul blast emerging from each close mouth would have enabled a blind man to enter one without touching a wall, and when girls wore clothing which had been kept in such houses no perfume could come near concealing the fact. When toilets had to be added to the older tenements this was done by building them in a sort of brick tower attached to the staircase, one on each floor to serve the four, six and sometimes eight families involved. In winter these froze, and the contents flowed down the stair . . .'

Vermin flourished in such an environment and disease still more so, not least in those city wynds where inhabitants even stored their own excrement to help pay the rent. Experienced professional men – doctors or ministers long exposed to the usual hardships of the Scottish countryside – were aghast at what they found in her cities. 'I never knew what destitution was, among the poor in the country,' recorded one pastor. 'I never saw a case of destitution that I could not relieve before the sun went down; but here there are thousands of cases that you cannot relieve . . .'

Improvement, until after the Great War, would be painfully slow, though windowless hovels had largely vanished by the 1880s and the number of 'single ends' had declined to 13 per cent of the Scottish total by 1911. And cramped, unhappy conditions could not be blithely explained away as old, obsolete housing stock. 'Clydebank, for instance,' Smout points out, 'was a small village of 816 inhabitants in 1871 and a brand new town of 30,000 by 1901: ten years later, four-fifths of its houses were of two rooms or less.'

Marxist historians have argued that such gross inequity is inevitable in the joyous march of economic history: the rich grow fatter and entrenched in power, as the downtrodden masses stay poor, or grow poorer still. But it is not borne out by experience elsewhere. In America, for instance, the new industrialism brought widespread social benefits. Nor did it continue its pitiless course in Britain: since the Great War, and especially since the Second World War, there has been much more general material progress and a widespread rise in living standards, even in west-central Scotland – and as Britain's relative wealth and, emphatically, her standing in the world fell so rapidly away. Ken Loach's bleak if engaging 2002 film *Sweet Sixteen* – set in Greenock and using largely a local cast without previous acting experience – is a troubling study of alienation, hopelessness and near-Darwinian morality in the post-industrial Scotland of the new century: but his characters, clean and pink and neatly dressed, toting mobile phones and clawing for advantage in the black economy, are not 'poor' in any recognisable sense from the perspective of, say, the 1930s. Their true deprivation – reinforced by a failing political order and welfare system, addiction and family breakdown and the ugly built environment, even against magnificent Clyde scenery – is emotional and spiritual.

The wicked order of things in industrial Scotland endured so long – and bequeathed an abiding legacy of bitterness and distrust, rather than the quiet social consensus that took root elsewhere, even in Imperial Germany – because of the gross imbalance of power between the princes of commerce and the mass of ordinary people; because of the extraordinary sense of entitlement among those who benefited most; the entire failure of the Scottish churches (distracted for most of the century by denominational empire-building) to confront the new order of things; and, of course, because until very late in the nineteenth century most men were denied the vote.

Accordingly, and with significant backing from the machinery of state – which they largely controlled – the winners of the new Scotland could engage in the determined abuse of power amidst general genuflection before laissez-faire economics and the positive duty of government not, in any way, to interfere with the business of making money.

That gained all the more force from the impact on ruling-class consciousness of one event late in the eighteenth century: the French Revolution. It is impossible to overstate the genuine terror this bloodbath inspired among the rich and mighty of Britain, especially after the slump (and widespread unrest, with strikes and protests) that followed the end of the Napoleonic Wars. For almost a generation, most of Scotland's educated class dreaded similar frenzy in their own little land. The fear of 'sedition' strongly coloured Thomas Chalmers's attitude to social change and permeates the memoirs and journals of one of the age's great Scottish observers, Lord Cockburn: even in his circles, the moneyed and legal echelons at the top of Edinburgh society, one careless word could land you in serious trouble; all the more so when the past Jacobite threat, and the government's counter-measures in Scotland, had but lately receded. As late as 1820, the '45 itself was still – just – in living memory.

By default, the energy of protest boiled further down society, among the lower middle class and the urban artisans – like the colliers, the many surviving and independent small-scale coal-miners; but especially the handloom weavers of the west, not least in Paisley. They were thoughtful, well read, of dissenting religion (most supported the Secession Church) and of decided attitude. Late in 1812, though, they had launched a disastrous strike, ending in entire failure early in the New Year after nine futile weeks. The supremacy of capital over labour was now established and not readily overturned.

In April 1820, widespread unrest – as Scottish gentry nervously raised militia, and a still more fearful government cultivated spies and launched assorted *agents provocateurs* – culminated in 'A Committee of Organisation for Forming a Provisional Government', who on 1 April erected placards around Glasgow and clamoured for a national strike. Days, later, on Monday 3 April, there was indeed widespread downing of tools, as a contingent marched on the Carron Iron Company works near Falkirk to seize weapons. At Bonnymuir, they were attacked by hussars; meanwhile, militia marching with hastily-seized prisoners to the jail at Greenock were beset by local sympathisers. The authorities – with abundant troops and determined will – quickly crushed the 'Scottish Insurrection'. Three leaders – John Baird, Andrew Hardie and James Wilson – choked slowly on the noose; afterwards, and gratuitously, Wilson's corpse was beheaded. There were many other arrests and 20 prominent in the 'Radical War' were eventually transported. Down south, just a year before, the appalling 'Peterloo Massacre' in Manchester – when 40 cavalrymen charged a peaceful demonstration, killing 11 people and wounded 400 more – provoked such uproar in English cities that for a few days revolution seemed a serious possibility. The Tory government hastily passed new, Draconian laws, banning 'combinations' – trades unions – and meetings of more than 50 people, and enacted besides the vindictive Stamp Acts, imposing a tax on pamphlets and newspapers that might otherwise rouse the masses.

The courage of those involved in the events of 1820 is undoubted, but there is strong evidence of provocation by government agents and, in all, the fiasco only hindered endeavours for reform.

And the Stamp Acts vividly underline an inconvenient truth for the enduring advocates of Adam Smith and untrammelled free markets. Such virtue as it may have only stands if it is indeed free and without interference for all involved. In fact, the boss class were very happy for all sorts of intervention and legislation – in their own interests and against the poor, reinforcing their power at every turn. We have already noted how those who made money from renting out slums to Scotland's workers could plot to stifle any public housing provision. Employers – especially shipbuilders – deplored, in the most outraged and moral tones, competitors who lured away tradesmen with better pay.

'As we think it is most unfair to entice our men away by offering exorbitant wages,' complained Charles Connell to Barclay Curle after losing an ironsmith to that yard, 'we would be glad to know if you approve of what your Foreman has done. We would just like to point out that if once we begin to outbid one another in this way, it would be the most effectual plan we could adopt to increase the rates of wages all over.' The free market, as T.C. Smout observes – relaying this story – 'was evidently only supposed to work in one direction'.

Through the early decades of the nineteenth century, the winners in Scottish society built a lucrative industrial system on Scotland's unusual abundance of cheap labour. They were helped because the new wave in radicalism – the disciplined Chartist movement of the 1840s – was restrained by the prudent, generally religious caution of its leaders, as eager to improve the education and aspirations of the poor as to assail the present political order. New power looms destroyed – with great speed and considerable suffering – the handloom weavers who remained the intelligent backbone of dissent. After two serious depressions in the 1840s – the first threatened such unrest in Paisley that Cabinet ministers and even the Queen hastily funded relief from their own pockets – artisan weavers were rapidly beggared, and no longer a class of any political importance.

Scottish industry barons faced besides a society still so divided by skills, religion and values as to be for decades incapable of concerted action. Hardie's heartless boss was only a craftsman baker, not the moneybags capitalist of caricature; but such lines of demarcation – for instance, the gulf between the time-served tradesman and the unskilled labourer; the shopkeeper and his boy; the clerk and the fitter; the foreman and the riveter; the builders, bricklayers and joiners and plasterers and plumbers, and the builder's neatly coiffed secretary – stratified working-class Scotland until very recently, and the sight of separate canteens, separate toilets and even separate entrances still disturbs visitors even from America. To the present century, on arrival at the Lewis Offshore Yard at Arnish, near Stornoway, one stared at two car parks. One was vast, unasphalted, muddy and potholed, littered with ankle-deep puddles and riven by ruts. The other, by the little office-block, was tarred, with neatly outlined bays – and beside it a cold sign: 'THIS CAR-PARK IS FOR ADMINISTRATIVE PERSONNEL ONLY. THE WORKERS' PARKING IS TO THE RIGHT.'

There is hard evidence, too, that Irish immigration was actively encouraged by powerful entrepreneurs, if only to depress wages still further: the Irishman would do jobs no one else would endure, and for less money. As early as 1792 – when the first post-Reformation Roman Catholic church was built in Glasgow, for Highland immigrants – a group of manufacturers led by the formidable David Dale, all Protestant, bankrolled the project and pledged £30 annually for the support of the priest. When labour was still distinctly short, the Catholic Schools Society was founded in 1817 with the active assistance of Protestant bosses. 'The manufacturers of this country,' noted Kirkman Finlay, 'could never have gone on without the emigration from Ireland, or the assistance of Irish weavers; and, having them, would they retain them in an ignorant and debased state, or help them to attain to the character of a population who were able to read and write?' By 1825 – well before the mass of Irish arrived – the Society had five schools with 1,400 pupils, and (despite attacks from hooligans) Glasgow's Roman Catholic cathedral was completed in 1816.

The new laws notwithstanding, from '1817 onwards organised unions appear in many places,' notes Smout, 'especially in the western counties of Ayrshire, Lanarkshire, Renfrew and Dunbartonshire fighting wage reductions, limiting output to maintain the price of labour, and in some places trying to operate a closed shop to keep out strangers. The owners freely retaliated by importing Irish blackleg labour, which began a tradition of bitter racial and religious hatred that marred life in the West of Scotland throughout the nineteenth century and is not dead today.' Such use of desperate Irish migrants to break strikes and subvert early trades-union endeavours was bitterly resented, and abiding folk-memory of it undoubtedly fuelled twentieth-century trouble.

The Combination Laws were repealed in 1830, and trades unions at last began to multiply, but they would take decades to achieve serious clout. For now, the law remained firmly weighted in favour of capital. The instinctive reaction of employers, when markets grew tight or times grew hard, was to cut wages and increase hours. Though they inveighed most righteously against the wickedness of unions and strikes, they could (and of course did) form combinations and cartels of their own; and agreed tacitly to rig wages; and kept one another informed of known 'agitators'. Such, like Keir Hardie's father, were 'locked out' until they learned the error of their ways, or simply dismissed.

The old paternalism of Scotland's rural parochial life found no successor in modern industry. Into the 1860s, any worker declared to be in breach of contract to his employer was invariably arrested. Most believed – with reason – that the odds lay heavily against them in any case that came to court; few could afford legal defence. As late as 1901, the Taff Vale judgement – ordering a railways union to pay £23,000 in damages after a strike – could criminalise industrial action; as late as 1909, the House of Lords passed the 'Osborne Judgement', which ruled that trades unions could no longer donate money to fund the election activities and wages of Labour MPs.

In any event, between all the social fault lines, it took remarkably long for what we would now call 'working-class consciousness' to develop. 'This came later,' observes T.C. Smout, 'but it is surely reasonable to assert that socialism, when it came, did not so much "preach the class war" as open the eyes of workers to the extent to which it had already been fought against them for generations. The wonder is they did not see it sooner.'

It was an age of double-think and propaganda. Trades unions were wicked, because they forced the price of labour above its 'natural' level; but 'employers deserved their wealth because they considered themselves finer people than most of their workers . . . the middle classes who accepted this myth could feel that those who never made it into their ranks were morally inferior: when the cheap labour was Irish, it was possible to add a racial and religious overtone to that feeling of superiority. How could you share decision-making in the work place, or build up a partnership in industry, with a proletariat you considered drunken, ignorant and superstitious?' And one of the most striking aspects of the history of the Left in Scotland, even to the present century, is how economic radicalism has been generally allied to profound social conservatism.

By the 1850s, Chartism had collapsed, and for decades thereafter ordinary, working Scots and progressive forces gave general support to the Liberal Party. Though it enjoyed sustained success – with the exception of the 'Khaki election' in 1900, during the Boer War, the Liberals won an absolute majority of Scottish seats at every poll between 1850 and 1922 – it was a weird coalition. There were Whig aristocrats, from the Duke of Argyll and other nobility to preening Edinburgh lawyers; the new, professional middle class, who hated the Established Church, liked to moralise against the few pleasures of the poor and feared trades unionism; and 'Lib-Labs', who sought factory acts and union recognition and thought the provision of free, wholesale education for the poorest in society much more important than the denominational fights for school control that continually delayed it. All upheld, though, a conscious ethic of self-reliance: thrift, discipline and temperance, saving a little something each week for a rainy day, seemed much more a service to the poor than higher rates and taxes for their public benefit.

The Liberals were decisively split by Gladstone's obsession with Irish Home Rule in 1886; indeed, it is from the subsequent 'Liberal Unionist' tradition that modern Scottish Conservatism, until very recently, drew most support. Though Scottish national spirit did feature fitfully in Victorian politics – and gained ground from the 1880s, with a dedicated government department and so on – it was more emotive and cultural than the nationalism of our own era. Much more significant was the dawning realisation among Scotland's 'Lib-Labs' that, while eager for their votes, the bland middle-class folk who retained firm control of Parliamentary candidate selection would never relinquish it to working men. Though it would be the 1920s before the slippage became a catastrophe, Liberal support began now to erode. The latest Reform Act of 1884, which enfranchised some 6 million ordinary men in the British countryside, alarmed many who felt they had most to lose.

Few realise that the first significant success of an (agrarian) socialism was not on Clydeside, but in the Highlands: at the 1885 general election, the Crofter's Party, heavily indebted to the Irish Land League for its best ideas and to the new Evangelicalism for its self-discipline, won four seats on the new electoral roll and, within two years, won the Crofters Act of 1886, bestowing at last security of tenure and neutering the worst of Highland landlordism. The new force did not last long thereafter, wilting back into the Liberal Party, which, finally shorn, over the Irish issue, of its landed aristocrats, was no longer in their thrall. As a consequence, the Liberals – to this day – retain substantial Highland support.

In industrial Scotland, however, they now faced the competition of an intelligent Socialism, though it would take some decades to bear substantial electoral fruit. Keir Hardie's original Scottish Labour Party – founded in August 1888 – seemed more interested in Scottish home rule than the liberation of the proletariat, and was formed after his limp showing as an 'Independent Labour' candidate at the Mid Lanark by-election that April; though with a high local profile as a miners' leader, and his genuine piety (he was a stalwart of the Evangelical Union), Hardie had won just 617 votes. He later founded the Independent Labour Party, in Bradford, in 1893, which soon absorbed the SLP. But when the 'Labour Representation Committee' was formed in London in October 1900, the Trades Union Congress was much more important than the ILP, which happily affiliated itself with the new body but kept an abiding, separate identity against fraught times.

It would be 1905 before the Labour Party avowedly adopted its defining aspiration: 'the co-operative ownership by the workers of land and the means of production', and only then, as Smout dryly notes, did it become 'explicitly socialist . . . away from the world of Tom Paine towards the world of Karl Marx'. Indeed, what became the enduring Clause 4 – drafted by Sidney Webb, adopted as late as 1917 and pledging 'common ownership of the means of production, distribution and exchange' – was much more of faith than hard policy: as Harold Wilson would decades later crack, only 'fundamentalists' ever saw it 'as a policy declaration – more practical Party members as the Party's equivalent of the detailed architectural passages of the Book of Revelation.' Hardie's own socialism was much more a matter of religious, moral conviction than 'philosophical theorising or scientific analysis', as Bruce Glasier concluded – owing something to the fervour of the Covenanters and still more to the tent-hall emotionalism of the Evangelical Union. All his life Hardie detested drink: as long as he led the Labour Party, no Labour MP was allowed in the House of Commons bar. He thought of evolution, not revolution; hated talk of class warfare. If pushed to detail specific policies, they sounded both worthy and impractical – a coal-pit owned outright by the village, he would suggest, run by elected representatives.

It is no surprise that in a country of such robust Presbyterian heritage and a love of detail and argument, men dreaming of a new Jerusalem should take so avidly to socialism. Nor – with many big personalities and a modern trend to denomination and faction – is it any surprise that Labour faced at least noisy socialist rivals. Few, though, would care for details of the nascent Marxist smorgasbord: the Social Democratic Federation (SDF), or the Socialist Labour Party (SLP), or the Scottish Republican Socialist Party (SRSP), or the Socialist Party of Great Britain, or – not to be outdone – the forces who finally came together in the Communist Party of Great Britain. The movement that would count was born in October 1900: a quarter-century later, it had already formed a government, and was permanently established as the progressive alternative in Britain to the Conservative Party, a status which – for all its troubles and adventures through over 80 years since – Labour has never forfeited. But let us now look in detail at 'Red Clydeside'.

Socialism readily won leaders and lieutenants in Scotland. It took years, though, to win many votes. Hardie and MacDonald were just two early ILP leaders who had finally to launch a Parliamentary career in England. Unions remained weak, without the muscle or guile to win a major strike; in 1897, the Amalgamated Society of Engineers lost emphatically a bitter Clydeside shipyard dispute. Though 10 Labour councillors were elected in Glasgow in 1898, they proved inept and silly: most lost their seats in 1901. It would be as late as 1933 before Labour won control of the city.

The early Scottish Labour movement in Scotland had a keen nationalist edge; this would be greatly weakened by the Great War and from 1945, and well into the Thatcher years, the Left in Scotland would largely remain determined supporters of undiluted Union, the principal reason why the 1970s' devolution schemes faltered and failed. There was, one fears, a racial, anti-Irish tinge to this early patriotism. But it had one important consequence. Scottish trades unionism made an early run for autonomy, refusing to come under the new London-based Trades Union Congress (TUC) after it denied affiliation (at the behest of craftsmen) to local Trades Councils, which represented unskilled workers.

A separate Scottish Trades Union Congress was accordingly established in 1897 – enduring to this day – and embracing these Trades Councils, which only served to highlight the TUC's undue cosiness with the Liberal Party and, in the long term, greatly strengthened the Labour movement in Scotland. Friedrich Engels might in the 1890s have described the Scottish Liberals as 'the most advanced bourgeoisie in the world', but their Parliamentary ranks – in 1910, the Liberals would hold 58 of Scotland's 72 seats – were a mass of businessmen and lawyers, who could not long command the allegiance of those voters they employed and indeed had long exploited.

It took time to detach skilled workers from lifelong Liberalism. And the churches were a serious obstacle. All the Presbyterian denominations viewed socialism with alarm, though they did increasingly question conditions in Scotland's cities. Socialism had been expressly denounced by Pope Pius IX in his infamous Syllabus of Errors in 1864; priests, too, denounced the new politics. Besides, the disdain of men like Hardie for the Irish as a people and 'popery' as a religion was all too evident.

But a new, remarkably vital, cultural life grew in Scotland's cities from the church of Marx. Soon, Glasgow – for instance – boasted Socialist Sunday schools, the Clarion Scouts and popular lectures from a range of gifted speakers on a range of Socialist topics. Hard as it might be to imagine, a thousand would tramp out on a Glasgow winter evening to hear John MacLean, a Govan schoolmaster and pillar of the SDF, hold forth on Marxist economics. There were night schools, philosophy clubs and seminars; there were Clyde and countryside excursions. A clever young man, Tom Johnston, in 1906 launched a vigorous ILP newspaper, *Forward*, 'with its socialism, radical liberalism and home rule', record Christopher Harvie and Peter Jones. 'Many young writers, painters and artists were attracted to the propaganda of socialism, including Edwin Muir adrift on the urban tide of Glasgow, or John MacDougall Hay who assaulted the greed of nineteenth-century employers in *Gillespie* (1914). They generally assumed that socialism would be accomplished within the frame of a Scottish state, but at the same time their ideals were essentially internationalist.'

Meanwhile, *Forward* – mindful of the finer things in life – included concert and theatre reviews and even advertised piano lessons. One ILP enthusiast, Hugh Roberton, founded the Glasgow Orpheus Choir; by the 1930s it would be one of the most celebrated in the world. This was not just a passionate new politics. It was, socially and emotionally and for thousands of people, all but a new religion. Yet there was still but a bridgehead of hard political advance. The 1906 election only returned two ILP MPs north of the Border, and both owed their election to a local deal with the Liberals. The workers were yet far from seizing the citadels.

Then two things broke in Labour's favour. First, continued innovation in factories – as well as a manufacturing recession – enormously strained Liberal loyalties. And then, in the wake of that rapid shift in fortunes, there fell the cataclysm of the Great War and its unexpected empowerment of skilled Clydeside workers.

Clydebank was still centred on two enormous employers. John Brown & Company, who had made their name and fortune in Sheffield steel, had bought out the troubled Thomson's concern in 1899, gripped by the possibilities of its site and works. The slips could be readily extended (especially as the business included the housing around it) and could besides be realigned with the mouth of the River Cart opposite, allowing the construction of enormous new vessels. The work was done, and in a few years the men of Clydebank had begotten a succession of magnificent ships for Cunard – the *Saxonia*, the *Carmania*, the *Caronia*. In 1906, there followed the still more splendid *Lusitania*, a mighty transatlantic liner.

But Clydebank was besides the town of the Singer Manufacturing Company, founded by Isaac Singer in New York in 1851; their site at Kilbowie was their largest in the world. By 1911 it employed 11,000 people – a very high proportion of them women. Its distant owners kept shipping over and installing the latest American machinery and dividing labour (in the logic of what became known as mass manufacture) to such extremes of monotonous specialisation as to be soul-destroying for their employees. Thomas Bell gives a wincing instance:

I remember Arthur MacManus describing a job he was on, pointing needles. Every morning there were millions of these needles on the table. As fast as he reduced the mountains of needles, a fresh load was dumped. Day in, day out, it never grew less. One morning he came in and found the table empty. He couldn't understand it. He began telling everyone excitedly that there were no needles on the table. It suddenly flashed on him how ridiculous it was to be spending his life like this. Without taking his jacket off, he turned on his heel and went out, to go for a ramble over the hills to Balloch.

In Professor Smout's phrase, 'this kind of technological substitution for skill' began to worry many tradesmen through industrial Scotland and especially on Clydeside. Might they soon be replaced by far cheaper employees – boys or even women – with nothing more to do than mind machines? Already, two humble but important crafts – baking and pottery, now heavily automated – employed far fewer people by 1905, and scarcely any skilled ones.

For long, an able artisan who worked hard could earn good wages – enough to climb socially; enough one day to set up as a sub-contractor on his own account, perhaps employing a few workers. But Clyde shipyards were bigger now, preferring in-house tradesmen and using ever more sophisticated machines; work for the self-employed fast evaporated. In what was always a cyclical industry, there were frequent closures, so that more and more skilled men had now to endure spells of unemployment. The failure of the 1897 ASE strike was especially serious as, humiliated, her workers lost their long-standing control of work-floor processes: employers soon 'drove the men to antagonism and an elaborate defence of restrictive practices which was scarcely dismantled before the 1980s', sighs Smout. 'Alienated labour was plainly losing interest in helping "masters to compete." Nothing has been more catastrophic for the long-term health of British industry than the inability to pursue consensus in the workplace.' In the winter of 1907 to 1908, there was frightful unemployment throughout Britain, and on Clydeside, by that Christmas, 7,000 were sustained only by a hastily raised relief fund. By the autumn of 1908, *The Times* reported starkly that in Govan some 16,000 people 'were on the verge of starvation'. Weeks earlier, 35,000 turned out for a Socialist demonstration, including hundreds and hundreds of the most gifted – and redundant – craftsmen. 'A boy from school now does the work of three men,' cried John Hill, who headed the boilermakers' union. 'It is mostly machine-minders who are wanted and a line from some well-known Liberal or Tory certifying that you are not an agitator or a Socialist is the chief recommendation in the shipbuilding and engineering trades. Thus today we find the ranks of the unemployed largely recruited by men of intellect: men of genius, and men of high character and independent means . . .'

By 1911, patience with the continued anti-trades union ethos of Clyde manufacturing was dangerously thin and, on top of the old tricks of force, intimidation, lock-outs and imported 'scab' labour, the rising mania for 'scientific management techniques' forced more to work harder, in still more mind-numbing tasks, for less and less pay. That year, Singer managers forced yet another reorganisation on female 'cabinet polishers' at the Kilbowie plant with a yet higher workload and less wages. A dozen immediately struck. To general astonishment, within two days almost everyone else who worked at the factory came out in sympathy – men and women, fitters and tradesmen, administrative and manufacturing staff, Protestant and Catholic – in a display of unity hitherto unprecedented. Remote management responded savagely. The works were closed; transfer of production to other European plants was threatened; any hope of employment elsewhere on Clydeside was ridiculed. The strike finally failed. Most voted to return – unconditionally – to work in a secret ballot. Singer later launched vindictive reprisals, identifying and sacking over 400 workers it held most responsible for unrest. (They included Arthur MacManus; in 1920 he became the first chairman of the Communist Party of Great Britain.)

Yet it proved a Pyrrhic victory for the captains of local industry. The timidity which had prevailed generally on Clydeside through the first decade of the new century now dissipated. Whole new classes of worker, hitherto fearful, acquiescent, were now radicalised – not least women. Between 1910 and 1914, four times as many working days were lost to strikes as in all the preceding 10 years. In 1912, west-central Scotland alone saw 70 industrial disputes, including a national strike by miners for a minimum wage. In 1910, 129,000 workers belonged to groups affiliated to the Scottish Trades Union Congress: four years later, it was 230,000. Pressure for better pay, safer conditions and trades union recognition became clamour. Scottish employers now nervously formed their own associations against 'agitators'.

By July 1914, Glasgow had 18 ILP councillors, of whom the ablest by a country mile was one John Wheatley – clever, industrious, gently religious. In 1906 – few grasped its significance at the time – Wheatley had founded the Catholic Socialist League, which in due time was affiliated to the ILP, dedicated to convincing brethren there need be no conflict between old faith and new politics. He had besides struck on important new political territory – a campaign for decent, publicly owned houses, available on easy terms to ordinary working people. He saw no reason why the mass of Scots – those who did the most living and toiling and dying – had to tolerate crowded and often filthy conditions.

The Great War exploded in August 1914 and was unhesitatingly opposed by most of the ILP leaders and other princes of the Left: Hardie and MacDonald, Wheatley and Johnston and MacLean. Only the year before at Basle, at the Second International, they had gladly taken the pledge that the working classes of Europe should not again take up arms in a European capitalist war. To their chagrin, British workers were overwhelmingly swept up, instead, in ecstatic patriotism. Sixteen of Glasgow's ILP councillors hailed the campaign, and most of the trades unions. There was a mad dash to enlist and, indeed, Scots volunteered in greater proportion than anywhere else in Britain. A quarter of Scottish miners joined up. An entire battalion was swiftly raised from Glasgow Corporation's tram department: by year's end, 1,756 had joined, 1,000 within the first 24 hours. Most were duly slaughtered at the Somme.

As for the *Lusitania*, she was sunk with colossal loss of life off the coast of southern Ireland by a German torpedo in May 1915. Abiding outrage at the 'atrocity' – which did much to swing American opinion behind intervention in the First World War – should be tempered: she was a British-registered ship, she was undoubtedly carrying war materials and she was a perfectly legitimate target. The German Embassy in Washington had conscientiously warned US citizens – even taking out advertisements in the press – not to sail on her; and had as much right – by the accepted rules of war – to sink her as they had, in Belgium, to shoot Edith Cavell for smuggling British servicemen back to military action. But Britain, awash in jingoism – and still free of conscription – was not a place for rational discussion; any opposition to the war itself seemed more heroic than prudent.

Ramsay MacDonald, who thought it a mere dynastic conflict between imperial houses, called to the last for a negotiated settlement. He accordingly found himself on the wrong side of most Labour MPs, some of whom were recruited to the government. The wider party was hopelessly split: at the 'coupon' election of 1918, he would lose his Leicester seat. Nevertheless, when businesses with German names were being attacked in English cities, and violent mobs quickly broke up the few hardy anti-war meetings down south, anti-war speakers in Scotland (notably John MacLean) were at least afforded a courteous hearing, even when most did not agree.

In Clydeside, for all the jingoistic noises, two immediate issues increasingly worried working people – both arising from rapidly expanding war production and pressure from the government to produce yet more; its manufacture already shaken by the rush of so many men to the colours. People now poured into Glasgow from all over Britain, from Ireland and even from America as shops, yards and factories clamoured for labour. We have already noted the deplorable Clydeside housing. With an influx of some 20,000 men and women, it became desperate. And landlords took swift advantage. Rents went up and up: in Govan alone, hard by the busiest shipyards, rents rose by 24 per cent, as factors exploited both the housing scarcity and the absence of so many men at the front who might otherwise have made trouble.

In 1915, the housewives of Partick and Govan would endure it no more. They launched a famous rent strike, refusing to accept avaricious increases and to hand over another penny until they were reversed. They were rapidly joined by other determined women around the city. A similar campaign took off in Birmingham. Soon something between 15,000 and 20,000 grim little tenement households in Glasgow were involved. Factors tried to evict, only to find themselves repelled in city closes by women of all denominations and political bent – their efforts marked not just by physical ruthlessness but righteous anger, not least when so many had men on the high seas or entrenched in France and Belgium.

The government was slow to react – many of the landlords involved, after all, were Liberal – but the situation became intolerable. Placards like 'While my father is a prisoner in Germany, the landlord is attacking our home', 'We are Fighting Landlord Huns' and 'We Want Justice' were widely reported in the press. The Glasgow Rent Strike won besides powerful allies from the ILP, suffragettes and influential lawyers. Liberal ministers now drew up a rent control bill, but the very idea was deplored by the Tories, now part of the wartime coalition under Herbert Asquith. It was only when the munitions minister – David Lloyd George – threw his muscle behind it that things began to progress. He had reason to fear: shipyards and engineering shops on Clydeside now threatened to strike in sympathy. And before the Bill could be passed, one rapacious factor summonsed 18 defaulting tenants to the Sheriff Court, bidding to arrest their wages. Workers now furiously downed tools. Thousands marched on the court. The Sheriff made his sympathies plain – with the housewives – and the factor hastily withdrew his action. Six days later, on 23 December 1915, the rent control measure was law. The women and workers of the Clyde had stood shoulder to shoulder – and won.

But the shop floor saw still more trouble than the close. Only one shipyard – Fairfield's, in August 1915 – witnessed serious industrial action. Gordon Corrigan's somewhat partisan account suggests that on the Clyde, 'that hotbed of workers' militancy', local union officials deliberately defied a national 'industrial peace' agreed hastily at the onset of war, but by men who had 'little or no control over local officials'. Corrigan does not grasp that the TUC had no authority to speak for workers in Scotland, but insists that 'in defiance of national trade union leaders the Clyde strike went on for a month, and while a face-saving formula was eventually cobbled together to end it, local militants knew they had the upper hand.'

Words like 'militancy' only enforce the enduring might of the Red Clydeside legend, especially when history is filtered through English Tory prejudice. There was in fact no further trouble on the Clyde shipyards throughout the First World War. It was the engineers of the city in other vital trades – Barr and Stroud (who made precision-engineered optical instruments, like periscopes), Weir's (who made steam pumps), Beardmore's of Parkhead (who at their peak employed a prodigious 40,000 men, forged steel for practically everything and now avidly made huge guns) and Albion Motors – who repeatedly fought a succession of little fights William Gallacher, a rising Communist, would later dub 'The Revolt on the Clyde'. Admittedly the atmosphere was confrontational from the start, with not a few shop stewards who doubted the fervour of their official unions for confrontation. In February 1915, the Amalgamated Society of Engineers declined to authorise a strike by 10,000 workers seeking a modest pay rise. Hardliners now quickly formed the robust Clyde Workers' Committee (CWC): they included Gallacher at Albion Motors, John Muir of Barr and Stroud, and Arthur MacManus – the Singer's martyr – who now flew the people's flag at Weir's. They believed fervently in workers' control, a cause trumpeted by the hard-left Socialist Labour Party; so did an associate, the young David Kirkwood and another Beardmore employee, though he was an ILP man and no revolutionary.

They had legitimate cause for alarm. The young William Weir, now in charge of the family business, had formed an alliance of local industrialists and was determined (taking full advantage of war conditions and confident, if it came to the push, of government support) to smash traditional Clyde workplace practices – and, hopefully, the rising Labour movement generally. Here was an opportunity to bring in new machines, new methods and cheaper and much more biddable labour – especially women. And in an extraordinary misjudgement, the government in 1915 appointed William Weir its 'Munitions Controller' of Scotland, granting this rich class-warrior serious power and at once forfeiting much goodwill among Clydeside workers.

Two issues became central: the imposition of 'Leaving Certificates' – which a skilled worker in the given war industries now had to obtain if he wished to enlist in the Forces – and 'dilution': the drafting of unskilled (and often female) labour into plants and factories in a bid to increase output of war *materiel*. Both threatened the freedom and post-war job security of the skilled men and their CWC tribunes; but even in wider Labour circles (to say nothing of the general public) there was at first thin support for the CWC, especially during a war now going bloodily and badly wrong.

On Christmas Day 1915 – not then, nor for half a century yet, a public holiday in Scotland – David Lloyd George arrived in Glasgow, determined to exhort workers into patriotic obedience and perhaps hoping besides to exploit some new goodwill after his action on rent. He addressed a public meeting, wittering on – as Emanuel Shinwell would 60 years later tell John Doxat – about a 'land fit for heroes'. It was patronising. It was irrelevant. It was a disaster. He was heckled incessantly, cleverly and hilariously. For most of the time the minister for munitions – determined to preen over rents – could scarcely be heard.

Anger about 'dilution' spread: less about the issue – everyone agreed something had to be done to pump out many more armaments in a war Britain was now in real danger of losing – than the refusal of either the government or industrialists to sit down with the unions and negotiate its terms. Engineers had real cause to suspect that Weir and his chums were but taking advantage of the war to extend the power (and profit) of the bosses – with tacit government support. Lloyd George did need to reassure the workers of Clydeside. He calamitously failed to do so.

Tom Johnston wrote a delicious (and accurate) report of proceedings for *Forward*; under the astonishingly illiberal powers of the new Defence of the Realm Act, Lloyd George foolishly had the paper suppressed, assuring colleagues that Glasgow was 'ripe for revolution'. The CWC nevertheless fought all the harder against dilution and, in January 1916, another radical journal, *The Worker*, was muzzled. That March the government finally hit hard. With cynical rhetoric about 'German agents', prominent shop stewards, including David Kirkwood, were arrested and deported to Edinburgh. It was a crass blunder: Kirkwood, who was genuinely liked and respected by Beardmore, had so deftly organised things at Parkhead (to general workers' satisfaction and to unprecedented levels of war production) that a delighted Sir William had bought him 'the best hat in Glasgow'. Kirkwood's treatment now provoked a large demonstration on Glasgow Green, where a gaunt and lantern-jawed schoolteacher, James Maxton, gave an incandescent speech. 'Not a rivet should be struck on the Clyde,' he proclaimed, 'until the deported engineers are restored to their families.' He, too, was now arrested and bundled off to Edinburgh's Calton Jail.

Thus – storing up untold trouble for the future – the government got its way, forced through 'dilution' in factory upon factory and smashed the CWC. The shock of the 'Easter Rising' in Dublin that spring – a farcical failure only celebrated today because of the government's witless insistence on executing the ringleaders, including Socialist Labour Party leader James Connolly – undoubtedly dampened spirits on the Clyde.

By war's end, though, things were again restive. For one – years after the hysterics of August 1914 – its human cost was now heartbreakingly evident. For another, many on Clydeside were greatly stirred by the revolution in Russia: socialism, it seemed, was about to deliver – somewhere – a workers' paradise. At home, conscription proved contentious, especially when ex-empted, skilled workers seemed mysteriously to lose exemption should they show a taste for industrial confrontation.

Rationing, introduced late in the war and run with incompetence and visible corruption, bred much resentment. Clydebank saw just one of many outrages, in a public order still largely run by the well-off for the well-off – and that included the local Rationing Committee. Fifteen hundredweight of sought-after margarine had just arrived. The Clydebank and Dalmuir Co-operative Societies – whose membership was, between them, 60 per cent of the local population – were awarded one hundredweight each. The Rationing Com-mittee's convenor – a grocer and a district-court judge – awarded himself eight hundredweight. There was outrage. The deputy food control commissioner of Scotland was forced to the extremity of politely telling the convener he had made 'an error of judgement'.

And the giddy wartime profits of manufacturers were in high contrast to niggardly, begrudged increases in workers' wages. Only 10,000 turned out for Glasgow's May Day March in 1916. In 1917, it drew over 70,000. By year's end, David Lloyd George – by Cabinet coup and a sly deal with the Con-servatives – was enthroned as prime minister, one of the ablest, most un-principled and – in our time – the most corrupt ever to hold the office.

Imprisoning the most rumbustious leaders of the Left had proved fraught. When John MacLean was sentenced to five years' imprisonment in 1918, the uproar was such that the authorities deemed it prudent to free him after he had served but seven months. He returned to Glasgow, from chilly Peterhead Prison, in December 1918; the Armistice had been signed only weeks earlier.

With Germany defeated and the Empire safe, the folk of Clydeside now asserted themselves, especially as demobilisation loomed and the cessation of munitions toil threatened widespread unemployment. The easiest way to save jobs was to curb the working week, from 54 to 40 hours. So the CWC was revived – styling itself the 'Ways and Means Committee' – and early in 1919, as negotiations went nowhere, began to organise a general strike, from 27 January.

Emanuel Shinwell was a perky 34-year-old campaigner of London birth, Polish-Jewish heritage and warm Glasgow accent, and his career in public life was prodigiously long: leaving school at 11 to train as a tailor's apprentice, 'Manny' Shinwell became an activist in the splendidly titled Amalgamated Union of Clothing Operatives in 1903, and gave his last speech in the House of Lords on 22 January 1986, when he was a sparkling 101. Since 1906 he had been a formidable delegate in the Glasgow Trades Council and Shinwell now toiled, with just a hint of malice, to get as many workers 'out' as possible. It proved less general a strike than had been hoped, though 40,000 workers did obligingly down tools. There was particular resistance among municipal employees – power stations continued to hum; city trams to trundle – so Shinwell decided to lean hard on Glasgow's lord provost and (blithely unaware of the drama he was about to unleash) called for a vast rally in George Square, right in front of the City Chambers:

> . . . and a delegation should interview the Lord Provost and ask him to intercede with the Prime Minister. I was a member of the Town Council and had access to the City Chambers. The demonstration practically filled the square: probably 80,000 people were there. Among my colleagues were David Kirkwood, also a Town Councillor, and William Gallacher. No speeches were made. It was decided Kirkwood and myself should enter the municipal buildings, leaving Gallacher with strict instructions to maintain order.

> The Lord Provost was disinclined even to listen to us. Meanwhile, it appeared that a tramcar was making its way through the square, to the great annoyance of some demonstrators. There was something of a scuffle. Unable to get anything useful from the Lord Provost, Kirkwood and I left. By this time hundreds of police were in sight and began using their batons in brutal fashion. Unfortunately, some of the crowd were forced up a side street, where there happened to be a lorry stacked with bottles, which they began to hurl at the police.

> During my public life, I have seldom been critical of the police . . . in my experience they have proved their worth. But the action of some during the demonstration in George Square was deplorable. Within a few minutes, the Sheriff appeared and read the Riot Act. When I left the Chambers, the police had succeeded in dividing the crowd, so I stood on a seat and tried to persuade people to leave the square . . .

> About one-thirty in the morning there was a knock on my door. Several policemen came in. One said, 'We've come to arrest you . . .'

There is no reason to doubt Shinwell's estimate of the George Square crowd: photographs show one ocean of flat caps, with the Red Flag waving portentously. He did not, of course, see everything – such as the rather convenient arrival of a sheriff to read the Riot Act. If anything though, he understated the brutality of police: David Kirkwood was viciously truncheoned by an officer and then arrested. Veterans afterwards were eager to foster the legend that, for an afternoon, Scotland teetered deliciously on the verge of revolution. 'A rising was expected,' William Gallacher would long afterwards sigh blissfully, from his Communist fastness in West Fife, wishing decades later they had all thought to march on Maryhill Barracks and subvert the troops. 'A rising should have taken place. The workers were ready and able to effect it . . .'

But it was the government – and in particular the Scottish Office – whose hysterics made such drama out of a demo. Robert Munro, secretary for Scotland, assured the Cabinet that Scotland was on the brink of Bolshevik revolt. He might well have had grounds to wonder just how loyal troops stationed in the city – in very great number, as demobilisation had scarcely begun – would now prove. It was certainly at Munro's insistence that, by overnight train, a show of force was sent at once from London. Amused, only mildly alarmed Glaswegians got up that Saturday morning to find a howitzer glowering by the City Chambers, six tanks in the Cattle Market, armoured cars in George Square, machine-gun nests peeping from assorted public buildings and a great many nervy, rifle-toting English troops. It was a show of force unparalleled anywhere in Britain, even through far more serious and bloodier disturbances, especially in the 1980s: tanks have never again been turned out on the British mainland to quell public disturbance, real or imagined. Yet, soon, wee wifies were bustling out with mugs of tea, as fatuous officers worried aloud about 'fraternising with the enemy'. And the strike, already faltering, lasted only two more weeks, as the authorities pressed for the trial of its revolutionary ring leaders.

Emmanuel Shinwell found himself consigned to a bare cell at the local nick, without as much as a mattress. A detective told him grimly, 'You will get five years for this.' 'For what?' 'For rioting.' Shinwell all but laughed aloud, and later slept as best he could on the hard floor. In the event, the Court of Session was not greatly awed by the evidence led in prosecution; certainly, there was nothing to justify either accusations of rioting or incitement to riot. The presiding judge in fact acquitted 10 of the 12 accused, and only 3 men were convicted and sent to prison – and for terms that scarcely suggested any imminent capacity to bring the state to its knees. Gallacher went down for three months and Shinwell for all of five, to the infamous Calton jail which he would describe in 1984 as 'one of the most squalid prisons in the country . . . The food was abominable. From the prison doctor and governor my treatment was most objectionable. By the chief warden and his colleagues I was treated with the utmost consideration. No privileges, of course: I practically lived on the horrible porridge, and bread, throughout my sentence. I must admit I was much healthier on my release than on my entry . . .'

For the rest of his 102 years, Shinwell recalled that weekend – branded so indelibly on the abiding image of Glasgow, and which certainly cemented the glory of Red Clydeside – with profound suspicion.

Why was it that the Sheriff appeared so readily? Why were hundreds of police available within seconds of the tramcar incident? If there was any incitement or intention to riot, why was no evidence to that effect given at our trial in Edinburgh? Incitement to riot was certainly never the purpose of the demonstration. We later learned that a member of the Government told the Prime Minister that he thought the demonstration was intended to start a revolution. It was only eighteen months after the Revolution in Russia. What happened in George Square – the presence of police, tanks in the streets and soldiers on rooftops – was a deliberate act on the part of Lloyd George.

But a long and generally distinguished career lay before Shinwell, including high public office and finally a peerage, despite faltering performance in the post-1945 Attlee government. The events of 1919 made his name; others who had besides, in 1914, been general obscurities in what was still little more than hobby-Socialism (men like Wheatley, Johnston, Kirkwood, Maxton and Gallacher) were now heroes of the people. And David Lloyd George had already sown the dragon's teeth of his own permanent destruction, and that of the Liberals. (So, at least as his Scottish standing went, had Churchill, detested thereafter to the very end by thousands who could not forget either his prodigality with Scottish blood at Gallipoli or his enthusiasm for tanks and guns in George Square.)

At the 1922 general election, Labour doubled its Glasgow vote, taking a hefty 42 per cent of the entire poll and 10 of the city's 15 seats. All the Liberals were beaten. In Glasgow Central the prime minister himself, Andrew Bonar Law – a sturdy Scottish Unionist – narrowly avoided defeat. Over Britain as a whole, 142 Labour MPs were elected, emerging decisively as the Opposition party to Bonar Law's Tories, and eclipsing the hopelessly split Liberals, now in two warring factions under Asquith and Lloyd George and fighting each other in many divisions.

Events and prevalent mood had played decisively into Labour's hands. The advent of the Irish Free State – after several years of fabulously inept, even brutal policy by the Lloyd George government – saw tens of thousands of Catholic votes switch unhesitatingly from the Liberals to Labour; there was new confidence to Scotland's new Roman Catholics, especially since the 1918 Education Act now guaranteed their own state schools. A languishing economy and remorselessly rising unemployment – amidst evident recession – made mock of a 'land fit for heroes'. Certainly it no longer seemed nearly as quixotic to have opposed war in 1914, especially when housing conditions – to take just one instance – were, if anything, worse than ever.

Keir Hardie had died in 1915: but his brother George took Glasgow Springburn with a majority of nearly 10,000. Shinwell was elected for Linlithgow; James Maxton for Glasgow Bridgeton; John Wheatley for Glasgow Shettleston. West Stirling returned Tom Johnston as its new Member of Parliament and – in the Dumbarton Burghs constituency – the people of

Clydebank and the county town voted by the thousand to secure the election of David Kirkwood.

Estimates of the host who converged on Glasgow's St Enoch railway station to cheer off the new Labour Members range exuberantly from 120,000 to a mere 40,000. There was unbridled joy. The new MPs had made appropriate speeches, 'promising to work unceasingly for decent pay and conditions in industry, to eradicate monopoly and avarice, and to have regard for the weak and those stricken by disease'. They put their names to a pledge by ILP lawyer Rosslyn Mitchell – who, next year, would win Paisley – to 'abjure vanity and self-aggrandisement'; and 'that their only righteous purpose is to promote the welfare of their fellow-citizens and the well-being of mankind'.

In the event, save perhaps for Tom Johnston and John Wheatley, none of the 'Clydesiders' ever realised really great things. And 'The Red Flag' was eventually enjoyed, of course, and the 'Internationale', and 'Jerusalem'. But first someone had raised – and the vast congregation exuberantly sang, in a day when most Protestants still knew their words by heart – the 23rd Psalm, and then the 124th, in echo of far older Scottish roots to this remarkable movement:

> Now Israel
> may say, and that truly,
> If that the Lord
> had not our cause maintain'd;
> If that the Lord
> had not our right sustain'd,
> When cruel men
> against us furiously
> Rose up in wrath
> to make of us their prey . . .
>
> Ev'n as a bird
> out of the fowler's snare
> Escapes away,
> so is our soul set free:
> Broke are their nets,
> and thus escaped we.
> Therefore our help
> is in the Lord's great name,
> Who heav'n and earth
> by his great power did frame.

4

THE WINDS OF WAR

She towered over all, a vast and gigantic thing of steel, immobile and static, and – as if mindful of the perpetual pall of smoke, and as if they had anticipated the rain which today, this 26 September 1934, came down relentlessly and in rods and curtains on Clydebank – the men of Cunard White Star and of John Brown & Company had painted this great hull, No. 534, a sleek and vivid white, all the better for the hundreds of photographers and the cine cameras of Pathé and Movietone.

Cunard directors had been awkwardly caught out, though, over her final name – still, but a minute or two from launch, a closely guarded secret. Sir Percy Bates and Sir Ashley Sparks had a standard, Cunard company form for nomenclature: the same *ia* vowels at the end of each: *Carpathia*, *Mauretania*, *Lusitania*. This, they had grandly resolved – the biggest ship ever built anywhere in the world – would be the *Victoria*. But the old Empress was not, in 1934, long dead – three of her children were still alive – and, as a matter of good form, this needed the approval of the Sovereign, her grandson.

So off to the Palace had tripped Sir Percy and Sir Ashley and – as can happen even to the most rational of men – they found themselves weak at the knees in the presence of royalty, quite incapable of plain English. 'Your Majesty,' burbled Sir Ashley, 'we are pleased to inform you that Cunard wishes your approval to name our newest and greatest liner after England's greatest Queen.' The King beamed, and thanked them, 'My wife will be delighted.' What could the knighted directors then do but start, glance at one another, make obeisance and withdraw? To correct the King was out of the question; to abandon Cunard tradition the only answer. There followed yet further embarrassment – a classy little Clyde cruise-ship, launched only in 1933, already bore the name of the Queen Consort. Sir Percy and Sir Ashley had now to make representation to Williamson-Buchanan Steamers and beg them to add a numeral to the name of their turbine-powered pride and joy. They graciously acceded, and in due time Cunard presented the *Queen Mary II* with a fine portrait of the lady herself.

Now, this implacably wet day, the Cunard supremos were but lost among other dignitaries, tripping into a specially built (and, mercifully, covered) gallery, high above the slip and concluding in a protruding, canopied platform for the final rite. Well ahead was the Prince of Wales, already 40, still unmarried, blond and small and slight, very much second-fiddle today, his face at once noble and weak. Ahead of him, in yet higher precedence, walked the Queen, tall and be-toqued and Victorian: only once, ever, after the Great War, had this clever and cultured woman (the worst thing about Hitler, she liked to say, was that he spoke such execrable German) dared to don a skirt significantly higher than her ankles, and such was the wrath of her partner in life that she never dared to do it again. And there – ahead, as always, even of her – smaller, a little stooped, immaculate in the uniform of an Admiral of the Fleet – progressed George V, King, Emperor of India.

David Kirkwood, still MP for Dunbartonshire Burghs, now 62, back in opposition, misunderstood and attacked by former close comrades and increasingly tired, had today special grounds for satisfaction. No. 534 had been conceived even as the world reeled from the Wall Street Crash; in 1930, Cunard had proudly announced that John Brown & Co. had won the tender for the building of this 1,000-foot, 81,000-ton behemoth. Her keel was laid down on that Clydebank slip on 31 January 1931. The whole town seemed to ring and resound as thousands toiled around her, inside her, on top of her; and within months, No. 534 rose high and yet higher over the river and the gables of Thomson's Buildings and Clydebank herself, and her launch was tentatively pencilled for May 1932. Then – a fortnight before Christmas, 11 December 1931 – the fist fell. The mounting Depression had overwhelmed shipbuilding worldwide. Cunard had perforce to pay all outstanding bills; to survive, work on No. 534 was suspended immediately. All workers were laid off – save for a few to mount guard over the hull – with no word as to when they might return. For weeks – months – there seemed every possibility the half-built glory might even be dismantled for scrap. Meanwhile, she sat there and rusted.

Though he would never hold government office – and principled, fastidious and his own man, had always an uneasy relationship with comrades – Kirkwood was a formidable politician. As a veteran of William Beardmore & Son (like every born shop steward, he always dreamed of running the company himself) he knew how industry worked, especially in the great things of steel and the games of high business. Kirkwood knew, besides, just how much can be achieved in high places if you genuinely do not care who wins the credit. And he had that capital of irreproachable integrity: a man who had endured prison for doing as he had deemed right. Much of Kirkwood's endeavour thereafter was of necessity covert. The goal was a hefty government subsidy. The means – as became quickly evident – was to secure that loan by firm merger of the last great Atlantic lines standing (or, in the case of White Star, haunted to the last by the *Titanic*, tottering). It was not easy. But the deal was duly done. Cunard White Star Ltd were up and in business by December 1933; and with a loan from the National Government of £9.5 million not only to resume No. 534 but to build, thereafter, a comparable sister – and, considering all the troops these majesties would in a few years bear over the Atlantic for the liberation of Western Europe, that money may just have won the war.

Kirkwood had saved the ship, the yard, the town. But the rain pounded on, coursing on the glass, and out there still implacably stood tens of thousands of people, and out of his view tens of thousands more – in all, some 250,000 people gathered to see this launch – and the tough old fellow felt chill even in his dull dry suit, and felt silly besides, and just a little unmanned.

The National Anthem billowed in the Clyde air, from bands and throats, as the King took his place at a bulky microphone, already ailing – he had never really recovered from a wartime accident and grave 1929 illness, and had not 18 months to live – and stood gravely until 'God Save The King' was done, saluting; afterwards, the Queen bobbed just a little, with a gesture of her Württemberg hand.

He read, slowly, in a voice guttural and with a hint of autumn leaves in the wind in his beloved Norfolk countryside, and to our ear oddly unaristocratic. Though he had no dramatic art or natural presence, and just read, the sincerity still moves you today. Not two years before, he had given his first Christmas radio talk to Empire and Commonwealth, and neither his son nor his grand-daughter ever broadcast so well.

'I thank you for your loyal address of welcome to us,' said King George V. 'As a sailor, I have deep pleasure in coming here today to watch the launch by the Queen of this great and beautiful ship. Today we come to the heavy task of sending on her way the stateliest ship now in being. I thank all those here and elsewhere whose efforts, however conspicuous or humble, have helped to build her.

'We send her to her element,' said the King, in careful earnestness, 'with the goodwill of all the nation as a mark of our hope in the future. She is being built in fellowship among ourselves. May her life among great waters spread friendship among the nations.'

He moved aside, just a little, and the Queen – who, privately, when there was not the least call for probity, liked an elegant cigarette, two bottles of chilled hock and a roaring chorus round the piano of 'Yes, We Have No Bananas, We Have No Bananas Today' – came forward now, as below men swarmed with hammers at just about the most dangerous point of the drama, pounding clear and away the final props and stays that kept No. 534 absolutely on the vertical: for fraught seconds longer, high and dry, the vast steel creation was on her own. The Clyde, just beyond her stern, had been heavily and urgently dredged – just in case – and, River Cart or no River Cart, helpful attendant tugs or no helpful tugs – great drag-chains, weighing a full 2,500 tons, had been coupled to her bows, to brake the final and remorseless ride to her destiny.

The Queen took hold of a beribboned bottle of Australian sparkling wine – its glass earlier and heavily scored, to encompass the vital bursting with absolute certainty – and gave the first and last broadcast of her life.

'I am happy to name this ship the *Queen Mary*. I wish good luck to her and all who sail in her.'

The bottle flew, and exploded in gratifying foam, and almost before the froth flowered in the air the *Queen Mary* was moving; and she moved for a long time, as a quarter of a million throats roared and sirens howled and ships blew whistles and shot maroons, and on the flickering newsreel footage she slides and slides to this wailing cacophony, and as the vast propellers kissed water and she slid on and on, the cables tightened and the great bundled chains moved reluctantly with her, clawing and rolling at the ground, oddly shaggy, and did their job: the *Queen Mary* did not smite the Clyde, far less shoot calamitously across it, but assumed it. It took only 75 seconds; 75 years on, the footage still aches with the tension of it . . . but in those moments No. 534 became a ship; vast and inert metal became a living thing, and were Clydebank remembered for nothing else – had she failed, indeed, to rise from the ashes of March 1941 – Clydebank would be immortal today, for this Clydebank built the *Queen Mary*, and though a bigger ship fast followed, and ships larger still took life near and after the Millennium, no greater ship has the world ever seen.

The *Queen Mary* – she would finally begin her Atlantic service on 1 July 1936 – normally cruised at 29 knots, but was capable of 34, driven by four mighty steam turbines coupled to what were then the biggest propellers ever built: each, of manganese-bronze, weighed 35 tons and was 20 feet in diameter. The turbines themselves were built by John Brown & Co., but much else was also designed and made on Clydeside – her mighty compasses, for instance, were by Kelvin, Bottomley and Laird Ltd of Glasgow and all her electric pumps were from another city firm, Drysdale's. The liner had the finest onboard telephone system afloat and (not least with the uncomfortable White Star baggage) her designer, John Brown – no relation to the company, and who would live to a great age – paid obsessive attention to safety. There were 66 watertight doors in bulkheads through all the low levels of the *Queen Mary*, and each could be monitored from the bridge; 38 of these were powered, all sounded an alarm seven seconds before they began to descend, and each could be opened manually if someone were trapped. All this required electricity, and this – to say nothing of her propulsion, her 22 onboard lifts and even her cooking plant – required great boilers and steam-driven turbo-generators: she had no fewer than 24 water-tube boilers for the engines alone, all Clyde-built; three additional double-ended Scotch boilers gave heat for the 'hotel services', and seven turbo-generators produced 10,000 kW of electricity, not least for her 30,000 light bulbs.

Particular care was taken against fire. Flame-retardant materials and paint and finishes were used throughout, and electrical fittings (like lights and heaters) were scrupulously planned to minimise risk. A remarkable 'Lux-Rich' smoke detector system was installed in all areas – such as cargo spaces and baggage-holds – that could not easily be patrolled, linked to both visual and audible alarms in a central fire station, allowing the officer of the watch to see at a glance where smoke had been detected. They could then immediately activate an extinguishing mechanism, using carbon dioxide gas to smother any flame, and in this alone the *Queen Mary* was decades ahead of her time. Everywhere else in the ship was covered by a fully automated sprinkler system.

Each shower head could operate independently of others; there were besides over 200 2-gallon fire extinguishers and 313 lengths of fire hose, each 60 feet long and 2 inches thick – and even the film-projectors (she had seven, for assorted onboard cinemas) had an inbuilt CO_2 fire-quenching technology. Each of the *Queen Mary*'s lifeboats was motorised – and could be single-handedly launched in less than a minute, thanks to the ingenious winding-gear; and three great 'Tyfon' whistles, powered by steam at a pressure of around 140 pounds per square inch, adorned the forward funnels. Each whistle was 6 foot 7 inches in length and weighed a stately ton; each was tuned to 'A', two octaves below the middle A of a piano, and was 'one of the most far-carrying sounds ever devised': the whistle of the *Queen Mary* could be heard 10 miles away.

The new star of the oceans could convey 776 cabin-class passengers, 784 tourist-class passengers and 579 third-class passengers, and we need scarcely detail the opulence of her apartments – modern, stylish and beautiful. Six square miles of carpets and rugs were laid through her staterooms and public lounges and restaurants, most woven by Britons Ltd, of Kidderminster. Her curtains, bedspreads and covers totalled 13 square miles of the finest fabric; her blankets were by Priestley Brothers of Halifax, and her linen-stewards had 500,000 pieces for the laundering, including 30,000 sheets and 31,000 pillowcases. Passengers ate and drank from 200,000 pieces of glass, earthenware and china; 16,000 items of tableware and cutlery. The horologists of St Albans built her 596 onboard clocks; Waring & Gillows of London crafted most of her wood-panelling and furniture. And one need list but a few of the celebrated figures who, over the decades enjoyed her comfort as *Queen Mary* surged through the North Atlantic – the Duke and Duchess of Windsor; the Shah of Persia; politicians of the order of Churchill and Morrison and Eisenhower; stars of stage and screen, from Chaplin and Coward to Crosby and Astaire, Erroll Flynn and Bob Hope, Gracie Fields and Greta Garbo, Gloria Swanson and David Niven, Elizabeth Taylor and – naturally – Richard Burton – to see that this was no mere ship, but the personification of an age.

Yet she would survive the Second World War. Clydebank – as a built environment and, in certain real and human respects as a community – would not.

High were the hopes with which, after the 1922 general election, the princes of 'Red Clydeside' entrained for London. In the event, of all those men – all decent; some quite gifted – only three, really, would accomplish very much, not least because it would be almost quarter of a century before Labour would win an absolute majority in the House of Commons, and by then only Emmanuel Shinwell was still young and vigorous enough for government. But their general failure significantly to advance the interests of that class whose blood had been shed so prodigiously in Flanders reflected the floundering landscape of British politics.

It is hard to disagree with A.J.P. Taylor's flat judgement that the two decades between 1918 and 1939 are a 'dark period' in British history – best remembered for economic mismanagement and botched foreign policy. Contrary to mythology, there was no 'lost generation' as a consequence of hostilities: of all the British men mobilised, only 8.6 per cent were killed – half the French slaughter, and at a net loss per annum less than the average outward flow of emigrants in the years 1912 or 1913. Nor had those at home endured anything like the rationing and privations the next world war would impose. During the struggle, wages had risen steadily and in the immediate years after the Armistice there was a minor boom, so that 'by November 1919,' writes Denis Judd, 'there were only 300,000 unemployed, a tolerable enough figure for the times. The average man who had stayed at home and done his job probably expected the government somehow to hold down price rises, encourage the building of new homes and see to reasonable wage settlements. These proved to be high hopes.'

Much more had died with the Great War than the might of European aristocracies and high-minded liberal idealism. In the summer of 1914, Britain had been the richest country on earth; her national debt but £650 million. By 1919, it was £7,435 million. Assets overseas had been flogged off to finance the killing, and the country was heavily obligated to America – colossal borrowings offset against huge sums owed Britain herself by battered allies on the Continent, which they could not (and, in the case of the new Soviet Russia, would not) pay. The national economy sagged back to stagnation by the end of 1920.

By 1921, unemployment was over 1 million, and never fell below it again until the outbreak of war. For much of the period, over 2 million British men were out of work. For all Lloyd George's promises, there was an acute, enduring housing shortage. The 1930s brought dreadful agricultural recession, with hundreds – thousands – of little farms collapsing; Britain grew the more dependent on imported food, and was thus dangerously vulnerable when hostilities began. Inflation became a concern and so, throughout the inter-war years, interest rates were held stubbornly high. This benefited those 'hard-faced men who had done well out of the war' and had their millions in the bank; but it depressed demand and denied capital investment to heavy industries who might otherwise have started making retail goods people actually wanted to buy.

Not that British Empire armour had intimidated, at least, the women of Clydebank. Late in August 1920, after the passage of the Rent Restrictions Act – it imposed a new 10 per cent surcharge on standard rates – townsfolk fast revolted when factors went chapping on doors to collect what practically everyone thought was daylight robbery. Insisting that they would pay no more than in 1914, wives and mothers launched the Clydebank Rent Strike, consciously modelled on the 1915 battle in Glasgow – though without, this time, the advantage of a major war, and with no parallel campaign in the city itself. The Scottish Labour Housing Association – with branches everywhere by now, and with John Wheatley's brains behind it – supplied the moral argument. Working folk could not afford the increases. Even if they could, the flats in which they lived were not worth it. It was wicked that owners should profit from such housing; and in any event, they asserted, the state was morally obliged to build decent houses for working men.

Clydebank's unusually close-knit community was well suited to concerted action. In Radnor Park, for instance – dominated by the 'Holy City' – almost everyone worked for Singer's. The town was already steeped in the politics of the Left, from ILP to Communist, and, after the fears and hardships of war and the expectations stoked wickedly by David Lloyd George, the Bankies were angry. This Rent Strike never had much prospect of long-term success, though in detail still makes a good story – protracted battles in court; righteous Socialist rallies and resolutions; strong, fleet women swiftly organising bands in defence against evictions, or swapping nameplates from one door to another. And as there followed dozens upon dozens of vindictive and largely pointless court-proceedings against some of the poorest families in Britain, even the *Glasgow Herald* – a most bourgeois, Unionist paper – was by July 1921 uneasy.

> The courtroom was crowded, and the passages were thronged with people who were waiting for their cases to be called. Their appearance gave a somewhat vivid impression of the distress prevailing in the city. Most of them were poorly clad, and not a few showed traces of the pinch of poverty. There were women wearing shawls and carrying children in their arms, and bent old men who seemed to find the climb upstairs to the courtroom a tax on their strength. Here and there could be seen disabled men with crutches, and a large proportion of the crowd were unemployed, as the subsequent proceedings in the court showed. . . . About 300 decrees for ejection were granted.

The people – the women – fought on and, though they would lose, they were not humiliated. The Clydebank Rent Strike, its gruesome publicity for the 'boss class' and the opportunity afforded ILP Parliamentary candidates to attest to the corruption of a failing Liberal order, were central to the election breakthrough of 1922.

Politics between the wars was dominated by two realities: the flailing struggle against general economic woe, and the messy but remorseless replacement of the Liberals, by Labour, in the main two-party order of British politics. The central figure, Stanley Baldwin – thrice prime minister, between 1923 and his retirement in 1937 – should not be underestimated: Churchill himself regarded Baldwin, scion of an iron-foundry dynasty and one of our very few prime ministers with a serious business background, as the ablest politician he had ever known. No one did more, for instance, to defuse class as a dangerous factor in post-war affairs, facing down the oddly mannered General Strike with calm common sense. Baldwin, too, had one determined resolve: that David Lloyd George – of low character and whose post-war government had been notable for extraordinary belligerence at home and abroad – should never again hold office; in the event (and few in 1922 would have thought it possible) the Welsh Wizard never did, though as late as the crisis of 1940, but for his cynical defeatism, the old man was still a contender to resume the premiership. Lloyd George had hung around just long enough (maintaining personal control of a fat and dubiously built campaign fund) to seal the ruin of the Liberals, for most of the inter-war period in two or even three competing factions.

Ramsay MacDonald, as A.J.P. Taylor argues, had notable achievements. 'For they were great. MacDonald created the British Labour Party and defined the social democratic outlook which still keeps it going. He established Labour instead of Liberal as the predominant party of the Left. The successes of British foreign policy between the wars, and these were not few, were his doing. His oratory rivalled that of Gladstone. As prime minister he proved that Labour was fit to govern. Until his lapse in 1931 he was regarded almost universally as the greatest Socialist leader in Britain.' By temperament, though, MacDonald was cautious; he was oddly in awe of 'gentry' and there was more than a streak of personal vanity. He should not in 1931 have succumbed to the desperate beseeching of King George V (who genuinely liked MacDonald) to remain as prime minister. It not only destroyed his own personal happiness, but through critical years left Britain without an effective Opposition, a factor often overlooked in the sleepwalk to appeasement.

In fact it was John Wheatley, really the ablest of the 'Red Clydesiders' – if prone to wild language: in June 1923, he was briefly suspended from the Commons for attacking Tory plans to cut grants to child welfare centres as 'murder' – who delivered the biggest domestic achievement of pre-war Labour government. Though MacDonald's first, 1924 administration only held office for nine months, and he did not greatly like Wheatley personally, that was enough time for his Minister of Health to pilot an important Housing Act to the statute-book. It was really a framework for new partnership – between political parties, local councils and representative groups of builders and men who worked for them – but it would be generously subsidised by central government and had hard objectives. Through 1925, 190,000 new 'council houses' were to be built, all to be made available at modest, controlled rents: such annual production would continue, and accelerate, to some 450,000 new homes in 1934. Though Labour lost office weeks after the Housing Act was passed, the new Baldwin government was more than prepared to live with it, and 508,000 houses were built under its terms. Among the first in Scotland are the handsome 'Wheatley houses' by the Knightswood corner of Anniesland Cross, as the Great Western Road becomes the Boulevard. The next decade saw Glasgow building attractive, generously spaced homes at Knightswood and Mosspark, of such garden-city charm they are highly sought after today.

The second Labour minority government, though – from 1929 to 1931 – was unlucky and inept, and by yielding to King George V's importuning after it fell and heading a Tory-dominated National Government, MacDonald only split the Labour movement; though his weak 'National Labour', a bastard thing, did not long survive. There was a still more pointless maverick. Though perhaps today the most famous of the 'Clydesiders', James Maxton – whose pinched features all but personified Glasgow's grinding poverty – was more posture than substance. In 1932, at his insistence, the ILP was disaffiliated from the Labour Party – it was at this point David Kirkwood broke with it – formed a stupid 'Popular Front' with the Communists, and ended up as a 'pointless rump' with just three MPs, locked in socialist La-La Land and insanely pacifist. As often happens, too, with hard-Left motor-mouths, Maxton ended up as really rather a pet of the Commons, held in general affection and patronised to death,

'Great oratory,' sighed Shinwell many years later, 'but apart from his oratory – nothing else. He wouldn't get up until twelve o'clock in the morning, that was his trouble.' And, while Tom Johnston's accomplishments as wartime secretary of state for Scotland were substantial, his legacy to our long-term governance (an indefatigable quango-land Scotland under, as Smout rightly damns it, 'the rule of the expert and the consensus of the well-informed', was not helpful.

Maxton and his ILP rump apart, only two other forces flickered in Scottish politics through the 1920s and 1930s. An unexpected and in some respects quasi-Jacobite new force was Scottish nationalism, crowned in 1934 by the union of the practical, Left-leaning National Party of Scotland (founded by a Glasgow student, John MacCormick, with such clever allies as Eric Linklater and Compton MacKenzie) and the distinctly right-wing and grand little Scottish Party, which boasted the Duke of Montrose and other posh supporters. But the SNP would be of little account for many years and, as European war loomed, harboured irresponsible and unsavoury elements: several, in the national crisis to come, were jailed.

And, of course, there was the Communist Party of Great Britain, operating at an open level in its own right and by more subversive 'entryist' tactics within the wider Labour movement: there were not a few Communists in Clydebank and still more volubly in the Vale of Leven nearby, where communities like Renton and Alexandria were pleasantly dubbed the Little Moscows. From 1935 Scotland even boasted a Communist MP: the redoubtable William Gallacher would represent the highly politicised coal-fields of West Fife until 1950. By the 1970s, a quarter of the entire CPGB membership would be in Greater Glasgow and, in the city itself, the party had actually more activists than Labour. No one became a Communist for riches or ambition, and many were fine men and highly esteemed shop stewards. Unfortunately, the CPGB took its slavish orders from Stalin.

And fatefully book-ending the era was the hapless Neville Chamberlain, who attained the premiership – unopposed – in the summer of 1937, with one of the finest administrative brains ever seen in politics. Yet no one, in the Great Depression, cared about clever pen-pushing, well-organised local government or sly protective tariffs. When Chamberlain became prime minister – with visionary plans for domestic reform – he found himself instead overwhelmed by foreign affairs. And he was at the helm when we stumbled into renewed war. 'It was Chamberlain who had tried for so long to appease Herr Hitler,' writes Peter Lewis, though Chamberlain had been prime minister for less than two years by September 1939, 'who had boasted of "peace in our time" on the strength of Hitler's signature on a piece of paper during the Munich crisis, who had been so transparently eager to compromise and who had been so easily fooled . . . he was not made of the stuff to unite the nation when at last he was reluctantly compelled to go to war. . . . Now that Poland was crushed there had to be another reason for going on with it, but Chamberlain's government never gave one. Although often asked for them, it refused to declare its war aims and showed a far from wholehearted desire to wage total war, seeming to prefer a minimal war which would disturb life little and cost as little as possible.'

Visiting Clydebank today, almost 70 years after the Blitz, there is a notable strand in recollection alongside, inevitably, the memories of March 1941 terror and bereavement. Her oldest residents still quietly grieve for the townscape the Luftwaffe largely destroyed: they are still, seven decades on, sturdy octogenarians moving about by envisaged, long-vanished landmarks – and it is worth describing that pre-war town.

The greater Clydebank of the late 1930s was a town roughly bracketed by the two chain-ferries concluding the cross-river passages of the Clyde Navigation Trust – from Renfrew to Yoker in the east, and from Erskine to Old Kilpatrick in the West – and centred on two great highways: Dumbarton Road (which goes all the way from Partick to the eponymous town and, between Yoker and Clydebank Cross, styles itself confusingly Glasgow Road) and the long, remorselessly climbing Kilbowie Road, from Clydebank Cross to the Boulevard at Duntocher and Hardgate. Despite some deliberate infilling in 1906, Kilbowie Road was (and remains) a steady, at times steep brae, and was especially wearying for horse-drawn traffic. Trams here were the first on the Glasgow Corporation network to be fitted with air-brakes and it is said, according to John Hood, 'that instructors would test the mettle of trainee drivers by allowing trams to run freely down the hill and then gauging the drivers' reactions'. Several, it is said, lost their nerve and leapt in panic from the cab.

Though a densely populated town – dominated by tenements – Clydebank boasted two spacious cemeteries, at Dalnottar and Kilbowie, and (as we shall see) some gracious parks. The inter-war years brought some diversity of housing – the first council terraces and, up in the rising and leafy parts by the Boulevard, many pleasant new bungalows for its middle-class and clerical residents.

The years between the wars were often hard. In the shipyards, there was no meaningful job security: men were laid off by the thousand when the order-book was empty, and re-hired at the discretion of the detested foremen (who, naturally, took advantage of the situation to weed out known troublemakers).

Another trick was the exploitation of 'apprentices' – in fact, skilled men who had fully mastered their trade and served their time, but were kept nevertheless in apprentice status and, more to the point, on apprentice wages. Health and safety awareness was laughable. Riveters, pounding away over the years, literally deafened themselves; it would be decades after the Second World War before the lethal danger of asbestos – used widely by 1940 as an insulator for hot machinery and so on – was grasped by the wider community, though there is hard evidence that industry knew of its perils far earlier. Men – 'white mice' – worked in choking clouds of the stuff all day; they squeezed at evening into packed trams on Dumbarton Road; wives beat thick asbestos out of their overalls, as little girls and boys scrubbed it off their father's boots. Bankies did not just work with asbestos, they made it – it would be the 1960s before the local Turner's plant shut up shop – and it would be the 1990s, long after the last shipyard fell silent, before its legacy was confronted in full horror.

In her addictive novel, *The Holy City*, Meg Henderson darkly captures the reality of the town's industrial life – and practices that survived far into the Fifties.

> The riveters like Tommy MacLeod were still considered the hard men of the yards, but as Marion saw, they had to be. . . . they still worked in all weathers and often outside, on the deck of a ship or on the shell of a ship under construction. In winter they would be holding pneumatic hammers so cold that their hands stuck to the metal and frostbitten fingers were common. They worked with sweat dripping off them from the heat of the rivets and the furnace heating them, while inwardly they froze because of the weather. Often they could be seen balancing on two wooden planks a hundred feet above the ground, the planks bouncing beneath their feet as they worked, and nothing to steady them or break their fall if they lost their footing. Accidents happened all the time and it was said that there was a death for every ship built. Whenever someone was killed the workforce would take the rest of the day off and within the yard they would take up a collection for the family of the man concerned. But there would be no compensation from the management, and nothing was allowed to stand in the way of shipbuilding, least of all respect from the bosses. . . .
>
> At 7.25 every morning the first hooter sounded at Brown followed at 7.30, the official starting time, by the second, and the closing of the main gates. At the timekeeper's wooden hut each man was given a small, round brass disk with his works number stamped on it. But the hut was a good ten minutes' walk from the main gates, and the only way the entire workforce could get through on time was if those who arrived early also passed through early – for no extra pay. A man's working time, and so his pay, began as he picked up his metal check, not as he entered the gates, so if you missed the 7.30 am starting time because of the inevitable queues at the gate, you were deemed to be late and were therefore 'quartered'. This meant that men who had been on company soil for ten minutes had fifteen minutes deducted from everything they earned, basic pay, piecework

and overtime. So in the perpetual battle between the management and the workforce, a new strategy was worked out. The men who arrived early refused to collect their metal checks until 7.30 on the dot, and the queues that built up were so huge that a great deal of time, and therefore money, was lost processing the workers. This brought the practice of 'quartering' to an end, not because of its basic unfairness, but because the way the men hit back cost the company money. It was a victory though, one of the few the workforce managed to force out of the management.

When work finished for the day the men were held wherever they were, even on board half-built ships, until the hooter sounded. Then they would scramble in their thousands down the gangplanks to get home, with accidents avoided only by luck. As they pushed and edged forward the gates would remain firmly closed until the last second. You could see them as you passed, crowded behind the gates like cattle, then bursting forth to freedom as the hooter sounded. Yet to hear the grand speeches on launch day, you would think the bosses held the men in the highest esteem: they were the skilled tradesmen who had built the most famous ships sailing the seven seas, as well as the reputations of the yards. It was the law of the yards: words were cheap, but men's sweat, men's lives, were cheaper.

They hurried home, these riveters and platers and fitters, the machinists and cabinet-polishers of Singer's and everyone else, through the smoky streets of a vibrant, characterful town. Blitz survivors, decades later, would recall it wistfully as such an intimate, friendly one. 'Clydebank was a great place, really was,' Mrs Richardson would tell Billy Kay for his 1981 Radio Scotland documentary. 'In Clydebank you never walked anywhere but you always got, "Hello," – always did. Didn't matter what you were, up high or down low, you were always classed the same. Up each tenement close there were nine families – a bedroom and a kitchen, that was all. The toilet was outside, on the stair, that's the way everybody lived at that time.' 'There was a lot to be said for the old tenement buildings,' Kathleen McConnell chipped in. 'People cared about each other. John Knox Street was always full of characters, good, down to earth, solid folk.'

The decades have no doubt rather rose-tinted such recollections: towns as tormented by episodic unemployment and hardship as Clydebank in the 1930s were no more immune to unhappiness, domestic violence and community strife than anywhere else – and perhaps worse in the likes of Clydebank, which (for its size) had an inordinate number of public houses. Kilbowie Road alone boasted the Clydebank Bar, T.F. Ross's Public House (both at its foot, Clydebank Cross), the Kilbowie Bar and the Rossdhu Bar. McCallum's Bar honoured the corner of Dumbarton Road and Bruce Street. At the corner of Radnor Street and Robertson Street, Tennent's public house likewise paid homage to Bacchus; the Duntocher Bar sat just east of Somerville Street on the Glasgow Road. Perhaps best remembered – and surviving into my own lifetime – was Connelly's Bar, on Belmont Place off Glasgow Road and officially called The Restaurant: the Bisley Bar, on the North Elgin Street corner of the same highway, had also traded notionally as an eating-place. And there were many other local hostelries, from the robust to the sordid: Dalmuir had so many drinking-places it became notorious for Sunday excursions (by tram) from Glasgow, the journey being sufficiently long by the strict licensing laws of the time to qualify the parched Sabbath tourists as *bona fide* travellers – at prices almost as extortionate as those gleefully charged at their final destination, Balloch.

At the opposite end of human nature, the Risingest Burgh supported many churches. Perhaps the best known (because it survives) is the handsome Church of the Holy Redeemer, completed on the Glasgow Road in 1903 in place of an earlier, more modest Roman Catholic chapel. Only a block separated this splendid building from St Columba's Episcopal Church, with its thin and elegant spire. St James Church, near John Brown's, was the oldest congregation in town, born as the 'Tarry Kirk' and soon more grandly accommodated in Gothic, 1876 premises.

Most majestic of all – and opened as a Free Church in 1894, in the stead of earlier premises which had imprudently stood in the way of the North British Railway – was the Union Church, which went through United Free and Church of Scotland incarnations; but the 'Cathedral of Clydebank' finally succumbed in the 1980s to fire. Radnor Park Parish Church – opened in 1895 and known locally as 'Brown's Church,' after its first minister – has had a still more fraught history, surviving a fire in 1909 and further, serious damage in the Blitz. Highlanders were catered for by Free Church and Free Presbyterian preaching-stations, under supervision from Glasgow. The Salvation Army had a lively town-centre presence and a celebrated band, which played doggedly on through both world wars, with James Borthwick as bandmaster for almost half a century between 1915 and 1961.

But it was also a town of cinemas – such as the art deco mass of La Scala, up in Radnor Park, or the New Kinema picture-house, which backed onto Bannerman Street, and of such wooden-seated, seedy accommodation it was known in affectionate scorn as the 'bug house'; and the Bank Cinema, which had originally opened as the Gaiety Theatre. It was besides a place of mannered sports, such as the Clydebank Bowling Club in John Knox Street – to say nothing of Clydebank Junior Football club (its deadly rival was Yoker Athletic) and some very attractive recreation areas.

Dalmuir Public Park was the first in the whole burgh, opened in 1906; the Whitecrook area – one of the last corners of the district developed, with a notable laundry on Barns Street – soon boasted a 201-acre 'Whitecrook Public Area', with a huge purpose-built pond for model yachts. This had cost the Town Council £5,000 (using unemployed labour) and was opened in November 1925. Nor had the many pubs of Clydebank a monopoly on catering. By the late 1930s, the town abounded in jolly Italian cafes – the Regal, at the bottom of Kilbowie Road, and the Singer Cafe, further up the hill, were both owned and operated by the Tedeschi family; and Thomas Capaldi plied his trade at Radnor Park, though the oldest Bankies maintain that Simione's Cafe, at the corner of Canal Street, made the best ''Tali' ice cream in all Clydebank. The City Bakeries premises, on Glasgow Road, were highly popular between the wars as a venue for weddings, especially once they added an attractive upstairs restaurant, the Windsor Rooms, celebrated for its high teas and a welcome respite for the busy shopper.

Scarcely anyone – save the town's few professionals – had a private car, and it would be well into the Sixties before supermarkets began to take root in Scotland's cities. The Clydebank housewife typically went shopping in the morning, be-scarved and basket-toting, round a range of specialist vendors, from McGoldrick's Dairy on John Knox Street to Callaghan's confectionary at Clydebank Cross to a branch of R.S. McColl (opened in 1915) which proudly advertised 'Russian toffee, treacle toffee, cream caramels and peppermint lumps'. There were grocers and butchers and fishmongers and hardware stores and drapers and fruiterers. Radnor Park alone, at one point, boasted over a hundred shops – 16 grocers, 15 confectioners, 11 dairies, 10 newsagents, 2 post offices and a bank, to say nothing of a butcher, a barber, a chemist and Capaldi's ice cream parlour. Private businesses in Clydebank were besides kept on their toes by the Co-operative Society – or, until their merger in 1908, societies, for (in very Scottish fashion) the town proper boasted three, sometimes at daggers drawn: the Clydebank Co-op, the Radnor Park Co-op and the Dalmuir Co-op, each of which ran a range of stores and services.

In 1939, Clydebank acquired a branch of F.W. Woolworth, a stylish white-tiled art deco building with red and gold signage: nothing for sale cost more than sixpence. Glasgow Road – then the heart of the town, with Kilbowie Road shooting north from Clydebank Cross – was a hub of respected businesses: John McChleary's shoe shop, James MacCulloch (tobacconist and newsagent), Francis Spite & Co. (chemist) and Alexander Aitken ('Grocer and Tea Merchant'). Margaret Gray (newsagent, confectioner and tobacconist) sold besides 'Dr Plum and Irwin pipes, Biro pens, and Bestway and Weldon's fashion books and knitting leaflets'.

A glance at just one of the town's great employers – Singer's – tells us much of this community. By the 1930s, aerial photographs vividly bring home the sheer scale of this plant, which had sprawled well beyond its originally 46-acre Kilbowie site – a maze of sheds, offices, workshops, gigantic brick chimneys and multi-storey buildings. The six-floor Cabinet Department was completed, for instance, by Robert 'Concrete Bob' McAlpine in just six months in 1904; and the campus extended yet again in 1906, over the North British Railway Line: the company had to relay the track, and the lost Kilbowie Station was succeeded by a new Singer station, which survives. With over 10,000 employees, no fewer than 14 special trains had to run between 6 and 7 a.m. just to bring them to work, and the plant itself, by 1911, needed yet another train station – Singer Lye, little more than a mass of platforms. (It is said the carriages laid on for Singer employees were so basic many brought their own candles for the commute.) A special tenement block on Kilbowie Road – Singer

Terrace – had been erected by the company just to house its 'foremen, firemen and watchmen'.

Singer had, as we have seen, occasionally fraught industrial relations, and the Great War was a serious setback, but the company had largely recovered by the late 1920s and weathered the Depression better than most. Its employee relations steadily improved, with a range of activities and recreational endeavours. By 1928, according to Sheila Struthers, Singer workers not only enjoyed their own bowling club, but 'a Ladies Athletic Association, Football Association, Boys' Recreation Association, Operatic Society, Chess and Draughts Club, Hockey Club, Pipe Band, Badminton Club, Camera Club, The Singer Players (amateur dramatics), Tennis Club, Golf Association, Orchestral Society, Whist Club . . . and a rather dubious-sounding Physical Culture Club (keep fit). It's a wonder that anyone ever got any work done.' But all this reminds us not only of the community largely obliterated in March 1941, but of the genuine fun and fellowship to be had in a past, gentler and now distant Scotland, pre-consumerist and pre-television and with much greater social interaction – as the winds of war blew over central Europe, and finally, from 3 September 1939 in raging fury.

The indolence and fatuity of Chamberlain's leadership in those early months of conflict is seen in the reaction of Sir Kingsley Wood, his air minister, when – bewildered as to why the RAF was dropping little but leaflets over Germany – one MP suggested an incendiary raid might usefully destroy the Black Forest. Sir Kingsley was positively scandalised. 'It is private property! You will be asking me to bomb Essen next!' Essen was home to the Krupp armament works: Herr Krupp's millions, as Lewis wickedly notes, 'were the kind of private property the Chamberlain government apparently respected'. The one field where Chamberlain and his ministers excelled was the installation of a huge bureaucracy, from the laughably titled Ministry of Information (it was, of course, a ministry for wholesale censorship) to a rigid structure for civil defence. Air raid protection wardens soon became no less powerful, and in many parts far more hated, than policemen; and eminences were appointed as area or regional commissioners with little respect for lack of talent, character or practical experience. These were months – with years more ahead – of scolding, nannying, finger-wagging bossiness, bombarding the populace by every medium and at every opportunity for the duration of the war.

The testy, know-it-all culture of this new war is captured in a typical leaflet, 'When you go to shelter – what you should know'.

Bedding should be aired daily . . . Try not to lie on your back – you are less likely to snore. . . . Make your family gargle before they start for the shelter: make them gargle again when they return. *Don't spit: it is a dirty habit.* If you see anyone spitting, it is your duty to tell the warden at once . . . Keep your feet dry. One of the easiest ways of catching cold is by sitting with wet feet. . . . Entertainment: a certain amount of entertainment is good for us all, but don't let it become a nuisance . . . Try to find a home for your pets. If you can't, take them to a vet. You cannot take them to a shelter . . . Pay No Attention To Rumours.

Rumours, though, inevitably flourished against a backdrop besides of vacuous exhortation. Though, 70 years later and in another national crisis of sorts, 'Keep Calm And Carry On' has found a new market on mugs and T-shirts, it had actually very little exposure in the 'Bore War'. Much more visible – and far sillier – were the posters declaring

YOUR COURAGE *YOUR* CHEERFULNESS
YOUR RESOLUTION
WILL BRING US VICTORY

which, as should have been grasped, infuriated ordinary British people. Who were this 'us'? To many it sounded like the rich, the rulers, the Establishment and the boss class. 'Living in London,' lamented a Canadian diplomat, Charles Ritchie, 'is like being an inmate of a reformatory school. Everywhere you turn, you run into some regulation designed for your protection. The government is like the School Matron.'

Neville Chamberlain that April of 1940 boasted that 'Hitler had missed the bus'; by the end of June, the Führer was the master of Western Europe. Even Chamberlain's fall was as hapless as everything else. The calamitous campaign in Norway was conceived and directed by Winston Churchill. His incessant interference and change of orders wrecked its execution and cost troops and lives. Yet the debacle took down Chamberlain and installed Churchill in his place; still, the Birmingham technocrat remained leader of the Conservative Party, and might well have directed much of importance at home, but – as Taylor sighs – Chamberlain then 'was struck by cancer, and died'.

It is still widely believed – largely because of a noted 1940 anti-appeasement polemic, *The Guilty Men*, by Michael Foot (who died in March 2010, even as this chapter was being written) – that far-sighted men of the Left had long denounced appeasement and warned repeatedly against the threat of Nazi Germany. That may well have been true of Foot himself, one of the very few radicals of his generation who never flirted with Communism, Fascism or pacifism, but it is simply not borne out by the record: anyway, Foot would not begin his own Parliamentary career until 1945.

In fact it was 1935 before Labour MPs even began to reassess their position; most stubbornly certain that war was still unlikely and morally unthinkable. As MacPhail points out, the Baldwin government's 1935 proposals for rearmament 'met with criticism from nearly all sections of the Labour Party and the trade union movement' and, though avowed pacifists were a minority in the Parliamentary party, they included its leader, the decently silly George Lansbury. More fatefully, for Clydebank, they included their own Member for Dumbarton Burghs, David Kirkwood. 'I am all out for peace in the real sense,' he declaimed at local elections in October 1935, 'and would not send a Clydebank boy to war upon any consideration. No war for me under any circumstances.'

In fact, only one Scottish Member of Parliament struck out early, consistently and loudly against appeasement – a Tory lady, Katharine, Duchess of Atholl, member for Kinross and West Perthshire and the first woman ever elected for a Scottish seat. The story of the 'Red Duchess' (she earned the epithet, quite unjustly, for vocally supporting Spain's democratically-elected government against the violent Franco insurgency) is colourful and faintly depressing, reflecting as much the inveterate sexism of that era as the obdurate refusal of practically everyone in high places to grasp the Nazi threat. Katharine Atholl's brave (but foolish) decision to force a by-election in the autumn of 1938 over appeasement, against all sensible counsel – she lost, albeit narrowly, after a singularly nasty campaign by Tory opponents – put permanent end to her political career, and little honour has ever been paid to her courage.

It is important, as Iain MacPhail warns, not to assume that local Labour reluctance to co-operate with the National Government's belated measures for civil defence was down even substantially to starry-eyed pacifism. There was a legitimate feeling that National Government 'defence measures were no substitute for a foreign policy which was based on collective security instead of being one of appeasement'. Yet, even with the benefit of hindsight, it is still difficult to respect the decisions of Clydebank Town Council, under absolute Labour control from the burgh elections of November 1934.

In September 1935, Clydebank councillors met to consider Scottish Office Circular 3026, which gave advice to local authorities for early preparation against air attack – especially to make early arrangements for co-operation with other districts and burghs. The Council rejected such notions decisively, by 10 votes to 5. In March 1936 – as German troops marched into the Rhineland – Clydebank Town Council were again defiant, balloting by 13 to 5 not to send delegates to an air raid precautions conference. As months passed and the European situation darkened, that became an increasingly rare stance. By January 1937, only three local authorities in Scotland still refused to follow National Government directives – Tranent, Wick and Clydebank. By year's end, they lost the choice: determined now on compulsory arrangements, Chamberlain's Cabinet had pushed the Air Raid Precautions Act through Parliament. Clydebank Town Council did not resist further, and in the spring of 1938 started at last to prepare against any future aerial bombardment by Germany.

It seems incredible – again, through the happy spectacles of hindsight – that so many for so long could not have believed the avowed intent of Hitler and the Nazi regime, and only started at the eleventh hour to ready for a war that would have been readily averted by earlier rearmament and tougher diplomacy. But through two critical decades the Soviet Union – which alone had the weight to threaten Germany from the east – was to all intents and purposes a pariah state. The United States had from 1920 retreated to parochial isolationism. The tanking economy and a limp cultural pacifism in Britain (to say nothing of the cynical French politics through this period) precluded serious rearmament and a robust line with Germany until it was too late; it is still dubious whether going to war in 1938 could have actually forced German retreat in the Sudeten crisis, and we were far less equipped for it than was the case 12 months later.

Nor should we underestimate the impact of the Great War – fought on a scale Britain had never experienced and bringing casualties beyond the worst imaginings – on political opinion. It haunted the men of the Left, like the dutiful and conscientious David Kirkwood, whose autobiographical reflections of 1914 (when he was toiling in the Parkhead Forge) reflect the perfectly honourable agonies of his class and generation. 'I hated war. I believed that the peoples of the world hated war. Yet I was working in an arsenal, making guns and shells for one purpose – to kill men in order to keep them from killing men. What a confusion! What was I to do? . . . I resolved that my skill as an engineer must be devoted to my country. I was too proud of the battles of the past to stand aside and see Scotland conquered. Only those who remember 1914 can understand the struggle of mind and the conflict of loyalties which so many of us experienced.'

And Kirkwood wrote those words after the Second World War and in a very different national climate; a decade before, his language reflects the Peace League delusions of 1935 and the universal truth that war is usually a rich man's game and a poor man's fight. And at the other end of the political pitch, one should not lose sight of a genuine, wholly admirable revulsion in the heart of Neville Chamberlain and Tory contemporaries – many whose sons had been claimed by the Flanders mud – that world war should never again waste Europe and decimate a generation.

Rudyard Kipling, Herbert Asquith, Arthur Conan Doyle and renowned Scots musical-hall comedian Harry Lauder were just some of the many significant public figures bereft of boys between 1914 and 1919. It is notable, though, that among the few MPs who did from an early stage repudiate the wisdom of appeasement were several who had actually fought – Clement Attlee, Alec Duff-Cooper, Harold Macmillan (who even resigned the Tory whip for a spell) and Anthony Eden, who quit as foreign secretary late in February 1938, and could well have positioned himself, granted the necessary spirit, to outflank Churchill and become prime minister in May 1940. Men who have actually endured battle – learning, their lives depending on it, that he who hesitates is lost – are much more likely to grasp both the tide of affairs and the depths of human nature.

And clouding all in the 1920s and especially the 1930s, owing more to science fiction than sober reflection – and undoubtedly twisting British policy – were grotesque notions as to the scale, the casualties and the civil impact of terror bombing.

'The bomber,' fretted Stanley Baldwin, in his final term, 'will always get through,' and dwelt lugubriously on 'tens of thousands of mangled people – men, women and children' before a soldier or sailor was even scratched.

In truth, the naiveté of British foreign policy in the fateful 1930s owed much to near-universal belief that the next war, waged largely from the air, would entail national annihilation. When air raid sirens wailed in London just as Neville Chamberlain finished his radio address to the nation, that Sabbath afternoon of 3 September 1939, thousands instantly concluded the end was nigh. (It proved a false alarm.) Winston Churchill himself, gazing out at Whitehall, had vivid thoughts of apocalypse. 'My imagination drew pictures of ruin and carnage and vast explosions shaking the ground; of buildings clattering down in smoke and rubble, of fire brigades and ambulances scurrying through the smoke. For had we not all been taught how terrible air raids would be?'

Indeed it had become, as Tom Harrisson puts it, 'near-obsession . . . The pattern of British politics and forward planning was gradually overshadowed by visions of shattering bombardment on the civil population. Along with this, latent where not explicit, went the broad assumption that much of this population would either be killed, shell-shocked or reduced to panic. They would not be able to stand up to the experience . . . This fearful concept of coming "reality" was supported by scientific argument, statistical estimates of the highest order. Predictions came from extreme left as well as extreme right. The foremost international theorist of the theme was a Fascist general in Italy. The foremost alarmist in Britain was the country's leading Communist scientist.'

The 'Fascist general' was Guilo Douhet, a senior Italian officer of great enthusiasm for bombing, and his book *The Command of the Air* – published in 1921 – was taken up avidly in military academies all over the world, and by statesmen besides, and for the most part unhesitatingly read as gospel verity. That reflected partly an abiding bewilderment and horror after the wretched war of attrition on the Western Front; and the age's continued fascination with technology; and perhaps what has been aptly judged the 'Jupiter Complex' – something deep in the political mind that is drawn both to the low political cost in dropping bombs on unpopular foreigners, and a sense of righteous service as the Fist of God.

Douhet argued that in future war should – and must – be waged not against armies, but entire peoples; that sustained, weighty, awful bombing of cities would soon break the morale of an entire populace; that at length they would rise against their own government for immediate peace, and indeed immediate surrender. Only a great bomber fleet of your own – or perhaps very many deadly little fighter-planes – might serve to deter such an assault; but Douhet was adamant – there was no effective defence when such bombers duly came.

His hypothesis (which, in fact, was largely discredited by the actual experience of the Second World War) spread through capitals and parliaments everywhere like a bacillus. It invited fatalism and despair; it coloured attitudes; it moulded national policy. Churchill himself, in July 1934, talked up London's entire vulnerability to air attack to the House of Commons: 'the greatest target in the world, a kind of tremendous, fat, valuable cow, fed up to attract beasts of prey'. A week later Professor Frederick Lindemann, already Churchill's pet expert and a world authority in aeronautics, assured readers of *The Times* that the imminent war by bombing 'might jeopardise the whole of western civilisation'. Late in 1935, Clement Attlee – now Labour leader – again invoked its imminent end, should war on such terms break out.

Government experts had calculated – and advised – that 100,000 tons of bombs would pour on London in the first fortnight of hostilities; more, in fact, than the capital finally received in all the six years of the Second World War. Fumbling with Great War evidence – which proved highly misleading – the authorities decided there would be 50 casualties per ton of high explosive dropped. They also confidently expected wholesale poison-gas attack on British cities, which is why – in 1938, and at colossal cost – 38 million gas-masks were manufactured and distributed, including a grotesque 'Mickey Mouse' version for small children and a sort of rubbery hold-all for babies. The vast Air Raid Precautions (ARP) scheme had begun besides – 100,000 wardens; 60,000 auxiliary firemen – and every house was exhorted to lay in a long shovel and a bucket of sand (for smothering incendiary bombs) and buckets of water and a stirrup pump besides: in fact these pumps were never available in sufficient numbers. There were besides the highly inconvenient restrictions of blackout and, for the first weeks of the war, this was absolute (no street lighting, no torches allowed, no car headlamps) until it became obvious that the number of road-deaths had doubled, to say nothing of assaults on women; meanwhile, ARP wardens – who spent most of the day, in folks' eyes, lounging about – grew despised for initiating fatuous prosecutions, over the likes of a loose living-room curtain or someone lighting a cigarette at the avenue corner.

From January 1940, at Churchill's urging, some common sense appeared; very dim street lighting was allowed at junctions, and torches dimmed with tissue-paper were permitted, and headlamps with special slotted covers. The biggest failure – because, with the flop of the 'Phoney War', tens of thousands had returned to towns and cities when the Blitz indeed began – was the commanded evacuation of schoolchildren and young mothers. There were odd benefits – for millions of British people, living in relative comfort across the countryside, new exposure to the wretchedness of too many urban gamins contributed greatly to post-war agreement on a range of social policy – but evacuation caused distress and ill-will, undoubtedly exposed thousands of children to abuse as skivvies or worse, and by being launched so prematurely accomplished very little good.

The villain of the piece – the officials who, for their own ends, talked up the prospects of catastrophe as much as possible, and thus engineered these precipitate schemes – were bureaucrats of the Royal Air Force and the Air Ministry, who spent much of the 1920s dreading absorption back into the Royal Navy, as the Admiralty eagerly pressed.

In 1924, Air Staff forecasts of putative civilian woe sounded bleak enough: 3,800 Londoners dead in the first three days of war, and 25,000 dead in a month. By 1937, though, they happily peddled statistics of a whole new dimension, still based on the 'fifty dead per ton of bomb' which seems to have been but apocalyptic guess. The figures were besides cleverly expanded in terms of hard cash and essential expenditure. Advising – quite calmly – that, in the event of war, the National Government could expect 1,800,000 civilian casualties, some 600,000 of them dead, the Committee for Imperial Defence indicated that compensation would total £120,000,000 at 1937 values. Working on the same assumptions, the Ministry of Health declared the need for 2,800,000 hospital beds. The Home Office, not to be outdone, assured the Cabinet some 20,000,000 square feet of seasoned timber – a month – would be required for all the coffins; as that was manifestly impossible, contingency plans were made instead for mass graves and quicklime. There were wild discussions about insurance, which Lloyds of London had made plain they would not underwrite; in the first three weeks of hostilities, they concluded 5 per cent of all property in Britain would be destroyed.

In October 1938 the Cabinet accepted those weird sums – the impact on Chamberlain, who was nothing if not a balance-sheet man, can readily be imagined – and by then he was promised 500 tons of bombs on London in the first day and night, with 700 tons daily thereafter, brought by ruthless daylight raids and with very high accuracy. And all this was just the vision of men who did vaguely know what they were talking about; in the newspapers, and the clubs and salons of London, still wilder scenarios were forecast – influenced, quite literally by science fiction, for H.G. Wells's nightmarish *The War in the Air* was confidently assumed to be both expert and sober. Not that there is much sobriety even in the title of one hysterical essay, 'An Expert's Prophetic Vision of the Super-Armageddon That May Destroy Civilisation', by Colonel James Fitzmaurice, recent head of the Irish Free State's somewhat limited air corps:

> A hideous shower of death and destruction falls screeching and screaming through space and atmosphere to the helpless, thickly populated earth below.
>   The shock of the hit is appalling. Great buildings totter and tumble in the dust like a mean and frail set of ninepins . . . The survivors, now merely demoralised, masses of demented humanity, scatter caution to the winds. They are seized by a demoniacal frenzy of terror. They tear off their gas masks, soon absorb the poisonous fumes, and expire in horrible agony, cursing the fate that did not destroy them hurriedly and without warning in the first awful explosions.

One sage, Lord Halsbury, declared a single gas-bomb would kill everyone between the Thames and the Serpentine. Negley Farson, a renowned reporter, was assured by pundits there would be 30,000 to 35,000 casualties a day. The new Air Raid Defence League forecast 200,000 in ten days; John Langdon-Davies, who had personally witnessed the Luftwaffe raids on Barcelona, warned of 'silent approach' by attacking glide-bombers, and added helpfully that anti-aircraft guns could never be used, as their noise would shatter eardrums. Professor J.B.S. Haldane, the archetypal rich, aristocratic, loungelizard Communist, expected tens of thousands to flee Britain's cities in entire hysteria; and that German planes would deliberately mow them down by machine gun to block the main roads. Diverting himself with nightmarish descriptions of bomb-blast, Haldane called for anti-panic measures and robust crowd control.

It is often those who speak loudest for the common man who most despise him: all this was compounded, at the highest levels of national life, by general disdain for the mental and emotional strength of ordinary people, influenced perhaps too by the very sudden collapse of German civilian morale late in 1918 – though founded on hunger, not bombing. At best, the masses were so many biddable sheep; under pressure, they would panic, and at the worst murderous Reds would emerge from beneath every other bed.

Along with all the horrors of the generally predicted Armageddon, as Harrisson sighs, the 'proletariat were bound to crack, run, panic, even go mad, lacking the courage and self-discipline of their masters or those regimented in the forces. The alternative view – that a Belfast plumber might manage as well as an Irish Guards officer – was rarely seriously advanced . . . much of this population would either be killed, shell-shocked or reduced to panic. They would not be able to stand up to the experience. Thus the properly motivated, disciplined armed forces would be threatened by collapse on the home front, stabbing them in the back.' (Not that the intelligentsia might greatly care: by late 1938, a surprising number of self-consciously informed and clever people spoke aloud about simply killing their own families, rather than letting them endure the entire Gehenna of aerial war – though none, of course, ever did.) Even today, our perceptions of the Second World War are coloured more than we admit by this all-pervasive patrician prejudice: of the hundreds and hundreds of British films made during or inspired by the conflict – and made through decades after 1945 – it is extremely rare to hear, in a part of any importance, a regional or working-class accent. The national deliverance, we all grew up thinking, had been wrought by the posh.

All this was founded on a central premise: that Nazi Germany intended a war of strategic bombing (that is, the wholesale destruction of industrial areas and major population centres by very large planes carrying a great weight of explosive) rather than tactical bombing (small, fast-moving planes carrying limited explosives and working in close battlefield co-operation with advancing troops.)

But the Third Reich had no such plans and, when the Second World War was launched, it had no such aircraft; by the time it began belatedly to build big strategic bombers, its factories and cities were themselves under sustained attack. It is remarkable how easily, conditioned by popular *Vorsprung durch Technik* notions of German efficiency and her capacity for immaculate and obedient organisation, we forget that – as a direct consequence of being a murderous, criminal state led by little more than a B-movie cast of adventurers, gangsters and psychopaths – the Third Reich was in many respects utterly incompetent. Hitler himself deliberately encouraged (from foggy, Darwinian notions of the benefits of competition) much overlap, confusion and cut-throat struggle between different departments of state. Furthermore he habitually gave detailed and absolute orders about subjects, campaigns, battles and armaments and tactics he knew nothing about.

But Hermann Göring himself – the bullish and genially vicious Reichs-marshal – probably bears more responsibility than any other Nazi for defeat in a war Germany, objectively, should have won. Certainly he was not remotely equipped to plan, build and direct her air forces. Of big appetites and lazy temperament, he had not the self-discipline for serious government and only survived at the top of the Nazi regime because, though faltering even by 1939, he was too popular with ordinary Germans safely to be dismissed.

Though a highly-decorated First World War flying ace – Göring had commanded the Richthofen squadron – and, for some years after that conflict, a stunt-pilot with a flair for aerobatics, none of this entailed the technical heft to build good aircraft for modern war. In any event, since treatment (in hiding) with morphine for wounds received in the failed Munich putsch of 1923, Göring had serious addiction issues, to say nothing of a strange effeminacy – he regularly wore make-up, was whispered to paint his toenails and had a signal weakness for gaudy, often ridiculous uniforms. Granted astonishing powers by Hitler in 1934 – his effective deputy and designated successor; in charge of Prussia; commanding all German civil and military aviation, most important strategic commodities and the foreign exchange reserves – Göring besides became astonishingly corrupt. 'Most of the Nazi leaders complained that he was lazy,' writes Len Deighton, 'a condition not helped by addiction and obesity. During the Second World War he certainly devoted far more time to buying, exchanging and plundering paintings and works of art than he did to running the Luftwaffe.'

Though he became a buffoon, Göring was not in essence one. Those who dealt with him at the Nuremberg Trials after the war, or who had close experience of him in prison, were struck by his bearing, intelligence, entire grasp of a mountain of documents and utter self-control (not least because the prison psychiatrist had firmly weaned him off paracodeine tablets). He was popular to the very end with millions of ordinary Germans, who identified with his pleasures, appreciated his unfailing public cheerfulness and could barely hide their glee when, in 1946, he cheated the gallows by cyanide. He was nevertheless, it must be stressed, a profoundly evil man: Göring estab-lished the concentration camps and launched what became the Gestapo, and it is now known his authority was immediate, and probably pivotal, in author-ising the 'Final Solution' early in 1942. We should be thankful that – the lucky triumphs of the Battle of France apart – his Luftwaffe failed at every important crunch of the war.

That was partly because Göring's vast new Air Ministry in Berlin – a surviving marvel of architecture, with 2,800 rooms – was, in typically Nazi fashion, grossly overmanned with squabbling, plotting, competing officers and planners and bureaucrats, united for most of the time only in determination to outflank and preferably to destroy one another. It was partly because, like much else in the Third Reich, such an atmosphere and its hierarchies – in a regime where the danger was not, should you fall foul of authority, of being charged, tried and imprisoned, but of being cast into a concentration-camp abyss outside the rule of law all together – made it tough for the bravest of men to tell the truth to power. And, not least, it was because Göring placed his chief confidence in those as flawed and wicked as himself. Erhard Milch, his second-in-command at the Air Ministry, was – as Deighton points – out – little more than a 'competent bureaucrat, with unusual administrative skills' whose judgement 'was entirely inadequate'.

Nor was Ernst Udet – placed confidently in charge of the Luftwaffe's technical department, simply because he had flown with Göring in the Great War – any better. The war record was certainly impressive: Udet, who had made one of the earliest emergency parachute-jumps, was the highest-scoring German ace to survive the conflict: only von Richthofen, the 'Red Baron' himself, had downed more Allied planes. Udet had also found work as a stunt-pilot (and was besides a rather good cartoonist) and was never really happy outside a cockpit: with childish delight in display and bravado, and a playboy by inclination, he had no experience of industry and not the least managerial skill.

Udet had an undoubted weakness for the theatrical. It was his idea to fix a terrifying siren to the Stuka, a doughty but rather dated little dive-bomber which could come down in screaming attack from a near-90° angle, and destroyed many tanks early in the war; but few German pilots cared for such flying-circus aeronautics. That was just Udet's problem, as Richard Overy points out; his 'infatuation with aerial acrobatics led to the neglect of long-range bombardment in favour of smaller bombers that could dive down and destroy even small targets on the battlefield'. When Göring did, belatedly, order development of a long-range 4-engine bomber, Udet insisted it be able to dive and thus delayed delivery of even a usable design by three full years. As the scale of his ineptitude grew evident even to him, Udet drank more and more heavily; late in 1941, now in a thoroughly bad place and while on the telephone to his girlfriend, he shot himself through the head.

In all, it typified the self-defeating indiscipline of a demonic regime. Though they witnessed the very first jet-powered flight – by German technology – Milch and Udet flatly refused to see any potential in the idea. They meekly stood by as the Luftwaffe was placed in entire subservience to the German army – co-operating closely and at all times with ground forces, a strategy maintained for the rest of the war. Though charged with the anti-aircraft defence of the Reich itself, those endeavours too proved hopeless. Far more attention was given to pace and drama and the operatic movement of *blitzkrieg* than ever to the more prosaic realities of the battle in the air. In the critical weeks of the Battle of Britain, the Messerschmitt 109 was at least as good a plane as the Spitfire and certainly better than the Hurricane; but – fully fuelled – its operational range was only 90 minutes, as Angus Calder points out, which

> meant that it could fight for only a few minutes over Britain before it had to head for home. Its stablemate, the twin-engined Me 110, was so unwieldy in combat that it was a liability. The dreaded Stuka dive-bombers had been effective enough against frightened men on the ground, but the RAF found them excellent target practice; they were slow and weakly armed. The Heinkels, Dorniers and Junkers of the German bombing force had also been designed for co-operation with the army rather than the 'knockout blow' which opinion in Britain had expected before the war. They were relatively fast but, as the winter of 1940–41 showed, they did not carry the scale of bomb load required to knock out a major industrial country. It was the British, not the Germans, who had planned giant four-engined bombers for such a purpose . . .

In fact, the Luftwaffe was really, as Deighton puts it, little more than 'a form of long-range artillery, providing support to the army in short sharp wars that the sensitive German economy could endure', all the more so as through the 1930s Germany's foreign exchange was most limited. All imported raw materials were in short supply and the army always had first call on them. Without Göring's ferocious weight behind the idea – which never came – there were not the stuffs to build a fleet of huge, serious strategic bombers, nor any likelihood of the fuel to fly them. (Udet's suicide was probably tipped by the gross shortage of aluminium, without which the aircraft Göring had promised Hitler could simply not be built.) In 1936 the one senior figure in the German military establishment who was convinced of the necessity to prepare for strategic bombing – General Walter Wever – was killed when the ailerons of his aircraft locked on what should have been a routine flight.

There was also a deft little shove from the British, where Marshal of the Royal Air Force Sir Hugh Trenchard and Field Marshal Jan Christian Smuts – he, unaccountably, was held in great esteem in Whitehall and was eventually appointed a War Cabinet adviser on home defence – had long hailed the age of the great bomber. While on a trip to England in 1937, Udet enjoyed an official visit to the RAF and foolishly, in the company of Sir Victor Goddard (a fervent supporter of heavy bombers) complained about mounting pressure on him to produce such planes – but, remembered Sir Victor coyly, Udet 'then cited the disadvantages in manoeuvrability of large bulk; he cited the difficulties which would be involved by engine breakdowns and found various other reasons, all of which I endorsed . . .'

So Germany soon abandoned 'plans for heavy bombers', observes Harrisson, 'in favour of speedy planes, fighters, short-range dive-bombers. Only reluctantly did more desperate pressures send the Luftwaffe "indiscriminately" bombing. Then, late in 1940, their enormous bomber weakness enormously alleviated the burden to be borne by British civilians, whereas Trenchard's enduring vitality had, eventually, the obverse effect upon the unhappy inhabitants of the Third Reich.' By May 1945, Allied forces – executing a determined policy of strategic bombing, and with increasing skill, and using large powerful planes like the Wellington and the Halifax – had dropped 964,644 tons of bombs on Germany, and 305,000 to 600,000 Germans had been killed. British civilian casualties from bombing, in all the Second World War, amounted to 60,595.

Yet, even in Germany, popular morale never collapsed, any more than it did in Britain; as late as April 1945, Berlin postmen still doggedly made their rounds in a capital reduced largely to rubble. And war production (sustained by this point largely by slave labour) ground steadily on. In December 1944, German industry (even as death came screaming by day and night) produced 218,000 rifles and 1,840 armoured cars. Strategic bombing undoubtedly hampered Third Reich endeavours, diverted untold resources from the fronts both west and east, and significantly shortened the Second World War. But the prophecies of 1930s doom-mongers failed signally to translate into reality.

And, however darkly beneficial they may have been for the RAF – securing its survival and the means to build effective fighters and serious bombers – their effect on Britain's civil defence was largely malign. The National Government planned not for daily, ongoing survival, but for hecatombs. The emphasis, Tom Harrisson laments, was 'overwhelmingly on death and destruction, or crippling hurt, with little consideration for other, less obvious and in the event usually far greater side effects on humanity: confusion, anxiety, dislocation and distress'. It was at an early stage decided not to build deep air raid shelters, lest the working masses simply vanish into that refuge and refuse again to emerge. The vast plans for evacuation of children and young mothers from urban centres were another unhappy, largely self-defeating fruit.

Though ARP measures were rolled out across Britain, the main obsession was the defence of London. Here, at least, central government and the London County Council could quickly co-operate, and as residents – and potential casualties – senior ministers and officials had immediate interest in effective planning and, when the Blitz began, the rapid execution of rapid decisions. In the rest of Britain – what ministers were pleased to describe as the 'provinces' – things were far less efficient and there was much more diffusion of decision-making, hampered besides by much rivalry between local authorities. A system of 12 regional commissioners was unveiled in February 1939 granting vast emergency powers in the event of the anticipated cataclysm. In Scotland, the honour passed in 1941 to Lord Rosebery, an amiable aristocrat who attained the post largely because his late father, a high-minded insomniac, had served briefly as a hapless Liberal prime minister: Rosebery the younger was a noted patron of the turf.

Bombing on a serious scale began in September 1940 as Nazi Germany began finally to accept defeat in the Battle of Britain and – after a fortnight of trying to destroy airfields rather than the RAF – launched the 'Battle of London', three weeks of bold and largely ineffectual daylight raids by fighter-escorted bombers against the capital. It was a final, desperate bid to accomplish the sort of knock-out blow that would clear the way for invasion, as winter remorselessly approached. The turning point fell on 15 September 1940, when 200 heavily-escorted German bombers converged on London. The RAF met them east of the city, and a second wave besides, and by nightfall had turned back the assault, downing nearly 60 German aircraft. Two days later, Hitler grimly cancelled 'Operation Sealion'. There would be no invasion of Britain that year, though until 30 October desperate, daylight raids would continue. Thereafter, battered German bomber squadrons began protracted, destructive but strategically pointless night-time raids on the British capital, on a Wagnerian scale and of frightening intensity, and it is this beleaguered winter that is the Blitz proper, as – night after night, week after week – London was bombed and bombed and bombed.

Through October 1940, the Luftwaffe also began to vest effort in attacks elsewhere. On 15 October, 170 people died in a raid on Birmingham. On 14 November, the Germans launched their infamous attack on Coventry, a centre of the British motor industry and with a great many vital factories, 12 directly involved in aircraft manufacture. Five hundred and forty-four people died, and two-thirds of Coventry houses were rendered uninhabitable; a 100-acre area in the city centre was flattened, all railway lines into Coventry were blocked and of the great medieval Cathedral only two towers survived. For a day or two there was entire confusion, and Mass Observation files record a degree of panic and hysteria and such phrases as 'Coventry is finished' and 'Coventry is dead.' Rationing had to be suspended. For several weeks, all drinking water had to be boiled.

Coventry is important because it was the first practical test of a new German system for terror raids. They had initially relied on a radio-based system of navigation, *Knickebein*; beams from two different radio stations on the Continent could be arranged to intersect over a British target, and aircraft could then fly along either beam and launch their attack at that invisible junction. But the British found out about it in June 1940 and had soon worked out how to block or deflect the beam – though the technology (a point of which Meg Henderson makes much) was never brought to Clydeside.

The Germans – now only raiding at night and at most strength when there was a good moon – rapidly devised a still better system, with three different radio signals, and decided now to head an attack with a 'pathfinder' force, the Kampfgruppe 100, who would carpet the town or city in question with incendiary bombs. The aircraft in their tail would then simply steer for the flames and it was this, more than anything, which proved so fateful for Clydebank.

But Coventry also starkly highlights the limits of bombing. Factories might have been destroyed, but not the machines inside them; streets might be so much rubble, but workers continued stubbornly to toil. Practically all the huge roofing of the Morris Motor Engine Works had been blown away; but, in the first week after the raid, five-sixths of all employees showed up for their shift, doughtily clad in coats and waterproofs, working on beneath smoky open skies. The Germans – too busy boasting now of *coventrien*, 'to Coventrate', chose inexplicably not to attack again. Within six weeks, Angus Calder notes, 'Morris's production of tank engines, airscrews and other vital components was back to normal.'

Wider raids would continue. Bristol was in turn 'coventrated' on 24 November 1940. There would be especially serious attacks on Southampton and Portsmouth. Manchester, Merseyside, Sheffield and Leicester suffered much. Hull – its travails today almost forgotten – was piteously battered; being on the east coast, it was a very easy target. Liverpool, of all great cities, probably endured most after London

None of this should distract from the sustained assault on the capital, which remained the prime target: 19,000 tons of bombs blasted the city between September 1940 and May 1941. But its sheer scale – acre upon acre of suburb for temporary refuge; the miles of Underground railway (rapidly granted for shelter, after the people had determinedly seized it anyway) and the great retail economy – allowed life to go on with some fraught normality whatever the Germans threw at it.

And the repetitious, near-nightly attack also gave the ARP wardens, fire brigades official and auxiliary, and a host of other agencies sufficient practice and experience rapidly to improve their skills in firefighting, defence and general emergency endeavour. London weathered the ferocious raid of the City proper, on 29 December 1940, in a rain of flame so terrible it is still remembered as the 'second fire of London': there were no fewer than 1,500 separate blazes in this one relatively small area, and firefighting was all the harder as, with a very low tide, it was unusually difficult to draw water from the Thames. But St Paul's Cathedral, in one of the most iconic images of the war, rose defiant and surviving amidst the sea of cataclysm around it, and only 163 people perished, for very few lived in the actual City. The Germans continued, rather more fitfully after New Year, to bomb London, and the last night of her Blitz – on 10 May – would be the most frightful of all; but by then, of course, the Luftwaffe had emphatically found the coasts of Clyde.

On a steamer from Carradale, north of Campbeltown on the Kintyre peninsula, in these early weeks of 1941, a lad of 17 – in a day when boys of that age looked rather younger than they do now – hunched over an exercise book, his brow furrowed, his pencil scratching. Jim, small, jug-eared, a little weak of chin and intense of gaze, had not wanted to go to Glasgow at all: he was nevertheless going, on the first leg of his journey by boat and train, to begin some ghastly course at the behest of his fretting parents.

James Alexander MacKinven, young and geeky as he looked, was a compulsive writer, and the book of blue covers curled in his hand was full of it – weighty poems, light verse, comic verse, earnest schoolboy compositions.

Most, as Jim himself was darkly aware, were rather juvenile, a little overdone, sickly or at times pretentious. There was a lugubrious one about Dumbarton (which he had hated); and two (jolly, but still too sentimental) about his pet Glasgow evacuees in Carradale, Oliver and Will, whom his family had taken in and which wee gaffe-prone keelies had afforded no end of culture-clash entertainment.

But, just lately, Jim felt at last he was finding some skill, and a voice that would not only be a good voice, but truly his own voice; though of late he had lost his taste for the couthy, the funny, the kailyard. He scratched an adjustment or two to one of his most recent, 'Undertones', which had a brisk rhythm to it, and a faint note of preaching, and that melancholy which for a change was not affected, and which increasingly lay on him, and which he could not shake off.

'Neath the waves that roll and rumble there is something said in silence,
Silence to us for we cannot hear below
That wild noise the whispered phrases in a million different mazes
Where the strangest creature gazes
Sitting cold eyed, there, amongst the strangest things that grow.

'Mid the wind that shrieks and rustles there is something said in silence,
In a language ne'er for us to understand,
In the lonely cliff's white ledges its weird tale it swiftly wedges,
To the grey graveyard it pledges
Trusting all who form that sacred solemn band.

In the World the world should care for there is something said with clearness
Ringing richly like a pealing calling bell,
Have we not oft heard its pealing
And its sound come softly stealing,
Wrapping us in clouds of healing?

List, my friend, learn, love and preach that lasting knell!

Jim shivered again, and closed his book, and tucked his pencil away. No, he did not want to make for the city, and Clydeside. At all. He had a really, really bad feeling about it . . .

II

THE TERRORS OF THE NIGHT

He that doth in the secret place
of the most High reside,
Under the shade of him that is
th'Almighty shall abide.

I of the LORD my God will say,
He is my refuge still,
He is my fortress, and my God,
and in him trust I will.

Assuredly he shall thee save
and give deliverance
From subtile fowler's snare, and from
the noisome pestilence.

His feathers shall thee hide; thy trust
under his wings shall be:
His faithfulness shall be a shield
and buckler unto thee.

Thou shalt not need to be afraid
for terrors of the night;
Nor for the arrow that doth fly
by day, while it is light;

Nor for the pestilence, that walks
in darkness secretly;
Nor for destruction, that doth waste
at noonday openly.

A thousand at thy side shall fall,
on thy right hand shall lie
Ten thousand dead; yet unto thee
it shall not once come nigh . . .

Psalm 91:1–7 – Scottish Psalter, 1650. These verses were made precious to a Clydebank woman who survived the assault of March 1941. They are sung today, for the most part, only in the Highland Presbyterian tradition, whose Clydebank services – Free Church and Free Presbyterian – did not long survive the Blitz.

5

'ALL ON FIRE ...'

Thursday 13 March 1941 had been the loveliest spring day, and Clydebank prepared to turn in for the night on the finest of evenings, as low golden sun yielded graciously to a high moon, and the first nip of frost pinched in the gloaming. 'The rooks were building their nests in the tall trees at Mount Blow,' Iain MacPhail would muse in 1974, still haunted by the pastoral ordinariness of it all, 'carts of blaes were being delivered at the local tennis courts, and with the advent of double summertime' – a wartime tweak to extend the working day for farms in a beleaguered and hungry Britain – 'allotment-holders were using the extra daylight after working hours to make a beginning with the spring work.'

As spades bit into winter-impacted soil, and last year's wizened and discarded potato-shaws were piled on compost, hundreds more played after a hard day's work. The local cinemas – five of them – boasted full houses this evening, as workers relaxed at the Regal in Dalmuir, or at La Scala, or the Bank, or the Palace, before the sugary joys of Shirley Temple and Jack Oakie, or the pleasantly creepy *Daughter of the Tong*, or assorted documentaries, B-movies and light features. Alex Hardie and his family had headed into Glasgow for a night's entertainment at the Queen's Theatre; hundreds more, after a long working day, had washed up and donned their best and made for assorted dance halls. Many more, of course, simply wound down for the night at home, clearing things away after high tea and preparing for that sombre wartime ritual, tuning in the bulky family wireless for the nine o'clock news.

But men in authority were in no position to relax. Around 7.30 p.m., word came through from the Civil Defence District Control 'War Room' in Glasgow: a German radio-navigational beam had just been detected, bearing right through Clydeside. Town councillors had spent the early evening disposing of business on various dull committees: Housing, and Fire and Lighting, and Cleaning (the last that night, MacPhail notes dryly, had to consider a letter of protest about plans to close the public convenience on Whitecrook Lane). By eight o'clock, though, such high municipal affairs were done, and several of the Clydebank town fathers made for the 'Control Centre' in the basement below the Public Library: the town clerk, Henry Kelly, was also civil defence controller for the risingest burgh, with James A.G. Hastings as his deputy.

Kelly had put in untold hours, over many weeks and months, in a near-impossible position. Determined to play political games, Clydebank Town

Council had not even begun to prepare – far less realise – any air raid precautions until late in 1937, when finally compelled to comply by writ of Parliament. In 1982, Hastings would nevertheless insist to Billy Kay that 'once the 1937 Act came into being, we certainly got the go-ahead from the Town Council and we got any support that we needed from them; they not only supported us, they pushed us almost to exhaustion. The net result was that they were in the forefront of the local authorities with their preparations by the time 1939 and 1940 came along.'

But the town's human geography had precluded anything approaching adequate shelter arrangements: only households with gardens, for instance, could take advantage of the new Anderson shelters made available (though these were cramped, and very prone to flooding), and the simple but surprisingly effective Morrison shelter – a weighty steel table, with caged protection at the sides and which, designed for erection indoors, made a life-saving difference in tenement flats – would not appear till the early summer of 1941. Many brick-built communal shelters had been built around town and in assorted back-closes, but these had no hope of surviving a direct hit and, as whispers from the south attested, were often so shoddily erected as to prove veritable deathtraps. They were, besides, dank and moist and windowless and not made any more attractive by basic, smelly and often unstable chemical toilets.

The best that could be done in Clydebank, for the most part, was the bracing of ground-floor closes. 'Entries' were bolstered with heavy steel framing; and at either end – on the street front and by the rear close – baffle-walls were built, lest blast from explosion on a street howl through this humanity-packed tunnel like the barrel of a gun. (With the imposition of blackout besides, painful human collision with these brick barriers – habituated tenement denizens constantly forgot they were there – was frequent.)

Kelly and Hastings were also uneasily aware of the 'phoney war' problem: months and months of very little happening had fostered much complacency. The programme of Clydeside evacuation late in 1939 had largely unravelled, women and children flooding back to their men as apocalypse failed to materialise. 'At the beginning of the war,' Patrick Donnelly remembered 40 years later, 'the whole family were evacuated to Tighnabruaich, that's across from Rothesay, and we stayed there for a few month. We couldn't stick the country life kinda thing, we stayed in the Marquis o' Bute's house; it was like a big haunted house and we couldn't really stand it. I think most people actually came home. You've got your home and it doesn't really matter how bad things are, you'll just go back to it and just accept it. . . .'

Then – amidst a chronic labour-shortage, and abundant overtime – it was an ongoing struggle to recruit enough bodies for the various voluntary services and turn them all out even for training evenings, far less in an actual emergency.

Still, Kelly and Hastings had done their best. By March 1941, Clydebank boasted 462 ARP wardens, 50 of them full-time. All had regular tours of duty, all were obliged to report when the siren wailed and they were organised in five distinct districts corresponding roughly to electoral wards, each with its own control centre and assorted wardens' posts. (But facilities were mean: at one station, Boquhanran Church Hall, there was no telephone, and messages had to be brought by runner.)

Though they could be hugely unpopular, ARP wardens were for the most part conscientious and soberly-minded men. Joan Baird – best known today as a stalwart of the Clydebank Asbestos Group – has kindly furnished her father's ARP log, an officially-issued and hard-covered notebook wherein Thomas Thompson, ARP warden for the D1 sector of Dumbarton, had to keep his meticulously handwritten record, countersigned regularly by the head warden. Thompson's burdens can be grasped from his last entry before the Clydebank Blitz:

The fortnightly meeting of Wardens and messengers was held, at the Post D1, on Sunday 9th March 1941. Mr John McColl Head Warden presiding. The minute of last meeting was read and adopted.

Arising out of the minute, we are informed that the order for coats has been sent to the makers, and we hope will soon be supplied to the wardens.

The report of examination of Gas Masks shows that 99 Gas Masks had been examined at the Post, represent [sic] 41 families. A discussion took place – should wardens volunteer for fire-fighting.

It was generally decided that the duties of wardens would not allow them to undertake more responsibility.

Owing to pressure of business, Miss D Murray apologises for being absent from our fortnightly meetings. The meeting decided Mr McColl should bring up before the Head Wardens meeting that despite all our efforts, D Group cannot get more fire-fighters.

This was all the business, and the meeting finished with a vote of thanks to the Chairman.

Names of wardens and messengers attending meeting will be found in Part-Time Wardens Book.

There were around 90 messengers or 'runners' in Clydebank – almost all lads in their teens and drawn from the Scouts or the Boys' Brigade, most with bicycles and the luckiest with motorcycles, and whose heroism in the final reality of bombing is attested and remarkable. There were also the casualty services, under the local medical officer of health: there were two first aid posts set up for treatment – at Elgin Street and in Boquhanran School – and four first aid party and ambulance depots, where 16 trained squads (eight of them full-time) trained to go a-running to locate, treat and if necessary bear back the maimed and wounded. They had the use of 23 ambulances, and 18 cars besides for any bloodied victim still able to sit up.

The town also had eight rescue parties – four of them, again, full-time and trained – which drew largely on the building trade and were primed to pick through or clear the rubble of ruined buildings to extricate the trapped but living (even as bombs still fell and in most dangerous conditions). As all had gone into the war convinced attacks by poison gas and perhaps other forms of chemical horror were certain, Clydebank had besides decontamination squads – and on top of all this, of course, there were the local police (bolstered by special constables) and the fire brigade (bolstered by auxiliary crews).

Fire, as things would prove, was the deadliest reality of all; and firefighting the area in which the town was most vulnerable. The Auxiliary Fire Service – with basic man-handled trailer-pumps and equipment – called for young, fit men, who were naturally in short supply in a town dominated by war industry and still scarcer as the few in surplus were called up to the fighting forces. Besides, long before March 1941 the pattern of German bombing was well established – early 'pathfinder' raids showering a conurbation with small, quiet, but insidious incendiary bombs, which smouldered pleasantly in yards and on roof-leads but, unfought and unsmothered, soon launched serious flame – by which in turn the real bombers could close in on the target below with some accuracy.

The lessons had already been painfully learned in London. There should have been rooftop volunteers all over Clydebank to spot and kill those incendiaries (which could readily be dowsed by a bucket of water or even sand). And, early in the war, there were such patchy endeavours; but, by this Thursday night, they had been almost entirely abandoned. The government had besides put much effort into exhorting domestic precautions, such as keeping filled buckets to hand; and, since 1939, it had urged everyone to buy a stirrup pump. But these were never cheap and, more to the point, never manufactured in anything like sufficient numbers: when John Anderson, righteous Home Secretary from September 1939 to October 1940, intoned on the radio that he wanted 'every householder to get a stirrup pump and to learn to use it', there was dark, knowing laughter all over Britain.

There is controversy to this day as to the adequacy of Clydebank's fire-watching by March 1941. After London's flaming horror in the last gasp of 1940, the government belatedly grasped the scale of the problem across Britain and passed new compulsory arrangements, insisting that every company and factory organise fire-watching at night on its own premises; and that, in addition, local authorities make plans for every street. Only days before the attack – at a lively public meeting in Clydebank Town Hall on 25 February 1941 – there were claims and counter-claims as to the town's organisation and readiness. But the meeting was thinly attended, suggesting much local complacency. Few were even present to hear the call to attend free fire-prevention lectures.

It was declared that Tom Johnston (the old Labour warhorse had, just a week earlier, become the new Secretary of State for Scotland, after a stint as ARP regional controller) was worried about Clydebank's readiness. One councillor praised the folk of John Knox Street who had shown enthusiastic interest. An ARP warden insisted that in his patch – the Second Ward – there was 'hardly a close not organised for fire-fighting'; he had been able to send up a list of over a thousand names to the authorities, and the problem was at the top – no one was co-ordinating or directing. Late-night and overtime working, someone pointed out, made it very difficult for many to attend training; there were besides landlords and factors who had still failed to clear lofts of lumber and junk that could readily ignite. As for all the McAlpine houses at Radnor Park (the 'Holy City') Cllr King warned prophetically that roof access was a serious problem (only a hatch in every third close) and that, with flat roofs slathered in tarmacadam, there was a disaster waiting to happen should incendiaries fall. The shortage of stirrup pumps and sandbags was bewailed by another Clydebank resident: Provost David Low insisted the ARP Emergency Committee was doing 'all in its power' to secure enough of them.

But time, in fact, was almost up. On Thursday 13 March, there were but two stirrup pumps in one ARP ward; indeed, an anxious meeting in the Chestnut Drive home of a conscientious warden as to how more pumps and buckets might somehow be wangled had hastily to be abandoned when the sirens howled. That thousands of residents had indeed put in their names in for firewatching duties is undoubted; it is equally plain that no one in a position of responsibility had done anything effective to organise them. MacPhail does rightly point out that, in a district dominated by high and tightly-packed tenements, even dozens of trained and properly-directed firefighting crews would, really, have made very little difference. The problem was that Clydebank, unlike London, was granted no learning curve under a long period of sustained and patchy attack. There was really – counting two consecutive nights as a unit – but one concentrated assault: catastrophic and total.

There is certainly some evidence that many Clydebank folk, by March 1941, were living in a fool's paradise: not a week before the attack, Tom Harrisson and his Mass Observation team had just completed a quiet but inquisitive stint on Clydeside and submitted their report, in an atmosphere heavily coloured by continued industrial unrest and a protracted apprentices' strike in the local shipyards. (This was not, as many seem to think today, impudent and unpatriotic strike action by young boys. It was angry endeavour by fully-trained, fully-qualified journeymen at John Brown's and elsewhere who were still cynically consigned by management to apprentice status and an apprentice's meagre wage – fostering yet more ill-feeling on top of many years of industrial insecurity, blandly rapacious bosses and grim social conditions.)

Locally, only 30 per cent of those polled informally by Mass Observation expected heavy raids 'soon'. Twenty-eight per cent did not; a full 42 per cent were 'vague or indifferent, largely ignoring the whole issue'. Some resented the uncertainty and ongoing unease, wanting to 'get it over with'; Harrison quoted one elderly housewife: 'I wish to goodness it would come and *be done with it.*' A surprising number gave 'many and varied reasons' why they thought a local blitz unlikely. There were odd air-pockets over the Clyde, posing a risk to German planes. There were all the high mountains north of the Firth – a hazard for night-flying. There was 'a magnetic element' in the hills, 'which dislocates aircraft engines'. Besides, the Germans would never even locate the Clyde 'in a network of hills and lochs'. There were plenty of anti-aircraft defences and guns. It was all too far inland. It was all too far overland. It was all too far from German bases; anyway, the Germans were not antagonistic to Scotland – and so on. Glasgow's own Lord Provost, Sir Patrick Dollan – whom Harrisson describes slyly as a 'sunshine politician' – kept up a jolly, chaffing line in public. Bombs would not wreak the mayhem in his municipality as they had in London, for 'Glasgow houses are more solidly built'; and Greenock would certainly never be bombed, such was its foul weather: 'It always rains except when it's snowing.'

There were two themes in disturbing contrast. Many ordinary folk thought the Germans were deliberately sparing the area, as 'revolution might develop here so long as bombs *don't* stir up the people.' But some 'leading citizens' actually snarled in the hearing of Mass Observation diarists that

> what Glasgow needs is a few bombs . . . a number of important Glasgow people hold the view that the Germans are leaving Glasgow alone and will continue to leave it alone precisely to produce the effect which is now being produced, namely of gathering unrest and selfish interest. It is not that Clydeside workers are against the war or for peace. They want to win it as much as anyone, though there is a considerable Maxtonish minority. It is rather that Clydeside workers are *also* having a war of their own, that they cannot forget the numerous battles of the past thirty years, and cannot overcome the bitter memory of industrial insecurity in the past ten years . . . Bombs now might well focus the hatred outwards. Much would depend on where they fell and how the subsequent problems were dealt with.

And such class-war contempt still echoed in 2010, as the lively Eric Flack could recall be email:

> I live and my folks have lived in Drumchapel since about 1900. My grandpa owned a factory at Yoker making ships' propellors. Anyway he was involved with the Conservative Party in Dunbartonshire in the 1930s. I think he was a Tory candidate's election agent. Anyhow he told me that the 'Council' in Clydebank was due to its large number of Labour/ Socialist/Communist people putting all thoughts of civil defence to a low priority. There would be peace. My grandfather maintained if the British government had not 'leant' on Clydebank Town Council there would have been no air raid shelters or any form of civil defence when war broke out. Civil defence was low priority but Singer's/ Brown's etc knew they would be targeted and went ahead with their own internal works civil defence programme as the 'town council' did not want to be involved in the 'internal workings of these companies!' . . . These companies had to organise their own civil defence and bought their own equipment out of their own company's money if they had any – ie fire hoses, stirrup pumps, axes, uniforms, sand buckets etc. My dad spent nights on the factory roof fire

watching. I don't know how much the Communist Party influenced affairs in 1940/early 1941 in Clydebank. They sided with Russia and there were stories of warships having 'spanners' put in engines to cause damage etc. during this period.

Censorship helped the British government of 1940–41/42 etc not to reveal to the public just how bad things were. When you read the Bearsden Invasion leaflet for 1942 you realise just how bad things locally were perceived. In the case of Clydebank censorship suited local politicians as they did not want it shown how incompetent they were. Thus there was a more rigorous self censorship locally by Clydebank Town Council . . . My grandfather's thoughts towards the Clydebank Council were pretty dire. He once said to me 'The people voted for them so the people are partly responsible for electing people who were still going on about peace when Hitler was marching into Poland. All of them were bloody incompetent and it showed. Give Davie Kirkwood a rifle and send him to the Front. Then he will know what peace is really like. No, we needed to make a stand because Hitler was going to pick off each country in Europe one by one.'

All the factories on Clydeside had received warnings 18 months or so before war broke out and the factory managers had to organise local factory fire wardens/guards etc. The Clydebank factories got virtually no help from the town council. Glasgow Corporation were much more 'on the ball'. The problem lay in Clydebank Town Council with the controlling ILP pacifist element plus the small communist element who exercised a lot more power than their small numbers justified . . . People look back on those times now from a distance with 'rose coloured glasses'. People were very poor. It was easy to strike up grievances over tea breaks etc. I have worked in places like that where each 'union' prohibited men to do other men's jobs. There was very real demarcation lines in the shipyards. Have a look at the strikes in the period 1939/40/41. The Barr and Stroud women's strike. My mother in law worked in it at the time and her opinion was that it was a lot of 'daft lassies' arguing over a few pence. And most of these lassies after a few weeks 'couldna do a proper man's job any way !' However who was really behind that strike? It's difficult to be objective now from 70 odd years. I suspect it suited Clydebank Town councillors to underestimate deaths and injuries etc . . .

In fact – as Harrisson has also documented – the region generally, and Clydebank, was by March 1941 much better prepared for post-blitz measures, at least, than most English cities. There was good liaison between departments ('much closer than found anywhere else'). An emergency feeding-plan had been well thought through, 'with ten peripheral cooking centres and with mobile canteens ready to be mobile'. There were cooking facilities around Glasgow, prepared by the city's Education Committee, for 20,000; and an impressive 102 'Rest Centres'. There were elaborate plans for moving the newly homeless into identified, indexed billets within the area; the authorities wanted to minimise 'trekking'. There were but two serious vulnerabilities – the

inadequately built and insufficient air raid shelters, and firefighting plans that
owed more to hope than experience.

There is still wild talk that high authorities deliberately sacrificed Clydebank, and even the assertion that the Royal Air Force and others saw the area
as 'bait', perhaps with more than a tinge of anti-Left political motivation –
articulated most recently by Meg Henderson, in her readable if at times ranting
novel, *The Holy City*, centred on Clydebank's experience through the eyes of a
(fictional) Blitz survivor, Marion MacLeod:

> With precise co-ordinates the Germans were able to send out a radio-
> navigational beam to the target area for their bombers to follow. The boffins
> on our side could not only pick it up, but they could 'bend' the beam . . .
> Hindsight is a wonderful thing, but no matter how many times Marion
> considered it over the years since, it seemed incredible, unforgivable, that no
> one thought Clydebank would one day get hit. There was all that important
> industry, the shipyards and the munitions factories in [*sic*] the Clyde, and by
> 'bending the beam' away from English cities, like London, Liverpool,
> Manchester and Birmingham, the Luftwaffe had a clear run to Clydeside.
> Why did no one spot it?

This is, though, conveniently to ignore that there were serious raids that same
night on Merseyside and elsewhere; and that the Germans had been forced
generally by March 1941 to shift to coastal targets as the British defending
authorities came to more sophisticated grip with their technology.

'The 12 HE-111s of Kampfgruppe 100,' details Andrew Jeffrey, citing
German time, 'were due over Clydeside between 2154 and 2225 hours. This
unit had, for some months, operated in the pathfinder role equipped with the
"X Great" radio beam navigational system. The role of lead pathfinder had
passed, in January 1941, to III/KG26 commanded by Major Victor von
Lossberg, when their Heinkels were fitted with the more sophisticated and
longer range "Y" beam system. Both systems had been identified, and counter
measures taken, by the end of February 1941. Their beams compromised, the
Luftwaffe had turned its attention to ports which, being on the coastline, were
easily found. Hull, Belfast, Merseyside and Clydeside were among those
attacked . . .'

The Clydebank authorities – given only notice of an hour and a half of a
probable raid – could not even have begun to evacuate the town in that time;
and when things are falling out of the sky and huge bombs are blasting great
areas with fire and shrapnel, people are generally safer under cover – even
cowering in their own homes – than milling in fear by the thousand through
streets or huddled on open land, to say nothing of the serious problems posed
for emergency vehicles and the swift movement of personnel and resources
when streets are choked by panic.

But the captains of Clydebank's civil defence, Kelly and Hastings, were
further hamstrung by remote and implacable authority. Much of their

time was largely wasted 'implementing the instructions contained in the innumerable circulars emanating from government departments', as Mac-Phail sighs – much of it the absurd, micro-managed procedures decreed for this and that contingency, however unlikely. The hard-pressed officials had to contend with hundreds of orders in 1940 and 1941 addressing, for instance, 'a breakdown in telephone communications; the reporting of parachute mines dropped in the Clyde; the rendezvous points for reinforcements during air raids . . . the control of mobile canteens after a raid; gas vans and fixed gas chambers for gas training; ventilation conditions in public shelters; leather boots for Rescue Parties; methods of dealing with incendiary bombs; greyhound race meetings etc. etc. The Department of Health in Edinburgh was no less assiduous in their distribution of information and the Emergency Committee's files . . . grew thicker and thicker as the war proceeded.'

Yet any plans involving local authority spending on civil defence had, absurdly, first to be approved by this or that office of central government, MacPhail further records, 'and too often the burgh officials found their proposals changed or rejected simply because they differed in some degree from the official instructions contained in the original circular'. So eminently sensible decisions in Clydebank were once and again howled down by distant civil servants in Edinburgh, far from local realities, no doubt suffused with more than a little contempt for a dubious Labour-led council in grimy western Scotland, and obsessed with only the due ticking of boxes in their own London-framed guidelines.

And there was repeated denial of reasonable requests. For months before March 1941, Clydebank's sanitary inspector had beseeched the Department of Health for permission to secure (in large numbers) some sort of decent coffin, however cheap: even cardboard or papier mâché. Approval was constantly denied, and he was helpless to act. Kelly had besides fretted over an obvious shortage of fire-hoses, and tried time and again for Scottish Office approval to increase the local stock: he, too, was frustrated. They felt, Clydebank councillors and officials began darkly to joke, as if all the distant civil servants they had to humour were but 'inverted Micawbers, sitting in their office chairs, waiting for something to turn down'.

What was most bitterly recalled – when it was far too late – was Edinburgh's insistence that Clydebank's Control Centre be located in or near the Municipal Buildings. Everyone of authority in the town wanted it somewhere peripheral – by Old Kilpatrick or up by the Boulevard, say – rather than hard by the Town Hall, scarcely a stone's throw from John Brown's shipyard which, surely, was the top German target on all Clydeside. But the bureaucrats were implacable. It had to be hard by the seat of local government power and they especially favoured the basement of Clydebank Public Library, as its dimensions almost exactly matched the official specifications for such a base of ARP operations. The civil servants duly won. The Control Centre duly took a direct hit on the first night of Clydebank bombing, just as those on the spot had so fruitlessly warned and – though, mercifully, no one was killed, and the damage was limited – it was thereafter much impaired.

There were, these last few days, assorted, ominous straws in the wind. For one, there was increased – and notable – German activity over the Clyde. A local priest, Father Patrick Sheary, remembered that at February's end 'something like lights came down as if German planes were taking photographs of Singer's and the Clydebank area in general. We were all out watching the way the sky was lighted up and we were actually saying to ourselves, "They must be preparing to come to blitz us." ' Another man, still in his teens in 1941, recalled the wistful, halcyon-days atmosphere. 'There was an apprentice's strike on in the Clyde shipyards and the weather couldn't have been better. It was like a summer's day in March and we played a lot of football in the afternoon. Well, I was in the Royal Artillery at the time, on ack-ack, and so we were trained for spotting planes. On the Tuesday afternoon, I think it was, there was a plane flying pretty high, and I said, well, it looked like a JU 88 – it definitely to me was a reconnaissance plane going over but never thought any more about it. But I've thought plenty of it since, because of what happened on the Thursday night. . . .'

From early on Thursday morning, as Andrew Jeffrey's research attested, radio navigation beams from the Luftwaffe were detected across central Scotland – and the quiet rumble of this and that weather-assessment German flight. But the first action of the day was, of all places, amidst the mountains of Lochaber, as a JU 88 piloted by Oberleutnant Fidorra flew hungrily across the Highlands in the broad daylight of early afternoon. His target was the British Aluminium factory at Fort William but, perhaps a little disorientated and certainly not anxious to hang about as an all-too-visible target, Fidorra let fly with no great care: he loosed his bombs long before the waters of Nevis and Lochy, and they exploded harmlessly in high hills some four miles from the town.

Across central Scotland, at this and that hub of command, brows were furrowed: big Bakelite telephones rang and rang again. People mustered to their stations; by dusk, civil-defence control rooms everywhere were fully manned.

On Glasgow's Queen Victoria Drive, sweeping from Scotstoun to Knights-wood, one family made ready for the night at No. 135. There were three generations: Sydney and Mina Hutton, and their son Gordon – on leave from the Army – and their married daughter, Mrs Hylda Richmond, with her little sons Brian and Alan. In Knightswood itself, at Bankhead School, dozens were quickly assembling – it was a first aid post and command centre for the immediate locality: youths to run messages; young women with bandages and plasters and the usual requisites for major or minor trauma; some 20 men of the Auxiliary Fire Service.

At Peel Street, in Glasgow's Partick, was James MacKinven from Carradale, that clever lad of literary inclination, and who liked – at least in Argyll –

generally to wear the kilt. His parents, Peter and Ellen – aspiring people – ran a summer tearoom. James himself had studied at both Keil School in Dumbarton and the Campbeltown Grammar School and, still only 17, was both a promising musician and aspiring poet. Jim happily pounded the piano at local dances; he took that blue-boarded notebook with him almost everywhere, for thoughts and jottings and verses. Indeed, he had a powerful and already rather famous friend – the novelist and general force of nature that was Naomi Mitchison, who had grown fond of James MacKinven and recognized his talent. A mother of a goodly brood herself, she was happy to see the lad when he called by shyly to show his latest scribbles. He had, besides – and unusually for his age and even at that time – a strong religious bent. He loved to go for great bracing walks – one of his surviving poems is a righteous denunciation of the motor-car – and he much preferred the countryside, hill and shore to the grotty nature of town and city. Something of his playful nature, his way with words – and, besides, a vivid evocation of a pre-war kitchen – is evident in this account of the facilities at the family home, where they served summer teas in a parlour.

The kitchen has three doors so that one can disappear easily if an unwanted visitor should make an appearance. It is oblong in shape; dark at one end and very bright at the other. The shelves that run along the wall at the dark end have always been burdened with marshmallow tins. The washing cloths hanging by the sink look weary and run down. While the ceiling is pure white, the floor is splotched with red, green, blue and brown; the bunker is scrubbed white; the oilcloth that hangs limply over the table is a bright blue and the coal scuttle by the fires is burnished copper.

The range is a metallic monster and stands midway between the two ends and along one wall. The ribs resemble red hot fangs; the top of the range which is divided into two by the fireplace is shiny black surrounded by thick comforting steel. Below the ribs there is a slit – the mouth of our monster, and below the ashpit its stomach. Across the front of the hood, above the fire, are the words 'Pull Forward'. They always puzzled me. The oven door is sturdy – studded with steel like a knight's armour, and the rack directly above the fire like a solemn stretcher.

At one end of the mantelpiece are two irons dull, vacant-looking; in the middle a crisp clock that looks exceedingly important, and at the other end a tea-caddy on which a bird with a long beak and wild eyes looks and looks at you from every angle. And the lemonade bottles standing on a dresser at the dark end are so like soldiers at attention with coloured uniform and tin helmets. The cups lie along the shelf sleepy, lazy, waiting on the next meal.

McLean's Powder, Andrew's Liver Salts, Optrex, bottles here, bottles there are crowded into a corner of a shelf as if terrified. That hot water bottle hanging by the window always made me feel as if it were going to cry suddenly with the pain the hook caused passing through its ear to hold it up. The pot standing in a dark corner to the right of the range with handles sticking out here and there looks like an unskilfully pruned tree.

There is a teapot on a little shelf beside the window. It always reminded me of a little duck sailing along triumphantly. A kitchen would never, never do without a kettle. Queer thing a kettle – it seems to stare eternally upwards with that knob on top of the lid. I think the white-scrubbed bunker by the sink feels it terribly when the frying pan is taken away from under it. Very often – in that frying pan – I have noticed a grumpy old potato stuck fast among the grease that had solidified in ripples like a pond in winter. The boiler above and to the right of the fire, which makes a sobbing, sad sound occasionally and then without warning a rumbling like thunder is very particularly galvanized. It does brighten that dark side to some extent.

In summer the kitchen is noisy. Somebody frying ham and eggs; the mechanical grind of a tin being opened; somebody switching an ice-drink; the dull pop as a bottle is opened and the snappy click of the ice cream measure all sound simultaneously. The floor becomes dirty. That shiny black on top of the range bubbles excitedly with spilt coffee. The bright end is easily the scene of the most action for the freezer is kept there, the spoons are there, the cups and saucers are on a shelf at that end and the tumblers too, and the milk-shakes, and the trays that are kept behind the door. The dark end is not absolutely deserted. Lemonade is kept there and coffee-pots, and coffee on shelves above the lemonade; plates and jam-dishes too in a press. The swing door leading into the tearoom is at the dark end also. It is in the tearoom one second and in the kitchen the next. And the waitress, lest she forget her orders, shouts rather hysterically on one note – soh on the scale of C or thereabouts. She makes up the bills on the long narrow table that runs along the wall opposite the range.

I like the kitchen. Always a smell of cooking in it. At night after the buzz of the brass rail that is so vigorously polished in the morning it is covered with sweating dishcloths tired of drying dishes. The handle of the door opposite the range leading into the shop is smeared with ice cream. The lemonade straws that looked with a hundred eyes in the morning now only look with three or four, and the squat little gas stove full of coffee is more than ever like a bulldog.

There is a door at the bright end which leads to the back door or to my bedroom. And so I leave the kitchen – to the back door, you think – no sir, to bed.

There is more than love and note of detail in this prose; there is the hurt of homesickness. Jim MacKinven had wanted to train for journalism and could readily have got an apprenticeship at the *Campbeltown Courier*. But his parents were sniffy, hostile. They persuaded their Jim to pursue something more prestigious for the present. So, keen in any event for a taste of urban life and independence, James had just arrived in Glasgow to begin a dull accountancy course at Skerry's College. He was tired, lonely, frustrated: and so, sir, this night of Thursday 13 March, to bed.

Elizabeth Bailey – 13 years old – had played outside, since school, with classmate Esther Anderson, of 66 Crown Avenue, one of the great tenement canyons looming on the hillside above Singer's factory. It was still just chill enough for cardigans to be worn over frocks, but decades later Elizabeth could not forget 'the most exciting fun, running and jumping; it was a taste of summer soon to come, as it always did with all our childish pursuits. . . . I remember there was the most beautiful of sunsets in the sky away down the River Clyde above the dark rock of Dumbarton where the ancient castle stands. The weather being so mild we played on much later than usual. I then went with Esther to see her to the bus for her short journey home. It was just too late for her to walk; I normally walked part of the way with her. A smile, a wave. "See you tomorrow." ' Esther would not see the morning, though it would be months, amidst the entire dislocation and confusion, before Elizabeth Bailey learned that her classmate and her father Thomas Anderson, himself but 33, had both been killed.

From six that evening, German bombers had been taking off from their bases on the Continent, assuming formation and droning towards their target: Clydebank, which had been exhaustively photographed in recent reconnaissance and which the Luftwaffe had code-named 'Gregor'. It is now generally accepted that the town was expressly targeted – not the accidental centre of a raid planned for Glasgow and Clydeside generally – and that, despite some bombing of Liverpool on the way up, that Clydebank was not some Plan B. We should remember, too, that in 1941 the town was much more physically distinct from Glasgow than it is today, since the sprawl of cheap housing in the post-war decades through Yoker and Garscadden have merged them in general conurbation.

'The main attacking force was Luftflotte 3, based in France,' writes Les Taylor in probably the best military analysis of the assault, 'although bomber groups such as . . . KG 26 also participated' –

> Their tactics were by now tried and tested. Instead of the bomber 'stream' favoured later by the RAF, German bomber formations employed a multi-directional approach to their targets in order to confuse the defences, calling it the 'all points of the compass' approach. This technique required the attacking force to be divided into three or four waves, each timed to arrive over the target from different directions and at different times in order to avoid collisions. Consequently, the first Clydebank raid was divided into three waves, each over an hour apart, which tormented survivors on the ground who assumed that the break between each one meant that the raid was over when it was not. The force that set out on that first night was estimated to comprise some 236 aircraft drawn from a variety of bomber groups, but headed by one in particular, Kampfgeschwader 100, the Luftwaffe's elite pathfinder force, who would lead the attack.

By nine, fully alerted, RAF fighters were already circling above assorted Scottish bases, from Dyce by Aberdeen to Drem (in East Lothian) and Prestwick, near Glasgow. At seven minutes past nine, as the first Luftwaffe engines were heard, sirens rose along the eastern Scottish coast. Three minutes later, the ominous yowling began on Clydeside as the Germans came in over Bo'ness and Linlithgow, Stonehaven and Angus and the Mearns, and the very first already looming in the Glasgow night.

According to Taylor's analysis – speculative to some extent but credible from the known evidence – the whole force came up the west coast of Britain, each wave peeling off on its own circling tangent over the Irish Sea and making its own feint or detour round to Clydebank. The KG-100 'Pathfinder' Group, navigating by the X-Gerät radio-beam technology, made deliberately first towards Edinburgh, close enough to trigger the sirens and alarm the city's outer defences into action. 'Then the force abruptly turned due west and headed for the Glasgow area,' suggests Taylor. 'The bombers would now be over the surprised defences of their primary target in less than fifteen minutes.'

This first assault – from the east, coming in over Stirlingshire – attacked from 21:00 to 23:30, with flares and incendiary bombs in great quantity from a height of 12,000 to 19,000 feet. The second wave of Junkers and Heinkels came in at midnight, circling over Argyll to bear on Clydebank from the north; it navigated visually – for the Pathfinders had now set up a glowing, fiery welcome – and bombed with high explosives between midnight and 02:30, from a level of 7,000 to 12,000 feet. There was then a marked pause – about half an hour – before the third wave of bombers peeled in from the south, straight over Ayrshire and Renfrewshire, and pummelled Clydebank from 03:00 to 05:30, with comparable cargo from comparable height. Such are the bald, technical details of war from the air.

At Govan's Leckie Hall, it was weekly training this Thursday night for volunteer ARP wardens. They had as yet heard no word of warning as they dispersed into the street. At Dalmuir, the sirens had barely ceased when the approaching aircraft could clearly be heard. Flares – 'Molotov Chandeliers', as they were wryly known – were already floating in the sky, and in west Dalmuir Anne Greig, now Mrs Anne Holmes – then only five years old – can remember that horrid green, phosphorescent glow to this day, and the fire that shortly augmented it, and the shock of seeing the velvet totality of blackout so affronted. She and her family stayed in the bottom flat at 5 West Kitchener Street; right across the back-court, at 78 Jellico Street, lived still more extended family – her grandfather, Patrick Rocks, and his wife, and his elderly mother-in-law (Anne's great-grandmother) and uncles and aunts and cousins besides. Her grandfather, himself an ARP volunteer, was already bustling out on duty.

Already, over Clydeside, the first 'Thermite' incendiary bombs were falling – not 2 feet long, grey, of deceptively simple and unmenacing appearance, packed with magnesium and other ingredients in an insidious brew. Most ignited on impact, and did little more than smoulder; but they burned for a long time, and with a heat that could chew through slate and steel, and they landed by the dozen and by the hundred on fields and in woods, in roof-valleys and through the flimsy coverings of stores and sheds, and they landed amidst the mountains of lumber in Singer's timber-yard, and bounced on the bitumen-thick flats of the Holy City, and for the most part stayed there, and flamed hungrily away.

In Scotstoun, a little girl called Elma was five, and her family, like so many families this night – folk had grown blasé after so many false alerts and blastless warnings – braved neither a communal shelter nor the dubious comfort of a tenement close, but instead huddled in a cupboard under the stairs. Her father, an ARP volunteer, was out fire-watching, and in the strange glow he saw something coming down, big and ominous, not screeching but floating, on its own parachute. It was one of the most terrible weapons of this night, a 1,000-kg 'Luftmine', fat with high explosive and of vast lateral blasting power, and he had the wit to duck as it bore remorselessly down on Queen Victoria Drive. The explosion demolished an entire row of villas, smashed in the windows of his own home and many more, shook properties across the suburban railway and resounded, vibrating and awful, for miles; and this may well have been the first bomb proper of what we remember as the Clydebank Blitz. Of the Hutton place, no. 135, little more than a crater survived; the entire family present were slain in an instant, and something of evil and terror still lingered in this gap 30 years later, to little boys tripping past on their way from school.

It was those outside – travelling home – who first realised that something frightful was happening. One Clydebank lady was out with her sister, socialising at Blanefield in the shadow of the Campsie Fells and on the other side of the Old Kilpatrick Hills. 'And we were with two boyfriends and one o' them drove a car. It was the sky, the sky was all lit wi' red, just a red flow in the sky, and comin' over Windyhill, you could see the whole o' the Clyde valley . . . *Clydebank seemed to be all on fire.* . . .'

The narrative of this terrible night is, inevitably, one fat with horror and laden with entire confusion. There are the sober recollections of those in leadership – trying to rescue the trapped, retrieve the injured and fight fire and explosion in chaotic and terrifying circumstances, with inadequate to utterly broken communications and the general collapse of infrastructure. And there are the hundreds and hundreds of stories of survivors, though most related now – 70 years after the event – are largely of those who were then but children, and lived to tell the tale. And then, as conjecture and the stuff of nightmare, are the last hours and moments of the hundreds who did not.

But the night in which Clydebank to all intents and purposes died – as a built and known geography and as the community that was just preparing to sit down for the evening news and then turn in for its slumber – was defined by two elements of bleak providence. Though there was at first lively anti-aircraft fire from four 3-inch guns mounted at Duntiglennan Farm, behind and above Duntocher, near Drumchapel – which may have forced the raiders at first to keep above the level desired for accurate bombing – they soon, pitiably, ran out of shells. Anyway, the honed skills of KG-100 (first attested at Coventry) had sown sufficient incendiaries to light three near-perfect beacons, greatly assisted by extraordinary visibility. Just beyond the east of Clydebank, the Yoker distillery went up; the stench of alcohol, thick and giddying, and pouring in liquid flame into the Clyde itself, is for many just one sensual and frightful memory. Then, way out west at Dalnottar, Old Kilpatrick, the Admiralty oil storage tanks ignited.

And in between, close by the town centre, a lucky incendiary or two had lit all that seasoned timber piled in such enormous quantities in Singer's yard – guarded by just one aghast and overwhelmed watchman, with his bucket and his shovel and his lonely little stirrup pump. This was a 'vast store of wood', records MacPhail, 'estimated as worth at least £500,000', and that was the Singer timber alone; there was government-owned lumber there too and in great quantity, and it would all burn and burn. Horrified ARP wardens dashed to the scene, but all that wood was already roaring in curtains of flame. They flung buckets of water, tried to organise a hose; they flailed uselessly with sand and earth and even dustbin lids as planks blazed all the higher for the searching Luftwaffe. The factory itself – devoted now as much to armaments as sewing-machines, and whose skilled workers turned out, for instance, Sten guns for the war effort – would survive largely undamaged; but that inferno in its precincts damned Clydebank.

The Germans, plane upon plane still flying in, could not have been better assisted had the town thoughtfully laid on floodlighting. The bombers simply ran up and down the length of these three conflagrations and, indeed, aircraft homed in by the dozen on Clydebank which might otherwise have devastated much of Glasgow. A report later submitted by Luftwaffe headquarters – and which, like most of the neat and detailed paperwork amassed so methodically by the Third Reich, survived for the study of the victorious Allies – cannot hide their satisfaction after this Clydeside adventure. Officers happily recorded that 'from 22:30 to 06.47 hours' – Germany was an hour ahead of British time – '236 bombers attacked along the length of the River Clyde with about 272 tons of high explosive bombs and 1,650 incendiary containers.'

The operation was not perfect. Some of the Glasgow bombing pattern, especially, suggests that not a few German pilots mistook the broad sweep of the Great Western Road – silver in the night – for the River Clyde, and so wrought residential devastation here and there while missing the targets that mattered. Just north of Great Western Road, 44 houses were destroyed, 80 were substantially damaged and 441 superficially blasted. Scotstoun – already hit by the odd bomb early in the war – took yet more: Eastcote Avenue, and the corner of Crow Road and Sackville Street.

There was besides a 'Starfish' decoy scheme nearby – a fake, minimal shanty town in the Old Kilpatrick Hills, much of it assembled by the guidance of movie-set professionals and replete with clever illusions of a town and its street and transport: piles of flammable material, fake headlights and tram-flashes and so on. This was all now set a-going – by electric controls – early in the raid and tricked quite a few planes into dropping bombs where they exploded to no account.

But in truth the most vital arm of defence over the Clyde – the Royal Air Force – was badly compromised. Fighter Command, in March 1941, was experimenting (as it was wont to do) with yet another arrangement of 'combined operations' against a night-time German air raid: this granted full leave to anti-aircraft crews on the ground to blast away with all their might, to their flak's natural ceiling of around 12,000 feet, while all available fighters were kept above harm's way by absolute orders to remain at various levels above a minimal 14,000 feet. But there were not nearly enough anti-aircraft batteries and they were not, for the most part, so located in the circumstances of this German assault to be of much more than psychological advantage. The pilots of 602 (City of Glasgow) Squadron – flying four Spitfires; there were only 30 fighters, in all, over Glasgow this night – were stacked at a lofty 19,500 to 20,000 feet – far too high to be in any danger and, more to the point, far too high to be of any use. As Jeffrey details, they 'looked on in horror and frustration as large areas of their city were set alight'.

Only one, Flying Officer O.V. 'Pedro' Hanbury, managed a short burst at a bomber silhouetted against the flames and searchlights after he deliberately disobeyed orders and left the height band at 23:30 hours. In all the night, only three German planes were brought down. One RAF patrol over Ayrshire, a Blenheim of the 600 (City of London) Squadron, took out one of KG-100's Heinkels, attacking twice until it crashed around 10 p.m. at Drumshang Farm, near Dunure. All four crew survived to be taken prisoner, though only one was uninjured. Those aboard a JU-88, felled by another RAF pilot off Amble on the Northumbrian coast, all lost their lives. Another bomber connected with the Clydeside attack was destroyed, probably on its way home, at Bramdean in Hampshire. Otherwise, all Clydebank's defence hinged on what was done on the ground, and that – inexperienced, battered and overwhelmed – offered little more than damage-control.

It was a night, it seems, for practice everywhere; and in Clydebank Tuesday and Thursday evenings saw auxiliary ambulance men at their training. One became a hero. Hugh Campbell, based at the Dalmuir depot – and who had come through a Zeppelin raid on Edinburgh in April 1916 – was putting vehicles away when an incendiary bomb thumped by the entrance to the very basic lean-to sheds. He kicked it briskly away, and had just run to telephone the Control Centre when a real bomb exploded a street or two away. Then word came – Campbell was to proceed to Beardmore's Diesel Works with his crew; en route, they passed a pub as it was blown up. They were returning with casualties from Beardmore's when another bomb blasted at their ambulance, smashing a weighty manhole cover through its roof. The shaken volunteers emerged from the wreckage to find two of their casualties were dead. Sore and trembling, Campbell himself nevertheless trotted painfully away, through a hail of bombs and showers of debris, in search of further transport. The depot was within the mile and in due time he was back at the wheel of another ambulance, gathering everyone else and taking them to hospital. Hugh Campbell did much more through Friday and into the weekend, as well setting up a dressing station at Clydebank Town Hall – for four days and nights, according to Iain MacPhail, he had no sleep – and was later, justly, awarded the OBE.

By 9.30 p.m., the attack was in earnest. Incendiaries and high-explosive bombs – little ones, 50 kg or so, calculated by the Germans to frighten both citizens and firefighters into the safety of shelter – poured down on the lower, riverside reaches of Clydebank. It seems that those diesel works at Dalmuir were among the very first localities to be hit – though inevitably, with so many witnesses over so large an area, there are other claims. The early explosions fell so near the Forth and Clyde Canal it may have been deliberately targeted; certainly, a factory on Stanford Street and a Livingstone Street tenement were blasted near the start of the raid. The tenement at 69 Livingstone Street simply collapsed, and a 19-year-old woman – at the moment of impact, she was holding a neighbour's baby – was blown under the kitchen sink by the detonation. She survived; the child did not. Though trapped for five hours, her legs crushed and in inconceivable pain, she was able somehow to converse in upbeat tones with frantic rescue workers, until a very small ARP warden finally clawed his way to get her out.

At the Sick Children's Hospital on Garscadden Road, taut but determined nurses had rushed for heavy blankets to drape over the cots of their infant charges. Minutes later, a stick of bombs rained by outside, and the windows burst inwards, showering glass everywhere and over all this bedding – but not one child was injured. Explosions, perhaps from the same plane, shook Knightswood and Drumchapel – Trinley Road and Cowdenhall Avenue, Baldwin Avenue and Fereneze Crescent, Fulwood Avenue and Friarscourt Avenue, where No. 73 caught fire and people had with great difficulty to be rescued.

And still, every 10 minutes, watchers at South Queensferry reported still another incoming wave of German bombers . . .

It is difficult for our generation in Britain to have any comprehension of the experience of bombing; and, unlike the people of London – who grew so hardened to it that, as George Orwell would note, it became positively bad form to relate unsolicited personal tales of near escapes and frightful bangs – the people of Clydebank had only this one dreadful 48-hour exposure. But there are still many alive – then quite small children – haunted by those long-ago engines of German planes, which some maintain could readily be distinguished from those of RAF defenders. Many during the war 'claimed to be able to tell "one of theirs" from "one of ours" by ear – "their" engines throbbed and came and went with a curious moaning sound, like that of a vacuum cleaner'.

There was 'something menacing' about the noise of the air raid siren itself, relates Peter Lewis; the 'preliminary rattle in the throat, the first upward swoop to a full-pitched howl, the swerving down and up like a wailing roller coaster took people's stomachs with it'. Churchill himself described it as 'banshee howlings'. J.B. Priestley turned almost poetic: 'as if the darkened countryside, like a vast trapped animal, were screaming at us'. Some compared it to the hallucinatory, scary noise one used to hear while going under an old-style ether anaesthetic. Others, for many years after the war, would have heart-stopping flashbacks at the hum of a car accelerating or the mounting *woooo* of an approaching train on Glasgow's subway. And Lewis is still more vivid on the immediate experience of being around as death rains from the sky:

> The unearthly sound of a bomb falling really close by was different from the whistle you heard from more distant bombs. It was like 'the sound of tearing silk', as if someone 'was scratching the sky with a broken fingernail', like 'a great sheet of air being ripped through', 'something between the rustling of a paper and the letting out of the bath water.' So people variously described it. But the effect was more than a tearing sound: one could *sense* the motion of the approaching bomb. 'They rushed at enormous velocity, as though dragged down by some gigantic magnet' . . . 'It developed into the roar of an express train,' George Orwell noted: 'The commotion made by the mere passage of a bomb through the air is astonishing. The whole house shakes, enough to rattle objects on the table. Why it is that the lights dip when a bomb passes close by, no one seems to know.'

Anti-aircraft guns and the general barrage, thought Priestley, sounded 'as if gigantic doors were being slammed to' in the sky. A distant bomb shook the ground in a palpable 'crump'. If you were closer, the blast actually preceded the sound. In England, Barbara Nixon – who was out on her bicycle – left an almost incredible account of an explosion during the Blitz:

> Suddenly, the shabby, ill-lit five-storey building ahead of me swelled out like a child's balloon. I looked at it in astonishment that bricks and mortar could stretch like rubber. At the point when it must burst, the glass fell out. It did not hurtle, it simply cracked and dropped out, allowing the strained building to deflate and return to normal. Almost instantaneously there was a crash and a double explosion to my right. As the blast of air reached me, I left my saddle and sailed through the air . . .

There are many similar tales of weird explosive forces during all the bombing Britain endured in the Second World War. People were 'hurled on amazing journeys round corners . . . sucked up chimneys or stripped naked where they sat'. The tallest buildings 'fluttered and swayed like aspens, without falling. Posters were ripped from hoardings. Windows buckled inwards but sometimes straightened out, uncracked.'

Buses 'were blown into first-storey windows. Front doors, like magic carpets, went flying down the street.' One man recalled his experience in striking language: just as he grasped his front-door handle 'a bomb fell and blew the house out of my hand.' Another Blitz survivor could scarcely credit what she had observed in one attack. 'I remember seeing a roll of material

inside a shop window which had rolled underneath the window and come out
on the pavement. The blast had bent the glass and sucked out the material
before the window snapped back into place intact . . .'

And Clydebank – amidst the narrative of destruction, death and horror –
would have such stories too. Constable Iain MacAulay and a colleague rushed
frantically through the blazing town and up Hornbeam Road in their Wolseley
car: a bomb landed straight ahead, there was an explosion and their windscreen – rather than being blown in – was simply sucked out. On Radnor
Street, an alarm-clock was blasted out of a house – and found sitting neatly on
top of the dustbin. In the Mannings' home on Young Street, absolutely
everything was destroyed – except for the dog's bowl. One distressed survivor
had lost his beloved canary – the cage was intact and undamaged, and the door
still shut and fast, but his pet was quite gone and not as much as a feather to be
seen.

But that was a concern, tiny and intimate, for daylight and for Saturday. As
midnight neared, and the rain of fire and explosion continued, and this and
that corner of Glasgow shook in damage and death, Clydebank – at the vortex
of this assault – was fighting for her very life, as the bare streets themselves
yawned suddenly in craters, as water gushed and flooded from shattered
mains, as electric lines here and there were severed and telephones suddenly
went dead in appalled civic hands.

The town's amenities seemed fast to be melting in flame. The stately Scottish
schools erected in recent decades had valleyed roofs with abundant nesting
places for incendiaries; great central halls and galleries, perfect for fanning
draughts; varnished, polished pitch-pine floors under great thin skylights. First
one academy and then another ignited. By midnight, on Kilbowie Road,
Radnor Park School was irretrievably ablaze. Not far away, Boquhanran
School was soon likewise in flames. St Stephen's at Dalmuir and the original
premises of Clydebank High School were likewise torched in this first night of
raiding. Two schools at Old Kilpatrick were utterly destroyed; four other
campuses saw serious damage. Churches, too, were devoured by flame,
without respect for Pope or Protestant.

It is true, as we shall later explore, that even in the short run the impact of
the raids on Clydebank's weighty contribution to the war effort was not
significant: for the most part, machinery and slipways survived unscathed, or
could be repaired within days or weeks. Yet much damage there was, and not
just to wood or whisky. There was a serious fire at John Brown's shipyard,
which was not quickly subdued. By Rothesay Dock, a store packed with
rubber caught fire, and that acrid stench too became part of the night's folk-
memory. At Dalmuir, the Royal Ordnance Factory churned out important
munitions; fire wrought havoc, and after a huge 1,000-kg bomb landed on
Turner's Asbestos Works there was much consumed there too. Near the
burgh's western edge, at Old Kilpatrick and Dalnottar, the Admiralty kept
over 70 great tanks of oil: on this first night, three were bombed and one sent
roaringly ablaze. (On the second night of raiding, ten more – eight at Dalnottar

and two at Old Kilpatrick – would catch flame.) These infernos, notes MacPhail, 'were of such magnitude that they could be seen by RAF planes at Dyce . . . It is little wonder that the later units of the Luftwaffe had no trouble in finding the target area and concentrated on Clydebank, where the fires were, rather than on Glasgow.'

Even without their own jeopardy of bombing, Clydebank's ill-prepared, under-equipped fire services would have struggled in such conditions. But units themselves were hit and, even by midnight, firemen were quite over-whelmed. Though Clydebank Fire Station itself survived, all three Auxiliary Fire Service Stations were disabled – one utterly demolished; two others so badly wrecked they could only be evacuated. Meanwhile, telegraph poles tumbled everywhere; for a few critical hours there was virtually no commu-nication with the Control Centre. Gas mains were ruptured and, apart from the obvious risk of yet further fire and explosion, the 'town gas' of the period was fat with toxic carbon monoxide. And then, of course, there was all the damage to water supply.

William Smillie was sub-officer in the town Fire Brigade, and his haunted testimony paints vividly the conditions in which he and his comrades fought against great walls of flame:

> I went to Second Avenue and saw three incendiaries lying on the road. I was earthing them over when I heard someone shouting, 'For God's sake come and help us.' A shelter had collapsed and there were men in it trying to hold the roof up with their backs. I put my crew in and ran for a rescue squad. A gas main was leaking and, when I got back, four of my crew were unconscious. I got them to the stage when they were vomiting but on their feet and then we tackled a burning tenement in Montrose Street but before we'd got far with that a screamer came down and blew me over the wall and into the churchyard unconscious. When I came to, the pump was dry; the bomb had taken half of Kilbowie Road and the big water main with it, and left Clydebank without water. The hydrant was dry, so we used the crater. I got the men together and we had another go at the tenement and then after that a four-storey tenement in Kilbowie Road and then some villas. We did those jobs and then we reported in.
>
> A call came in right away to say that No. 57 Livingstone Street was alight. I went there. No. 57 and every other number in Livingstone Street was alight. It was a great place for lodgers, which meant that nearly every room had a fire in it. Bombs had landed and blown most of the fires out on to the carpet. I was on the job there from Thursday to Sunday.

The Luftmine had smashed the town's largest water main, a 15-inch pipe by Kilbowie Road. Its broken ends jutted out from either side of still another great new hole in the ground, and 'firemen's hoses fell limp in their hands', as Jeffrey puts it. By Saturday, the other two – 12-inch and 10-inch respectively – would be bombed or blocked as well.

Now they had to fight fire with water-laden tenders in tow, or pump the stuff up even as they worked from the canal or the Yoker Burn or the Clyde itself. (Radnor Park's near total devastation in the Clydebank Blitz was a consequence of simple topography: few of the available pumps could draw water up from the Forth and Clyde Canal at sufficient pressure for hoses and that elevation to be any good, and – like other, high parts of Clydebank – the area could, at last, only be left to burn.) Meanwhile, of course, frantic word went far and wide for help elsewhere. Though Glasgow, too, had fires to dowse – and Dumbarton had not escaped unscathed either – they sent what men and engines they could; in all, from Stirlingshire and even Edinburgh, from Coatbridge and Motherwell and Kirkintilloch and Helensburgh. By four o'clock on Friday morning there were 64 major units in Clydebank to help – and little enough that was, against what seemed like a whole town ablaze.

The Regional Fire Brigade Inspector had also come puffing from Edinburgh and, making brisk assessment of the scale of the disaster and immediate and due priorities, ordered all to concentrate on three operations: subduing the blazes at Singer's timber yard, on Rothesay Dock and the general bonfire that was Radnor Park and Kilbowie.

But there were wretched complications. The gross damage to so many streets – heaped with rubble or rent by craters – greatly impeded movement, especially for 'self-propelled' engines; the small Auxiliary Fire Service units, which men could haul, were actually of more immediate use – save that their short hoses and weak pumps granted little 'throw' of water. Nor were the town's hydrants readily found by visiting crews strange to the town: in the 1940s, fire-hydrants were not painted bright and vivid yellow. Then, besides – and here was a lesson that should have been learned from the English experience – there was simply no uniformity, between one local council's brigade and another, of hose couplings. Many of the visiting firemen found they could not extend Clydebank hoses with their own, or even – should they find a hydrant – make fast to that. In 1981, one hero of that night in Clydebank – Deputy Town Clerk, James Hastings – could not hide his frustration.

> We had, let's say, about three hundred or four hundred [incidents], – and we only had about ten rescue teams, perhaps ten fire appliances, half a dozen or more ambulances – first aid parties, perhaps another ten – that we just couldn't cope, and why I say that the thing was chaotic outside was that they had all been sent out and there was nothing more we could do until reinforcements came in from outside. The telephones went – we were dependent on runners. And these were just young lads, they weren't supposed to operate while a raid was in progress; in any event, instead of perhaps twenty or thirty of them reporting, there was only a few reported because, quite naturally, when their houses had been bombed and there was a chance of more aircraft coming over – their parents weren't going to let them out of the shelters to go through a raid to come down and work with us. So communication was just absolutely hopeless.

There were fires all over the place, you see. Hot ashes from domestic fires got in among the debris from a building – this set it alight. Sometimes the explosion itself had fractured a gas main and set the gas mains alight. My impression was that the whole town was on fire and very little was being done about it. But it transpired that what had happened was that the fire crews had run out of petrol – there were only two pumps left in the whole town that weren't damaged. They couldn't get petrol, they'd been hauling the hoses, the wet hoses over debris that included a lot of glass and nails and sharp edges – a lot of their hoses were torn to bits. We found another thing and that was that a lot of the equipment that came in from other areas to help us out, their appliances couldn't be coupled up to our mains because there was no standardisation of mains outlets and fire-hydrants in Scotland. So quite a lot of them were standing about doing absolutely nothing. They just could not operate . . .

But still they fought on, in terrible conditions, through and past dawn and hours after the last German plane had rumbled east or south, and everyone was still hard at it on Friday. (At a quarter to three in the morning, with bombs still dropping and through the gravest danger, a Co-op baker had borne urns of hot tea and a great many rolls to the Town Hall in his little van for the briefest refreshment of the firemen.) By ten in the morning, there had been more fitful endeavours in like mercy, but the men were now close to exhaustion, with much of the town yet ablaze and the high likelihood of a renewed raid at nightfall. By half past three on Friday afternoon, with 33 pumps still labouring and firemen pushing on like so many sooty, soaking zombies, it was obvious their task could not be completed by nightfall. The Luftwaffe would locate the area again with laughable ease.

Early that morning, around 8 a.m., Lord Rosebery himself had materialised in Clydebank. Rosebery would end the war in a very brief stint as Secretary of State for Scotland, once Labour had quit the Coalition and forced Churchill to seek a general election. As Scottish Regional Commissioner for civil defence – newly appointed, after Tom Johnston's elevation to the Scottish Office – Rosebery now toured what remained of the town and seems to have been particularly disturbed at what he beheld at Rothesay Dock: two fires raged on, and one was entirely unattended. He was certain that direction of firefighting in Clydebank was beyond inadequate. Rosebery's views were no doubt informed by the opinion of the Glasgow Firemaster, Martin Chadwick, who had been responsible for regional reinforcement arrangements and genuinely believed Clydebank had demonstrated no 'competent operational control'. Firemen, he insisted, had arrived from Glasgow and Edinburgh and found no officer able to direct them to any of the points of crisis in Clydebank. They were left standing on the street as their own officers tried to ascertain what was going on; some units had given up and returned to the city. Chadwick himself had finally taken charge and ordered such groups as were available and unoccupied to make for Dalnottar and fight the blaze there.

The man at their elbow, Sir Stephen Bilsland, the district civil defence commissioner, was adamant that 'the whole machinery of local authority control had broken down'. It was a harsh assessment of the situation, and less than fair – coloured, more than they might have admitted, by contempt for small municipalities and especially those governed by Socialists – but, after they had seen this smouldering and broken day, and with no time for a full and informed account, it was understandable.

That evening, word came through that the 'beam' was indeed once more trained on Clydeside and the Germans would return within hours. Rosebery acted immediately and sacked the man in charge. Clydebank's Firemaster, Robert Buchanan, was to be superseded for the night, and the town's operations put in the direction of Paisley Fire Brigade's Second Officer.

It was a humiliation of the first order for Buchanan, who had been seriously ill in December, and most unjust for a man who had done his best in impossible circumstances. Scapegoated for the consequences of enemy action, Scottish Office incompetence and the impossibility of any effective firefighting in such conditions, Robert Buchanan would tender his resignation to Clydebank Town Council in April. By November, he would be dead.

And, beyond the echelons of power and the fraught direction of emergency services under falling bombs, the incalculable tragedy of ordinary people was already wrought, and on huge, life-changing scale.

6

'NOT AS MUCH AS A RIP OF HAIR . . .'

There are details of the Blitz all the surviving Clydeside children seem to remember. One – because it was the normal ritual whenever an air raid warning sounded, as so frequently in the early months of the war – was of their mother calmly picking up the important papers: birth certificates, the identity cards mandatory even for wee ones in those years of crisis, insurance policies, savings-account books, cherished photographs. Most kept these to hand, in a biscuit-tin or a little case.

And those children of darker experience – who saw their home obliterated or their family sundered by death – seem with near-photographic intensity to recall the last fragile moments of normality, as the sirens wept and the first thumps and bangs began, and things to shake, and as adult voices tightened.

Writing in 1999, still not old, James McBride in 1941 was a very small boy, and he lived with his mother, father, brothers and sisters at 9 Kilmun Lane, Maryhill, in north-western Glasgow. Several weeks previously, his father had been called up, and gone to serve with the RAF.

James could remember everything nearly 60 years later. At the alarm, on 13 March, they all hurried downstairs as usual to the flat of the Hamiltons, deemed safer as it was right off the ground floor close. Soon the bangs began, and the thunder of guns. Everyone talked brightly; games were played; the hours passed. He did not feel at all frightened and in due time the all clear was sounded and he and his kin shuffled back upstairs and into bed, and the next morning there was talk 'of the terrible things that had happened in a place called Clydebank. I'd never heard of this place before and, in those days, it was a long way away.'

But that night – Friday night – was quite different. Once more the sirens sounded; once again they tripped down to the Hamiltons and 'what happened to us a while later is branded into my mind and will remain there until the day I die.'

I see the picture of where everyone was. It's as if the moments are frozen in time. If you can visualise a single end with the usual hole-in-the-wall bed. A deal table and chairs scrubbed almost white. There was an armchair either side of the fireplace. My mum was sitting next to me in the armchair. I was sitting on the fender in front of the fire with my back against the gas cooker. Mrs Hamilton was in the other armchair nursing baby Charlie. Margaret, my sister, was on a stool between us. My brother Billy was at the end of the table with Mr Hamilton, and my sisters, Sadie and Grace, were playing some kind of game.

Suddenly there was a whistling noise in my ears, then choking dust and darkness except for a tiny glow from the remains of the fire.

I shouted and screamed for my mammy, shouted for everybody by name but no one answered. After a while I heard groaning and, when I called out again, Margaret answered. She was buried and in great pain. We screamed and shouted and the Hamilton's dog barked and barked adding to the noise.

I must have passed out, because the next thing I remember, I was in an ambulance, wrapped up in a blanket and sitting on someone's knee. I remember I had no trousers on. What happened to them I don't know, anyway I didn't care. I was taken to a casualty clearing station. I remember being given very sweet tea and being very, very sick. I was then taken to a hospital, and, the following day, I was again taken by ambulance to another hospital, quite a long journey away, the Law Hospital in Carluke. I knew nothing of what had happened to any of my family or what was going on.

It was two weeks later before my father came for me. Until then he didn't even know that I was alive. He thought we had all died that night. Someone visiting the hospital had recognised me and passed the information to him.

I remember I was playing on the balcony outside the ward and, seeing someone in an air force uniform, somehow I knew it was my dad. I rushed to him and threw myself into his arms. We both cried and cried. He didn't need to tell me. I knew my family were all dead.

My grandfather, grandmother and uncles stayed in Kilmun Street across the back court from us. Grandad McBride, cousin Bertie McBride and uncle James Buick, who was home on leave from the forces, were all killed that same night. My grandmother survived . . .

Smouldering morning saw hundreds – thousands – emerge, exhausted and shaken, from their shelters, to the first sight, in Clydebank, of a town so devastated that large tracts of it had simply ceased to exist and where, quite disorientated by the smoke and dust and the loss of recognisable features, many struggled to find their bearings and their way back to homes wondrously intact, or violated, or flattened.

The first tales of frightful incidents were already circulating.

Patrick Rocks had worked far into the night at Beardmore's. It was still not dawn when, as the planes retreated and the bombers faded away, he picked his way to Jellicoe Street through what was left of Dalmuir. Wedged between the blazes at Singer's and Old Kilpatrick, this sturdy community had been pounded through the night, and, within an hour of the first bomb, water, power and telephone had all ceased to function. Rocks meandered through wreckage with mounting alarm. When he rounded the corner, his heart lifted to see light through the window of his flat. Then, a few steps on, he realised it was but the moon, and the glow of flame, through one tottering gable.

Two bombs had exploded on Jellicoe Street, with awful consequence – on the bank of the canal and on the tenements opposite: at No. 78 alone, 31 people had been killed in a matter of moments. Save for two married daughters – who lived elsewhere – Rocks's entire family had been wiped out: his aged mother-in-law, his wife, one of their daughters and all six of their sons, their daughter-in-law – Bessie – and five grandchildren, the oldest of them only six. 'We lost four generations of the family,' his grand-daughter Anne would recall many years later, 'my great-grandmother, grandmother, uncles, aunts and cousins . . .'

She remembers being roused from bed with her two sisters, just across the back-court in the bottom flat of 5 Kitchener Street, as the sirens sounded: their parents brooked no fuss, and plumped the little ones on the coal-bunker in the lobby, draping them with layer upon layer of coats and blankets. (In another fraught Clydebank home, Tom McKendrick records one terrified girl would actually toss her startled baby niece *into* a coal-bunker as a bomb screamed down. The family was entombed for hours, but all survived.)

As a relatively safe flat, Kitchener Street neighbours from upstairs were soon crowding it, as the guns began to roar and the bombs began to fall. 'There were therefore eight families in our flat – mothers, fathers, children,' remembers Anne. 'There were some people hiding under the kitchen table, children crying and wetting the floor in fright, other people being sick . . .' Her parents scurried back and forth, cleaning up, consoling, returning to check on their own nervous little girls.

Anne's uncle, John, had been at the dancing in Glasgow, and now appeared; the trams had stopped at Yoker, as the attack took hold, and he had walked undaunted from there through flaming Clydebank all the way to Dalmuir, and paused to check on his sister before making for 75 Jellicoe Street. 'He spoke to me and Mary and Susan in the hall, laughing and making fun of all the coats around us, asking if we were playing at wee houses, making us laugh, playing peekaboo with him. I needed to go to the toilet at that time, so my uncle took me. I remember looking at the top of the toilet window and seeing the sky red. I was very frightened and asked my uncle why it was red as it was night time. He told me God was polishing up the sun to make it nice tomorrow and I was not to worry . . .'

Once he had restored the mite to her bunker perch and solemnly buried her in layers of thick cloth, John Rocks insisted on going to his parents. His sister begged him to stay until the raid was over, but he was adamant: he was determined to make sure all was well at 75 Jellicoe Street – and so out he went.

The bombing was worse now, and Anne's parents all the more anxious. It was decided everyone should now pile into the Anderson shelter in the back-court. They took the youngest girls first – Mary and Susan, with blankets and food and clothes – and her father told Anne to stay right where she was as he would return for her within the minute. She did not quite obey him. She climbed onto the draining-board by the sink, to look out for him, and at that moment bombs began to fall in a curtain on Jellicoe Street itself. Her father burst in, seized her and off they went, and there assorted Greigs and their neighbours huddled together, tight as puppies and wordless in dread, as death poured about them.

It would emerge, days later, from a neighbour – Jean Gibson – who had come and gone, that Anne's old great-grandmother had refused absolutely to leave the flat at 75 Jellicoe Street for the shelter 'as she had been there before and nothing had happened, so she would stay in the house. My grandmother would not leave her mother and the rest of the family would not leave their mother. So no one went to the shelter. At 78 Jellicoe Street, two Rocks families lived next door to each other. My mother's eldest brother Pat and his wife Bessie and their five children had managed to get a house there. My Uncle Pat worked beside my grandfather at Beardmore's, Dalmuir, across the canal from where they lived. He was due to go on night shift, but had asked my grandfather to change shifts, as when the sirens had gone before Bessie had panicked trying to get the children ready. So, on that night, my grandfather was working and Pat stayed home with his family . . .'

In their turn, as the night grew the more alarming, the massed Rocks had repaired to the ground-floor flat at 78 Jellicoe Street. Jean Gibson – in one of these casual decisions that can, in entire innocence, spell life over death – now scurried home to be with her own people. Young Mary McLaughlin, engaged to wee Anne's uncle Francis Rocks, chose to stay; so did a friend, John McCormick. Mrs Rocks took a little granddaughter on her knee; then her son John, dashing from the Greigs' place over by, came panting in. Seconds later, as far as could ever be ascertained, a descending parachute-mine made its direct hit on 78 Jellicoe Street, killing every one of them. And it was to this scene the scant survivors of the clan at daybreak emerged:

After the all clear sounded and we came out of the shelter, my mother looked towards my grandmother's house and saw Jellicoe Street flattened. She started running, screaming for her mother, trying to move all the debris and rubble by hand, my father trying to pull her away, and Susan, Mary and I crying, not knowing what was going on. When my father finally managed to get my mother home, he went to French Street to get my granny to look after us while he went to search the shelters to see if any of my mother's family were there. He told me years later, when we used to talk, that as he searched that morning he went into a shelter, and there were five young girls sitting, arms linked, eyes opened, all dead from a bomb blast. He said they looked as if they had been to the dancing and had taken shelter on their way home when the bombing started.

When he returned home, he was told all the Rocks family from Jellicoe Street were dead. My mother was devastated. Of her family, three survived – her father, her sister and herself. When my grandfather returned from work on the morning of 14th March, his mother-in-law, his wife, his sons Pat, James, John, Francis, Joseph and Thomas, his daughter Theresa, daughter-in-law Bessie, and five of his grandchildren were all dead, his home was totally destroyed and all he had was what he was wearing – working clothes . . .

Yet Jellicoe Street – where a single explosion killed no fewer than 31 people – was not alone: other, solitary bombs had wrought horrific casualties. Elsewhere in Dalmuir, at 12 Pattison Street, 14 people – who had also taken refuge in a street-level flat – were blown to bits by one direct hit. Minutes later, a communal shelter behind No. 5 was likewise struck: all inside died.

Nor can Glasgow be overlooked. One mine drifted into a tenement on Lime Street, just off Victoria Park Drive South, at 22:15 on Thursday 14th. Nine died; five were badly injured. Another Luftmine blew up atop a shelter on the back-court between 148 Earl Street and 1571 Dumbarton Road, further west in Scotstoun, wrecking tenements all about and igniting a multitude of fires. The blast demolished, in all, three packed communal shelters: 66 died, and 60 more were hurt. At 22:42, bombs dropped by a single plane just south of the river – on the Govan Road, around Shieldhall Farm and by the King George V Dock – took 37 lives. And, almost an hour later a number of aircraft bore down on Partick, loosing five bombs and another mine: they hurtled down on Peel Street, across from the West of Scotland Cricket Club, and on Hayburn Street, and on the stretch of Crow Road nearby: the Germans may have been aiming for the suburban railway, which crosses Dumbarton Road close by. A slew of tenements on Peel Street was reduced – as Andrew Jeffrey describes – 'to a pile of smoking rubble'. There would be 50 dead.

That was a distinctly blue-collar part of town; but the Germans did not respect suburbia either. More of their lethal cargo rained on Hyndland, bourgeois then as now. One 'heavy bomb' flattened No. 3 Queens Gardens and substantially damaged those tenements to either side. A stately villa at 26 Turnberry Road was hit by a mine: 'the house was totally destroyed and no trace was ever found of the two occupants, who were simply blown to pieces.' Still more frightful was what just one parachute-mine did to Dudley Drive: it made landing between Nos. 8 and 12, quite annihilating three entire closes: three others had later to be demolished. There were 21 injured and 36 dead: had not so many residents hastened to the shelters at Hyndland School, the casualties would have been frightful. As it was, this solitary explosion left 500 people homeless. Still another mine blew up over the offices of Yarrow's Shipyard, on the edge between Scotstoun and Yoker, killing 67 people – though here there was a notable tale of rescue.

But two Glasgow blasts eclipsed all others. Almost on the dot of midnight, a Luftmine descended on Tradeston, going off with terrific force between a tram and a tenement on Nelson Street, just by the corner with Centre Street. The blast was such that it slew instantly three French sailors at the Broomielaw, on the opposite bank of the river: in total, 110 people were killed, 11 of them in this crowded tram (though 20 more were brought alive from its wreckage). At 101 Nelson Street, 40 people were trapped; gutted buildings tumbled like cards atop an underground shelter at No. 90, trapping another 41. A photograph taken on 14 March of that ravaged tram-car was deemed so disturbing its publication was flatly forbidden for the rest of the war.

One could detail many more incidents in the Second City of the Empire. A bomb dropped by the same plane wrecked the SCWS warehouse at Morrison Street, and is thought to have killed or trapped six people. No remains were ever found. Two mines sank into Kelvinside: two folk on the street at the corner of Queen Margaret Drive and Kelvin Way died in a second. A warden's post opposite 14 Queen Margaret Road tumbled: ARP officer Alex Munro crawled from the wreckage, but his young colleague, Marian MacDougall – lately a pupil at Hillhead High School, and a Scottish hockey internationalist – would die on her way to casualty. Three more people died at 8 Queen Margaret Road and some 500 shops and houses were damaged by that single blast, as well as the great Kibble Palace glasshouse in the Botanic Gardens and the BBC studios in what had once been Queen Margaret College. Kelvindale took hits: Cleveland Road, Dorchester Avenue, Chelmsford Drive and Leicester Avenue were all devastated by the impact of just two bombs. There was a brief lull between two in the morning and around 03:25 hours: then another, baleful shower of bombs and incendiaries, largely aimed at established fires in the north and west of Glasgow. Just about the last of the raid centred on Maryhill, around 05:35 hours: six houses at Glenburn Street were demolished, and six died, 'including the Young family at No. 267,' relates Jeffrey. 'The bodies of their daughters Agnes and Margaret were found in the back garden.'

Knightswood, cut by the swathe of the Great Western Road, took not a few hits – one of my primary teachers, Jeanette Mumford, would over three decades later tell us of the bomb at 394 Alderman Road that shook her own family home; there were more explosions at Baldric Road and Kestrel Road. But for sheer awfulness – especially as so many of the dead were schoolboy volunteers – what befell Knightswood's Bankhead School has a horror all its own.

It was hit early, the Luftmine descending on Caldwell Avenue finally detonating on Bankhead School's west wing, seething with first aid volunteers and Auxiliary Fire Service stalwarts and not a few teenage message boys. The alarm was raised almost immediately by telephone, for a large ambulance and rescuers bowled from the Esk Street depot within four minutes of the explosion. But they found entire carnage and, at 22:35, bleak word came to Main Control of the city's Auxiliary Fire Service from the superintendent at its Knightscliffe depot. 'I have received message per runner Bankhead Depot wiped out by landmine. They request all assistance I can give . . .'

Amidst the rubble, 46 people died, or died soon after rescue. They included Bankhead School's janitor, Alex Fraser, and all his family; 20 AFS officers and men; women who had, moments earlier, been taking stock of their first aid supplies, and preparing to head out for the succour of others; teenagers poised to dash hither and yon with their bicycles, bearing instructions and appeals and information vital to that night's endeavours in an emergency unparalleled.

Bankhead School burned remorselessly till near dusk on Friday and, for weeks afterwards, as the site was cleared, ghastly things would be found: an arm, a hand, a charred leg, teeth or a head. A buckled tin helmet was picked up that summer and turned over: inside was a piece of someone's skull.

Stories like this abound. Weeks later, Dan Trushell, from Kilbarchan, came to Clydebank to help salvage slates from wrecked buildings. Small and slightly built, he could be sent onto precarious ruins, and he was there when a mate picked something up in a roof valley – and gasped, and blanched: it was a child's decomposing hand. In March 1941, one little boy in Knightswood – Bryan Cromwell – was only five, and exposed to things few adults could have processed, as he grimly recalled half a century later. 'I saw bits of bodies lying about the street in Broadley Drive and Killoch Drive among the debris. I think I just stared curiously at the lumps of burned, charred flesh and bits of uniform attached to limbs. I don't remember being horrified by what I saw, just a feeling of detachment, like it was all unreal . . .'

Message boys – gutsy scholars, young enough to abound in energy and too young, perhaps, to be paralysed by imagination and terror – were among the many local heroes of March 1941. Most, despite their derring-do – dashing about Clydebank and assorted quarters of Glasgow by motorcycle or bicycle or on foot, as fires roared and bombs fell and buildings sagged and collapsed into this and that highway – survived to tell the tale.

'Those who were members of the ARP and Casualty Services were unanimous after the raids in praise of the messengers, generally youths connected with organisations like the Boys' Brigade and the Boy Scouts,' noted Iain MacPhail, '. . . they had a task which was probably the most hazardous of all but to them it was an exciting adventure; and when telephonic communication was impossible on the first night, they had the added thrill of knowing that the messenger service was of supreme importance in saving lives. They managed to survive the Blitz comparatively unscathed but one unfortunately was killed – Robert M. MacFarlane, who met his death on Broom Drive.'

Another Clydebank messenger, young William Sharp, acted decisively when bombs wrecked Boquhanran School and its first aid post: he began coolly directing ambulances to an improvised facility at the local Wardens' Control Centre, in the new campus of Clydebank High School on Janetta Street. In Glasgow, the heroism of Neil Leitch of 21 Hayburn Crescent – he was only 15 years old – has not lost power to move. As Andrew Jeffrey describes, he

. . . was one of the many messengers who braved the bombs that night. Four of them were killed. He was carrying a message from Bankhead School to Partick Fire Station when he was blown from his bicycle by a bomb and suffered both bruising and shock. Recovering his senses, he continued on his journey, delivered the message and was given First Aid before setting out to return to Bankhead School. On his way there an oil-bomb landed close to him, blasting off his clothes and causing him severe burns. He died soon afterwards and the *Glasgow Herald* reported that he bore his sufferings 'with the greatest fortitude.'

We have seen the (cruelly maligned) part played by local firemen, in impossible conditions, and something of the heroism of ambulance drivers. The chaos of the night posed the same dreadful burdens on first aid volunteers and all who sought to tend the maimed, injured and dying – disrupted communications, fire and flood, blasted facilities and cratered roads. But still – the mass of them young women – they fought and toiled.

From the start of the attack on Clydebank, as MacPhail has detailed, there were a dozen organised 'First Aid Parties' and what seemed like ample transport. But the assault on their own facilities from the swooping Germans added greatly to their difficulties. It was not long before a parachute-mine devastated the Elgin Street School, and its First Aid Post, and put much of their equipment out of action. The electric light failed; the water supply faltered and disappeared. Working frantically, volunteers retrieved as many medical supplies as they could and repaired to the playground shelters, where they treated over 190 cases by the uncertain, swaying light of hurricane lanterns. As rapidly as could be managed, the injured were borne to the Blawarthill Hospital in Yoker. It was soon jammed to capacity with the burned and bloodied from Clydebank and western Glasgow, and casualties thereafter were carried to Canniesburn Hospital and, as that too filled, yet further afield to infirmaries at Robroyston and Killearn.

In monumental mischance, as we have seen, the first aid post at Boquhanran School was also struck early 'by high-explosive bombs and incendiaries'. Again, supplies, stretcher-borne victims and the walking wounded were hastened to the outside shelters, with all the more urgency as fire took firm hold of the school's upper floor. The commandant at Boquhanran, William Smith, kept 'magnificently cool' through everything the night threw at him and his gutsy crew. He sent two volunteer nurses to the casualties directed by young Sharp to Janetta Street and took advantage of the lull in the bombing after two to evacuate all his patients to that hastily cobbled refuge; the fire at Boquhanran Street was now out of control, the heat grew oppressive and there was real danger of buildings toppling on top of everyone.

Through all this, the wee Clydebank ambulances and their determined drivers fought as they could to retrieve the injured. 'Ambulances were hit by incendiaries and caught fire,' John Grindlay – who drove one – remembered in 1986, 'or they could not get past the damage in the streets. We had to pull people out and carry the injured from one ambulance to another. I only saw one woman panic. Somebody thumped her and that shut her up . . .'

Soon the whole east corridor of the school at Janetta Street was lined with stretchers; this corner and that clotted with the walking (and often very noisy) injured. Many also had relatives in tow: brooding grannies, quiet and wide-eyed children. With incendiaries once more dropping about them, Smith had the presence of mind to organise fire-patrols, and such first aid personnel as could be spared were soon patrolling the sprawling premises and moving quickly to dislodge and extinguish the little thermite bombs as they glowed on roofs (the white glare of burning magnesium is yet another memory fast in the Clydebank consciousness, and how remorselessly it ate through metal and tiles) or thunked about the playground. And all the while, as Andrew Jeffrey writes, the 'corridors echoed to the screams of the injured and the dying'.

We know of one plucky young woman, Mary Haldane, just 21, and who in normality worked as a cashier at a local business. Tonight she was a volunteer ambulance attendant, waiting on the rickety facility at Radnor Park. She had only just turned up on an urgent call to Livingstone Street when a bursting bomb blew her ambulance onto its side. The other ambulance, still nearer the blast, was smashed to pieces, killing some occupants and further, dreadfully injuring others. Miss Haldane went immediately to its rescue and, amidst the fires and falling rubble of this death row, toiled on Livingstone Street continuously until daybreak. She would rightly be awarded the OBE for her gallantry.

This same night brought forth one more tantalising heroine; for no one – not even Iain MacPhail, who knew practically everyone in Dunbartonshire and researched those events when memories were still fresh and most involved were still living – could ever identify her, though Janet Hyslop – a strong woman even in a place that abounded in them, who had served briefly as a Clydebank councillor and was the only female head warden in the place – was in 1981 able vividly to recall her to Billy Kay. She it was in charge at Radnor Park Church Hall when the bombed-out Boquhanran School refugees appeared, and Mrs Hyslop had just started to get to grips with the 60 casualties when the cry was raised that the telephone lines were down. Her son was a messenger (and, indeed, one of the striking apprentices; he had been at a meeting in Glasgow earlier that evening) and he was sent at once to the Control Centre at Dumbarton Road for some ambulances. When only one showed up, he was sent out again by his determined mother.

Unfortunately the First Aid Post got a hit, so of course the folks all knew me – 'Right, we'll go to the Warden's Post. And about two or three o'clock in the morning [*when, as we have noted, there was a marked pause in the bombing*] a young woman walked in. She came over to me because I had a white helmet, wanted to know – where was the doctor? So I explained to her that this was a warden's post, not a First Aid Post and there was no doctor, and she walked away. I'm sorry to this day that I didn't find out who that young woman was because she went, as I learned later, to the hospital, and said, 'Look, boys, Clydebank's needing you . . .'

MacPhail had managed to establish, by 1974, that she was a student nurse, off duty this Thursday evening and who – near her home in Giffnock, on Glasgow's south side, had gradually grown aware of the devastation in the west. She had hailed a passing ambulance and, learning it was on a dash to

Clydebank, came along as a volunteer. She quickly grasped that the First Aid Post at Boquhanran School had been destroyed, and had now learned from Janet Hyslop that there was no qualified help at Radnor Park. Pausing only to collect a critically injured baby, the girl hurried back to the ambulance and – by a combination of charm, authority and urgency – got it with all haste to Glasgow's Western Infirmary, amidst a fresh shower of bombs and dodging not a few craters on the Boulevard and the Great Western Road.

The Infirmary, at the border of Partick and Hillhead, was no less a hive of frantic endeavour on such a night, with doctors and nurses attending to casualties rolling in regularly from the city's West End. There was little hope of luring any professionals to Clydebank. But the girl did not hesitate: she went in immediate pursuit of medical students. There was a clutch from senior year – their finals were only 10 days away – and their instructions, in the event of an air raid, were to wait for the 'All Clear' to sound, before joining the assorted medical units which would then go out to tend the injured in the field and where, of course, the students would work (as decreed in normal times) only under the supervision of qualified doctors.

Even so, they had tried – all, by midnight, had hurried to the Infirmary, determined to do what they could amidst what was evidently a murderous German attack. But rules are rules and stern senior doctors, then and now, what they are; and in any event there was no shortage of qualified men in the Western. Not allowed near the casualties, the students were reduced to writing up details of injuries and other dull clerical chores; and one was frowning at his clipboard when the student nurse, hotfoot from Clydebank, accosted him: 'Doctor, is this baby dead?'

The child, as the young man soon assured her, was quite alive – and, indeed, the infant did survive. But the nurse had found a friendly ear. She explained the desperate position in Clydebank: a hall packed with hurt people, many grievously wounded, without help or medical necessities. Other students were quickly called over. No less quickly, they had prevailed on their surgeons to let them hurry west. But Dr McQueen, the medical superintendent, showing what Jeffrey properly damns as 'scarcely credible bureaucratic small-mindedness' flatly refused to release any supplies, and least of all morphia – the most urgently needed medication for horribly maimed and screaming casualties. More, he declared forcefully he would 'accept no responsibility' for whatever the students chose to do.

But they would not yield. They turned instead to a ward sister, Isabella MacDonald, and she quickly unearthed what she could – dressings, bandages, the requisites for suturing, antiseptics and swabs and sterile instruments and so on, tying everything up in eight enormous bundles in eight crisp white sheets. But she would not (and could not) defy Dr McQueen and give them morphia.

The trundle back to Clydebank in the jammed ambulance was the stuff of nightmares. Like everything else on the night-time streets under the regulations of the Second World War, its headlamps were dimmed, gridded and visored. The driver could scarcely see where he was going and, when he hit something with an enormous bang, all were flung about inside and for moments there was anger, howling and confusion. They became very quiet when, standing briefly outside, they saw what they had struck – a vast, intact parachute-mine. They made away then with all speed. (When the exhausted little band returned by the Boulevard, many hours later, the mine had detonated, leaving a great crater, which had by then swallowed a single-decker bus.) On the outskirts of Clydebank, they were then halted by a policeman, who of his own authority declared they could go no further, what with wreckage and unexploded bombs. Time was lost explaining the position to him, and the officer could not even direct them to Radnor Park, finally suggesting that they make 'for where the fires are greatest'.

At the church hall, the parish minister – the Reverend James McNaught – and Janet Hyslop toiled as they could, amidst hideously injured and anguished people. Mrs Hyslop never forgot her heart lifting as young men appeared from nowhere, pulling on white jackets, carrying their bundles of desperately-sought hospital things. The word rose thankfully on all sides: 'The doctors have come, the doctors have come . . .'

Doctors they were not – quite yet – and few can ever have had careers so launched, tending ghastly wounds with scant equipment and no useful pain relief, as bombs whistled and landed and exploded and buildings seemed to be collapsing on all sides about them. (Mrs Hyslop 'went out periodically to check how things were. That was Second Avenue, there – got a direct hit and the place was just obliterated . . .' Even more creepily, the terrace was brought down not by blast but by explosive vacuum: the entire front wall sucked out and down.) Sensibly, the assorted makeshift ambulances – including the one the student nurse had commandeered – were put to the urgent task of ferrying patients away from the hall to the assorted hospitals, away from the immediate danger of the Luftwaffe, and back post-haste to convoy still more. 'When asked by the students if they would undertake the task,' MacPhail records, 'which involved driving along roads almost impassable in places with the constant risk of being shattered by the explosion of delayed-action bombs, the drivers all pledged themselves solemnly before God to do so, and right nobly did they keep their word.'

Finally – eyes heavy, hands trembling with exhaustion, their garb splattered with blood – their work was done, those in most need away to hospital. The 'All Clear' sounded; the dawn rose on what remained of Clydebank. There was no available transport, so the nurse and the students simply set off on foot for Glasgow: two of them, in fact, had that same day to sit examinations at the Royal Infirmary. Before long, as MacPhail continues, 'a large Crossley car came along and they were given a lift. Almost immediately afterwards a delayed-action bomb exploded in a field . . . great piles of earth and stones pouring down on top of them, fortunately without serious injury. The car was brought to a standstill by the blast and when the students emerged to examine the damage, they discovered that the edge of the bomb crater was only eighteen yards from the car.' At half past eight on this broken morning, as the father of one of the students later told local dignitaries, 'they returned to the hospital, bloodstained and weary after having lived through what will most probably be the most terrible experience of their professional lives.'

But, as for the young woman who had of her own volition taken passage to Clydebank, ascertained its crisis, dashed back to Glasgow, organised aid and made the fraught journey once and twice more – cheating one unexploded bomb on the way out and a full-blown blast on the way back in – we do not know, and can never now learn, her name.

Women, though, were not confined to applying plasters, mopping brows, beseeching students and doctors and laughing off unexploded parachute-mines. A large number toiled heroically in March 1941 as air raid wardens, sharing all the peril and much of the responsibility of their male colleagues. Helen Robertson, for instance, whose ARP post was in the hall of the Radnor Park Church, had been at first a full-time warden at a modest £2 a week, but as the 'Phoney War' oozed on she was reduced to part-time service. In her 1999 account, her practicality, tough good humour and profound humanity are most evident – and the sense of being no less vulnerable, in March 1941, to the Germans than any other Bankie who was not in uniform. There is also a sharp reminder of a terror of the time now readily forgotten: the fear of German invasion, not least by paratroopers and cunningly disguised spies, at any moment.

The night of the Blitz I heard it on the wireless at nine o'clock, and I opened the budgie cage and I shut up my fire because I thought if there was a blast it would save the fire being blown into the house and creating a big fire. Then I went down with my tin hat on and got my neighbours into the shelter . . . Before that every few weeks we used to take turns at visiting the shelters, because they were pretty damp. What you did was you put a candle in a flower pot and then put another flower pot on top, and that took the chill off the air, so that if the shelter had to be used at least it wouldn't be running damp. So with my neighbours we got down to the shelter. We weren't long there till I heard *Wheeeeeeeee!* And I remember very calmly just thinking to myself that was 'probably the last sound that I'll ever hear.' However, the bomb exploded, and even though my eyes were shut, I still saw the flash and, suddenly, my mouth was filled with dust. I ran out the shelter and saw the neighbours further up the street running into what I could just describe as a big cloud of dust, for the building had been struck with the bomb that I had heard and I remember shouting, 'Stay where you are! The shelter held!'

I ran through our close and round to the front and there was just a heap of rubble in the street. But people emerged and I remember saying, 'Anybody that's able to walk come with me.' The fact that you had a tin hat on; people seemed to think you were immune. However, I took these people and put them in the shelter in St Stephen's School, and I said to them, 'Now, I'll need to go up to Boquhanran School to get an ambulance, and if anybody is able to walk, come with me.' Two wee girls set off with me up Albert Road and I remember incendiaries were falling just like flowers on a carpet, hundreds of them, and it was no use trying to put them out, at least if they burned out on the street they were doing no harm. Whenever we heard a bomb coming down we would take shelter together.

Just before we got into Boquhanran School, a man appeared with a rifle on his shoulder, and a great-coat (it was March, remember, a cold night) and he said, 'Can I help you?' Now we had been told that if the Germans came they wouldn't be dressed in a Nazi uniform. They would be in disguise. So I waited till this man spoke before I answered, and I said, 'I have these wee girls and we're trying to get into the school.' So he helped me and we got them into the school. We just got in and the woman that was there says, 'Have you got the form filled up?' Now we were issued with forms that you put the name and address of any casualties on, and I remember saying to her, 'Nelly, nobody's gonnae have had time to fill up any forms. It's just like H*** out there!' They knew nothing, because they were in the sanctuary of the school.

I left the wee girls and came out, and told the ambulance to get down to the end of Second Avenue because I knew there must be some people seriously hurt. I had just got out at the school and, quicker than I can tell you, the whole roof was just one blaze. There were two or three landmines floating down, though to me a landmine was a big round thing, but these weren't – these were big, long cylinders calmly floating down, slowly, beautiful in the bright, moonlight night. So I got to the junction of Boquhanran Road and Albert Road, and Bill Girvan was there with an auxiliary fire appliance. I said, 'Bill, get up to the school as quick as you can, for that roof's on fire.' And he says, 'Helen, I can't move. I have no water.'

So back down I went and it was chaos. Two closes were flattened. Luckily the ambulance was there before me, and a Mr Malcolm was standing in the ambulance with blood on his head. I said, 'You come out of there' – a tin hat made you a heid-yin – 'you're able to walk.'

And he said, quite calmly, 'It's my wee boy. I'm just helping him into the ambulance.' I lifted the end of the stretcher. I had the feeling the wee boy was dead, but I said where he was going they knew better how to deal with him than I did. So I helped him into the ambulance. It was a good job I had that ambulance because incendiaries fell in the school playground and burned out all but two ambulances.

However, I got back down to my place. The minister, Mr Philp, stayed in Boquhanran Church Manse near the foot of Albert Road and I knew he was often very late at night and his wife could be a wee bit nervous, and I thought about her being in that big house herself (although he had been a miner and he had shored up below their stairs and it would have held up to anything except a direct hit). So I went to see if Mrs Philp was all right and, just as I got to the gate, him and her came out the house, and I asked them where they were going. He said, 'Oh, we don't know, but we just feel it's not very safe.' So I took them through our close which was still standing and put them in our shelter. During this, of course, it was very noisy, with the roar of the flame and the incessant drone of low-flying planes. One plane, I remember seeing it plain as anything, was actually below the level of the flames. There was a No. 9 bus at the terminus at our close and that plane machine-gunned that bus. There was a high wall between us and Albert Road houses and we could see, right along the length of the wall, machine-gun bullets . . .

Whatever insouciance might later be affected by many survivors of the Blitz, Willie Green admitted to Billy Kay he had been terrified. 'During a lull in the early morning I went up above ground and I saw Clydebank burnin' – complete panic. People don't talk much about their fears, but I can assure you I was scared that night, and more so, I think, being helpless. You know, if you had a crossbow and just firin' aimlessly, you'd feel you're sorta doing something, but just to sit there . . .'

Anger would perhaps build in the days and weeks ahead as the townsfolk recalled how defenceless they had felt and how little sign of meaningful measures they had seen. There were, of course, some anti-aircraft guns – notably, those guns at Duntiglennan – but, brave as their crews proved, they had availed little; the location was chosen very much for the defence of Glasgow proper, and they were entirely out of ammunition by 2 a.m. Yet there was one doughty group in the town that night who blazed back at the Germans with abandon, and who thus cemented a niche in Bankie affections for ever.

As hap would have it, a Polish destroyer – the ORP *Piorun*; it means 'thunderbolt' – was berthed in Rothesay Dock, by John Brown's yard, in mid-March 1941. Polish – or, more accurately, 'Free Polish Navy' – she might legally have been, and she was in for a refit after her first weeks in service on convoy escort-duty; but she was an N-class destroyer of British design and Clydebank, John Brown's construction, launched only in May 1940 and commissioned on 4 November. Tens of thousands of Poles – those at sea in September 1939 had an obvious advantage – had managed to escape as the land was overrun by the Nazis from one front and the Soviets on the other; and Polish airmen had proved notable heroes in the Battle of Britain.

These Polish sailors would win local glory now. More than the *Piorun* was at stake. Berthed alongside her was a brand new British battleship of the mighty 'King George V' class, the *Duke of York*, which Brown's had newly built and were fitting out as rapidly as possible. The great, gun-bristling vessel was naturally of keen interest to German aircraft, who dipped in to attack time and again; and they were tempted besides by other luscious targets: the monitor HMS *Roberts*, the destroyer HMS *Nizam* and the convoy-escort HMS *Blankney* also sat in this fitting-out basin.

But the Polish crew of the *Piorun* – most young; lads in their late teens – had more reason than anyone else in town to hate the Germans, and they were not prepared to stand idly by. Their ship, too, boasted anti-aircraft guns. The sailors manned them and started to blaze away. Nevertheless, inevitably, incendiaries bounced about the *Duke of York*, and soon she was on fire. Still the Poles refused to yield. The guns of the *Piorun* hammered on, and other sailors dashed about the *Duke of York*, kicking incendiaries into the Clyde, dowsing this and that blaze with buckets of sand, buckets of water, brooms, whatever came to hand, as bombs plunged and parachute-mines drifted all about them; and still the guns of the *Piorun* pounded until her youthful crew had used all the available ammunition.

It was maintained in local lore for years – MacPhail is deliciously sniffy at this point – that the Poles not only downed an aircraft but, when the hapless pilot's parachute bore him remorselessly onto the deck of their destroyer, they seized him 'without further ado' and flung him into the furnace. For all the Polish courage, as one lady of the town dryly put it 40 years later, they would have been as well flinging matches in the air for any prospect of bringing down a Heinkel or Junker; but there is no doubt that, with such vigorous banging-back from the ground at the heart of Clydebank, German aircraft lingered much less long about the Rothesay Dock and John Brown's than had been their certain intention. The boys of the *Piorun* may well have saved John Brown's shipyard. What is certain is that they saved the *Duke of York*; though sufficiently damaged to delay her delivery by some months, she would have a distinguished war. The Poles would justly win an Admiralty commendation; their tough little ship would have a still more dashing adventure in the Second World War.

Other public servants had their part in all this; and probably men of no other agency, as MacPhail points out, 'were so continually under stress as the police. Fortunately none of them lost his life but fourteen of the regular force had their homes completely destroyed . . . six of the Police War Reserve were in the same position.' Over two dozen more found their homes so badly damaged as to be uninhabitable. Almost all were on duty from Thursday evening through to Saturday, and granted but five hours' gritty sleep on the Friday. Even that, in many instances, was given over not to their own rest but to making desperate arrangements for their families.

Two simply broke under the strain. One War Reserve officer served two successive nights on duty, and then vanished for two days. He would turn up at Carlisle Police Station, reporting himself in and utterly unable to explain how he had got there or what he had been doing. It was evidently what MacPhail describes as 'shell shock', now fashionably, if more clumsily, known as post-traumatic stress disorder. Another officer – a superintendent at Dalmuir, William MacCulloch – would lose his reputation. He had taken shelter with his family on Thursday night in the Anderson shelter behind their home at 16 Overtoun Road: a bomb then hit their house, quite destroyed it and blew in the shelter's sides. None of them was seriously injured, and one can understand MacCulloch's strain and alarm as with considerable difficulty he freed himself, his wife and his offspring. It is much harder, considering his responsibilities, to understand why he personally then took them out of the area altogether, to Windyhills on the road between Duntocher and Bearsden, and did not report for duty at any point on Friday – and it was politically impossible for senior colleagues to defend. After discussion between the chief constable and His Majesty's Inspector of Constabulary in Scotland, MacCulloch would be quietly transferred to Kirkintilloch, his usefulness in Clydebank at emphatic end.

The chief constable of Dunbartonshire himself – A.J. McIntosh – played quite a proud part in the town's ordeal. As the assault began, he was not only in Clydebank but at John Brown's shipyard, for there had been complaints about lights showing during air raid warnings and the politics of placating air raid regulations on the one hand, the exigencies of war production on the other, and the potential threat to a vital industrial facility from the air besides called for delicate handling at the highest level. The siren was on this occasion to be sounded, at an agreed time, so spotter aircraft could then rise to look down and report as to what light from the shipyard was visible. The chief constable was vexed when sirens started to howl ahead of the ordained moment. But then he grasped it was the real thing. The mission was abandoned. He hastened to the town's Control Centre, underneath the public library, and there – save for occasional sorties to his own Constabulary headquarters – McIntosh would remain until Saturday afternoon.

But the officer, perhaps, most remembered from the night Clydebank burned was Sergeant John MacLeod, and like most good men with that good name he was a native of the Isle of Lewis. MacLeod lived at 43 Albert Road, and he was hastening to his duty on Thursday night when bombs simultaneously destroyed houses on either side of him. Within moments, from one, he could hear the cries and wailing of children, and at once clambered through the smoking ruins and, with great difficulty, rescued two of them. He then made for another disintegrated home and, directing efforts and taking his turn to grope and shift and lift and pull, helped in the rescue of three further children and their mother, and extricated besides the still and broken body of a fourth. Thus Sergeant MacLeod proceeded, taking charge of further rescues at the very height of the raid, and, once all the injured and trapped of whom he knew were freed, he duly turned up for duty (as normal) at his station.

There was heroism all over. Take Boreland Street, in Knightswood: outside two adjoining homes – Nos. 77 and 79 – a bomb detonated on the pavement in the first hour of the raid. The house at No. 81 simply collapsed on itself, trapping inside all eight of the Hastie family. Within minutes, urgent efforts to help were under way. A 16-year-old schoolboy, Gerard McMahon, joined determinedly with two grim-faced ARP wardens, Alex Glennie and Alex Hamilton. They managed to haul most of the roof clear by the simple if risky expedient of a rope and a car. Glennie then clawed and tunnelled his way into the rubble with his own raw hands. Only yards away, curtains of flame roared some 20 feet into the air from a smashed gas main. Overhead, as the little group toiled on, shards and splinters tinkled down from detonating anti-aircraft shells in the glowing and roaring sky.

McMahon had put in 4 hours at this labour before nipping briefly back home to check on his own family. They were safe in their Anderson shelter, and he quickly extricated himself and was soon back on Boreland Drive. So they picked on, brick by brick, beam by beam, and – one by one – every last Hastie was brought safely out. Only a few hours later, in Stobhill Hospital at eight o'clock on Friday morning, Mrs Hastie was safely delivered of a baby boy.

Two other public servants in Clydebank deserve, too, to be memorialised – her leading water engineers. James MacWilliam was assistant engineer of the Clydebank Water Trust, and George Aitkenhead its foreman. As the fire-fighting emergency became clear and the wretched problems with burst mains, limited or failed supply and falling pressure left firemen but helpless spectators at this and that conflagration, MacWilliam and Aitkenhead rushed around doing what they could, heedless of bomb and blast and peril – shutting valves here and there, or opening others, to conserve what water there was at such pressure as could be attained in the circumstances. It was all the more difficult as the Town Council plans of the water mains were not accurate, and there many faulty valves. When the engineer turned up for a Water Trust meeting at ten to eight on Friday morning, colleagues were shocked to see MacWilliam hurt and bloodied by shrapnel – and had enjoyed besides no contact with or word from his family since the assault began, and yet persevered in his duty.

But heroism seemed to march this night in uneasy alliance with pointless, helpless horror: entrapment and torment, bereavement and maiming. In Tom McKendrick's little account of the Clydebank Blitz in 1986, as condensed by the late, darkly minded Angus Calder, one survivor – in March 1941 a young woman – recalled sitting in a 'comfy' shelter, playing cards with family and friends, when a bomb not one of them had heard coming 'blasted her brother through the door, tore her friends to pieces, smashed a concrete roof down on her mother's chest, crushed her father, and left her buried under her dead friends for eight and a half hours. "I was paralysed from the waist down. . . . my mother was killed . . . my friends were killed . . . my father and brother survived. . . ."'

Scorched by flame, shaken repeatedly by bombs, often soaked in filthy water or half-choked in dust and fumes, toiling hour upon hour without respite and with nothing at all to eat or drink, even the bravest Clydebank volunteers were falling over, in complete exhaustion, before break of day. Yet Tom McKendrick records memories of one fireman sustained by sheer willpower. 'They brought in this fireman. He had been injured by flying debris and his arm was split to the bone from wrist to elbow. They patched him up with what was available . . . it looked as if he had lost a lot of blood. He was really grimy and exhausted. After about twenty minutes he got up from the stretcher, mumbled something about "being no bloody use lying here" and went back to rejoin his unit. Where that man found his strength, God only knows.'

Nor were shelters for the most part nice, cosy places awash with good nature. They were damp, cold, usually jam-packed with frightened people, and frequently stank – many, terrified, wet or soiled themselves – and when folk did try to raise morale, things could sound almost delusional.

A Mrs Richardson recalled, 'We used to sit in the shelters and play guessing games, and sing, and then "I Spy" – used to laugh – "I Spy" in the dark. We'd light candles and once we got the "I Spy", the candle would be put out again and then lit again. And then the sing-songs, it was all the old fashioned songs, used to love to hear the old folks singing – you know. My mother used to sing *The Old Rowan Tree*, that was her song . . .' But Mary Rodgers, Clydebank-reared of Hebridean stock, had a darker tale. 'There was a church soiree and some of the audience went out and they thought they would be safer in the shelter. And others stayed in the church hall. When the all clear went, the people were just sittin' like mummies. The door had got blasted off and the blast went in and the people were just sittin' like mummies in their seats there . . .'

On one Clydebank street, aghast ARP workers saw a terrified girl – a young girl, perhaps seven years old – standing, screaming, in the high window of a blazing building. They had no ladders. Long moments later, the roof fell in, and she was gone. One of the earliest bombs of the raid fell on the tenements of 57–59 Whitecrook Street, with many casualties and deaths. One man had lost both his legs; he was being borne to an ambulance, gobbets of blood dripping on the road behind him, when still another bomb went off close to hand, at the entrance of Stanford Street, and blew off the legs of the ambulance attendant. So side by side they lay, helpless and barely conscious on the street, and quietly there, together, they bled to death.

Even in the early 1980s, Father Sheary was still haunted, night and day, by two incidents in which – in soft, tired Irish tone – he used the same poignant phrase once and thrice, recounting them for Billy Kay's radio programme.

There was a family called Semple, 'and Mrs Semple had quite a large family and they were all young. On that night, she had one in either arm and one on either side of her and she was standing in a close, and I think it was an aerial torpedo that struck against Jericho Street, but the blast that came from that took a child out of her right arm and took the child at her left side, leaving her with the child in her left arm and a child on her right side.

'They two escaped, she escaped, and she never saw as much as a rip of hair belonging to the other two children. Frightening – I'll never forget that as long as I live. They disappeared completely – she never saw them again, never, not so much as a rip of hair belonging to them, poor woman . . .'

The story Bridget McHard could relate in 1981 – at the time of the Blitz, she was a child of 11 – was, if anything, still more horrible; bombed down and trapped for hours with her family, and the awful end of a baby sister.

Well, I just remember this chap that stayed in the close, John Green was his name, tellin' us to cover wir heads – he saw something through the shutters of the window. Well, I remember puttin' my hands over my head and puttin' my head down, and that's all I remember until I wakened up and I was buried. It was a funny experience, really. I was buried in my mouth and nose, my face down, but I remember wakening up and this terrible dust – in fact I don't like dust from that time. I don't like dust. I seem to go in and out an awful lot. But I know I wasn't taken out until three o'clock on Friday afternoon, and that was from midnight the night before. The only time I saw daylight was when I was gettin' pulled out and I could feel the thing comin' over my face when I was gettin' pulled out. I'd one brother on one side of me and a sister on the other side of me – they were both killed.

But my mother was buried, she was in a cavity sittin' on a chair. The buildin' was on fire and wi' the firemen playin' the hose on the fire and the way my mother was situated, it was like a cavity, and it just filled up with water. My young sister was on her knee and she said that when she felt herself goin' away, or fainting, her hands slipped. She was tryin' to hold onto my sister Eveline and when she was dug out she was sorta pulled up the way and as she looked down she saw Eveline lyin' where she'd fell off her knee and she just told the man that was her wee girl. So if she wasn't killed then she was drowned because the water had come right up to my mother's mouth, she'd tae hold her head up. So that obviously Eveline, if she wasn't killed, she was drowned . . .

Amidst so much fire, and heat, and toxic gas, dozens of folk burned dead or alive, and somehow this tiny girl drowned in the Clydebank Blitz. Bridget McHard had seven brothers and sisters: only she and her mother survived.

Cuthbert Douse was but 19, and over 40 years on could not forget a sickening necessity as he and his father clawed and manoeuvred frantically to pull his grandmother from the wreckage after yet another parachute-mine. 'We had to dig with our hands but her arm was jammed by the window sill. I remember my father telling me to turn away because the only way we could get her out was to pull. I'm afraid he pulled three of her fingers out getting her out of the debris . . .'

Father Sheary's voice, old and tired, Irish and dignified, murmurs on the decades-old recording: 'I had married one of the Dorans just shortly before the Blitz and I was talking to him on the morning of the 14th and he went up to try and find his parents and they were blown to atoms. Two or three weeks afterwards I met him, I went back to see what was left of Dalmuir and I didn't know the place, to be honest with you – couldn't find out which was First Terrace, Second Terrace, or Third Terrace, But I saw Denis Doran and he was with his two hands pulling away there, bricks and mortar – and I said, "What are you doing?" "I'm looking," he said, "for a rip of hair belonging to my family." '

7

'WELL, THEY'RE COMING BACK . . .'

James Hastings, deputy town clerk of Clydebank, was one of the three local officials (the others were his boss, Henry Kelly; and the assistant town clerk, William G. Thomson) who had in turn to be available for duty when the alarm of approaching enemy aircraft was raised. Two of them had always to be on call – ready to report immediately to the vulnerable Control Centre beneath the local library – and it so happened that Thursday 13 March was Hastings' night off.

He had slipped through to Glasgow to relax with friends but had nevertheless (though not obliged to do so) left their telephone number with Kelly; and it was actually Kelly's failure to call – as the raid grew ever deadlier, and the continued barrage of anti-aircraft guns and the scream and impact of bombs rocked Clydeside – that moved Hastings to return in the small hours of the morning. He could get no further than the western edge of Scotstoun – the Kingsway, the ramping road from Scotstounhill into Yoker – before being forced to proceed on foot, through the terrors of the night along Dumbarton Road to the borders of his battered and blazing town.

'Immediately I got to the Clydebank boundary,' he recalled for Iain MacPhail three decades later, 'the whole scene was one of devastation. Actually, the very first building on the north side of the road was a public house called the Yoker Bar. It had been bombed and on the other side of it was Yoker Distillery and some of it was on fire. It is a ridiculous thing to say but if the German bombers had been briefed not to bomb Glasgow and only to bomb Clydebank, they could hardly have been more accurate at that end of the town.'

He found the Control Centre chaotic; its occupants hollow-eyed and harried. Until midnight, no fewer than 16 telephones had rung unceasingly with word of this calamity and that, or been lifted in turn to issue orders or divert trucks and engines: but soon after midnight all the telephone lines had failed, leaving Henry Kelly and the Control Centre staff at once beleaguered and helpless. Dunbartonshire's deputy chief constable, Kenneth MacLeod – the local force was dominated by Highlanders – had seen for himself the impossibility of their position. 'Piles of messages recorded by the telephonists lay on the table, messengers were coming in and out, and it was obvious that the staff were overwhelmed by the demands made upon them . . .'

By the time a dusty, puffing Hastings had arrived, about three in the morning, the electricity had failed too. His colleagues could do little more than note this and that from the scurrying message-boys, as in the uproar above and beyond the ambulance men, fire-crews, wardens and police officers coped as best they could on their own initiative. Just when it seemed things could be no worse – and only minutes after James Hastings had reached it – a German bomb hit the Public Library right above, and their base (which had, mercifully, been braced with timber and steel) shook sickeningly. 'There was a most damnable crash above. We were showered with glass, which percolated through the wooden reinforcements in the ceiling of the basement. No one was terribly concerned at the moment; we were alive and we shook the dust off our papers and got on with the job. The place was a perfect shambles.'

And so, by daybreak, was all Clydebank – much of it still burning, entire blocks of tenements wrecked, roads everywhere cratered or piled with rubble, the town everywhere reeking of burnt timber, burnt whisky, burnt rubber and – though few cared to dwell on it – the cooked, roasting scent, here and there, of human flesh. Scarcely a corner in Clydebank had been spared death; in some, though, the carnage was appalling. On Second Avenue alone – where Janet Hyslop, keeking from the Radnor Park first aid station, had witnessed the bomb that 'pulled the face off Second Terrace' – 80 people were dead: they included 10 of the Diver family at No. 76; 8 McSherrys at No. 161.

On Pattison Street, 43 had been slain; 31 on Dalmuir's Jellicoe Street; 27 on Napier Street; 23 on Radnor Street (including 9 of the Richmond family at No. 60); 20 on Glasgow Road.

Many had shunned damp shelters for the familiarity of their own homes, and died; some had obediently retreated to shelters that then fell victim to a direct hit. In many instances, as we have seen, folk fled to neighbours (particularly those in ground-floor flats) or scurried through the perils of the attack to check on friends or relatives; or had been on their way home from this ploy and that and begged refuge where they could – all factors which greatly complicated efforts at rescue and later, when hope was gone, the identification of the dead. Right now, 'as dawn broke,' records Andrew Jeffrey, 'the people of Clydebank emerged from their shelters into scenes of almost unimaginable horror and devastation.'

A huge pall of smoke billowed over the town from the blazing oil tanks at the Admiralty depot in Old Kilpatrick; and fires everywhere burned unchecked. All Kilbowie seemed still to burn: the flat-roofed tenements of the 'Holy City' were but a gutted shell. John Brown's shipyard, the Turner asbestos factory (three bombs had hit it, and two had detonated: it would take 91 Bomb Disposal Squad officers over a fortnight to locate and deactivate the third), the Rothesay Dock – all struck. Two ships – colliers, the *Clermiston* and the *Belhaven* – had been hit there: the *Belhaven* sunk and the *Clermiston* so eviscerated by fire she was but fit for scrap. 'Burning and blasted houses,' laments Jeffrey, 'smouldered in Parkhall, Radnor Park, Kilbowie and along Dumbarton Road. Rubble, slates, broken furniture and glass were everywhere and corpses lay in the street.'

'Right from Second Avenue right up to Radnor Street,' Mrs Richardson would tell Billy Kay in 1981, 'all these houses were down, and it really was full of people lying about. Sometimes you seen just trouser legs or legs or arms – and as you went up Kilbowie Road, you know, the bombs had fell there and it was wee tram cars used to run up there and the tram lines were up, you know, like a jigsaw. And then, right along Crown Avenue, I think there were about three closes left in Crown Avenue standing, the same down Second Avenue, just two closes left. And you think back – "Did you come through that or did you not?"'

James Barclay, a 12-year-old boy at 36 Bannerman Street, remembers the drama of the night before – how he proudly remarked to his mother that, by the peculiar drone, the aircraft materialising above were definitely German, not thinking how much it would upset her; screaming women who had to be dragged away from tenements to safety as their life-savings burned; his father and a neighbour scurrying to smother an incendiary bomb that had landed in the lobby; the local ARP warden – Jimmy Christie – being helped into the close, his chest bleeding with shrapnel. In the morning – and he has drawn a little map, seven decades on – every other tenement on Bannerman Street seemed to have come down. His cousins and their parents at No. 34 had only the clothes they were wearing. The entire gable at No. 45 had disintegrated, 'and you could see the . . . ranges of all the kitchens with all the pots still lying on the cookers'.

It was, Mr Bain told Billy Kay, 'like a nightmare. There was buildings still burning; there was masonry, huge sandstone slabs, you know, had fallen down after the fire. The whole place was really in a turmoil. It's just the look on the people's faces, the lost look, you know, really lost.' Beyond grief, pain and fear, everyone recalls that sense of dislocation – rising to the day in a town where they could scarcely find their bearings. 'It is a traumatic experience,' mused Willie Green, 'you know, because you see the town you've lived with disappearing. In Scotland I think this is the only place . . . a whole community you knew and grew up in, things that you'd known all your life, suddenly disappeared.'

MacPhail's account of the scene this Friday morning is as bleak as it is characteristically restrained.

The Pattison Street survivors and others all over Clydebank, many of them now homeless, emerged from their shelters to see the town shattered and burning. Tenement buildings were gaping open as if a huge knife had slashed off one side; and at piles of debris rescue parties were already working to extricate the living and the dead. Almost every road was impassable at one point or another; the Fleming family from Cedar Avenue, like many others in Dalmuir West who had lost their homes, made their way to the Town Hall by Mountblow Road, the

Boulevard and Kilbowie Road, where the water mains had been damaged by a direct hit and the tram rails reared up to the sky in distorted shapes. The Watsons from Pattison Street, on their way up to Radnor Street to see about a relative there, saw the bodies of the killed people, covered in blankets and laid out along the pavement in Second Avenue as they passed along . . .

In the Control Centre, exhausted Clydebank officials took anxious stock of the position, even as pitiless officials from Edinburgh bore down on them in a spirit of criticism rather than support.

There were desperate things which had simultaneously to be addressed. The ongoing fires had to be fought. Somehow, besides, the thousands of dislocated, wandering townsfolk had to be helped in their immediate needs – food; shelter; clothing; accommodation – and, though neither Kelly or Hastings was at all eager to encourage 'trekking' or organise an evacuation, they already knew Bankies were clearing out of the town on an enormous scale. Rescue endeavours had to continue unceasingly, with dozens of people still trapped or buried amidst the ruins of their town.

Whatever strictures might have been levelled, especially, at Clydebank's firefighting endeavours the night before – and a less hasty assessment than that of Rosebery, Bilsland or Chadwick would take a fairer view of their impossible position under such concentrated assault: Bilsland himself would eventually concede that 'even with a perfect organisation (which Clydebank was far from having) the damage from fire would have been extensive,' – the town's measures to deal with immediate human needs on Friday were surprisingly effective. That reflected thorough local planning in the months preceding and was all the more remarkable considering the necessity in many instances now to improvise, with so many lost halls and venues.

Ten 'Rest Centres' had been prepared: two had not survived the night and a third was so close to continued blazes as to be unusable. Numbed townsfolk rapidly converged on those open and operating, and on Clydebank Town Hall itself. Volunteers – a couple of local ministers, an official from the Public Assistance Board and various public-spirited ladies and youths – managed with speed to organise at least minimal catering: tea with bread and margarine. Mobile canteens were summoned to Clydebank, or trundled rapidly in of their own initiative, many manned by the Women's Voluntary Service and coming from Glasgow, Stirling and still further afield. The armed services in turn took a little longer, but by evening had come up trumps: assorted military kitchens were erected in Clydebank, – 'soup and milk puddings,' notes MacPhail, 'hot and of good quality, arrived in containers, and everyone seemed to get something to eat.'

As a near-local – a Dumbarton lad of Lewis parentage; his family would themselves be bombed out of Dumbarton in May – Iain MacPhail was, in 1974, too tactful to point out some weaknesses in the relief operation. Andrew Jeffrey goes too far in the opposite direction, asserting that the rest centre effort 'collapsed completely', and that such 'was the immediate ferocity of the raid that not one of the volunteers turned up for duty'. He is on firmer ground in arguing that locally recruited helpers 'were always going to be torn between care of the homeless and concern for their own families. The service really only ever worked well when staffed by volunteers drawn from outwith the immediate area under attack. When forty WVS volunteers were drafted into Clydebank from Glasgow and Giffnock on the Friday, the service began to operate more effectively.'

Bureaucratic and officious as it might have seemed, there was an urgent need to register everyone who turned up seeking help or direction, so that authorities could assess the scale of need and make more permanent arrangements for abode. Many local refugees had lost important papers – National Identity cards, or food-ration coupons – and Ministry of Food officials soon converged on Clydebank too, to issue emergency cards. Most of the form-filling and box-ticking was done by local teachers, who had in most instances the benefit of local knowledge; they also – in shades of their day-job – doled out little bottles of fresh milk.

But no one had anticipated the scale of the damage to the town or the sheer weight of human numbers. One 'Rest Centre' – the Scout Hall on South Douglas Street – had been equipped to help and accommodate 150 people. By Friday evening, nearly 400 jammed into the little place; on Saturday, almost twice that again. The scale of the crisis was only just beginning to dawn on Kelly and Hastings: so extensive was the damage to their town that, of its 47,000 population, 35,000 were by Friday afternoon already homeless. Even when homes were smashed about and salvageable, new and seemingly trivial problems could break morale, as Michael Burleigh writes in the German civilian context. 'After a major raid, public transport was inoperative, factories and workshops were covered with dust and rubble, there was no water to wash or shave with, or electricity or gas for cooking, heat or light, and something as commonplace as a plate or spoon became a cherished possession . . .'

Clydebank was not just blitzed: great tracts of it had been pulverised, or incinerated, or both. Take the problems caused by just one bomb: the blast on Kilbowie Road, just north of its junction with Montrose Street, which had tossed William Smillie over a wall like a rag doll and smashed the town's biggest water main. Daybreak revealed a crater 30 feet wide and 12 feet deep. The explosion had also burst the gas main and a sewer, and spectacular photographs survive of the contorted tram rails, curled up and high like so much spaghetti. Repair squads from Dumbarton and Glasgow soon made a start on fixing the damage, but were rocked by a second explosion – a delayed-action bomb, from a flaming property nearby – which showered them all in painful debris. By late afternoon they had only been able to restore a partial water supply, too filthy to be of anything but industrial use. (Still another delayed-action bomb would detonate on Sunday, further down Kilbowie Road, and burst the mains yet again.) For days to come, 'bowsers' – mobile water tankers – had to meet the needs of most Bankies and, for weeks

Above. Striking shipyard 'apprentices', Clydebank, late 1930s. Most of these young men would in fact have been skilled, time-served tradesmen kept deliberately on apprentice wages. Their shabby respectability is evident, and still more their cheerfulness – and how thin they are, and how small. (By James Russell, Scottish Ethnological Archive)

Left. A majestic 1936 photograph of the *Queen Mary* – fitted out, complete, and at last leaving her birthplace under her own power, dwarfing all around her. (National Archives of Scotland)

Right. Jim MacKinven and his father, Peter, around 1939. (Miss Catherine Ritchie, Carradale)

Below. A Glasgow tenement back-court early in the Second World War, complete with communal brick bomb-shelters. Often shoddily built, they offered no defence against a direct hit or even a parachute-mine at close range, and proved – at Clydebank and Scotstoun and elsewhere – veritable death traps. (Glasgow City Council)

Above. Spirits undaunted: women and children queuing exuberantly for coke at the Tradeston gas-works, Glasgow, during the war – prepared and irrepressible.

Left. Clydebank from the air, as surveyed – in chilling detail – by the Luftwaffe, only months before the assault of 13 March 1941. The assorted war-industries are naturally identified. (West Dunbartonshire Council)

Glasgow-Clydebank

Schiffswerft John Brown und Co.

Clydebank

Renfrew

Clyde

An exhausted fireman at Clydebank, March 1941. Colleagues in the distance are hosing down the gutted homes of Brown's Buildings. Many of these men went two or even three days without sleep. And some died. (West Dunbartonshire Council)

'Trekking' – families quietly, implacably fleeing Radnor Street and what had been their Clydebank townscape. That pram probably holds all the couple now owned in the world. Many others survived with only the clothes they stood in. All visitors and officials were astonished by the unwavering, dignified discipline of Clydebank people. (West Dunbartonshire Council)

An iconic image of Clydebank, 1941 – ARP Warden John Stewart bearing a little boy to safety.
(West Dunbartonshire Council)

Bombs fell without regard for class, income or residence – this had been a comfortable, white-collar home on Clydebank's leafy Park Road. (West Dunbartonshire Council)

Just one stretch of Kilbowie Road, some days after the bombing. The bent, warped, buckled things in the mid-distance had been tramlines. (West Dunbartonshire Council)

Queuing for transport out of the smouldering town: Whitecrook Street, March 1941. (West Dunbartonshire Council)

The mass-funeral at Dalnottar Cemetery, Monday 17 March 1941. Tom Johnston, Secretary of State for Scotland, stands at the left-hand edge of the picture, bareheaded, dark overcoat, head bowed. The short, hatless man seen, grim-faced, behind the officiating minister is Sir Steven Bilsland. The horror of the young clergy is evident; and the grim resolve of the grave-digger. The heavily censored photograph gives away nothing of the sheer size of this trench or the number of bodies — laid to rest only in cheap bedsheets, tied with common household string. (West Dunbartonshire Council)

Indefatigable and enduring: the great Singer's Tower and Clock, glimpsed from a wrecked tenement kitchen. It was torn down ruthlessly by the American owners in 1963, deaf to all Clydebank entreaty – an outrage the town has never forgiven. (West Dunbartonshire Council)

afterwards and even after supplies from this main were restored, the water was not deemed safe to drink without double-chlorination and boiling.

Food, too, was a problem; shops had simply ceased to function. On devastated Second Avenue, the two SCWS stores had been quite demolished, save for one forlorn wall with a barred window and a potato bunker. No fewer than 38 of the little stores owned and run by the Clydebank Co-operative Society had been flattened; in all Radnor Park, only one shop of any description survived. Military endeavours to prepare hot, filling fare, as we have seen, meant much: by one o'clock on Friday afternoon, Andrew Jeffrey asserts that some 4,000 meals had been brought into Clydebank by road.

And, besides, there was electricity, or the near-total lack of it. That Friday afternoon brought too, into Clydebank, 6,000 matches and a mighty 2 tons of candles. The authorities also – in a glimpse into the comforts of an age and a rare spark of earthy humanity in officialdom – thoughtfully delivered 15 lb of tobacco and 70,000 cigarettes.

Sir Stephen Bilsland had by now set up a second high camp for bossiness in the town: an 'Advanced District Control' headquarters, in Clydebank Police Station. He had additionally given orders to organise still another, an 'Administrative Centre', to make firm arrangements for all the homeless. As men of his class do, he looked for its natural leaders to Edinburgh, and even by eleven o'clock minor eminences of the National Council for Social Service had reached Clydebank. But the first appointed venue commandeered for their exertions – the town's Pavilion Theatre on Kilbowie Road (and, as MacPhail tartly points out, it was really a music-hall-cum-cinema) – was scarcely suitable: it was blacked-out like the grimmest of convents and (most ordinary Scots could have pointed this out to Sir Stephen, evidently no patron of popular entertainment) had besides fixed tip-up seats and a sloping floor. All that could immediately be put to use was an upstairs corridor, which was soon choked with townsfolk queuing – this was a day of queues – for billeting certificates, travel vouchers and other bits of paper deemed essential from the harried clerks.

Within hours it was decided instead to use the West Church hall, crowded as it was: the Public Assistance Board and the Ministry of Pensions already reigned in pomp there. As if there were not enough government in Clydebank already, the Ministry of Information turned up besides in grating loudspeaker vans, and toured the streets to summon the people, who soon flocked to the Administrative Centre in great numbers.

Yet megaphone vans spoke, it seems, with forked tongue, inevitable during Friday's bureaucratic confusion and with continued doubt as to who was actually in charge. 'Loudspeakers blared out telling everyone to go to the Town Hall as quickly as possible and to take what food and clothing they could carry,' Anne McGuigan Curry would remember in 1986. 'When we got there, masses of people jammed the roadway, trying to get on to the buses, pushing and being pushed, not caring where they were going as long as it was out of Clydebank before the Luftwaffe returned.'

In perhaps the understatement of 1974, Iain MacPhail suggests that 'it is doubtful whether the opening of the Administrative Centre improved matters for the bombed-out people in the Rest Centre or for the burgh officials, as it led to a duplication of efforts.' It certainly became difficult to control the crowds, and a turf war broke out at one heated meeting between the District Commissioner's representative, a Mr Sillers (Sir Stephen was too important, or too self-protective, to risk such bruising encounters himself.), A.M. Struthers of the National Council of Social Service and W. Ballantine of the Ministry of Information. MacPhail quotes Struthers' account of the row and, while it is angry and more than pompous, it does give insight into the mentality of many high officials in Britain in the Second World War and even at the heart of immediate human tragedy:

> When we asked for definite information on the questions being asked, he (Sillers) waved a copy of the Department of Health pamphlet, 'Information for the Homeless,' and said, 'It's all here.' This left Ballantine speechless. He next wanted to know why we were setting up an Administrative Centre. It was explained to him that the decision was the District Commissioner's and not ours. We were merely trying to be helpful in a very difficult situation for everyone . . . There was a similar pointless discussion with Sillers on the transport of the homeless out of Clydebank that night. The reports from the Rest Centres, as well as our own observations, indicated that there was anxiety among homeless people. We wanted Sillers to take action to ensure that the District Commissioner's decision was carried out, but he just sat, a perfect example of the complacent official who regards voluntary social service workers as busybodies who should mind their own business.

As MacPhail very properly adds, most of the Clydebank Burgh officials, who had been up all night, were 'all but dropping on their feet – the Town Clerk, the Sanitary Inspector, the Burgh Surveyor, the Fire Master, the Public Assistance Officer, all desperately coping with a situation unparalleled in their professional lives. Actually, many of the problems confronting Struthers in the Administrative Centre in Kilbowie Road were already being dealt with by burgh officials in the Rest Centres . . .' The ineptitude of all this can be traced to the central assumptions of government in civil-defence planning: that it would be dealing with death from terror-bombing on an enormous scale, not really rather limited casualties followed by the untold and complex needs of thousands of homeless, hungry, frightened survivors.

And all the while, as help and supplies streamed in, Bankies streamed out. By late afternoon 'several thousands (the number is put between 2,000 and 10,000 and no check was made at the time) were leaving Clydebank,' MacPhail would write in 1974, 'or being evacuated, some trekking out of the town on foot, all their worldly goods in a pram or a "bogey", and others in buses after waiting for hours in queues.'

The bombing through Thursday night had killed some 480 residents; the attack to come within hours, scarcely less ferocious, slew but 50. All through Friday, Clydebank remorselessly emptied; far from striving to stem this undesirable 'trekking', the authorities now quietly welcomed it, and officers and commanders here and there tried now to help. The seriously injured were in any event borne continually out of town, by all available transport, to infirmaries here and there; relatives naturally wished to follow them. Clydebank was a town, officially, of some 47,000 people by the last census a decade earlier. Between war service, movement and the booming employment the number in March 1941 was probably much larger, but, by nightfall on Friday, it has been reliably reckoned only 2,000 remained, the mass of those men of working age.

There are still many alive in Glasgow – especially in Scotstoun and Yoker – who remember the long, straggling lines of shocked humanity tramping eastwards, out of their little town and into the city. 'Shocked and bewildered survivors,' says Jeffrey, 'shambled their way to safety. Their faces were caked with plaster-dust and soot and many were still in their nightclothes.' The psychic wound of this experience – residents of a proud little town walking east in disarray to cast themselves on the mercy of the great city they had long resisted and resented – went deep indeed. Cuthbert Douse was still shaken by the gruesome, finger-ripping rescue of his grandmother. He now managed with a few friends to cajole a lift by car into posh Hillhead, grubby as they were, and their reception still stung when he was interviewed many years later for the Channel 4 documentary, A *People's War*. 'I'll never forget the amazed expressions of the people there. They were only five miles from Clydebank and they had seen the flames, yet they looked at us as if we were a band of tinkers arriving from a holocaust . . .'

And there are photographs of other desolate little groups all about Clydebank that day, waiting for transport, or at least for direction, and clutching what they had chosen to salvage – some cherished ornament; a canary or budgerigar in its cage; a prized fur coat.

But they went in the other direction too. Kathleen Ritchie was a 17-year-old senior pupil at Dumbarton Academy and, with her family, had huddled anxiously in the kitchen, camping down with blankets and pillows and taking care to close the shutters inside the windows.

I do not know at what point during that night we ventured out and saw the flames. The sight of that vast, flaring noisy sky was beautiful, dramatic and utterly, shockingly horrifying. Some conception of what such a sight meant in terms of death, destruction, pain, suffering, bereavement and loss would gradually be borne in upon us. But not yet. We were witnessing something far too terrible for the human mind to accept.

Morning came eventually and with it the all-clear. Weather-wise it was a perfect spring morning but the sky was covered with a thick pall of heavy, black smoke from burning oil, so that we were in semi-darkness.

We checked round our neighbours. A friend came for me and we went to school. In front of Dumbarton Academy was, or is, a large area of common ground, known simply as the Common, and we were amazed to see that this was crowded with people.

As we approached we saw that they were dusty, dirty and dishevelled and many were only in their nightclothes. Some had a few belongings. Many had nothing. They were very quiet, not speaking or crying or complaining. They just seemed stunned. They had come there to the Common from Clydebank, but I'm sure most of them knew not how.

The school was abuzz with relief activity and Kathleen and many of her classmates were shortly lent bicycles and sent to a primary school in Vale of Leven – one of the many hastily improvised rest centres – and spent that day serving soup and meals and tea.

Later, we would hear more and see more and begin to understand more about what had happened in Clydebank. Not, however, from any of our Clydebank High classmates. Weeks later, we would perhaps hear of this one living with an aunt in Inverness, or that one in a croft in Skye, but most of us never saw any of them again.

The broader experience of evacuees we shall yet consider; we can sketch something of their flight. Again, we meet Dunbartonshire's formidable chief constable, A.J. McIntosh. The sirens had already sounded on Friday evening when, making for the shaken and debris-strewn Town Hall, he found 500 women and children still waiting to be evacuated in a building that could well stop yet more German bombs within the hour. McIntosh grabbed a telephone – wondrously, this instrument was working – and called the Scottish Motor Transport depot in Old Kilpatrick. His instruction was emphatic: the duty inspector was to send all the buses he could to Clydebank Town Hall. The buses duly arrived; the anxious folk, with cases and bundles, filed quickly aboard. Drivers wanted to know where they should go. 'The Vale of Leven,' said McIntosh briskly, 'or anywhere you can think of.'

Buses continued shuttling back and forth with brave drivers at the helm, westwards to Dumbarton or Helensburgh or the 'Little Moscows' of the Vale of Leven, like Alexandria or Renton; or east to, say, Milngavie, Bearsden or Kirkintilloch – all localities still within the bounds of Dunbartonshire County Council. Yet the tide from Clydebank was such that rest centres everywhere within its bounds were quickly overwhelmed. Conditions, James Hastings would later admit, 'were terrible for a while'. There were problems, at once petty and immediate, no one had foreseen – inevitable, in hindsight, when practically every position of responsibility in the long months of civil-defence organisation had been in the hands of mere men. For one, there was scarcely any baby food, nor had any been sent to the town; women were also clamouring for sanitary towels and, again, no one had thought to organise those either.

Mrs Richardson found herself a passenger in one convoy of buses, chugging east or west and at any price out of town even as the second raid began. 'We were leaving on buses, we didn't know what destination we were going to, we just got on the buses and we were going along Great Western Road and I think the Germans thought it was the Clyde – they mistook the Boulevard for the Clyde, and they were droppin' the bombs and the buses were rockin' backward and forward but the bus drivers still kept goin' till we got down and it was Bonhill we'd landed in.'

It was a pleasant, busy little quarter of the Vale of Leven. 'Well, when we landed in the church they supplied us with beds and blankets, beautiful blankets, and we were all lying around the whole church hall, up the centre. The older people, they put all the young ones down, sorted them in their beds, slept there all night, got up in the morning – we were taken to the barracks, down to Bonhill, and given breakfasts, and those that had to go to work were put on buses and that. We travelled like that all the time, up and down, and they couldn't do enough for us.'

There were other issues, too, at the back of everyone's mind – the mountain of dead bodies, collected or (for the most part) still to be gathered which, even in a chilly Scottish spring, would soon make things very unpleasant. There was concern, besides, about the lost, roaming and terrified domestic pets, hundreds themselves injured and suffering, most with paws already shredded by all that broken glass – yet which could quickly pose a public danger. And one all-consuming awareness underpinned the urgency of putting out fires and unearthing the living but entombed, and fuelled the brusque anger in high places about Clydebank's failed firefighting – that, on the pattern of the Blitz across Britain so far, a return of German bombers that night was all but certain; and all the ongoing, unmolested flames were so many welcome-lights for the enemy.

Little incidents served to lend these fraught hours of Friday daylight their own black humour. A councillor on the relevant committee hastened to check the state of the blasted library that morning, even though his own home had been destroyed. As he stepped fearfully through the vestibule, amidst dust and wreckage, he noticed a couple of books blown almost to the door. He stooped and lifted them. One was *A History of National Socialism,* by Konrad Heiden; the other was *Germany – The Last Four Years: An Independent Examination of the Results of National Socialism,* by 'Germanicus'. Another story, too, fast did the local rounds: the thrawn old man who, as the family had hastened for the shelter, turned back, insisting he had to fetch his false teeth. His son grabbed him back, hustling him along. 'Are ye daft? It's no pies they're droppin' . . .'

From Dumbarton, Fergus Roberts – town clerk of that municipality – had hurried through to Clydebank to see if he could give Henry Kelly any help, or at least some comradely consolation. The Town Hall was thick with dust and strewn with debris from the recent terrors, and Kelly was most emotional. He could say very little, but fumbled among the papers about him and wordlessly handled a pile of letters to Roberts. They were copies of those he had sent to Civil Defence headquarters in Edinburgh, begging for authority to buy many more fire-hoses, capped by a letter back blankly denying him permission.

James Hastings repaired to his own Clydebank lodgings on McGhee Street, in the blasted Kilbowie. Even houses relatively intact – like this one – had been weakened by blast: fallen ceilings, smashed windows, loosened roof-ties. Still, Hastings was determined to persuade his anxious landlady not to leave town; that everything would be all right and that the building was safe, and he was in the middle of kindly words to this effect when, as he would later tell Iain MacPhail, he leaned nonchalantly against the wall of the room they were in. It promptly collapsed.

All the while, the most pressing task continued of freeing those still entombed in the rubble of failed shelters and ruined homes, as those they struggled to reach – if conscious – ran an entire gamut of emotions, from extremes of terror to a weird, fateful serenity.

Kathleen McConnell twice related her own Clydebank Blitz ordeal, in a self-penned 1999 account and, if anything, a still more vivid 1981 interview (later published under pseudonym, at her insistence) with Billy Kay. On both occasions she lays before us – and with singular power – the extraordinary disorientation many others who survived entrapment in a steadily burning building could also recall, but few so neatly describe.

In March 1941, Kathleen was 12 years old, and the youngest of a family of five at 2 Napier Street. As most of her fellow pupils at Our Holy Redeemer's School were evacuated early in the war, the school remained closed and she had to travel to classes in Paisley – though teachers do not seem to have sympathised with the inevitable delays of a route by foot, tram and the Renfrew ferry. Her father was away in Campbeltown, serving with the Home Guard. Her brother Joe was studying to be a civil engineer, and supported himself in the process with an evening job at the Bank Cinema – a circumstance, this March night, that almost certainly saved his life.

The day, she would write, had

dawned like any other. Thirteen an unlucky number? It was for me! I was late for school that morning and had to pay the penalty by staying in at four o'clock to make up the time lost. It didn't bother me too much – there was a good film on at the La Scala and I was going there with my friend Chrissie. Little did I know what was in store for us.

The siren went about nine o'clock in the evening and at home my mother was in, my two sisters and myself and we thought, it was just another raid, you know, the sirens had gone before and nothing had ever happened. But before many minutes had passed, things began to fall down from the wall, glass splintering, and my mother decided that we'd better really go downstairs into the close.

We gathered our gas masks and dressed warmly. Mum carried her wee tin containing documents: birth lines, policies and the family photographs. We made our way to the close where the neighbours had gathered. We prayed the Rosary – how we prayed! By this time the noise was ferocious – shattering glass, the crumbling of baffle walls as they collapsed, incendiary bombs and the screech of ambulances as they went up and down the town.

And, talking in 1981:

> Oh dear, the noise was dreadful. I don't remember much until about midnight, it was well past bedtime of course and my mother put me down in a corner to sleep and she said that she was going out to the close for a breath of air and that was the last time I saw her.
>
> When I woke up I thought I was still in my bed and tried to, to turn over, but here the clothes seemed very, very tight somehow, you know how you pull? My hands were full of stones and they were hot at that. Oh, I knew there was something not right here and I shouted for my mother. Of course there was no answer. Then away down below me I heard my sister calling me and she told me that we had been hit by a landmine and that we were buried away and the building was on fire and she told me to shout as loudly as I could.
>
> I seemed to be sinking into unconsciousness, you know, off and on, but my sister made me come awake and we called out and called for help and I couldn't get my leg free, it was caught in one of those big girders and I was told later that every rope they put down burnt in front of their eyes. So I was going into unconsciousness until I heard Father White – one of the curates in the church at the time – and two men speaking, saying, 'Father, we'll break her legs if we pull her like this.' And he said – I remember his answer well – 'If she's to come out without her legs she'll have to come because the two of them will burn.'
>
> Well, when I heard that I'm telling you I fought like a tigress trying to free myself. Then I remember them pulling, pulling, pulling and with a final tug I came out . . .

Kathleen had been trapped by one of the steel braces in the hapless 'strutted close' shelter, whose efficacy – to say nothing of supposed 'baffle walls' that toppled obediently at the blast of the first nearby bomb – was so mocked in the reality of the Clydebank Blitz. Writing in 1999, she said candidly that it had not been the thought of roasting agonies or death itself that spurred her last frantic effort, rather, 'how could I play hockey, tennis, rounders without legs?' One rescuer, Mr McFadden, had managed to get a rope about her – probably in one of her bouts of unconsciousness – and she was hauled up, dangling in space, to their perilous perch in the ruin, where the priest embraced her and declared that Lily, her sister, could now be retrieved in turn – Kathleen's body had been blocking the way.

Kathleen McConnell even had sufficient spirits to act when Father White began to fret as to how she might now safely reach the pavement. There happened to be a soldier below. 'I'll take her, Father.' 'I'll jump, Father,' said Kathleen, and she did. 'By this time I didn't care – I just wanted away. I took one leap and was caught at the bottom by the soldier. We both laughed. I was safe at last!'

An appalled big brother quickly hosed her down with a stirrup pump. It was only then 'I realised that my good school uniform was singed with fire and I was saying, "Oh, how am I going to get this dry for school tomorrow?"'

So we were taken then to the Rest Centre in Elgin Street and that I'll never forget. The noise and the screams and the cries and in particular I remember my godmother who owned a wee sweetie shop at the corner of Napier Street, and the last I saw of her, her arm was severed from there – above the elbow – and the screams of her – and, even as a child, I'll, I'll always remember the silence when she died . . .

Kathleen's mother, Mary Kate, her brother Hugh and her sister Mary were dead too. The horror she had witnessed in that rest centre was repeated there and in others, many, many times. The air of unreality was such that – in a story that may be apocryphal – one badly injured old lady of 94, treated with whisky in lieu of morphine, immediately, deliriously concluded she was about to give birth to a baby.

Not all Clydebank's residents were sturdy working-class folk in crammed, less sturdy tenements: or the more fortunate still in good, 1930s council houses. The town had its limited professional and mercantile population as well, in villas and semi-detached dwellings of some comfort and pretension on its northern margins. But a private garage or a neatly trimmed privet hedge offered no immunity from the Luftwaffe, as Margaret Sinclair – now Mrs Forrest – could chronicle in 1999. Her father was a Home Guard officer-in-charge; her 12-year-old brother John was out on Thursday night at the Boys' Brigade, and 16-year-old Margaret and her 17-year-old brother Bill stayed in at their pleasant residence. Bill had just bathed and gone to bed when the sirens sounded, and – because of their relative comfort and prosperity – Margaret's account is all the more familiar, immediate and disturbing to our own soft generation.

Our house was a bungalow, but had a large head-height basement which had reinforced brick columns. My father thought we might be safer there than in an Anderson shelter in the garden, so part of it was made into a comfortable shelter. We had to go down the back steps of the house to reach the basement door and, just as we were about to do that, a terrible barrage of gunfire started and Mother felt it wasn't safe to go outside. My father had told us that, if at any time we couldn't make it to the shelter, to get under the dining-room table or under a bed. We quickly decided to go under a back bedroom bed, first me then Mother in the middle, then Bill. We had just been there a short time when we heard some explosions, then a loud whistling noise and a *whoosh* – then nothing.

It was 9.20 pm. I came to, hearing mother calling my name. Bill was also awake. It was pitch-dark. None of us could move. Mother said the explosions must have caused the ceiling to fall down and the legs to collapse with the weight. Little did we know then that the whole house was on top of us! Mother said if we all pushed hard together we might be able to move the bed, but it was impossible. We were trapped. Bill then said that he could move his right arm but he couldn't feel anything – there was nothing there. We could hear water gushing but didn't smell gas. We all realised by then that something more serious had happened.

Mother said if we all shouted together someone might hear us. This we did repeatedly but there was no reply. After a time we heard a voice shout, 'Is there anyone in there?' It was Mr Reid, the Air Raid Warden. When he heard our shouts in reply, he said he'd go and get help. It seemed ages before we heard voices calling to us – the rescue squad had arrived!

The Home Guards had been kept on stand-by during the raid. About 2 am, there was a lull in the bombing and my father decided that he and some of the men would check out the village and also find out if their families were all right. He found John safe in his friend's air raid shelter, then made his way home. As he got up the hill, he was aware of several vehicles and an ambulance ahead. Something had happened there, he thought. Then he saw that where his home had been was now a pile of rubble.

A bomb had fallen in the back garden. There was a crater thirty feet across and the house had collapsed like a pack of cards. Had we been in the basement or in the garden shelter, we would not have survived.

The rescue squad had been there some time and had managed to get mother out first, then me, and we were being attended by the ambulance men. My father helped to recover Bill who was found lying at the edge of the crater.

It was 2.30 am. We had been trapped for five hours. We were first of all taken to the temporary first-aid room set up in the Parish Church hall and seen by local doctor, Dr Anderson. Mother was able to walk and didn't appear to have any serious injuries apart from some lacerations (subsequently severe bruising came up all over her body) so she didn't go to hospital. Bill had back injuries and I had a broken pelvis and internal injuries. We were taken to the emergency wards opened at Robroyston hospital . . .

As Friday advanced, practical help in the outstanding – and, inevitably, more complicated – rescue operations came from an improbable quarter: some coal-miners from West Lothian. They were tough, wiry, resourceful, experienced in digging and tunnelling and the delicate parting of rubble, and many indeed veterans in underground rescue endeavours of their own. They seem to have hailed from Bathgate, and MacPhail has diverting detail of their attitude: they had turned up on the Friday to deal with the consequences of a particularly bad blast in Mountblow, but – like all rescue workers from outwith their burgh – were supposed to return to their own depots after 12 hours.

Yet Monday arose in West Lothian – perhaps even Tuesday – and there was no sign of these colliers; soon there was cross enquiry of Clydebank officials from their peers in West Lothian. The mystery seemed entire, until a clerk remembered seeing a neat tunnel in some wreckage near the canal bridge at Dalmuir, so professionally crafted he was sure it was miners' work. And indeed it was, and there they were found in a hut they had just erected (no less expertly) and having a quick brew of tea before diving into their next mission.

They had been toiling for days. They would return to Bathgate, they said pleasantly, if word came through that it itself had been bombed; for now, though, they would stay as long as they were needed in Clydebank.

'These miners had a different technique from the other rescue parties,' relates MacPhail, 'which generally tackled the rescue of buried people by standing on top of the debris and gradually throwing it off, whereas the miners constructed a little tunnel, about two feet high, from the street through the wall of the building and thereby got into the centre of the debris to the space where the people to be rescued were. One tunnel made by the miners was kept in being for some time as a kind of showpiece; and in the long run their method was recommended by the authorities in their manual of instruction.'

From her own experience in what, by virtue of its sustained bombardment over many weeks, was practically an expert role in the London Blitz, Celia Franklin has described grimly the realities of approaching a scene of domestic destruction.

The biggest problem when you got to a bombed house immediately afterwards was that there was such a cloud of dust that you couldn't see anything. You couldn't see the road even. You pushed your way through a choking cloud, this utter confusion of dust and silence. I would piece together what the people stumbling around told me.

You couldn't know how many were injured because – and this was new to us – people who are badly injured don't make any noise at all. The ones who are screaming are the ones who are just frightened or have grazed their knee or something. Screaming is almost always a sign that a person is basically okay. It was the silent injured that were the problem and there was no way of guessing how many there were. Places are terribly silent after a bomb.

Peter Lewis details what the aftermath of a recent blast was like. ARP workers and everyone else agreed the worst thing was the smell: 'the harsh, rank, raw smell which came from the dust of dissolved brickwork, masonry and joinery. John Strachey, an air-raid warden (later a minister in the post-war Labour government) wrote of it: "For several hours there was an acrid overtone from the high explosive which the bomb contained. Almost invariably, too, there was the mean little stink of domestic gas, seeping up from broken pipes. But the whole of the smell was greater than the sum of its parts. It was the smell of violent death itself."'

Even if people were for the most part uninjured and readily freed – a matter of shifting a beam or lifting some planks and furniture – there were other problems one might not expect, such as the near-impenetrable disguise of dust, filth and grime even when (like most ARP wardens, on a small local 'beat') you knew the casualties well. 'Endless confusion,' Strachey sighed, 'caused by the simple fact that it is usually impossible to recognise anyone without asking who they are.' Barbara Nixon, another veteran of the London ordeal, remembered one man, living but unconscious, so caked he 'looked like a terra-cotta statue, his face, his teeth, his hair . . . all a uniform brick colour'.

Bridget 'Bridy' McHard, reliving her ordeal again for Channel 4 in 1986, could relate to such experience after her own nightmare under a collapsed tenement. 'You came to and you drifted away again and you kept shouting, "Can anyone hear me?" and eventually I heard a voice saying, "We're getting to you, don't worry." I was pulled out by the legs backwards on my face and I actually thought I was in the dustbin. It looked like grey ash that you get out of a coal fire. My brother-in-law came up to me and kept asking my name. "Bridy," I said. "Do you not know me? I'm Bridy . . ."'

Many survivors of such attacks – indeed, the great majority – simply could not work out where they were on their own street, such was the obliteration or inversion of local geography, the dissolution of the familiar, the demolition of intimately known landmarks. Yet, as Lewis points out, 'under that debris there could well be survivors, buried but able to breathe – to be buried and not found was most people's greatest fear.

The rescue squads had a terrible but absorbing task. The only way to tunnel through the compound of rubble, broken furniture, rugs, linoleum, curtaining and crockery, all compressed into a sort of impenetrable pudding, was with their hands; they removed the debris by means of a chain of baskets. Every few minutes digging had to stop while everyone listened intently for the faint sound of voices or of knocking. Local air raid wardens tried to keep records of where in their houses people spent the night. But the rescue workers, mostly recruited from the building trade, became experts at knowing where to look for likely survivors in spaces under floors or in cellars. Bill Douglas, a structural engineer in the pre-war London County Council architect's department, was in charge of St Pancras rescue service. 'There were some patterns known as "V-shape collapse", where the floors had given way at either side and had pushed themselves into a V-shape. You knew you were much more likely to find people alive under the sloping floor. We tried to find places where the debris hadn't fallen and break through into any open space that we could find.'

Lewis also records that in the cities of England, at least, rescue workers 'regarded their work simply as a job – their pay was only £3 to £3 10s a week – and knocked off at the end of their shift, except when they knew a child was buried in the building. Then they would carry on desperately and continu-ously, no matter what the time. Sometimes they were angry to be relieved when they thought they had nearly reached someone; it was hard to leave before they could discover whether there really was someone at the end of the tunnel – alive.'

There is no evidence of such jobsworth attitudes in Clydebank. Most of the tales of the raid on Clydeside extend to the heroic and indeed the near-suicidal. In the immediate aftermath of the explosion at Yarrow's Shipyard, for instance, help was swift. A 'mobile unit' dashed from Knightswood Hospital within five minutes, and on arrival located nearly 200 men trapped in a basement below a 'massive area of wreckage', Andrew Jeffrey relates. Two determined young women – probationer-nurse Joan Anderson and staff-nurse May Stanley – crawled repeatedly through rubble and into this void to tend the hurt. At 01:31, early on Friday 14 March, alarmed colleagues saw a parachute-mine drifting down. One Home Guardsman simply threw Joan Anderson to the ground and flung himself over her. The blast smashed to pieces the yard's electrical and paint shops, and this soldier was injured. Anderson, shaken but resolute, worked on. In a later report, Dr A.S. McGregor described the performance of Anderson and Stanley as 'outstanding . . . the two continued to give succour to the wounded under difficult conditions from midnight until the early morning.'

At one point, Joan Anderson had to be held by the ankles as she fought again into the wreckage. In this Yarrow's disaster, 67 men died and over 80 were injured; most had to be freed by cutting-tools, in the uncertain light of handheld torches. There are, though disturbing tales of dilatory efforts at rescue elsewhere in Glasgow, as we shall see.

Reflecting on rescue-crews in Clydebank, MacPhail records there were eight of them – four full-time and waged. This proved, of course, not nearly enough for events, and even before midnight on Thursday 13 March, just before the telephones failed, the Control Centre had begged eight more units from Dumbarton. At half past three in the morning, they had beseeched another eight from District Headquarters in Glasgow. They would again be cast on Glasgow's mercies in the raid to come: 18 would arrive from the city, well before dawn, on Saturday 15 March. 'The work of these rescue parties was stated in an official report to be beyond all praise,' chronicles MacPhail. 'As far as can be ascertained, they managed to relieve all those trapped alive in buildings except where they were forced to abandon their task because of fire. One of the difficulties which faced them and which led sometimes to a loss of valuable time was the uncertainty of neighbours as to whether people were trapped or not.'

Some of the local crews were on duty – continuously – for three days: two of the foremen would be decorated with the George Medal, and two others the OBE. One – a volunteer, James Gray – arrived at a blasted tenement where a young woman was trapped in the basement. He tunnelled laboriously down to her, as fire broke out once and twice. Slowly, slowly, he jacked up and braced groaning joists as he advanced. It took him, in all, nine hours, and he would allow no one to relieve him because of the extreme danger. He brought the girl out alive. John Stewart likewise burrowed into a blazing building and, by the narrowest of openings, brought a succession of terrified people out; before he could retrieve the very last, the walls tumbled down.

David Logan, one foreman of a rescue unit, spoke in 1974 of two young bus conductresses – fondly remembered 'clippies' – of about 20, who happened on one scene of horror and unhesitatingly volunteered to tend the hurt. Logan never learned their names. When a heavy bomb went off, 50 yards away, the girls were sent flying: but they rallied, arose, brushed themselves down and set to their nursing again. 'I hope their story will be printed and that they will read it to know that someone has not forgotten the glorious work they did that night. They are the unknown heroines of the Blitz.'

One might have thought, through all this long and fraught Friday, James Hastings had more than enough with which to contend in Clydebank. But, amidst a myriad of burdens, he had one pressing worry; all the fire engines standing about, still and inactive, for want of petrol, even as swathes of the town burned on. He tried to secure supplies from Glasgow, but as of mid-morning the telephone lines were still dead. Hastings – who seems not once to have slept since the morning of Thursday 13th – toured Clydebank to gain full understanding of the position and found he had in fact two problems: fire-crews locally unable to operate for want of fuel and fire-crews unable to enter Clydebank for all the blockages on the roads. The deputy town clerk saw that as something he could immediately address and gave orders for work to begin at once on removing rubble and obstructions from the main arteries: the Boulevard, Glasgow Road, Dumbarton Road and Kilbowie Road. Everyone agreed, and labour began.

Clydebank, though, was entirely without petrol – filling-stations bombed overnight or such supplies as had survived already drained by fleeing motorists and desperate emergency vehicles. So Hastings travelled to Glasgow as quickly as he could, to the Bothwell Street local headquarters of yet another wartime outfit, the Petroleum Supply Board.

But, when James Hastings arrived, it was that sacred ordinance of British office life: the lunch hour. The place was practically deserted, save for typists and the office-boy, who were kindly and alarmed but quite powerless to help him. They did find one official by telephone, who grandly told the deputy town clerk of blitzed Clydebank that he would have to come back in the afternoon – an example, Hastings lamented to MacPhail many years later, 'of the sort of peacetime easy-going attitude that I had experienced from most of the Government departments at the time'. He pleaded, argued, described in frantic detail just how grave the situation in his town was, and would remember 'a devilish barney' with this preposterous civil servant, but to no avail.

On his way into the city, though, Hastings had glimpsed a fuel depot at Port Dundas; he now repaired there and, with moral courage and on his own authority, the depot-manager readily assented to his pleas and assured him that a lorry-load of petrol would be in Clydebank 'as soon as he was'. By mid-afternoon, it was being distributed around fire engines, ambulances, trucks and lorries, and the cars of vital workers and the motorcycles of the runners and message-boys, and there was no fuel problem thereafter.

A sort of tired, smoky order seemed to be settling on the town. Roads were being cleared and the rest centres starting properly to work. As hundreds continued to leave Clydebank, the pressure on resources and personnel began to ease. Food, hot drinks and even a smoke were readily available, and the assorted branches of this and that social service getting on with their job. Few noticed – or, by now, really cared about – the five German reconnaissance craft which, through the hours of daylight, snuck over central Scotland (one as early as a quarter past eight in the morning, over Glasgow), peering and photographing and pondering. One of the 16 telephones in the Clydebank Control Room had even started, at least now and again, to work. With what seems astonishing discourtesy, when it rang at six in the evening Hastings had no chance to pick it up before it was grabbed by a Mr Goddard, one of Sir Steven Bilsland's staff. The conversation was most brief. Goddard replaced the handset and turned to Hastings. 'Well, they're coming back.' The 'beam' was on, he said. Though, technically, the news was confidential – only the responsible civil defence controllers of the targeted area (Kelly and Hastings, in this instance) were meant to be told – the bone-weary deputy town clerk had to make sensible arrangements to defend, as best he could, what remained of Clydebank from yet further devastation.

Hastings hurried to alert the assorted heads of services and made sure skeleton teams were kept at all times in the centre of town – vitally, those for firefighting and rescue – and sensibly sent the mass of available units to the edge of his burgh, at Duntocher and Hardgate, where their chances of being bombed themselves were much slimmer and from whence they could readily be summoned as emergencies arose.

So another armada of German aircraft – 203, this time – converged on Clydeside, and the sirens duly sounded at 8.40 p.m. Almost at once, a last and thin exodus began: the few left in town making for the surviving shelters, and a hardy core heading for the hills. It was another beautiful, moonlit night with a hint of frost.

The first bombs landed, at Drumchapel, practically on the dot of nine. Ten minutes later, Dalmuir, Radnor Park and Kilbowie were being hammered yet again.

The clarity of the air did not last long, for soon a full 10 oil tanks at the Admiralty depots in Dalmuir and Old Kilpatrick were ablaze. There was besides a light fog over industrial Scotland from the small hours: the Luftwaffe would later minute that this had interfered somewhat with their bombing, and the Royal Air Force state that it prevented the launch of any night fighters. The Germans, as was their wont, also put on record that they had dropped 231 tons of high-explosive bombs and 282 incendiary containers on Clydeside, this night of Friday 14 to Saturday 15 March. They besides tweaked the target area, extending it 2 kilometres to the south-west and with several aircraft expressly instructed to attack the Rolls-Royce factory at Hillington, south of the Clyde in West Renfrewshire.

In fact, that proved a largely futile exercise: damage to the Rolls-Royce works – this plant produced aircraft engines, not smooth limousines – was limited to a few minor fires, soon put out, and a burst water mains. And Rolls-Royce workers at Hillington seem to have been remarkably sophisticated, as Willie Green would tell Billy Kay:

That first night in the shelter . . . it was quite remarkable because we found out there was quite a number of talented people – girls, who were singing opera stuff, of that quality – it was unbelievable. And of course whenever a bomb went off there was hysterics, you know, the girls screaming and the men saying 'Everything's all right,' and then probably encouraging the girls to sing again. We had no sort of inclination what was going on upstairs . . .

Almost all the German aircraft, this night, came from the direction of the Netherlands and came over the British coast between Tynemouth and North Berwick, MacPhail details. A few flew from the Channel Islands, crossing Wales and coming over Scotland by the Galloway coast. One, inexplicably, went as far north as Aberfeldy – perhaps a little lost – and then turned south to come over Glasgow. Again, there would be a lull – between 2 a.m. and 3.30 a.m. – before a last flight of German bombers arrived from Denmark, and of these five converged on Glasgow and the Clyde.

There were fewer bombs this time, and there seems to have been somewhat less focus on Clydebank, but the bombs were for the most part bigger – 'large bombs and mines,' says Andrew Jeffrey, 'which, as one observer in Clydebank noted, "leave little or nothing of the smaller type of houses, and their occupants, which receive a direct hit. In the case of blocks of tenements or larger-type houses, they leave only a large heap of rubble."'

One of these mines, Iain MacPhail tells us, was a typical whopper, a cylinder 'of thin metal, about eight feet by three feet, suspended by parachutes,' and it landed around midnight outside the ARP depot on Dumbarton Road, as Constable Charles Hendry – that speedy Blitz despatch-rider – came along on his motorcycle. The explosion demolished buildings on both sides of the street, killing four people and flattening the depot: this in normal times had been a store for Clydebank Motors, and now kept sandbags, petrol supplies and so on. Hendry quickly grasped that folk were buried in its rubble, and was keenly aware of the petrol. He called a rescue squad and they set to urgent work: Hendry himself brought four men out of the heap of smoking stone alive, and carried one – a fellow policeman, Iain MacAulay – a full 300 yards to the police station at Hall Street. As the night wore on, Hendry, a sturdy Aberdonian, was more than once blown off his bicycle by bomb-blast. MacAulay himself had survived an explosion only the night before – the one that inhaled his Wolseley windscreen out, rather than pounding it in. He needed but a week to recover from his injuries now.

Sergeant John MacLeod was again out, and called to one 'incident' where a bedridden old man was trapped in his house by an unexploded bomb in the garden. The raid was still in full force, with incendiaries and mines dropping all around. MacLeod went calmly inside and bore the gentleman out and to safety. He then efficiently directed the evacuation of the area.

The new Clydebank High School on Janetta Street was still doing its unscheduled duty as a first aid post when a parachute-mine blew in walls at its west end. The blast, mercifully, was well away from the stretcher cases already borne in as the night's bombing raged; they were in the lobby. Then the wardens' post in Parkhall was hit. A rescue party hastened from Helensburgh, and brought everyone out; this explosion had killed 11 people. There was, though, a serious problem in the higher reaches of Parkhall – there was still no available water supply – and one ARP warden, Robert Elder, of Chestnut Drive, resorted to dramatic action to save his own home as the roof began to blaze: he begged an axe off an AFS fireman and hacked away the flaming beams. He had inexplicably forgotten the ample gallons of water in his own loft storage-tank – perhaps a less dramatic solution – but his house survived; the adjacent block burned to the ground.

If anything, many Bankies would afterwards maintain that this was a meaner, more vindictive raid. Some claimed to have witnessed German aircraft dive-bombing – one seemed determined, in its plunge, to obliterate the Town Hall, but pulled out at the last second and sailed along Dumbarton Road, scarcely higher than the rooftops. (The pilot may have mistaken the road for the Clyde and the building for a significant ship.) Far less chivalrous – and plucky – are reports of planes machine-gunning streets and buildings in Dalmuir, which had another appalling night: when the infant department at Dalmuir School was torched, a laconic superintendent rang the Control Centre from his first aid post. 'Some very heavy stuff is falling,' he drawled, 'and the building is on fire.' Later a shelter at 2 Castle Street, Dalmuir, took a direct hit, as did the post of the singularly unfortunate ARP warden at Parkhall. Bombs sank the 5,270-ton steamer *Trevarrack* in Dalmuir Basin, and among the many more Clydebank homes which had survived the first night of bombing, but not the second, was that of the town clerk, Henry Kelly. Two mines battered what remained of Radnor Park and Crown Avenue.

'The second night of the Blitz was terrifying,' Father Sheary would remember four decades later. 'As darkness fell, the whole of Singer's from Kilbowie Road right up to the boundary of St Stephen's – it was all wood, and it had been hit with the incendiaries the day before. During the daylight we didn't notice the fire, but as darkness came over it appeared more like the Inferno itself. The red blaze of the burning wood, and the darkness of the night . . .'

But Glasgow again endured in its turn, as Andrew Jeffrey details. Another warden's post, at Drumchapel, was early rendered *hors de combat* by German bombs. The squad repaired hastily to a private house on Garscadden Road. Less than an hour after the raid began, a delayed-action bomb from the same attack went off at Firdon Crescent, next to Drumchapel station. Parachute-mines exploded all over Knightswood: Kaystone Road, Alderman Road (by Chaplet Avenue) and on Lincoln Avenue, by its junction with Archerhill Road. Six people were killed this night in Knightswood, and six blocks of houses were demolished.

Great Western Road was closed at Drumry by another huge bomb – it left a yawning crater – and incendiaries fell everywhere. (James McLymont, who farmed at West Millichen, north of Maryhill, put one sourly out by wielding his shovel and tossing it into the dung-heap.) In Bridgeton, a district nurse –

Cecilia McGinty – had to leave a pregnant woman when, at a quarter to eleven, another mine destroyed a tenement on Allan Street, near Dalmarnock Road, and with two doctors she went bravely into the wreckage to help free a trapped 44-year-old man, Thomas Sherriff. His right leg was hopelessly trapped – mangled – between a kitchen range and a stone staircase. There was nothing they could do in the circumstances but amputate his right foot, in less than 40 minutes and by torchlight. Sherriff later died in hospital.

That mine caused damage over a wide area, notably to the unfortunate (and self-evidently vulnerable) spirit-works of the Methylating Company: the conflagration was such that it was later mentioned by more than one Luftwaffe pilot. (They would also attest that the flames from Clydeside – especially those blazing oil tanks – were of such intensity they could be seen from many miles away as the Germans approached over the Irish Sea.) Six hundred people in the vicinity of the Allan Street explosion lost their homes.

Near Glasgow's Maryhill Road, the first of two mines went off at 23:48 hours, in a ploughed field by Duncruin Street. Warden R. Scott had been walking down the main highway, and was sent flying. The blast badly damaged St Mary's School and blew the second mine into Kilmun Street tenements. Scott regained consciousness to find himself lying in the middle of the street and surrounded, inexplicably, by precious wares – packets of Cochrane's Tea. 'Well, for once,' he chuckled laughlessly, 'I don't need a ration-book . . .' There was a busy Auxiliary Fire Service post at St Mary's School, but everyone escaped without significant hurt. Two tenements on Kilmun Street, though, were completely destroyed; and we have already met little James McBride, who survived the devastation from this explosion in Kilmun Lane. Other homes in the area were demolished, or set afire. There were many ghastly sights to greet rescuers on the Kilmun Street scene: one was a dead young mother, still clutching her infant to her blood-spattered chest. The baby had no head. In all, more than a hundred homes had been destroyed by this prodigious explosion; some 250 rendered uninhabitable; a hundred shops in the locality damaged. Glass over a mile away was broken by the force of it.

Scott – showing the astonishing resilience of so many men on these nights, even after his experience – hastened to his appointed post at the corner of Maryhill Road and Lennox Street, and found dozens of folk milling about, trying to flee the area. He managed to impose calm and order, and directed people to the tram depot on Celtic Street: by 00:25 hours, a hundred would be sheltering in its inspection-pits. But there were still enough bewildered folk around to undertake essential emergency work in the aftermath of the explosion. Coolly, Scott commandeered a tram, piled as many as he could inside and drove it to the rest centre at Eastpark School on Avenue Park Street. The journey from Maryhill to Bilsland Street – as the bombing of Glasgow continued – was excessively interesting; at several points, 'I had to get out and remove shrapnel that blocked the rails.'

Back in Maryhill, and resorting to what he would later describe as 'much scrounging', Scott begged enough provisions to fuel a small canteen he got up within minutes for rescue workers, bomb survivors and the homeless, though years later he could not hide his irritation at the general lack of gratitude and the vocal criticism of the rescue services.

There was a final flurry of bombs, well into the small hours. Knightswood was hit yet again: Broadley Drive, near the heap that had been Bankhead School, and Alderman Road; Lochlibo Avenue; Fullwood Avenue. Broken gas mains blazed; two houses were destroyed. Another unexploded bomb was found and deactivated in the back garden of 2 Fereneze Crescent. Bombs fell vaguely about the Clyde: Lanark County Council's sewage works took a hit, and another exploded on the Westhorn playing fields. Shieldhall Wharf and Stephen's Shipyard were hit. Shieldhall Power Station survived with slight bomb damage, and two unexploded mines had to be dealt with at the Clydebridge Iron Works in Cambuslang.

Nor did Dumbarton escape. A mine burst on No. 5 berth in Denny's Shipyard, damaging the laid-down keels of two vessels under construction there. Another smashed through the yard's canteen roof, but chose not to go off, and was later defused. In all, 60 Dumbarton residents died in the raids of 13–15 March; 217 were seriously injured; and 188 lesser casualties were reported. Mrs Joan Baird, then a little girl and daughter of local ARP warden Thomas Thompson, recalls their Dumbarton experience soberly in a June 2010 letter:

The hills behind us were set ablaze as a decoy to lure the planes away from Dumbarton town, though a number of homes in Dumbarton/Glasgow Road were hit and a detached house just behind us on the Stirling Road. (It lay an empty shell for years and was always referred to as the bombed house.) Had it not been for the forethought of lighting the decoys, I'm sure our town would have been severely destroyed like Clydebank – we were indeed most fortunate. When being led out to the shelter that night, we had to stop at our door as right above us was a plane shooting tracer-bullets down the searchlight beams – these made a *putt! putt! putt!*-ing sound.

Our front and back door left unlocked, mother had always baked and prepared food; laid out on the table in the recess, for the wardens on duty and the neighbours. The remarkable part of this that her wedding china was used throughout, not a breakage and I still have it.

My mother left me in the shelter with neighbours, while she tackled fallen incendiaries; she would lift divots of grass and dance on it to prevent it bursting into flames. She could smell burning coming from a neighbour's house two doors down and with an ARP warden entered the house to see a sofa smouldering – they managed to douse it and took it outside; undetected, our whole block of houses would have gone up and attracted the foe. Then she heard a shout to lie flat on the ground as the local gas tank went up – she felt the blue flame go over her body. At this point she was ordered back to the shelter; on entering she hit her shin. This was to be her legacy – six months later while taking a bath her vein burst and erupted and she was taken to our local cottage hospital. Months she lay in the hospital. Mother suffered dreadful pain and though after many years the leg healed for a while, the damage done to the veins meant constant breakdown causing ulcers . . .

Other attacks in central Scotland seem more erratic, from disorientated or retreating German aircraft. A mine fell on Blanefield in Stirlingshire, injuring eleven and killing three. More dropped around Killearn, Drymen, Fintry and Baldernock. Two mines burst on Browntod Farm near Hamilton, Jeffrey details. Renfrewshire, he reports, took repeated though for the most part harmless hits: four bombs near Newton Mearns, one at Barrhead Station, on the East Renfrewshire Golf Course and five on assorted farms around Eaglesham. A mine exploded on Barrhead's Kelburne Street. Quite a few more bombs and mines fell around Neilston – four close to the volatile, to put it mildly, Royal Ordnance works at Bishopton. There were maritime alarms too. The tug *Warrior* was passing the mouth of the river, towing the steamer *Ferncourt*, at four in the morning when she set off a mine; her crew had hastily to beach her at Renfrew. No fewer than 27 bombs fell around Erskine Hospital – full of disabled Great War veterans – and the chain-ferry nearby across the Clyde. Incendiaries started a bad fire at the hospital, eventually quelled. In both raids, in total, a dozen died in Renfrewshire – a remarkably light escape after such bombardment – and 78 were injured, but only 15 seriously. Four bombs fell on the Isle of Bute, on high ground behind Rothesay, concludes Andrew Jeffrey in his fine summary of the night, 'and one fell three miles west of Sannox Bay on the Isle of Arran'.

The Luftwaffe were not quite through with the river and Firth of Clyde, or – quite – with our town; but their total war with Clydebank was over. The sun had now thoughts of rising to the east. The last German aircraft retreated over the towns and hills of Scotland, and to their bases over a cold and implacable sea.

8

'A PICTURE OF HEART-RENDING TRAGEDY ...'

He was John Bowman; he was a young soldier from Clydebank, and he had – this mid-March weekend in 1941 – just won 10 days' leave from his battalion of the Cameronian regiment, stationed in a sleepy village in Suffolk. 'Hoping to surprise my family by not telling them of my visit,' Bowman would write many years later, 'I set off on the long, tedious journey back to Clydebank. A train to Glasgow Central, then a bus for Clydebank at Waterloo Street. When I asked for a ticket to Radnor Street, I was told the bus only went as far as Bon Accord Street, a mile short of my destination. Supposing this to be a war-time restriction, I thought nothing more about it.'

He had been travelling for hours and hours, up the spine of Britain, on a slow, crowded and halting train, and he had not the faintest idea what had been going on and what had happened.

But, as he alighted from his bus and began the tramp up Dumbarton Road, this morning of Saturday 15th, he was struck by all the scars on the buildings he passed – 'shrapnel holes', he would later record: superficial damage from blast. And worse – much worse – was to open out before him:

To my horror, as I turned into Kilbowie Road, I could see the beginning of the devastation that had been wrought on Clydebank. There was a bomb crater and a piece of tram-rail suspended on the overhead tram wires and, further ahead, piles of still smouldering debris of collapsed tenement buildings. Parts of Bannerman Street had gone, but I did notice the building between Bannerman Street and Montrose Street was intact and the Co-op butcher's shop was open, wide open, as the windows had been blown out. The shop manager, whom I knew, called me in. He told me not to make for the family home in Church Street. It had been demolished by a bomb. He told me my family had all been killed.

Stunned, I hurried away. I was making for Parkhall where I had some friends. En route, I passed Church Street. There was utter dereliction. Where the house had been was a crater and scattered about were the remains of Anderson shelters. As a large family, we were allocated two shelters, which my father had dug into the garden as one long shelter. In Circular Road, I met a lady I knew and from her I got new information. She told me my family had not all been killed. She had seen one of my young sisters leaving the area on a lorry going to Garelochhead. When she heard I had been travelling for twenty-four hours, this lady took me in and gave me breakfast. Her advice was not to go to Parkhall, as most people had been evacuated from there. Instead she told me to visit the information centre in a church hall in Kilbowie Road.

There I was given the grim news: my mother, a sister and two brothers were dead; two sisters were in Lennox Castle Hospital; two brothers were in Larbert Hospital near Falkirk. They had no information regarding my father, so they told me that I should go to St James Church hall, which was being used as a mortuary, because I might be the one who had to identify my dead family,

In the hall, I was shocked and appalled at the sight before me. There were rows and rows of dead bodies, burnt, maimed and disfigured, lying there waiting to be identified. I left the hall unable to recognise anyone. Outside, to my huge relief, I met my father. He was limping badly, but he related the story of what had happened on Church Street.

When the air raid siren sounded, my mother and other members of the family were at a social in the church hall opposite the house. Along with a few other friends, they went into the shelter, nine adults and four children. My other sister, on seeing the cramped conditions, went into a neighbour's shelter and thus survived the carnage and escaped to Garelochhead. My other brother, Albert, aged eighteen, was an ARP warden and was patrolling the street. And my father had moved a few doors along the street to talk to a neighbour when the bomb fell. When the building collapsed, a door lifted and then landed on his foot. He still managed to make for the place where the shelter was. Then he found Albert, lying badly injured, with a heavy piece of concrete on top of him. He tried in vain to lift it, and Albert told him to look after the folk in the shelter. Together with a neighbour, my father spent the night, while the raid continued, digging in the debris, bringing out the casualties. All nine adults were killed and the four children were injured.

My father and I spent the next two nights sleeping alongside a number of other people left homeless until an uncle and aunt returned to their home in Dumbarton Road and invited us to stay with them. It was a welcome change from sleeping in the church hall in Renton.

I spent the remainder of my leave going to funerals of various friends killed in the Blitz and visiting others in different hospitals.

These then are the images and recollections which I have of the aftermath of the Clydebank Blitz, when a long-awaited ten days of being with family and friends became the worst ten days of my life.

Clydebank was rubble.

Dr J.P. McHutchinson, in charge of Dunbartonshire's education, sadly minuted, 'Clydebank has had a bad knock, probably severer than Coventry. The gaunt and stark burned-out tenements, the gutted council houses, and over all huge columns of black smoke from the oil tanks made a picture of heart-rending tragedy . . . No praise is too great for the people. Even among those who have lost their home or all their earthly possessions, there has been no complaining.'

Entire streets were gone; many houses simply flattened, or – still more terrifying – but a deep, smoking hole in the ground. It was manifest, wrote Lord Rosebery to Herbert Morrison, 'that Clydebank had suffered a major disaster. The first impression one gathers on entering the town is that great harm has been done. Behind the facade of the main street, especially on the north side and beyond the Town Hall, there is widespread havoc. In particular the houses in street after street of the Radnor Park district are completely gutted, with only the gables standing, charred and gaunt, while the White-crook, Kilbowie and Mountblow housing estates, though not touched by fire, were heavily damaged by high explosives and parachute mines.'

There had been 12,000 homes in Clydebank: after two nights of bombing, only seven were entirely undamaged. 4,300 had been destroyed, or so wrecked there was no hope of repair. Many more would take months to rebuild. As exhausted officials in the dusty Control Centre took stock on Saturday – they were all but sleepwalking by now – they faced a still vaster problem of homelessness, to say nothing of the continued need to fight fires and, against the clock, to rescue dozens trapped in the new wreckage and, for all they knew, dozens more who – living – had been entombed since the first assault of Heinkels and Junkers.

One great building, somehow, had survived, even close to that fearful and ongoing blaze in its own backyard: the Singer's Tower, its great clock still working, the structure dusted and sooted and chipped a little, but standing still, as if signifying Clydebank might live. Yet the 'infrastructure', as we would call it in a more pompous age, had all but collapsed. Clydebank was again without gas, water or power, and scarcely a telephone worked. Roads every-where were obstructed or blocked completely; an additional complication was a number of live but unexploded bombs: a few, perhaps defective, but many deliberately primed by the Germans with delayed-action fuses.

Some gas, at feeble pressure, would be moving again by Saturday night, and electricity too. Water was a much more serious problem. Barrels and barrels were, for now, begged from Glasgow. 'As the population was much reduced,' records MacPhail, 'it was found that three lorries, each with twelve casks of sixty gallons each, were sufficient.' These barrels presumably now enjoyed their second career after more exciting contents, for some people 'in the Whitecrook area thought they could detect a winey flavour in the water from the barrels but it still made good cups of tea'.

Helen Robertson, that formidable young ARP warden, would recall her concerns in 1999, after her husband and a friend had been briskly sent forth with kettles to find a drinkable supply. 'They went away round by the chapel and they found water running down the street. They managed to fill the two kettles. The danger was the clean water and the sewage was all mixed up in below the streets. And when they came back with this precious water, we started to boil it and then it just dawned on us the lavatory cisterns were all full. Now they were all iron, so there was always a thick covering of rust, but we boiled it anyway, and I don't know that anybody ever suffered from it. . . .'

'We all lost everything. There were very few people who had anything left. There was so much damage it was incredible,' a survivor sighed in 1986. Ruby Stewart had survived the collapse of her Anderson shelter; on Friday, she had left town on a coal wagon. 'You had to go. There was no water. The police were all in. There was an organisation but it was chaos.'

She would remember, lifelong, other details of that weekend in her town. How, apart from rock and rubble, the streets were thick with broken glass: 'you were walking on three or four layers. It was like walking on ice.' It was far worse for the many, many wandering refugees who had lost their boots and shoes. And the dead – bodies everywhere, and bits of body. There were three on her own street, each 'covered with a grey blanket. Our pavement was full of rubble, so you had to walk past these bodies and I'll always remember, one of them: there was a bare leg out of the blanket, I don't know whether of a man or a woman. These bodies lay there for a couple of days . . .'

The recovery and interment of the dead was just one of many desperate concerns for William Cunningham, Clydebank's sanitary inspector, who now feared an epidemic. The hecatomb of human remains apart – lying forlornly in rows in this and that hall, or much as they had fallen in the street, or pieces of people visible everywhere, or inert and discoloured limbs protruding from debris – there was the town's broken and fouled water supply. The lack of functioning lavatories – or the wholesale demolition of buildings with water-closets – presented other obvious problems; people had wretchedly to make shift for the needs of nature as they could, amidst ruins or behind some heap or wall or with pots and buckets in crowded, sweaty, fetid halls: the lack of privacy and dignity was especially distressing for women. The town, within hours, reeked of filth as well as dust, smoke, fumes and cordite; and with virtually no means of washing everyone soon stank.

Already, man's oldest and seemingly indefatigable foe – the rat – was visible, scurrying everywhere, taking unclean, defiling advantage. And there were all those wandering, terrified and increasingly feral cats and dogs, some already nibbling at dead human flesh, and this seems to have shaken Clydebank's all but broken leaders more than anything else. The suffering of animals can move men at a level the worst human anguish will not touch; but there was horror, besides, and even a primal terror of all those dogs, 'some of them hysterical', writes Iain MacPhail, 'roaming around where their houses had been and desperate for food and water . . . Some of them began to form packs and one police officer, who came upon a small pack hunting in the darkness round the new High School building in Janetta Street, part of which was in use as a mortuary, confessed that the sight gave him an eerie feeling.'

Such scenes – a catalogue of general ghastliness – made many feel as if, in what had been their bustling and well-loved town, they had in two nights and a day been blown back into some new Dark Age. The Scottish Society for

Prevention of Cruelty to Animals was contacted urgently on the Saturday, but it would be Tuesday before anything was done. An animal clinic was set up on Kilbowie Road and later an office, on Glasgow Road, for the reception of lost, abandoned or discarded pets. In the circumstances, the authorities could provide no more than euthanasia. Nearly 500 sad little animals were put to sleep at the Glasgow Road facility alone; meanwhile, armed men besides – in the grim situation – hunted about the broken town, shooting lost dogs on sight. By year's end, some 1,800 cats and dogs had been destroyed in Clydebank and, in the days immediately following the bombing, there was another surreal spectacle – pet birds, which had lived and flown, flitting about shrubs and trees in the open air. When James Hastings gently accompanied Henry Kelly to survey what remained of the town clerk's blitzed home at Dalmuir, he remembered for the rest of his life half a dozen canaries, hopping around their parked car and singing in the soft March sunshine.

Birds still caged seemed to accompany many Clydebank homeless as if they were a talisman for good, or something portable of lost domesticity – more canaries, budgerigars, parakeets in cages elegant or plain 'which remained with them wherever they went,' MacPhail would recall, 'to the Rest Centre in Clydebank, to the Rest Centre in the Vale of Leven or elsewhere. In Clyde Street School, Helensburgh, which was used as a Rest Centre for some time, Dr J.P. McHutchinson, Director of Education for the county, saw one man asleep on the floor with his parrot perched on his chest.'

Not all sought solace in the feathered friend. Mary Rodgers and her Highland mother had their own robust religion, but they were Bankies besides, able – even amidst this catastrophe – to hail the spirit of their people, as the trek from the town continued. 'After the raid,' Mary would tell Billy Kay 40 years later, 'there was always people passing our house because we lived on the main Kilbowie Road and people were going away out to the hills. This particular day there was this group and this man obviously had a wooden leg, and he had another leg, a spare leg, and he'd a walking stick. He stood and he took the other leg from under his arm and waved it to us and we thought, well, that man had the courage to wave a wooden leg to us and maybe in his simple way of waving to us it would give us courage. You cried and you laughed at the same time.

'Then another day we seen this group and they passed the window and there's this man carryin' a good-sized portrait of the Pope. And although we were Protestants, my mother started crying. She said to me in Gaelic, "His faith is so strong in that picture itself that that man feels that he'll be safe."' And, on this 1981 recording – and in that Glasgow Highland duality – Mrs Rodgers switches effortlessly from grating, glottal-stopped Clydeside drawl to the perfectly accented language of Eden, 'Tha an dochas lan air aige . . . Tha a chreidimh san dealbh ud cho laidir agus gu bheil an duin' ud a' faireachdainn gum bith e sabhailte.'

On Saturday afternoon, even as Kelly and Hastings and Cunningham – he was so overwhelmed, now, he was generously relieved the following day by

A.M. McConnell, sanitary inspector of Kilmarnock – fought to gain a grip on things, a solitary German aircraft flew high, high overhead. It was evidently there to assess the week's work, though the smoke and mirk over all Clydeside was such the crew could have seen little of value. The Germans would shortly record that improved anti-aircraft fire on Friday night had complicated the mission, though a much greater nuisance had been searchlights, 30 or 40 of them, making one vexing 'dome of light'. There was puzzling reference to barrage balloons over Clydeside – pilots reported 30 to 40 of them, between 3,000 and 10,000 feet above the ground, far more than had in fact been the case. But the entire absence of opposing fighters was highlighted with evident satisfaction.

Fires were still being fought all over Clydebank on Sabbath afternoon, by firefighters hauled in from a still wider Scottish field, including – Andrew Jeffrey notes – men from Dundee and Ayrshire. The authorities had even put crews in Newcastle and St Andrews on stand-by before the second German raid, though they were never called. At one point – reflecting the lessons learned since the first, and with, of course, more notice – 400 fire engines and over 4,000 men were simultaneously in action against the Clydebank flames.

Evacuation and flight from Clydebank, of necessity in a town where normal life could simply not function for the time being, continued all through Saturday 15 March, and for days thereafter. An Old Kilpatrick boy, Wilson Stewart, would in 1974 recall 'the seemingly endless stream of people from Clydebank, bound for Dumbarton and beyond, with belongings in prams, carts, barrows, or carried on the backs of old and young, fit and obviously unfit people'. More buses were organised and the mistakes and confusion which had to a degree botched transport operations on Friday – people gathered in church halls for conveyance that never came; the belief of some officials that every school in the burgh had been flattened, leading them to dismiss as unreliable reports of groups in this or that seat of learning awaiting help – were not now repeated.

The exodus was hastened by rumours that the local state of emergency was now such that the authorities were about to place all Clydebank under military rule; after two nights of being bombed, townsfolk had fearful visions of being shot. (The gunfire resounding from assorted, localised endeavours to eliminate wandering dogs can only have fed it.) Probably, too, with communications so compromised and with little access to radio, there were fears besides of imminent German invasion. But the steady emptying of Clydebank – partly by the general instinct to escape, partly by official endeavour – through Friday and the weekend was dramatic, as MacPhail details; and in many aspects would have life-changing consequences:

Approximately two hundred buses were used in a shuttle service to transport the homeless refugees of Clydebank – an estimated 7,000 to the Vale of Leven, 3,000 to Coatbridge, Airdrie and Hamilton; 1,500 to Paisley, Bearsden and

Milngavie; 2,500 to other parts of Renfrewshire, Lanarkshire and Dunbartonshire. According to the report of the Scottish Regional Commissioner for Civil
Defence, dated April 3rd, there were, in addition to the 3,000 who were
evacuated on the 14th and the 12,000 on the 15th, at least 25,000 homeless
who left of their own accord by the 15th, so that by evening probably over
40,000 (out of a population estimated at well over 50,000) had left the town.
The report added: 'At no point during the ordeal through which the town had
passed or afterwards was there any sign of panic; all accounts agree that public
morale was magnificent.'

In the confused situation, it was possible for families to be split up and sent to
widely-separated reception areas. For almost all who boarded the buses,
however, theirs was an unknown destination: it might be Helensburgh or
Bonhill or Kirkintilloch or Blantyre, and for some the whole course of their
future lives was decided by the bus they boarded on Saturday, March 15th,
1941, in Clydebank.

Inevitably, and with the best will in the world, the ad hoc arrangements for
feeding and accommodation at assorted rest centres buckled repeatedly under
such a tide of humanity – thousands and thousands and thousands of people,
in perhaps the greatest and certainly the quickest flight in all of Scotland's
history, many bereft of everything save the clothes they wore. Officials – most
of them already worn out by the horrors of the last 48 hours – had but scant
notice to make any arrangements, and the laborious and bossy arrangements
laid out at the beginning of the war for such civil emergency were upended by
events.

No one had anticipated the sheer scale of destruction in Clydebank, or its
considerable 1941 population: it had, after all, been an official 'evacuation'
area. And the designated 'reception' area in the county – leafy, seaside
Helensburgh – was all but full; to say nothing of the culture shock, as we
would now say, between the determined villa-dwelling gentility of its citizenry
and the practical denizens of Clydebank tenements. The only available space
was in the clotted little towns of the Vale of Leven – an officially 'neutral' area
and where government departments had never made any arrangements at all
for the accommodation of bombed-out refugees. 'Schools and halls could be,
and were, requisitioned,' MacPhail laments, 'but no one had considered, even
as a remote possibility, that large numbers of evacuees would sleep, eat and
live there for a few days, far less weeks. As a result, conditions of overcrowding, bad from the outset, became intolerable and almost unbearable.'

There were many decent, good-hearted volunteers, but scarcely any were
trained for the crisis now engulfing them. Many rest centres at first had no
equipment at all save cups – 100 each; some centres, by Saturday evening, were
jammed with folk in multiples of that figure. There was no cutlery, there was
no bedding, and in not a few a single toilet was all the available sanitation.
Bread and margarine were not hard to beg from horrified local residents,
moved by the plight unfolding before their eyes, but a range of ridiculous

government agencies had tediously to be lobbied and organised (with all the complexities of rationing) to win tardy supplies of milk and more substantial food. At the South Church in Bonhill – where 250 Bankies made as best a shift as they could – the failure of promised Co-op pies to arrive in time for dinner could have caused serious trouble: instead (and the restraint and forbearance of Clydebank folk in this and much else should still command our respect) it was the spark that launched those politically astute folk to set up an Evacuees' Committee, chaired by a Mrs Campbell of what had been 35 Chestnut Drive.

Apart from endless cups of tea, effective catering was long in the execution. At another Bonhill rest centre, sacks of carrots and turnips were generously delivered; unfortunately, there was no means of cooking them. Indeed, this was a widespread problem. Hundreds of folk had to endure most of Saturday with nothing save a slice of bread and nasty wartime margarine, the night before, to sustain them. Yet moving glimpses of human ingenuity and Scottish generosity have been recalled. At Renton Secondary School – still another rest centre – the headmaster, his wife and staff toiled through Saturday, making near-industrial quantities of hot tea. One teacher had somehow sourced carrots and potatoes, and with Clydebank ladies helping in the peeling, a basic but hot supper was soon in the making. Yet there were no dishes, no knives, no forks. So the older schoolchildren were sent about Renton to beg for the loan of utensils. They were back, almost within the hour, not just with enough for some 320 people but a fat parcel of sandwiches, labelled in a gentle hand, 'For the teachers'.

Teachers generally formed the backbone of relief, finding ingenious means to immediate needs. Science masters at one school warmed babies' bottles over Bunsen burners. (In Clydebank itself, one man was even seen heating milk for the same purpose over the glowing end of a near-exhausted incendiary bomb.) Other staff coped with dramas beyond normal chalk-and-tawse experience. How could one deal with dirty nappies, or the epileptic who had a violent fit in the middle of the night, or the children hysterical with nightmares? Where could one quickly find sanitary towels, or vast quantities of toilet paper? At the Clyde Street School in Helensburgh, one woman gave birth in the head-master's study. Everywhere, older schoolboys willingly helped to clear space, carrying desk after desk out of classrooms and halls. No one had expected so many imploring requests from the myopic to help in the repair of spectacles: hundreds of pairs had been broken or cracked in Clydebank's ordeal. Shops were quickly denuded of razor blades, shaving soap, toothpaste, collar studs, safety-pins and so on. There never seemed to be anything like enough towels, or enough food, and the lack of privacy steadily drove many to near-distraction, on top of anguish as to relatives and loved ones, unseen perhaps since Thursday and their whereabouts – or if they were alive or dead – as yet unknown.

In 1941 the 32-year-old Alastair Dunnett, a native of Kilmacolm in Renfrewshire, had temporarily abandoned journalism for a civil servant's existence in the Scottish Office, and he had some part, days after the

Clydebank calamity, in making arrangements (he asserts) for an important
visitor to the hammered town: Sir John Anderson, Home Secretary. Dunnett's
memories of the occasion give us something of the atmosphere; and of the
priorities of a natural bureaucrat.

> Much had gone wrong in the administration there because the children had
> come home from the first evacuation and they had to be gathered up again after
> the first night of the assault and sent by buses to destinations which no central
> body knew about, and parents were desperate to trace them. The bombing had
> missed the shipyards but the factories were out of commission and of the 6,000
> houses in Clydebank only six had escaped damage. Many of course were utterly
> demolished, and there was to be further devastation on the succeeding night. I
> commandeered a truck from somewhere and took one or two people up to
> Singer's factory where we walked into the deserted building and purloined ten
> typewriters from the desks of the typing pool along with masses of stationery
> and copying paper. Returning to the centre of the burgh to the more or less
> intact Town Hall, I sent a runner out to find volunteer typists and these girls sat
> at desks and typed out lists of children which were coming in from the
> evacuation centres, often written badly on paper stained with rain. These sheets
> were posted up all round the town giving the names of the children, their home
> addresses and the new address where they could be written to. The morale was
> good in that town. For example, cigarettes were already short, but on several
> successive days I passed a tobacconist's shop which had been blown apart with
> hundreds of packs of cigarettes spilled out on to the pavements and I never saw
> from day to day any indication that even one had been lifted. All this happened
> shortly after Coventry was badly bombed and I put to John Anderson the idea
> that if he would make a statement to the Press saying that, in his view,
> Clydebank had been worse hit than Coventry, it would do Clydebank a world
> of good. He agreed at once because this was his view anyway, and women went
> about the streets for the next day or two saying to each other with great
> satisfaction, 'They gien us worse than they gien Coventry.' Anderson was a
> pedantic fellow, and one of his senior officials told me that at a later stage in the
> war, when he was sitting at his desk as Home Secretary, news was brought to
> him that a courier carrying papers to some other ministry had been mugged and
> his briefcase stolen. Anderson folded his hands severely and instead of saying,
> 'Have they caught the fellow?' he boomed, 'Has the miscreant been appre-
> hended?'

Dunnett, who would later edit both the *Daily Record*, and, for perhaps
rather too long, *The Scotsman*, had a complacent streak. It is highly doubtful
in Clydebank – where there were hardly any women left and when it was
almost impossible to buy a loaf, far less a newspaper, or listen in domestic bliss
to the wireless – that many heard of Anderson's odd compliment; and while
everyone was impressed by the discipline and stoicism of the Bankies, stealing
there certainly was – mostly by organised parties from Glasgow and, in the

months ahead, workmen sent into the town to rebuild and repair. Nor can any aspect of his tale so far be corroborated; there is no evidence that Sir John Anderson (who, in any event, was no longer Home Secretary but Lord President of the Council) ever visited Clydebank; or made a public comment of that nature – nor did Churchill, nor any member of the Royal Family, come to the town. The Queen had never to look Radnor Park in the face.

'One of the tragedies, you know, was that there was a certain amount of looting,' Willie Green would tell Billy Kay. 'Yes, I've heard of people who got stuff stolen. Men were re-fixing the houses, you know, wee simple things were stolen, like the wee tumblers out o' Woolworths, the wee tumbler stands, the wee things that cost sixpence, things like that were all gettin' removed. It's surprisin', people'll take anything.' Eric Flack confirms he was 'told of Clydebank folk who were looting being set on by angry folk. Looting is not much talked of but was something which did take place. It was blamed on the "Glasgow workies" sent to clear the place up.'

And, from Sunday 16th onwards, to the quiet fury of the few remaining Bankies and the frustration of those trying to restore some civic order, great crowds turned up from Glasgow to gawp, 'much to the annoyance of police, soldiers, wardens and others on duty'. Soon vans were turning up, driven by men who claimed they had only come to help. It was impossible effectively to police the whole place, and these vultures were soon picking around the ruins of this home and that and making off with valuable materials, household items, little precious things and so on in great quantity. Even when such things were witnessed, confrontation was dangerous. A week after the attacks – after a day's work and having missed the last bus to her Balornock billet – 'E.L' took refuge for the night in her grandmother's empty home. 'Although most people had left Clydebank, there seemed to be a lot of people tramping about on the stairs. Suddenly the door burst open and three or four men came in and emptied the meter. As I cooried down under the quilt, I heard them say, "The last meter was more full."'

In Clydebank itself, there was by now pressure on anyone who had no job to do to get out. 'Anyone who stayed unless they were necessary was really a handicap,' Green would remember. But the provision in the town proper for essential workers and the distressed generally – compared to the clotted endeavours in the Vale of Leven – was remarkably good.

The Public Assistance officials were already organised in emergency aid – largely the distribution of meagre but important funds, for people who had lost everything and had not a penny in their pockets. When the clerks ran out of cash on Sunday 16th, £3,000 in £1 notes was brought from Glasgow within 2 hours. There was a prodigious effort to provide food, and all the agencies combined with a will, with important assistance from the armed forces and Glasgow Corporation. Hot meals cooked in the city were swept to Clydebank Town Hall, which became the main feeding centre not just for ARP wardens and others but anyone who came looking to be fed. The city's 'Domestic Science' teachers were soon orchestrated by a Miss Murray to cook even more.

Mobile canteens puttered round Clydebank; army field-kitchens were erected. Many – not least those engaged in some dreadful jobs after the bombing – would long recall how sumptuously (by the standard of post-war rationing and all sorts of shortages) they were fed, especially at the Town Hall, as wartime restrictions were for a few days sensibly lifted. 'The one bright spot in our lives – food galore and as much sugar as you wanted,' a Bankie would wistfully recall to Iain MacPhail.

When the Ministry of Food later backed out and the Town Council had to run this service themselves with much more limited fare and normal rationing (half a teaspoonful of sugar per cup of tea), there was widespread and rather unjust local anger, the Council taking the blame. But it is in the nature of people, amidst disaster and untold loss, to take unusual comfort in tiny things and something seemingly as petty as the desired sweetness in your beverage took on extraordinary importance. The folk of Clydebank never revolted wholesale, but there is certainly evidence at times of high tension, especially as they sensed that, for distant government, renewed war production was of much more account than the comfort of workers; or that the convenience of administrators seemed to dominate many official endeavours for aid.

The most serious incident was a consequence of well-meant but thoughtless organisation of the continued evacuation. It is an extraordinary feature of the Clydebank Blitz that, after what were by most criteria the most destructive raids anywhere in Britain throughout the Second World War (and the only true Blitz anywhere in Scotland), there was so little serious damage to the town's industries. It is still more remarkable that work in those places scarcely faltered, if for some weeks through cold, rain and discomfort, amidst shattered sheds and with rubble underfoot. Even as bus after bus ran out to the Vale of Leven with distressed Bankies, buses rumbled back in every morning with thousands of men from these seething rest centres to their duties at John Brown's, or Singers, or Beardmore's, or other engine rooms of the national struggle against the Third Reich.

Men without families, or who had managed to make private arrangements (with, for instance, relatives in the Hebrides, or Dunoon, or Rothesay, or Dumfries) hunkered down uncomplainingly in the most limited conditions – in the open wreckage of their own homes, or in what were little more than caves in the rubble, or in a corner of the yard where they worked. Some, for weeks on end, simply lived in the Old Kilpatrick Hills. (Many, especially during protracted unemployment in the 1930s, had taken avidly to hiking, climbing and camping; and many, of course, were veterans of the Great War, and knew how to rough it as required.) Some camped for the night on the Parkhall Golf Course, unshaken by the sight of the bomb craters all over it (including one on the eighteenth tee, as Andrew Jeffrey deliciously notes). And the 'apprentices' strike' died with the Blitz, with everyone hastening back to work on Monday even before shop stewards had time formally to abandon the action.

John Brown's were certainly desperate to recover their workforce: for some chaotic days, it has been calculated that two-thirds of its 10,000 employees had been scattered across Scotland. As was now evident from experience elsewhere in Britain, bombing – as long as it was not concentrated and sustained over weeks – did not break civilian morale; it actually inflamed it. So the authorities and the great mass of Bankies were united, for the most part, in determined fury to regroup, to regain some sort of normality, and as quickly as possible resume with a will the production and repair of ships, weapons and machinery.

For now, men all over town – if enough of the family home survived – tried to make at least one room habitable, brewing tea on the street if necessary over an open fire. And there was an impressive official effort to rebuild. Within days, over 1,000 workmen were drafted into Clydebank. As much usable material as possible – slates, timber, intact bricks or blocks – was systematically salvaged from wholly devastated property as possible, and applied to the healing of the reparable. Everywhere cables were replaced, broken pipes and mains repaired, telephone cables re-hung. Within a fortnight, an impressive 2,095 blasted Clydebank houses were fully fixed and fit for comfortable occupancy.

But family men tried naturally in the first battered days to stay near their wives and weans at this or that rest centre, or at least in daily touch with them, as official efforts to make more permanent living arrangements for their families continued. (Apart from anything else, there was mounting pressure to free up local schools and resume classes.) And soon many of these men were returning at the end of long, wearying shifts to find their wives and children had been borne away by a bus that afternoon, and to where nobody knew.

It was a genuine oversight by authority, but reflected an entire lack of common sense and human imagination. Everyone exploded, from the tired fitters and tradesmen to the remaining women and children scared of being removed without notice. Rumour abounded. A quickly convened group of evacuees (held, significantly, in the rooms of the local Communist Party) denied buses their passengers when such a fast flit was attempted by officials from the Rest Centre at the Vale of Leven Academy. Furious folk then quickly got up a march on Clydebank and several thousand people were halfway to the town to protest when Sir Steven Bilsland himself, whose alarm must have been serious, met them on the road to give iron-clad and emphatic assurance that families would not be divided. (He might have made an even better impression had he not turned up in his Rolls-Royce, addressing the proletariat from its immaculate upholstery.)

He had nevertheless acted quickly to defuse the situation and avert what could have been ugly scenes in the town itself. Emotion rapidly ebbed. Whitecrook School was quickly fitted out as a hostel for many of the male workers, and people began to make jokes about all those 'blitz bachelors'.

By the Tuesday after the raids, there were no fewer than 42 mobile canteens in Clydebank – according to MacPhail, these alone fed something between 15,000 and 20,000 people; and the communal meals at the Town Hall would continue for weeks thereafter. English servicemen and officials were singularly impressed by Glasgow's wrapped and ready-sliced loaves, almost unknown south of the border and which greatly eased the preparation of sandwiches. The National Council of Social Service deftly co-ordinated the donation of all sorts of good things: on Sunday 16th, stately Edinburgh ladies arrived with 300 tins of sardines.

Sir Steven Bilsland has not, so far, seemed a sympathetic figure, and no doubt he had his Colonel Blimp pomposities; but, as the emergency continued and he stayed in Clydebank for a full week, running his Advanced Head-quarters from a billiards-room above a police station in Hall Street, he won more and more respect.

Every morning, on the dot of nine, he held what was effectively a cabinet of all the regular officials, municipal or otherwise: the town clerks and the sanitary inspector were given the same weight as the princelings of the Ministry of Food, the Department of Health, the Scottish Office and so on. Sir Steven enforced immediate accountability and had no patience with waffle. He sided instinctively with Clydebank's leaders against strangling Civil Service regulations or requirements. He proved to be a wise leader, with sound instincts as to whose counsel was worth having. Sir Steven was a 'man in a million', someone – probably James Hastings – would later tell MacPhail. 'He was a very sympathetic listener, a man who made up his own mind and, having done so, he stood no nonsense from anyone.' Many believe that the tough old thing, with his Rolls-Royce and all, did more than any other single individual to get Clydebank – or a new, grieving, but roughly functioning sort of Clydebank – back on her feet within a matter of weeks.

For some days the hired crews, the West Lothian miners and assorted volunteers continued with rescue operations, but there had been far fewer people in the first place to be bombed and trapped in Clydebank on the Friday night, and as day succeeded day and no more were found alive things, inevitably, wound rapidly down. The effort was such in Clydebank, and waged so doughtily and with good local knowledge, that it is likely few, if any, died slowly, undiscovered, under the ruins of buildings.

Parts of Glasgow, it seems, were another story. On Wednesday 19 March, around eleven in the morning, a demolition squad from a local building firm – Samuel Allison & Company – pitched up amidst the smashed remnants of Peel Street, Partick, to start clearing the site. They were met by a distressed, incredulous part-time ARP warden, a Miss Wilson, who insisted that – nearly six days after the bombing – 20 to 30 of her neighbours were still missing; many must be trapped in the wreckage; some might well still be alive – and no one was doing a thing about it.

Allison's men did not seem greatly moved. They pecked nonchalantly away. One angry resident, by Jeffrey's account, pungently described their labour as 'scratching on top of the debris like a lot of hens at a farmer's midden'. Miss Wilson, collaring a senior policeman – Inspector W.T. Brown – declared that the workmen seemed only to think, 'They're all dead now, so what's the use of exerting ourselves?' By evening, four bodies had been recovered. On Thursday morning, the remains of a four-year-old girl and her parents were leisurely removed.

Inspector Brown was growing anxious. By Friday, he had excellent reason to be. 'It is shocking to relate that this morning, Friday 21st March, it is reported that groans were heard emanating from the ruins of 31 to 39 Peel Street. I say without any equivocation' – and the italics are his own – '*that someone is guilty of criminal negligence.*' At 13:30 that afternoon, Fred Clarke was freed from the wreckage, alive – just – and in a dreadful condition after a week's foodless, waterless burial. Clarke, a 'War Reserve' constable in the police, and a Highlander – from Kingussie – had been lodging with the Docherty family, all of whom had been killed. He lived only a few more hours, dying in hospital that evening. He passed away but minutes before John Cormack, at 19:15 hours, was hauled living from the Peel Street debacle. He had been trapped all this time in his bed, a huge beam only inches from his chest; but the blankets, as Andrew Jeffrey suggests, probably saved him from death by exposure and hypothermia. Cormack, buried alive for eight days, would fully recover, and a recording of a radio interview he gave later that spring survives.

If anything, the stories from Hyndland's Dudley Street are even worse. There was a boy trapped in the wreckage after the dreadful blast on the Thursday night Blitz: he was alive, he was conscious and could be clearly heard appealing for help. Yet the waged rescue workers simply downed tools when Friday's blackout fell, and made for their homes. The lad's brother was so furious he complained formally to the police. 'He further alleges that offers from civilians to assist in the work of rescue were absolutely refused. So bitterly does this boy feel in the matter that he is writing to the Master of Works.' His brother, it would seem, did not survive.

In 2005, Thomas McSorley gave his vivid recollections online: a little boy's experience of a night Glasgow was bombed, and the insouciance – on the occasion – to which little boys are prone.

One night in 1941 we were warned by the siren that there was an air raid going on. It sounded so near, we knew it had to be a very big one. We could even see a glow in the sky to the west of Glasgow, where we knew the shipbuilding industry was located in Clydebank, a mere four miles away. We just had to see what was going on, so being young and fearless, we went to see for ourselves.

The only vantage point we could find was the playground of my school, Saint Joseph's. You see, due to the congestion of the nearby tenements, the playground was actually built on the roof of the four-storey building and enclosed simply by a very high net. Everyone, large and small, made their way to this brilliant vantage point as it gave us a panoramic view for miles.

From this height we could see the bombs falling and the buildings going up in flames, lighting up the whole sky like daylight. We could even feel the heat despite the distance from the raid itself.

Things got so serious, however, that we could actually start feeling bits of shrapnel whizzing about our ears; something we hadn't even given any thought to. The policeman on duty had the unenviable job of ushering everyone down from the roof before someone was injured.

The following day, myself and the rest of my pals searched the playground for any souvenirs we might find, and we were amazed at how many pieces had embedded themselves into the walls. Looking back, it is frightening – any of these pieces could have hit any one of us. At the time, however, we thought it was a great adventure, such was the innocence of our youth. It was only when we were told the extent of the deaths and casualties that the fact hit home.

By raw numbers – and these are a debate in themselves we shall later address – Glasgow had paid a higher price than Clydebank: there, an early, broadcast estimate of the death toll as 500, relayed to a local in the Home Guard, won the incredulous response, 'Which street?' The official tally puts Glasgow deaths at 647, with 1,680 injured. Some 803 had been taken to hospital; the Western Infirmary – nearest to some of the worst-hit localities, like Partick and Maryhill, had alone received 267. In all, 6,385 Glasgow houses had been damaged, with 312 quite demolished and 361 so wrecked that demolition was the only safe option. Many sites would remain little more than desert for decades; much of the chunk of Queen Victoria Drive, flattened by that devastating parachute-mine, served as a bleak blaes football pitch into the 1980s. Across the city, 25,000 houses, it was assessed, had sustained super-ficial damage; largely broken windows.

'Details of the bombing of Glasgow last Thursday and Friday nights are now beginning to come through,' wrote the Free Church minister of Storno-way, Revd Kenneth MacRae, in his diary on Wednesday 19 March. '500 were killed and 800 wounded [*these are of course less than half the true figures, reflecting reporting restrictions*] and among the former are Mrs MacLeod, Dudley Drive, and two of her daughters. Felt very much upset by such ghastly news. How inscrutable are the divine providences! How devilish the ways of man!' On Friday evening, MacRae told his journal, 'Heard tonight that so many of the Grant Street congregation (Glasgow) were killed that poor Mr Sutherland could not preach last Sabbath. Who can wonder at it? The poor man must be heartbroken.'

Yet Glasgow was an enormous conurbation and, without making mock of the human tragedy involved for individuals, streets and families, these were but scratches to a hippopotamus. Clydebank, much of which was flattened and which suffered in devastation and upheaval by far higher proportion, seems to have coped much better. The Corporation could not even get a shift on with clearing highways or gathering its own dead. On what was left of Nelson Street, bodies were still being recovered well into the new week. By Wednesday 19 March, as putrefaction became odiously evident and the job grew still worse, Main Control had to be begged for gloves and disinfectant. As late as Friday 21st, all that remained of one woman was picked up: two little feet, each still in its black laced shoe. The 'Incident Post' at Nelson Street was only closed on 8 April and the road did not open again to traffic until 10 April. Even then, days later, one survivor, a Mr Sutherland, whose home at No. 101 had been smashed to a heap, protested that the bodies of his wife and three children were still entombed. Search was resumed for two days, but not a trace of them was ever found. At 95 Logan Street – also blitzed, and where police and a rescue-crew and doctors had heroically, and in dreadful conditions, rescued several trapped victims at great personal danger – one body was not released from its gritty bed until late May.

In Carradale, by Kilbrannan Sound on the Kintyre peninsula, his family were increasingly hysterical for young James MacKinven, unheard of since the bombing of Thursday 13 March and the destruction of his Peel Street lodgings. Villagers had actually watched, dumbfounded, the great fiery glow to the north-east in the nights of raiding. But they had Naomi Mitchison in their midst: she was, besides, almost certainly the diarist retained in her district for Mass Observation, and there is no good reason to believe the account of the unfolding Carradale tragedy relayed by Tom Harrisson is not her own, for her part in helping the MacKinvens now is still remembered in the district. Her written account is an outstanding and psychologically astute portrait of most human, coping dignity amidst awful bereavement – all the worse for the parents who had pressed and wheedled their son to go and train in Glasgow, and now bore intolerable guilt.

Two uncles of James MacKinven – herring fishermen – made the difficult journey to Glasgow to help in the Peel Street search. A third, a deep-sea sailor, happened to be in port, and he too was summoned to the task. But the days dragged and, there still being no news, on Wednesday 19th Naomi Mitchison made the trip to the city too. She would not return to Carradale for two days and was evidently shaken by the experience; her Mass Observation diary for that night describes it as 'extremely moving' and impossible to write about at the time. She found the strength and clarity in the days succeeding.

Mr and Mrs MacKinven, highly distressed, had been with friends in a flat close by when Mitchison caught up with them. They had an emotional conversation about immortality. His mother Ellen kept asking if her lad had suffered; on blitz night she had an awful dream about whipping him, and awoke knowing 'something had happened'. They talked, the three of them, of pity. 'I have forgiven the young chap who killed him – oh, long ago,' said Mrs MacKinven. His father – 'P', Peter – said quietly of the bomb-aimer, 'He didn't know what he was doing.'

The three men were still digging in the rubble, in the stead of two others who were worn out from the day before. The official Demolition Squad had moved on to other work 'as the next house was likely to fall onto that side soon.' Mitchison and the MacKinvens stayed in the 'borrowed kitchen . . . holding a long discussion on heaven and hell, sin, guilt. Then –

D and S came in; they were wearing blue overalls, half undone at the neck; but the overalls and their hands and faces were grimed with plaster; their hands were cut; S was looking wild, his hair on end and his eyes bloodshot; D's face was blotched with black shadows round his eyes and mouth and grey with plaster. *We got him*, S said, we got Jim, we got poor Jim, I told you we would get him. Then S began wildly: I have been drinking, he says I am a black sheep, I had a drink after getting poor Jim. I stood up and put my arms around his neck and kissed him and my mouth was full of grit and my nostrils were full of the smell of plaster.

There followed a 'verbal post-mortem' on Jim MacKinven's death: he had died in an instant, and his mother was repeatedly assured he had not suffered. The third digger came in: this man was first engineer on a ship recently torpedoed while under convoy – but that nightmare, he asserted, was preferable to 'what he had just done'. He had now reported the discovery of the body to the authorities, and the boy would have to be formally identified. Meanwhile, S had somehow – no mean achievement in the Second World War – secured a chicken; this had been cooked, and was duly taken in a repast that also featured tea, girdle scones and rhubarb jam.

Mitchison stayed that night with friends in a 'hamlet' just outside Glasgow; the other detail suggests it was one of the little places adjoining Clydebank. 'She got there,' Harrisson relays, 'by a train, a bus and a car driven by a drunk.' She thought that the authorities had 'lost control' on that side. 'An army colonel had taken over in one place; he was feeding 1,000 "refugees". . . . he'd cheerfully spent £8,000.' She rejoined the grieving group the next day. 'They had been up and down having cups of tea all night.' They planned the funeral. Mrs MacKinven chose a 'white box for her wee boy'. She really did not want a church burial, but hadn't liked 'to offend anyone'. (This should not suggest the MacKinvens were irreligious: church funerals in the Highlands were then very unusual, and as late as the 1980s most on Lewis, for instance, were from the family home.) There was to be no mourning garb; she had bought a blue hat with a white ribbon. There was no thought of cremation: she wanted to lie beside him 'when her time came'.

Her husband went out to reinforce himself with 'a good plate of fish and chips and a Glasgow cake. S had disappeared – last seen with a tart (female, in trousers.) He re-appeared at night "with no hat and extremely drunk", bringing a bottle of brandy for Mother, whisky for father and making a general nuisance of himself too. They split up to sleep in two rooms. Our diarist shared a bed with Father, Mother and two other young women, all in white flannel nightgowns ("only mine had no sleeves.").'

And so they made the painful journey, largely by sea, to Carradale and 'wild reactions' there.

Found a car, driven by their cousin, and he took us off, driving fast. Sometimes Ellen said: I am being brave aren't I? This is how Jim would like me to be. I said, yes, and when we got in sight of Arran I quoted to her I to the hills will lift mine eyes, and she liked that and said He's there isn't he? And I said yes, and here;

time and place don't count for the free spirit. And she pointed out the wee cottage where her mother had been born; they were all crofters. Old Mac came to the door to see us by. She [*Ellen MacKinven*] only glanced at the cemetery. As we came to the village her face was set. I came behind her and at once a wailing crowd of sisters in mourning burst into the passage and all over her. She began to cry, they were all crying; J in black, brought us a filthy drink, lemonade and gin – none of us had much to eat on the boat and it went slightly to my head and more to Ellen's. They all began to cry over me too, especially M. M began saying the most frightful things about poor, wee Jim being too good for this world, he's happier where he is – all the *personal* things which I'd managed to get her away from. And how we are all going to die and it might be any day at all, and the old mother crying, and Ellen threw back her head and keened and howled and began calling for her wee boy. I went and held her hands hard and spoke loud and calmly to her till she bucked up; whenever I stopped for a moment one of the other sisters began. But I managed to get Ellen steady before P came back. He came straight to me and said I nearly broke down but not quite; I was brave. I said I knew he would be. Then I went into the kitchen; there was a meat meal for the men and I sat with them – I was very hungry. S began telling funny stories, mostly traditional stories about his boyhood. P smiled a bit. Then I helped to wash up; I had said to Ellen that now we were sisters. Everyone was running round, and I got a dry dish-cloth and wiped the cups and plates and brought them in again for the women. We had mutton and girdle scones and butter and cookies, and lots of tea.

Over 60 years later, on 13 March 2006, a contributor to one online message-board discussion about the Blitz in western Scotland had these slightly garbled details, garnered decades later, of James MacKinven's funeral.

Strangely, the most touching tale about the blitz I have come across, didn't come from Clydeside. A number of years ago while visiting my father in Campbeltown I had cycled over the hills heading for the tiny fishing village of Carradale which sits on the east side of the Kintyre peninsula looking over to Arran. I stopped at a little tearoom outside the village for a cuppa, and got chatting with, I think, the person who owned the tearoom.

This fellow told me how, as a boy, he had watched the men of a Carradale family, who were all fishermen, carry a long pine box from the quay and up through the village to one of the houses. He recalled that some of the men had been drinking, and as they made their unsteady way through the villagers flanking the road, a long line of people stepped in behind, and followed in silence. As the fisherman approached one of the houses many womenfolk and children appeared, and there was much crying and wailing.

It seems one of the fishermen had a son who wished to learn a trade on the Clyde, and had to attend a school in Clydebank. Following the blitz, they had received no word at all as to what had happened to the boy, and decided to go to Clydebank and see if they could find him. The men of the family went, searched the debris of the house where the boy was boarding, and found his body . . . he had been dead for quite some time. They obtained a box. It was this box, with the remains of the boy, which the tearoom proprietor remembered seeing, as the fishermen of the family carried the body of the dead boy home. He was one of the many victims in the bombing of Clydebank 65 years ago tonight.

Tom Harrisson rightly observed in 1976, concluding this poignant discussion of the bombing on Clydeside, 'The keening cries from far Kintyre show how the blitz touched every corner of the islands. No place escaped the impact entirely. But the direct blows were on the few great cities and more numerous small ones. In human terms the smaller on the whole suffered most, bomb for bomb, per head of population.'

Naomi Mitchison has left, on record and under her name, her own recollections of Clydebank a week after the raid – probably from her stay in the locality the night after Jim's body had at last been found – which the local Member of the Scottish Parliament, Des McNulty, shared with colleagues in their dignified debate to mark the sixtieth anniversary:

A week after the raid: still smoking. The people all looked incredibly strained and tired, grey-faced. A lot of buildings were burned out, others badly cracked and unsafe, some completely smashed. Off the main road it was worse; here and there houses were being demolished, blasting going on sometimes, traffic being cleared, here a railway bridge propped up, there a loudspeaker van telling people where to go for money or food. All windows gone: everywhere was the smell of plaster and burning, everywhere this incredible mess, everywhere people trailing about with a mattress or a bundle or a few pots and pans.

Yet, amidst destruction and death and, for thousands, the loss of practically everything they had owned in the world, there is abundant evidence that the MacKinvens' extraordinary, shell-shocked compassion for the young German airman was shared by not a few in Clydebank. Alex Nicolson, one of the volunteers from the Edinburgh Council of Social Service, helped at the emergency station in Clydebank Town Hall in the days immediately following the raids, and shared (in his wonderfully posh voice) an affecting memory with Billy Kay.

Different people were allocated different jobs. And they asked me if I would walk up and down the queue, which was increasing every moment, trying to find out what the people wanted, because in the hall there were tables with assistants sitting taking information, and I could direct them to the [correct] table. If they wanted immediate financial help because all their money had gone, if they needed clothing, food, or information about their own relatives, or to give information of people whom they knew had been killed. If we could get any direct information and just hand it over it saved the people waiting in the queue. I've never seen such dignity, such courage, and I didn't hear a grumble that whole day. During all this walking up and down, feeling perfectly useless but at least presumably doing something – I'd been into the hall with information and was standing in the door just coming out again when a man came up to me and gave me a bit of paper and said – 'This is the name of a child who was picked up in a shelter – dead. Would you take it in?' And I said, 'You're quite sure this is right and the child was dead?', and he said, 'Yes. She was picked up beside my own bairn who was dead too.' And then he stood for a moment and said, 'We're not going to do this to German people's bairns, are we? What good is that going to do?' And I thought, the *courage* of it. There was no resentment, there was no bitterness, it was just a thought, about other people's children.

James MacKinven had written his last poem, as far as can now be ascertained, only days before his death; it is called, 'Thinking', and shows a fast maturing talent.

> Down the ages the hills are there.
> Far away the streams move in places.
> There are pebbles in all the streams,
> there is watercress in some, crisp and fresh,
> bitter and refreshing – green; green.
> There is mud in pools of rain: dust on the broad highway,
> small fish in dubs by the shore lying gazing.
> There are dances and drums; people dancing;
> games – a smile, an outburst of laughter;
> a world – we in it are always wondering.
> There are ministers and civilization – Christianity and Germans.
> A parliament above us and dirt below.

III

AND SORROWS ALL DEPART

Sweet sacrament divine,
hid in thy earthly home,
Lo! Round thy lowly shrine,
with suppliant hearts we come;
Jesus, to thee our voice we raise,
in songs of love and heartfelt praise,
sweet sacrament divine,
sweet sacrament divine.

Sweet sacrament of peace,
dear home of every heart,
where restless yearnings cease,
and sorrows all depart,
There in thine ear all trustfully,
we tell our tale of misery,
sweet sacrament of peace,
sweet sacrament of peace.

Sweet sacrament of rest,
ark from the ocean's roar,
within thy shelter blest,
soon may we reach the shore,
Save us for still the tempest raves;
save, lest we sink beneath the waves
sweet sacrament of rest,
sweet sacrament of rest.

Sweet sacrament divine,
Earth's light and jubilee,
in thy far depths doth shine
thy Godhead's majesty;
Sweet light, so shine on us we pray,
that earthly joys may fade away,
sweet sacrament divine,
sweet sacrament divine.

Francis Stanfield (1835–1914). This Roman Catholic hymn, of unabashed Tridentine theology – as set to Stanfield's own plain tune – is loved by many in that tradition still in Clydebank; and in the English-speaking world over.

9

THE NAMING OF THE DEAD

Clydebank gathered her bodies.

With mild daylight weather, spring sunshine, the warming effect of ongoing fires – Singer's timber-yard would burn implacably for 10 days – and the continued depredation of hundreds of stray cats and dogs, to say nothing of rats, the task, all through this first shell-shocked weekend, was pursued with mounting urgency.

Contingency plans had been made in Clydebank, as everywhere else, for wholesale casualties in the event of a German air raid. A mortuary had been prepared at the town's greyhound stadium and a mass grave – a great long trench – had long been excavated in Dalnottar Cemetery, backfilled afterwards with loose soil. But a bomb had demolished the makeshift morgue on the first night of the assault, and still less adequate arrangements had hastily to be thrown together on Friday 14th. The Janetta Street premises of the new Clydebank High School had enough space for one area to be used for the holding of corpses; the hall of St James Parish Church was also used, and some cover was thrown together at Kilbowie Cemetery.

By Sunday, nevertheless, the smell of death was increasingly evident and repellent around the town; the job of recovery all the more horrific. Inevitably, many bodies were mutilated: frazzled by fire, limbs curled and fists clenched in the 'pugilistic' attitude of those, living or already dead, baked in flaming heat; or maimed, severed, crushed, disembowelled by explosion and shrapnel and falling rubble. A surprising number – and for some of the workers, this was more terrible than anything – were found dead without a mark on them, killed by the kinetic force of blast itself and what it had done unseen to their insides, such as those Mary Rodgers had seen dead in one church hall, 'just sittin' like mummies.' Even when workers had to deal with little more than ash, there could be great anguish, as Janet Hyslop would bleakly relate in 1981.

A couple came to me – their wee boy . . . they had got out, but he hadn't got out and they came to me, I think it must have been the day after. He was in Graham Avenue, so I said, 'Well, you go back and I'll get the lads to have a look' – they told me where to look. And he had been playing wi' marbles and that's what identified him was his marbles. He had been burned. And it was just bones really that were left. So they were a Catholic family, terribly worried about him, so we got the wee remains put in a wee box, got them buried as they would have liked, and when they came back I said 'Yes' – we'd found him. I didn't say how we had found him,

and I said 'Everything was done that you would have done.' There was that wee
boy just sittin' playin' wi' his marbles, and that had to happen to him.

There were besides sickening calculations to be made when confronted with
only bits of bodies, and from any number of people. Perhaps the ghastliest
post-raid duty for an ARP warden was to collect a basket of 'unidentified
flesh', as investigation of what had been a family home or a crowded flimflam
back-court shelter was completed.

'If enough remained recognisable,' Angus Calder would record of general
Blitz experience, 'a body would be taken to the mortuary, where attendants
and volunteers would work on it. One volunteer, useful because she was an
artist trained in anatomy, has written, "We had somehow to form a body for
burial so that the relatives (without seeing it) could imagine that their loved
one was more or less intact for that purpose. But it was a very difficult task –
there were so many pieces missing and, as one of the mortuary attendants said,
'Proper jigsaw puzzle, ain't it, miss?' The stench was the worst thing about
it . . ." She adds, "It became a grim and ghastly satisfaction when a body was
fairly constructed – but if one was too lavish in making one body almost
whole, then another one would have sad gaps . . . I think this task dispelled for
me the idea that human life is valuable." '

In Liverpool, one undertaker was prosecuted when it was discovered he had
resorted to putting sandbags in coffins and 'taking them to be buried', Marie
Price related. 'And he said, "What's worse, telling people that I couldn't find
any bodies or pretending that the bodies were in these coffins?" The courts saw
the sense of that.' He was acquitted.

There were so many lone, isolated scraps of body lying about openly on
Clydebank rubble – a hand, a piece of head; a chunk of flesh – that, in the
fraught circumstances, the authorities soon gave up trying to collect them all.
Men simply went about dousing them with quicklime.

Dealing with hundreds of corpses, as Andrew Jeffrey observes, was really
quite beyond the resources of Clydebank Town Council. The task was instead
assumed by the Scottish Home and Health Department, and on Sabbath
afternoon one of their officials – J. McRobbie – arrived in Clydebank. He
had been warned of the sights awaiting him, but they were nevertheless beyond
his experience or imagining. At the St James church hall, 170 bodies still lay –
amidst showered glass and plaster – as they had been dumped down by
overwhelmed workers and volunteers; 33 more corpses lay at the Janetta Street
campus; 21 in dank sheds at Kilbowie Cemetery. To compound his strain,
relatives swarmed everywhere, looking in fear and dread and black hope for the
features of a loved one. Inevitably, ghouls from Glasgow and elsewhere turned
up besides. 'There were no coffins and no preparation facilities,' records Jeffrey.
'There were nowhere near enough undertakers. There was no water to wash the
bodies and there were no vehicles to transport them in . . . Owing to shortage of
space, some bodies had to be prepared in the open at Kilbowie.'

His miserable duty was further complicated by two separate operations: the naming and collection of this or that Clydebank Blitz casualty by relatives (who would then arrange interment or cremation themselves) and the mounting list of unknown, unidentified and too often unidentifiable remains which were his ongoing responsibility and whose burial could not long be postponed. Nor, as MacPhail points out, could the normal and proper processes in law be forgotten, whatever the emergency: bodies claimed by relatives had to be formally identified, and a doctor had in every instance to sign a death certificate, and each passing to be recorded in the civil Register of Deaths as usual.

There were besides folk searching for those who turned out, days or even weeks later, to be alive – an inevitable consequence of the desperate efforts to evacuate – and there was immediate economic pressure, if the family bread-winner had died, to claim on the insurance policies widely taken out by the provident townsfolk. Nothing would be forthcoming without a death certi-ficate and people might well insist a wholly unrecognisable, smashed and roasted body without a scrap of authentication was their husband, or father, or son. There were, in addition, the remains of those who had not been local residents – just visiting on this weekend of all weekends – and those found in one home who might well have been visiting or taking shelter from another, not necessarily close by. Andrew Jeffrey points out two other elements in the chaos of it all – that many 'bodies had been thrown out of the ambulances to make way for the living. Further confusion was caused by those having been found some distance from where they had been picked up.'

Adults – and even little children – were exposed to sights that haunt them to this day. Helen McNeill, hauled out into the daylight devastation on Friday morning – they had huddled, with many other cornered patrons, throughout that first raid in the Regal Picture House – glanced into a pend as her mother hauled her along the street. 'A lot of people in there are sleeping,' Helen chirped, seeing pair after pair of legs sticking out from the cover of tarpaulins. Her mother said nothing, and dragged her all the faster. On the same morning, Myra Brady would recall in 1999, 'all I saw was St James's Church facing me and all the dead bodies. It was pretty horrible. Coal lorries packing the bodies into them. And I always remember that when they were packing them into the lorries, I actually saw someone move. Now whether they were dead or not dead, it frightened the wits out of me and I never forgot it. I used to dream about it, quite often, for a long, long time afterwards.'

Between the urgency of Scottish Office officials, the agitation of families and all the fog of tale and rumour, mistakes were inevitable and much of the abiding suspicion in Clydebank – to this day – that far more perished on those two nights than the authorities ever admitted rests on such embarrassments as that recorded by J. Alistair Robinson at century's end.

Born at 96 Radnor Street, I had moved out to the small village of Condorrat near what is now Cumbernauld New Town, prior to the Blitz. But my family still stayed at 100 Radnor Street and on the day of the Blitz my brother Harvey, after his return from work from Babcock's at Renfrew – for reasons known only to himself – went upstairs and filled the bath with water and left a pail beside it. Around 2 am, with the raid at its height, he found it almost impossible to light a fag in the communal shelter just across the road, due to the lack of oxygen. So he came out into the bomber's moon, went across into his house and found an incendiary in the process of setting the bathroom door alight. Instinct? I wonder.

My wife's uncle, Edward Donaldson, was one of the few Air Raid wardens killed in the raid and our local police sergeant at Condorrat, who had spent the night in Clydebank, was able to tell us some weeks later that he and other helpers were just too late to save him from suffocation, and he was buried in a communal grave apparently as unknown. Yet, three weeks later, my father-in-law and I were asked to go to Elgin Street School to identify a body as being Edward Donaldson. The body we saw was faceless, but we were assured it was he, and his identity-card, gas mask, steel helmet etc. were there to prove it. And yet, the police sergeant told us that the Edward Donaldson they had tried to save was totally unmarked. 'Our' Edward Donaldson was buried next day in a communal grave at Dalnottar Cemetery. So much for the government statistics re the number killed.

Many dead, it seems probable, were never found. A few were almost casually located in the years ahead. Though expressly forbidden to play in the burnt-out shell of a bombed Clydebank hotel, about 1947 the young sons of one Clydebank woman scurried home in alarm to confess they had been climbing 'in the Benbow and saw skeletons there'. She hurried to the local police constable, Kenny McLee, and the remains of three or four people were indeed belatedly retrieved: 'men who had been burned during the Blitz'. Around 1960, an 11-year-old Clydebank boy, playing archaeologist, dug into the floor of a Blitz-flattened dancehall and found a human finger – the flesh of course dissolved, but the little bones still jointed. He placed it reverently in a matchbox and buried it in quiet, solitary ceremony.

To this day, it is likely that Blitz casualties still lie in the buried, bulldozed ruins, in sites long since levelled or even built over. Dozens of bodies besides had been all but atomised by explosion or burned and crushed to unrecognisable grit. One distraught man, searching what remained of the family home time and again for his mother's remains, found nothing but a few of the glass beads she had been wearing. Tom McKendrick repeats a story that could have been related tenfold. 'My cousin went up to visit her friend in Napier Street. Two parachute mines had landed at the back of the houses. Her family went up to see if they could find her . . . they never found a trace of her body . . . all they found was one of her black patent shoes . . . then they knew she was dead.'

Internal injuries – such as a ruptured bowel – often caused decomposition to set in with alarming speed, even when a corpse was seemingly untouched. Exhausted nurses at one rest centre had laid out one body and performed the last offices at best they could, leaving it serene and presentable; to their horror, when the family appeared, it had within hours become so discoloured, swollen and distended the features were unrecognisable.

McRobbie, confronted with dozens and dozens of unknown dead, many mangled and all rapidly putrefying in a town with sanitary problems on every front, had no choice: on Sunday afternoon, laying the grim realities before Sir Steven Bilsland, it was quickly 'decided,' narrates Iain MacPhail, 'that these should be buried in a communal grave on the following day, Monday the 17th, that Union Jacks [sic] should be used as palls, and that the funeral, though not to be publicised, was not to be kept secret. Bilsland made arrangements for Tom Johnston, Secretary of State for Scotland, Sir Iain Colquhoun, Lord Lieutenant of the County, David Kirkwood, MP, and other notables to attend.' McRobbie had already ascertained there was no hope of securing any sort of coffins.

The mass grave at Dalnottar was hastily opened. McRobbie sent urgent beseeching to Glasgow and Edinburgh for minimal but essential aid. Clydebank's great neighbour furnished 12 gravediggers and 150 shrouds. Edinburgh sent a professional mortuary superintendent and eight assistants. But the city fathers of the Scottish capital balked at another McRobbie request: Union Flags for respectful ceremony. With witless malice, they declared the national standard could not be appropriately used 'at funerals conducted by a local authority'. The Royal Navy instead granted his petition and quietly furnished them. For the bodies themselves, no more could be done than wrap each in a cheap white bed-sheet, tied round the waist and neck with common household string.

The bleak if solemn service was scheduled for four o'clock on the afternoon of Monday 17 March. The police turned up to take photographs of each dead face – at least, of those still recognisably human. Yet more relatives now appeared as word spread and the deadline pressed. McRobbie had not enough staff to help maintain order, console the weeping and stricken, assist him in the vital bureaucracies; there were not enough people either to act as bearers at Dalnottar, and cramped space at St James Church hall had besides to be shared with the undertakers readying and encoffining the known and identified deceased. Then there was the difficulty of arranging transport. It was late in the day before he secured six vans to act as great industrial hearses to Dalnottar, but it was 15:30 before loading of the consignment collected to date – what was left of 67 Clydebank people – could even begin. McRobbie's crew had just begun when a broken father appeared, in search of the corpse of a three-year-old child; and four other little bundles had to be unwrapped – as everyone paused to go through their grim cargo – before the mite was indeed found in one of the vehicles, and could be handed over for decent burial in the family lair.

The mass funeral was, then, late – it was a quarter past four before the vans even started their journey to Dalnottar – and, in the event, rushed and faintly shabby. A few bodies were laid, less than ceremoniously, in the pit; and then proceedings paused for acts of Protestant and Roman Catholic worship, as the dignitaries – hatless in the crisp spring air – looked on. Smoke was still acrid and grey even on this high ground over the town; the smell of death quietly nauseated, and there were ongoing bangs and even explosions, as in the streets downhill unstable buildings were dynamited, rubble bulldozed into craters and the odd wretched dog shot.

A photograph of the occasion was taken; it would be neatly cut by censors, betraying nothing of the size of the mass grave or the sheer volume of casualties. Wreaths were then laid, and the eminences at once departed. They had, no doubt, things to do; and there may besides have been security concerns, with so many important folk gathered in the open air at one spot well visible to enemy aircraft. Some say that even in the groves of Dalnottar, canaries and budgies cheeped in the trees as the funeral proceeded. Indeed, it would go on for days. On Tuesday 18 March, another 54 unknown dead were laid to this bleak rest: 33 from the Janetta Street premises, 21 from the undignified proceedings of Kilbowie Cemetery. Meanwhile, of course, there were constant, ongoing private funerals. By a week later – 25 March – 281 Clydebank bodies had been buried; 116 of these had eluded identification. In Glasgow, 561 corpses had likewise been interred; many more bodies, in town and in city, would surface in the weeks ahead.

Sir Steven Bilsland was furious at such indecorous rites of burial – the confusion, the delays as men of eminence stood at Dalnottar waiting – and held Clydebank Town Council particularly responsible for its apparent, feckless failure to have better prepared itself for a multitude of dead bodies. He did not at first appreciate the burdens – to say nothing of the human ordeal – laid on the shoulders of local men amidst general Clydebank cataclysm; nor did he know that William Cunningham, Clydebank's sanitary inspector, had been lobbying the Department of Health fruitlessly for months for permission to buy cardboard or papier-mâché coffins. When the letters were quietly laid before Sir Steven, he was shocked. The mandarin apologised at once and fulsomely to the town's officials, and went after the Department with all guns blazing.

How many, precisely, died on or soon after those dreadful nights in Clydebank can never be known with any certainty. Many bodies were never recovered and the precise population of the town on Thursday 13 March, and who happened to be passing through, could not be ascertained. Even had it been government practice to publish casualty figures – which it was not, both for nebulous grounds of 'national security' and the anxiety to preserve 'morale' – it would have taken many weeks to compile even a rough figure. But the government handled the matter so clumsily as to infuriate townsfolk and only inflame rumour upon rumour.

'The official communiqué on the raids,' records MacPhail, 'actually stated that, though the attacks had been heavy, the casualties, though serious, were not expected to be numerous. Such a statement . . . was nevertheless based on the incomplete information at the time, the casualty figures for Clydebank being absent from the first return and only an estimate being included. This communiqué was followed a few days later, on March 18th, by a statement from the Ministry of Home Security that about 500 persons had been killed on the raids in Clydeside.'

It was on hearing of this report that one Home Guardsman in Clydebank had snapped, 'Which street?' A central difficulty was the flat refusal of Herbert Morrison, home secretary and minister of home security, to make any distinction between Glasgow and Clydebank, even when pressed hard in the House of Commons by John McGovern, MP for Glasgow Shettleston and one of Maxton's little Independent Labour Party cadre. McGovern bluntly accused Morrison of making 'misleading statements', and declared – rightly – that the figures published to date had caused great resentment in the region. Morrison – an abrasive, crafty chap who never suffered fools gladly and whose grandson, Peter Mandelson, would decades later be scarcely more loved in British politics – would later concede just a little ground to McGovern, stating on 1 April that around 1,100 people had been killed on 'Clydeside' and another 1,000 seriously injured.

In Scottish politics, shrewd men were growing alarmed. The solicitor-general, J.S.C. Reid, spoke urgently to the Secretary of State, telling Johnston that Clydebank people heard such numbers on the wireless with 'frank incredulity'. Meanwhile, on 3 April and from the Regional Commissioner's office in Edinburgh – that of Lord Rosebery – highly confidential figures were drawn up, dividing the lost and maimed as summarised by Johnston's 1995 biographer, Russell Galbraith: '647 men, women and children had been killed in Glasgow, population 1.1 million; 358 people perished in Clydebank, population 55,000; and another 78 people died as a result of the air raids in neighbouring counties, mostly Dunbartonshire. The figures for these seriously injured were: 973 in Clydebank, 390 in Glasgow; 219 in Dunbartonshire; and 20 elsewhere.'

But these figures would be firmly sat on and confidence in government figures for the Clydebank Blitz – and, indeed, thereafter, for anything else – had been vitiated in the district. The wildest talk inevitably took firm hold, and the business would flare again a year later when, somehow slipping past the minions of the Ministry of Information, a *Sunday Post* anniversary piece on 15 March 1942 lamented the '1,200 Clydebank people' who had paid the supreme sacrifice 'as the result of the savage two-night blitz on the town'. There was uproar. As Scottish Office men panicked, Clydebank Town Council now held a full debate on casualty statistics and pressed for the official details to be released, as 'exorbitant figures' were the talk of the burgh. Still the authorities refused for the duration of the Second World War to yield, though the death toll was quietly revised in yet another internal, confidential and most secret Scottish Office memorandum: for Clydeside, 'over 1,200' dead and 'over 1,100' seriously injured; for Clydebank proper, '528 killed and 617 seriously injured'.

It is easy 70 years on, as armchair historians in a far less deferential age and after decades of peace in Western Europe, to condemn this obsessive secrecy. But in March 1941 Britain was all but alone in a desperate struggle for national survival: bombarded from the air, throttled by her Atlantic seaways, perilously close to starving and with well-founded fears of invasion and conquest. The government cannot entirely be condemned for refusing to give out detailed information that would, inevitably, have at once suggested signal German bombing success in a vital centre of war production and invited, perhaps, yet more great flights of Heinkel 111s and Junkers 88s back over Clydebank to make good its failures.

There was besides a silly but understandable reluctance to admit to a mistake in the first official numbers. Other factors doubtless coloured attitudes in Whitehall: the general belief that Clydebank was a hotbed of Bolshevik sedition and – as Tom Johnston determinedly talked up at every opportunity, to his own pork-barrel ends – the spectre of Scottish nationalism. Though appointed Secretary of State barely a month before the Clydebank Blitz, Johnston had already used his hat as Regional Commissioner to lobby hard against sustained idiocies from London and their impact on local morale: the BBC's decision to end all Scottish regional broadcasting; the new Home Service's blithe habit, in the first weeks of the conflict, of playing incessantly 'There'll Always Be An England', and the tendency at every level to use 'English' as a synonym for 'British'. Indeed, there was furious booing throughout Scotland's cinemas when a newsreel described the emphatically Scottish Douglas Farquhar – who commanded the 602 (City of Glasgow) RAF Squadron – as an 'English' airman.

And, serving only further to distress and anger the people of Clydebank, the Ministry of Information officials toiled assiduously to make sure the town was not even named in subsequent newspaper reports, of which this article is typical:

BLITZ VICTIMS' FUNERAL

On Monday afternoon in a common grave opened at a cemetery in a town near the Clydeside many unidentified victims of the recent blitz, including little children, were buried on Monday. Even the cemetery where the interments took place had not escaped the assault of the Nazi bombers, for alongside the paths, on graves and actually inside the glass globes protecting marble wreaths burned-out incendiary bombs were to be seen.

The bodies of the victims, wrapped in white shrouds covered with Union Jacks, were transported in five large vans to the cemetery, where policemen acted as pallbearers.

Local emotion was only fuelled as the press, in the days following the raid, readily published accounts – in detail – of ineffably trivial bombing incidents. 'The Glasgow paper *The Bulletin* has a headline for 19th March 1941,' fretted Eric Flack in March 2010, 'on the lines – "35 cattle killed in raid on west central Scotland," with a photo of the Peel Of Drumry . . . The byre was hit and the cows killed. That was an example of censorship.' Even in the town itself, absurdly – over a month after the raids, on 25 April 1941 – the heavy hand of the censor prevented one overblown, unattributed account from actually naming Clydebank:

THE GREAT DESTRUCTION
BY A CLYDESIDER

In a Clydeside town it was a clear night of radiant moonlight and twinkling stars, just such a night as poets and lovers dream about when romance and happiness and the sheer joy of living go hand in hand. Home from work and with my hunger appeased, I was washing myself in keen anticipation of a quiet, studious evening after the tedious toil of the working day. Half in jest, half seriously, I thought, as I listened to the warning, of the speech by Macbeth: 'It is a knell that summons thee to heaven or to hell!'

When the raid began my impression was it was another reconnaissance flight by one or two German planes and I decided to stay in the house until the all-clear signal sounded. But the loud drone of bombers and the reverberating reports of anti-aircraft guns made me soon realise that not a moment was to be lost if I valued my life. Even then, however, I could not visualise the dreadful havoc and wanton destruction that was so soon to rend our hearts and bring ruin upon us.

My mother and young sister were already downstairs and, still in my working clothes, I, too, joined them. Several neighbours were there together for we had no shelter from air-bombing save our strong stairway and a kindly providence, if there is such a thing. Yet at the back of my mind I harboured the hope that we might all manage through safely and see our homes preserved.

Incendiary bombs rained down, flashing up the brilliant sky, shells from the guns lit the heavens, loud reports echoed fearfully and over all, menacingly, hovering like many ghoulish, mechanical birds of prey, droned the bombers scattering death and desolation. Amid shouts and frantic gesticulations, we all cowered low as the whistling sound of a bomb was heard near at hand. Then followed a deafening explosion and the falling crash of falling masonry, and clouds of choking dust and the cries of women and children. Miraculously, in that dark hell of horror caused by brutish man, not one of our party was killed.

Across from us a church was burning furiously and cottages and tenement buildings were also a mass of red flames. Accompanied by another man, who went upstairs in a vain attempt to do something, I went back to my home and hastily snatched an overcoat and hat and had sufficient presence of mind to cram some money I kept in a drawer into my pocket. Down I dashed again and found our party herded together in a corner of the stairway, brave and apprehensive.

The merciless mission of destruction continued hour after hour. Each blast and terrific crash and whistling bomb seemed to herald our approaching end and I felt my heart wrung to its depths when I contemplated the kneeling women and children and heard their prayers. Most of them were praying aloud, a few were stonily stoical and thus they crouched.

Their homes were gone, their possessions burning to ashes, and the terror of aerial warfare was let loose upon them; and all these inoffensive, peace-abiding people, like their counterparts in every land, asked little of their rulers but the simple boon of being left alone to live out their days upon earth in a certain frugal comfort and pleasurable anticipation of things to come.

This I saw for myself: that no man in our group behaved like a craven soul. They were dazed, bewildered, baffled, furious at their impotence to fight the desperate situation, but fearless in a night of death and destruction. Outside in the streets the firefighters pluckily and heroically fought with the all-conquering flames which, leaping and spreading into the air, burned and burned, a red hot, living mass of consuming wrath and ravagement. The scene vividly recalled to me my early innocent impressions of the end of the world by fire and the fury of an almighty Power.

So rapidly and dangerously did the flames burn that we were compelled to seek a safer shelter, if one could be found, out in the open. Despite remonstrances and protests from some of our little group, we went round by the debris-strewn backyard and stood awhile in the brick wash-house. It was a perilous place to hope for sanctuary but it afforded us a few moments' respite.

As long as I live I shall never forget with what bitter anguish and desolation of heart I watched the red flames blazing out of every window of my home. There went the fruits of long years of study and concentration, the tie-beam of my life, the one great, finest thing that had spurred me on through adversity and misfortune. All my pictures, all my drawings, sketch books, writings, treasured volumes, and all the creations of inspired moments totally destroyed and lost for ever! I wished then to die where I stood, for the aim and strenuous endeavour by which alone I lived had been wiped out. My years had been spent in vain.

Clothes, furniture, worldly goods, all these were nothing; but this other thing was my very self, my innermost me, a fine spirit that could never be replaced.

I made no whine of complaint yet, in my soul, I was, like Christ, in Gethsemane. I thought of all the poor people who were enduring the full force of the German blitz; how they were being killed and injured, and rendered homeless wanderers if they escaped death; the men, women and children sitting in Anderson shelters and the surface shelters, those unfortunates, so many of them, with no protection save their tenement closes and houses, and blind chance, everyone of them hoping to escape from this fiendish, murderous tornado of modern warfare. Hell was let loose upon Clydeside that night.

Lives were being wantonly sacrificed in this mad, insensate lust to kill and destroy, and hearts and high hopes were being ruthlessly shattered. With a heavy heart I turned away with my mother and sister on either side of me, to seek a shelter from the hail of death that descended from the sky. Somehow, in a providential manner, we came through the ordeal waiting and watching for the dawn amid the thunderous reports, the crashes and heavy explosions and the blazing, crackling buildings.

Brave deeds were done by fearless souls, men and women everywhere, and miraculous escapes from death were chronicled through the night.

The cold, red dawn saw parts of Clydeside a smouldering mass of ruins and heaped-up masonry and debris where death hovered, a place of stunned, questioning people, homeless and penniless, dimly trying to fathom the meaning of it all. The once proud, prosperous homes were laid low, families killed or ruined, careers senselessly shattered, toil, blood, tears, the destiny of the people. There was left to them the distinction of knowing that their sufferings and heroic fortitude had thrilled the world and, let it be added, made their habitations a haunt for countless, curious sightseers.

Never was there a time in which this same world was so full of noble talk about God and religious ideals, the sacredness of holy things, and vibrant with the eloquence of orators imbued with lofty aims of freedom and brotherhood and a better way of living once the war is over.

And there may be still more drastic and more devilish methods of extermination in prospect for the peoples of all countries.

O, you poor dead and wounded, innocent victims! You shall yet be avenged! You shall not have died and shed your blood in vain.

The heavy religiosity, near blasphemy and general delirium of this prose suggest a journalist who had learned his trade during the Great War. But official determination to suppress any national awareness of the Clydebank Blitz is resented in the town – and by thousands beyond – to this day. 'Official estimates of the damage and dead were deliberately played down, "for reasons of morale",' Meg Henderson rightly observed in an April 1999 newspaper article. 'Unlike modern conflicts, unlike Kosovo today, there were no TV cameras to bring the horror directly into the nation's living rooms but there were newsreel cameras. What Clydebank has never understood was why in Coventry and London the newsreels films were widely broadcast with proud boasts of 'We can take it', while in Clydebank the official view was that there had been little damage and few casualties . . .'

To this day, the secret 1942 calculation – 528 dead and 617 badly injured – is the most widely accepted figure for Clydebank casualties; the Commonwealth War Graves figure remains, to this day, only 448, because it excludes those grievously wounded who died, in hospital, a day or several later and outwith the bounds of the burgh. As for that 528, Clydebank people point out it excludes those who succumbed weeks or even months later to physical injuries; that it excludes besides the unborn; and that it excludes those who died, over the years, as an arguable consequence of mental wounds.

It is unlikely, fairly considered, that the official figure is more than a few dozen short, though many in Clydebank insist to this day that hundreds more perished. We simply cannot now be sure. And recent, exhaustive efforts to tally the local casualties by West Dunbartonshire Council – whose staff researched over months on the list of names for an additional memorial at Dalnottar; and who appealed through every available outlet for public help – stopped at 522 named local dead. These bronze tablets, with this solemn roll of honour and designed and cast by Tom McKendrick, were laid and dedicated in March 2009.

What is undeniable, even from the final government statistics, is that as a proportion of its population Clydebank lost more lives than any other British conurbation: the scale of physical damage was (and would remain) unprecedented. 'Glasgow lost many more houses in the same raids,' Angus Calder wrote in 1969, 'but its small neighbour had the honour of suffering the most nearly universal damage of any British town.'

The uncovering and defusing of unexploded bombs was another nagging pressure in the hours and days following the raid and, indeed, a chore that continues to this day: there is some Second World War bomb incident or other, most years, in west-central Scotland. In 1941 itself, there was but one practical distinction: bombs on land had to be attended to by Army Bomb Disposal Squads, but those in the Clyde or other areas of water fell to Naval Mine Disposal Squads. (The Senior Service also attended to undetonated parachute-mines, afloat or no, arguing – with some truth – that these were primarily intended for waterways.)

The dangers of such work need scarcely be exaggerated. Dozens and dozens of these brave men were blown up in Britain throughout the duration of the war and, from Northern Ireland to Iraq and Afghanistan, their skills have been deployed at no less risk since. They tried in Clydebank, Glasgow and elsewhere to be patient with unnecessary call-outs – under the universal coat of dust and dirt, it was hard for the amateur to distinguish at a glance between a half-buried domestic hot-water cylinder and a half-buried German bomb; but there were many false alarms. According to MacPhail, '224 UXBs (or unexploded bombs) were reported, but on investigation as many as 130 were discredited. In his report, the Major in charge of the Royal Engineers, like professionals in other walks of life, severely criticized the amateurs, the wardens and the policemen who had wasted the sappers' time when so many urgent cases were to be attended to.'

It was a fraught business. Roads about were at once closed, and houses nearby briskly evacuated, when a UXB was confirmed. There was then the nerve-wracking distinction to be made – and only by close investigation – as to whether a UXB really was a UXB (a defective or damaged bomb that had failed to go off, though it might be pretty unstable and nevertheless a menace) or a deliberate, insidious delayed-action bomb, never intended to detonate on impact but set by dastardly Germans to blast hours or even days later.

'These time bombs were called "tickers" by the sappers,' writes Iain MacPhail, 'who used a giant stethoscope to listen for the clockwork mechanism. The maximum delay for a time bomb was ninety-six hours' – four days – 'after which period, if they had not exploded, they were treated as UXBs.' And Angus Calder casts further light, from his magisterial history of the Home Front, over the general British ordeal of the Blitz.

Perhaps one in ten bombs dropped . . . were duds; but others were equipped with delayed-action fuses and all 'UXBs' had to be treated as if they were 'DA.' At first, all premises were evacuated and all roads closed within a six hundred-yard radius of each bomb. Only a handful of troops, Royal Engineers, were present to deal with them [*in 1940*] and by the end of October, though a special organisation had been created, there were three thousand UXBs waiting for treatment. Hundreds, even thousands, of people might be made homeless by one dud bomb. The cold courage of the bomb disposal squads was one of the marvels of the period. It was spectacularly in evidence when the most famous UXB of all entered the ground at an angle, very close to St Paul's, on September 12th, and began to creep towards the foundations of the cathedral. With great bravery, it was finally extricated on the 15th, was driven in a lorry at headlong speed through the East End, and exploded in Hackney Marshes, where it made a crater one hundred feet in diameter. . . . In September 1940, the King instituted the George Cross, an award for great heroism in the fighting forces. But most George Crosses went to soldiers, notably to men of the bomb disposal squads . . .

UXBs were an untold nuisance, as Peter Lewis outlines, 'awaiting attention, causing houses to be evacuated and streets to be closed for 600 yards in all directions. Their nuisance value was far greater than the damage to life that they posed – greater than the Germans realised, or they would have dropped more of them. A third of those rendered homeless were turned out by unexploded bombs, and police guards were placed outside their houses in case they were tempted to step back inside for something they had left behind – a bottle of whisky or a change of underclothing could be a great temptation.'

With all the road-closures provoked by a bomb that might – or might not – shortly go off, even pedestrians had a sorry time of it. George Orwell wrote of 'little groups of disconsolate-looking people wandering about with suitcases and bundles turned out by unexploded bombs'. As for himself, so many roads around his own Baker Street residence had been roped off that his usual walk home from work – some 300 yards – was like 'solving a maze'. Vera Brittain – her daughter, Shirley Williams, would make her mark in later British affairs – had been forced out of her Chelsea home by a UXB. Every day – several times a day – she would telephone her town hall for permission to return. 'No, madam, the delayed-action bomb behind your house has not yet exploded,' they would intone. Another woman would write her sister, 'I do hope your bomb will go off soon and not blow up 254 and that you have got out the things you need, including the wireless . . .'

All the men who had to attend to these lethal cylinders – the crews of Bomb Disposal – were volunteers. 'Somehow their faces seemed different from those of ordinary men, however brave and faithful,' Churchill himself would memorialise. 'They were gaunt, they were haggard, they had a bluish look, with gleaming eyes and exceptional compression of the lips.'

As one great strip of docklands, with tall and nodding cranes in much number along her banks, the Clyde could present another complication: the silk and lines of parachute-mines frequently caught on these. My own Govan-reared uncle, the Reverend Angus Smith, vividly recalls seeing one Luftmine in March 1941 dangling, in silent menace, from a high jib by the river near his home, and

MacPhail has a diverting account of how, with steely resolve, another suspended bomb was effortlessly disposed of in Clydebank's Radnor Park.

> Parachute mines were the responsibility of the Royal Navy Mine Disposal Squads. Forty-six UXPMs were reported (there seems to have been a number of duplicated reports) but thirty were discredited or had already exploded and sixteen were dealt with by the Navy. . . . Navymen complained about lack of definite information about the location of the UXPMs, which involved unnecessary reconnoitring. When the naval squad arrived the men took their equipment over to the east of Kilbowie Road where most of the UXPMs had fallen, and two officers, accompanied by the Deputy Town Clerk, Hastings, to show them the locations, went over to the west side. A parachute-mine was a huge affair, about eight feet by three feet, constructed of light metal and suspended from a parachute. There was one of them just off Radnor Street hanging from a damaged gable by its parachute cords and swaying in the breeze. Because of its precarious position, the officers decided to detonate it by rifle fire, which one of them effected with his fourth shot. A terrific explosion ensued (the blast of a parachute-mine was reckoned to cause damage to houses up to four hundred yards away) with the officers and Hastings seeking safety behind an ARP shelter.

It speaks volumes for what little was left, unwrecked, of Radnor Park that this was exercised; any additional damage was but academic. Before that winter, the town would be horribly reminded of the menace unknown, sunken bombs could pose. And bombs of the Second World War – many the more unstable after decades inhumed – can still kill: on Tuesday 1 June 2010, as the last chapters of this book were being written, a 1,100 lb Allied bomb blew up in Göttingen, Germany. It had been found seven metres deep in ground being opened for the construction of a sports centre, and houses in the general area were still being evacuated by the authorities when the 65-year-old bomb went off, claiming the lives of three bomb disposal officers as they prepared to remove the detonator. Two others were gravely injured; four more had to be treated for shock. The oldest victim, at 55, had been born a decade after the unconditional surrender of Nazi Germany and the end of the war.

We should here honour Iain MacPhail for writing on this issue with absolute authority: on being called up himself to active service in October 1941, he volunteered calmly for bomb disposal duties, and spent two years living daily with death, in this wracking service, at Southampton, Portsmouth and elsewhere, before resuming his teaching career.

On Monday 7 April 1941, just after half past eight in the evening, the sirens wailed once more; the enemy took his time, but the first bombs fell on Glasgow – in Aikenhead Road, near an important locomotive-depot at Polmadie – at 23:10. Then two fell south of the Great Western Road. One merely left a crater, blocking the Boulevard some 200 yards west of Garscadden Road. The other landed at Lock Thirty-five on the Forth and Clyde canal, bursting its banks. The Yoker Burn was suddenly inundated with a rush of angry, gushing water. Shortly it would flood (and block) Dumbarton Road.

Bombs sang down from a plane over Yorkhill Quay, one crashing in the river and others exploding in Govan, doing some serious damage in the Harland and Wolff shipyard, and more to houses on Govan Road and Water Row, where a perilous gable forced the closure of the Govan ferry for some days. Five people were injured by shrapnel. Parachute-mines exploded by Largs and by Greenock and 12 bombs fell on two farms by the Ayrshire village of Riccarton. At Gretna, right on the border, a 'trail of 50 kg bombs', relates Andrew Jeffrey, destroyed the Masonic Hall, killing 20 people and injuring 19.

More bombs fell on Gelston Street in Shettleston, causing many casualties five minutes later, two others landed in Springburn. One unexploded 500 kg monster would within hours be found, undetonated, 6 feet under the floor of a classroom at Possilpark School, Alexander Street. In the south side of Glasgow, as yet more fell, and a great many homes were wrecked, an officious janitor later refused to allow 120 refugees into the rest centre at Pollokshields Primary School without official instructions from on high. On Seaward Street, a two-storey cooperage was destroyed, and the same bomb ignited a chimney fire in a tenement close at hand. Just before midnight, bombs had a lucky strike on two Glasgow goods-train stations – at High Street and College Street. Sixty-five wagons were damaged and rails fantastically buckled. On Kent Street, one bomb killed 16 people. Charlotte Street, Soho Street, Bell Street and Bellfield Street were all hit and a shower of incendiaries was strewn between Glasgow Green and Lancefield Street; another huge bomb landed in the ICI yard at Lancefield Street and into the murky water of Queen's Dock, but neither did serious damage.

Hutcheson's Academy, one of the upper-crust city schools, had playing fields at Thornliebank. Four bombs now ripped into them; four more fell in Giffnock, between Arden Drive and Percy Drive. In a typical false alarm for bomb disposal crews, one was summoned the following day to examine a 'suspicious hole'; in a Thornliebank garden. It turned out the gardener had left it, while transplanting roses. South and west of Glasgow, the Germans flew and bombed: by Eaglesham House, on Pollok estate, in Linn Park. Eight bombs fell on Cathkin Braes. One, landing at a farm by Carmunnock, failed to explode. Jeffrey details thirty-seven more landing around East Kilbride and Strathaven (five did not go off) and a further scatter in Renfrewshire, on 'Paisley, Neilston, Patterton, Bishopton, Inchinnan, and Abbotsinch airfield, three dropping on the airfield itself. A huge 1,000-kg "Hermann" remained buried south of Renfrew airport until 1946 . . .' It survives, harmless and on display, at RAF Wittering.

The West End was hit again. Three bombs had gone off in leafy Westbourne Gardens, at its corner with Westbourne Road, and in Hyndland Road. Worse, another from the same stick lay unexploded on the front lawns of Redland Hospital. A senior ARP warden set up roadblocks, but they were evidently of inadequate construction as several vehicles – no doubt driven by terrified residents – simply roared past him, one going at 'quite thirty miles an hour', he would later record in shocked tones. Boy Scouts did service as stretcher-bearers, evacuating patients to Cleland Hospital in Lanarkshire; the bomb was defused the following day by a Lieutenant Gerhold of 91 Bomb Disposal Squad. Later that morning a delayed-action bomb detonated in the basement of 49 Polwarth Gardens; a bewildered collie was found probing wreckage in Westbourne for its dead owner. More bombs fell at Connell's shipyard, badly damaging a vessel under build, and in Mechan's ironworks. The soap factory of James Young and Co. was demolished. Eight folk were hurt at three in the morning when a mine fell on empty land at Springfield Road, Dalmarnock. The worst explosion of all had been two hours earlier, when one huge bomb and many incendiaries landed on Shawlands. No. 33 Deanston Drive collapsed and the two adjoining tenements, Nos. 31 and 35, were substantially demolished. On Afton Street, 10 people were trapped in a back-court shelter. Others had been pummelled with rubble behind James Gray Street.

Here would unfold another sad little Glasgow rescue fiasco. An ambulance-depot superintendent from Pollokshaws, Harry Pike, was searching in the Deanston Drive tenements for survivors when ordered out: falling down around him. A veteran of the First World War, Pike 'was back on the scene two days later when moaning was heard coming from the wreckage,' details Jeffrey. 'He crawled through a gap not much more than two feet square and into a cavity where he found two women, one seated in a chair and the other lying at her feet. Both died shortly afterwards, bringing the death toll at the incident to eighteen.'

The last bombs of the raid fell on unbuilt land by Easterhouse. The German attack of 7–8 April 1941 killed 29 people, badly injured 71 and slightly hurt 253; 4,000 people (though most but temporarily) were made homeless. The central Scotland targets apart, more bombs fell in odd Highland localities, dropped by lost or fleeing German aircraft: two on Loch Long, two at the head of Loch Fyne and two on the large and scantily populated Isle of Jura. A full 30 fell on Morar, much further north. Two German planes were brought down over England.

On 16 April 1941, at 03:45 hours, a lone aircraft dropped two 250 kg bombs at 1 Wallace Street and 1 Thom Street on Greenock, killing eight and hurting others. But the last and, in their own way, most terrible German raids on Clydeside began early on Tuesday 6 May. A substantial force – 183 enemy bombers – converged on river and estuary, as sirens howled belatedly at three minutes past midnight from Stranraer to Oban. The first bombs hit Maryhill at 00:25 hours, where the Maryhill East goods-station seems to have been a target. Two old women at 3 Falcon Terrace had a striking escape: it was all but levelled by three bombs, one in both front and rear gardens and one hitting the house itself. Yet, as Mr Scott the head warden later wrote, 'From the few stones that remained standing, two elderly ladies came back from the dead.'

Another bomb exploded in a back-court at 21 Crosbie Street, trapping thirteen people in a crude shelter: six were gravely hurt and three women would die. Another blasted the front lawn of the Maryhill Old Parish manse; yet, despite the damage to his home, the minister insisted on taking in many Crosbie Street casualties. And yet more bombs are detailed in Maryhill – Rosedale Gardens – and Shawlands (Midlothian Drive) and elsewhere on the south side. Two mines and a bomb exploded all but simultaneously in Drumchapel, on a field beside the canal and Blairdardie Road at 01:10 hours. There was widespread blast damage. There were besides more bombs on the margins of Clydebank, though only two localities within its own council bounds were hit. An exploded bomb damaged the Power House at Rothesay Dock; it would be defused by 91 Bomb Disposal Squad the following day. A Luftmine nearby damaged a gas main; down at Dalmuir Station, bombs damaged the 'up' track of the London and North-Eastern Railway line to Glasgow. Further UXBs were found along or near the same line at Renton, Dumbarton and Howgate; a branch line for the Earnock Colliery was hit near Burnback Road, Hamilton. Knightswood was yet again battered, fortunately without loss of life: four bombs fell in succession by the length of Kestrel Road. One demolished homes on Baldric Road immediately; another went off the following day, destroying 153/155 Kestrel Road – mercifully, no one was at home. Another house at the corner of Kestrel Road and Pikeman Road was blown to bits by the third, which also cratered the street and set a gas main ablaze. The fourth went off at 08:08, wreaking more havoc and also igniting a gas main.

Yoker was again hit: first by two mines: one of these never exploded at all and the other, on detonating, did some damage to railway buildings. At 02:15, five cottages were destroyed by bombs and 130 homeless people had to be put up, even as the Germans raged about overhead, in the Speirs of Elderslie Hall. (Morning would expose to appalled gaze two more unexploded Luftmines between power pylons at Kelso Park, west of Kelso Street. Factories had to be evacuated and the railway nearby closed until a naval bomb squad had made them safe.) Inevitably, Admiralty tanks at Old Kilpatrick and its environs won the attentions of the Luftwaffe: a bomb at 02:40 hours blew out many windows at Milton School and, five minutes later, according to Jeffrey, incendiaries poured in 'large number' around Milton and Dumbuck. They burned for over an hour but failed to light the underground petrol-storage tanks, largely because locally stationed soldiers (from the 13th Argyll and Sutherland Highlanders) turned out so quickly for firefighting. Two were later commended for gallantry; they had fearlessly tackled incendiaries in a pump-house at the Milton petrol depot, which could have blown up most of Milton.

A lone bomber killed four people in Kilmarnock as it passed south overhead at 01:51 hours and Dumbarton stopped a number of bombs and mines too, though a number failed to explode and, miraculously, no one was killed, though a few fires started and a number of roads were blocked. Thomas Thompson, mindful – like everyone else in these years – that careless talk cost lives, and against the possibility that his ARP log might somehow be seized by the Abwehr, gives characteristically little Dumbarton detail in his entry for 6 May 1941:

> The 'alert' sounded again this morning and began the worst Raid we have experienced in this district. Much damage was done to property and we regret some loss of life. A feature of this 'Blitz' was the excellent work of all services of the ARP and voluntary workers ably assisted putting out incendiary bombs. The raid lasted until 0415 when 'Raider's Past' was sounded. It was about midday before wardens and messengers were dismissed owing to land-mines, HEs, being dropped in D Group. Names of wardens and messengers reporting for duty will be found in Part Time Warden's Book.

'Other bombs fell around East Kilbride, Thortonhall, Busby, Bishopbriggs, Bothwell, Lesmahagow and at the north end of Little Cumbrae,' details Jeffrey, 'but did little damage.' The assault of 6 May is most bitterly recalled in three communities to the west – Paisley, Port Glasgow and – inexplicable as it seemed at the time – the pleasant, even sleepy village of Cardross, right across the estuary from the latter and several miles east of Helensburgh.

The west side of Paisley was hit at 01:13 hours by a spray of bombs and mines. One Luftmine went off in a yard by 34 Newton Street, the blast instantly setting alight the pump and tow-unit of an AFS fire-crew. Three of them died. Another scored a bull's eye on a First Aid Post at Woodside House on William Street. Despite the frantic efforts of rescue-crews, who toiled far into morning, 92 people were killed (including voluntary ambulance men, the ARP senior warden and a local doctor, to say nothing of many more). There were 20 people badly hurt besides. More bombs started fires in Bridge of Weir; another, landing on Queen Street, Renfrew, killed two and hurt six.

In Port Glasgow, it was the east end – by Woodhall station – that bore the local brunt. One bomb blew up yet another inadequate street-shelter, on Woodhall Terrace, and brought down a chunk of tenement close by. Over 30 people died. In Greenock – and much worse was yet to come – tenements on Belville Street were bombed: there were many dead and injured, and still another fired gas main. Firefighters had only just reached the scene when another bomb simultaneously smashed the water main and a 5,000-gallon 'coffer dam' facility erected as the emergency alternative. Nothing could be done but slowly, slowly, arrange and pump a supply from the town's Victoria Harbour, almost half a mile away, as the Belville Street fires raged. A panicked request from Greenock police that troops be sent in – lest there be looting – was sensibly declined, though more constables were dispatched just in case.

But wee Cardross – which boasted nothing of more significance than historical associations with Robert the Bruce, two elegant nineteenth-century churches, an old inn, a modest station and a gentle golf club – took an assault of astonishing ferocity. The alarm was raised around midnight on 5 May and from after two in the morning, the village was under sustained attack by the Luftwaffe. German aircraft flew time and again overhead, unloading in all 63 bombs, flattening houses – especially at the eastern side of the village – and blasting the premises of Cardross Golf Club. James Adie's mother was the respected 'club-mistress' – his father was at sea, and they lived in a tied-home by the club-house – and James, only 16, rescued his mother with some difficulty as the buildings burned down, incendiary bombs bouncing around them.

The following properties were destroyed completely [*writes Arthur F. Jones in his engaging 1985 history of Cardross*], Cardross Old Parish Church, and a cottage across the road (home of Mr William Nicol); Cardross Golf Clubhouse; 'The Cottage' (Mr Hay's), and a smaller cottage (Mr Keywood senior's), both in Peel Street; a cottage in Blairquhomrie Wood occupied by the aged Peter Wilson; Borrowfield House (Lady Denny's) – where Mr Ritchie's ('Bali Hi') now stands; 'Glenlee' (McIntyre family, Sawmill;) – only the shell remained, but it is now rebuilt; semi-detached villas (homes of Mr Shanks and Mr Vallance) on the main road between the Muirholm Hotel and Barrs Crescent; Hope Terrace opposite the Geilston Hall; an old cottage at the foot of the Murrays Road; Barr's Farm; Mollandhu Farmsteading and house.

Some notable properties which were damaged were: Ardenvohr House; Cardross Mill; the railway footbridge at the east end of the station; and Geilston Hall. In addition many more homes in the village suffered caved-in ceilings and blown-in windows, and there were many near misses. Several hundred craters were seen scattered throughout the village the following day.

James Retson, then a young soldier staying with relatives in the village, in 2006 penned a vivid account of the Cardross Blitz which captures fully the sense of civilian helplessness under terror bombing. His aunt Maimie, his uncle Donald and their children Agnes and Barbara had just survived the Clydebank ordeal in March and come

from Clydebank to my uncle's farm at Cardross, still in shock, especially Agnes who had been totally terrified . . . My mother, sister Una, younger brother John and I were already living on Barr's farm so the place was pretty crowded. Outside in the stack yard, Uncle Jim had marked out the site for our Anderson shelter. It was the safest place he could find, but the pieces lay, still unassembled, on the ground. Most of us were in the kitchen when the sirens sounded. All too soon we became aware of the sound of the German planes, a fluctuating hum that my uncle's family had come to know only too well.

Agnes was already trembling when the first incendiaries dropped. Una suddenly took flight and ran out of the house. Despite our fear and the hellish noise, some instinct made us follow at her heels. When we burst into the night the farm was alight. The horses and the bull, which had broken loose, were charging wildly between explosions. My aunt Nancy grabbed a bucket of sand and rushed to the barn to put out an incendiary, but the rest of us stuck with Una who was running towards the local 'big house', Belmont, the only building so

far untouched. She battered on the door shouting for her friend whose family
owned Belmont House.

How we got in, I can't remember, but I do remember the lady of the house
being manhandled into joining everyone else huddled under the huge dining
room table for safety. Suddenly the bombing really began. Even with my eyes
tight shut and my hands over my ears I was aware of the flash of flames and the
thunderous, ear-splitting noise. We all cowered together under the huge table
and I felt someone's warm pee soak my leg. I thought we were dead for sure
when I heard the next, terrible whistle growing louder and louder and felt myself
being hurled across the room. The blast blew off part of the roof and soot from
the chimney covered absolutely everything. I can still remember that dreadful
whistle and women screaming, and waiting to die.

The bombing went on into the night but we stayed put in Belmont House until
morning. It wasn't till then that we discovered what a lucky escape we had had.
Belmont was the only house left standing. Its nearest neighbour was a burnt out
shell. The bomb that had damaged Belmont's roof should have wiped us out,
but instead of landing on solid ground it had plunged deep into the midden
diverting the blast skyward, away from the house and saving us all.

Later we learned that my aunt Nancy was peppered with shrapnel while
trying to extinguish the incendiary and had been buried under a heap of rubble.
In the midst of the bombing, her brother Jim struggled to move the debris with
no help from his injured sister. She said later that she was finally galvanised into
helping dig herself free when Jim told her the rampaging bull was heading their
way. Afterwards she told me she was more afraid of the bull than any bombs.

Barr's farm had been totally flattened. The Anderson shelter site was now a
bomb crater and the stack yard completely destroyed. When I think of it now, in
many ways we were lucky but at the time that wasn't how it felt. Our home and
livelihood had been torn from us in one fell swoop and the shirt-tails I stood up
in were my only possessions in the world.

Across the Firth, in Greenock, another lad – Jim Reynolds – looked over
from the fated Belville Street to the blazing village and exclaimed that Cardross
Point was 'all on fire'.

Sixty homes in the village were wholly or partially destroyed; incredibly,
only one person was killed, 'but one or two elderly people did not survive
much longer,' maintains Jones, 'having received a great shock as a result of the
calamity in general or the damage to their homes in particular. Younger people
worked hard in the coming months to repair damage. The Weirs at Kirkton
Farm, who had suffered the loss of glasshouses, a boilerhouse and various
outbuildings, had within a year rebuilt the tomato houses and other buildings,
cleared the debris, and filled in the surrounding craters.'

The violent death of a neighbour apart, the destruction of the Old Parish
Church was felt most keenly of all. The site had been occupied since 1644 – the
ruins of a still older place of worship survive inland – and the elegant Gothic
building, with its imposing tower, built in 1826 and opened for worship in

April 1827. It could seat 800 people and had a commanding position, sighs Jones, 'with sheltering trees and an elevated position with fine views over the River Clyde'. Late in the nineteenth century, in the mounting pretension of High Presbyterianism, it had been adorned further with a stained-glass window, an organ and a new timber hammer-beam ceiling; what ordinary parishioners most appreciated was the widening of the pews, which hitherto had been so cramped one could not 'stretch a limb or lift one knee after another'.

Now this glory of the village had been destroyed by the Germans, first set ablaze by incendiary bombs then, as men from the vicinity rallied to fight the blaze, a single high-explosive bomb through the roof, demolishing most of the building in moments and sending the church bell crashing to the ground in apocalyptic din. Someone had the presence of mind, at considerable risk, to rescue the congregational records from the session-room. More bombs fell around the manse (which survived) and into the churchyard; the damage to headstones in the churdyard is such that the aircraft in question may besides have sprayed it with machine-gun fire.

But Cardross had not, in fact, been singled out for so hammering an attack. The village was bombed in entire error because a 'Starfish' decoy-site had been built rather too close to it, in the hilly ground behind the village and between Cardross and the Vale of Leven – notably the crowded little hubs of industry that were Renton, Alexandria, Balloch and Bonhill. Indeed, the 'Starfish' site in question had probably been built to lure bombers away from these busy little centres of population (and, still more importantly, Dumbarton) and, like all the others, was an ingenious arrangement of junk and scrap, fat with good burnable rubbish and replete with assorted special effects. As we earlier noted, technicians from what was then the very busy British film industry had gladly given counsel on these projects, which at their most sophisticated featured all sorts of different fires, simulated head-lamps, aircraft landing lights, the flash of tram-cables – using real pick-up arms – and all controlled electrically, by a network of cables. There is no doubt a range of 'Starfish' installations around the high and unimportant parts of Dunbartonshire did substantially dilute the German attack in this spring of 1941: in the raids of May alone, some 205 bombs fell harmlessly in this countryside between Renton and Cardross; and another 196 in all have been counted at Starfish sites north of Clydebank.

The night following, 6–7 May, the Luftwaffe once more swooped on the shores of Clyde. At Ardeer in Ayrshire, aircraft focused on the important ICI explosive works, pounded by two oil-bombs, 64 high-explosive bombs that duly exploded and nine more that did not. 'Twenty buildings were destroyed,' writes Andrew Jeffrey, 'and serious fires started which required the attention of thirty-four fire appliances, Despite this, the major explosion hoped for by the Luftwaffe did not occur.' Three people were killed, one of the bodies being never identified.

Kilwinning was treated to some 300 incendiaries. Stewarton and its environs were dosed with thirteen bombs and two mines, with more falling on Largs and Loudon: at 00:45 hours, another drift of incendiaries was laid over

Langbank. 'Bombs and mines were meanwhile falling across Knightswood and Drumchapel,' records Jeffrey. 'Two mines fell into John Brown's Shipyard in Clydebank at 02:47 hours, damaging a wharf and storehouses, and injuring ten. A number of bombs and incendiaries fell in Dumbarton, one of which struck the Child Welfare Clinic in Strathleven Road, another destroying a nearby gasometer. Bombs also fell around Helensburgh and Balloch.' Meanwhile 250-kg bombs hurled at Rutherglen did considerable damage and killed two women and five children. The one mercy was that neither this attack nor that of 16 April took further Clydebank life.

But the raid is best remembered for the havoc it wrought in Greenock, bombed this night so pitilessly that, of all Scottish towns in the Second World War, only Clydebank eclipsed it in casualties and devastation. Early bombs hit the town's Ardgowan Distillery and started a colossal blaze, 3 million gallons of alcohol igniting in heat and flame of such intensity the German air-crew would report they had hit the local gas-works. 'Burning whisky flowed down the gutters in Baker Street,' notes Jeffrey. 'It ran into the drain and flames sprouted from manhole covers further down the hill. The flames leaping hundreds of feet into the night sky provided a beacon for approaching bombers and illuminated surrounding buildings which were systematically destroyed . . .'

Greenock was arguably the most important port and shipping-centre on the west coast of Scotland, abounding in docks and shipyards and with a significant industrial base. But, as everywhere else, the venom of the bombing fell most mightily on ordinary people.

The town could have fared far worse. But since the attack that morning before, many had taken refuge in the railway tunnels on the east side, or fled town all together, and this undoubtedly reduced fatalities. Another 'Starfish' assemblage behind Loch Thom – mounds and mounds of flammable material quickly ignited to resemble a flaming town – besides diluted the German effort; daylight would reveal dozens and dozens of pointless bomb craters on its moorland. There was besides – as Les Taylor convincingly argues – some hard opposition in the air to the Luftwaffe, which did much to unnerve the Germans and greatly hampered their bombing effort.

Yet Greenock's ordeal this night should not be minimised. The great, inviting lighthouse that had been the Ardgowan Distillery turned fright into nightmare. In the second wave, Heinkels and Junkers poured bomb after bomb into the centre and east of the town. There was 'massive destruction', especially astride Baker Street. Three 250 kg high-explosive bombs and a parachute-mine blasted Dellingburn Power Station; more incendiaries followed. The Westburn Sugar Refinery, laid waste by more bombs and a mine, became a place of horror, employees trapped alive under mangled machinery and tumbled masonry as great rivers of molten caramel boiled over from the smashed sugar-pans. The ooze and torrents of boiling syrup held back those who had come to rescue the victims and, by half past two in the morning, the Greenock inferno could be seen clearly in Clydebank.

Unlike Clydebank, though – and by merciful providence – there was serious RAF resistance in the skies over Greenock: from the Defiant fighter-planes of 141 Squadron, stationed in the spring of 1941 at RAF Ayr. The portly Defiant had failed woefully in the Battle of Britain, once the Germans had cottoned on to its ill-designed armament; it had, for instance, no forward-firing gun. In the summer of 1940, 141 Squadron had been humiliated at RAF Hawkinge, by Messerschmitt 109s, which shot down five of their Defiants in a mortifying turkey-shoot. They were now in Scotland, in a night-fighter role for which their indifferent aircraft was much more suited; and they deserve more credit for saving much of Greenock than they have been granted.

'Over the course of the two-night Greenock raid,' writes Les Taylor,

141 Squadron . . . claimed two Junkers Ju-88s and a Heinkel He-111 as destroyed. But this modest kill rate hides the greatest success that the Defiants achieved against the Greenock raiders. They transformed the entire situation. Mingling among the bombers, they harassed them with their very presence, forcing them to scatter all over southern Scotland, abandon their bomb loads and race for home. The Defiants from Ayr may not have brought down many bombers, but they had fully redeemed themselves in combat. They should build a statue of a Defiant in Greenock. They were the vital factor in sparing Greenock and its population from the worst that the Luftwaffe were capable of doing to it, by breaking up the raid before it could reach its target and concentrate its bombing pattern on the town.

And thanks to the Defiant, never again would German bombers feel safe over Scotland at night.

By 01:40 hours, two 141 Squadron survivors of that 1940 disgrace – Squadron Leader Wolfe and Sergeant Ashcroft – flew their chubby Defiant furiously upon a German aircraft as it started to bomb Ardeer. The Junkers Ju-88 fled north. But, granted opportunity for cold revenge, Wolfe and Ashcroft showed no mercy. They thundered after the bomb-laden Ju-88 in their silly little plane, blazing away, over north Ayrshire, over Glasgow itself. North of Maryhill, a farmer below heard the machine-gun fire and saw the German aircraft wallowing overhead, bleeding fire. Minutes later, it crashed and blew up at the edge of Dunbartonshire, on hilly ground at Newlands, south of Lennox Castle Hospital. Staffelkapitan Hauptmann Hansmann, its commander, and Oberleutnant Coenen were killed outright. Two comrades had just had time to bale out: one was captured, with no fuss or ill-feeling, by a Home Guard who found the shaken German sat on a golf course, all but immobilised by a badly sprained ankle.

The rape of Greenock continued. Four of the town's churches were destroyed; a collapsing tenement on Antigua Street killed four people in one crash. Just before three, the Town Hall was set on fire. In Rue End Street, there were frantic – and successful – efforts to rescue 30 people from a basement shelter beneath another tumbled tenement. Many horses were, with great difficulty, led alive from the flaming Beaton's Stables on Dalrymple Street. And, with only two clear arterial roads through the town – cratered repeatedly, blocked time and again by falling wreckage – the efforts of firefighters were gravely hampered, as they struggled to reach this or that emergency. Four aircraft at an assembly-plant for RAF Greenock were blown to bits; assorted works and foundries – notably the engineworks of Rankin & Blackmore – were badly damaged. But the docks, shipyards and berthed vessels were all but unscathed; only Lamont's dry dock and Scott's head office stopped German bombs.

The leaders of this gritty burgh did not cover themselves in glory; 'many of those on whom the efficient running of the town depended,' notes Andrew Jeffrey, 'had been among the first to leave . . .' Civil defence services in Greenock all but collapsed, and it was the doughty help of naval ratings from the many ships at the Tail o' the Bank, Major Small of the 14th Argyll and Sutherland Highlanders put on record, who 'gave invaluable help to Greenock and undoubtedly steadied the people of that town'. All through the day preceding, there had been virtual mob scenes as hundreds of desperate townsfolk fought and clawed to board buses out of the place. Though Greenock was twice the size of Clydebank, and the raid somewhat less severe – there was, besides, much regional benefit from the Clydebank experience – emergency catering, the rest centres and so on floundered badly under considerable pressure and amidst smashed infrastructure: mains water, gas and electricity would be down in much of Greenock for days to come. Greenock Corporation, unlike Clydebank Town Council in the first few days of emergency, was allowed to function as a front, for appearance's sake; but everything important was decided by the district commissioner and executed by his staff.

In the two nights of raiding, according to official figures, 246 Greenock residents were killed and 626 injured – 290 seriously. Fifty-two more were described as 'missing – believed killed'. Ninety-five Paisley folk had been killed and seventy-two in Port Glasgow; there were five other Renfrewshire casualties. In all, the two nights of bombing had cost, it was reckoned, 455 lives. Several quarters of Greenock lay in ruins and the work of rescue, demolition, bomb disposal and the clearance of blocked roads lasted for weeks; indeed, the last unexploded parachute-mine – at Renfrew – was not located and made safe until August. Some 12,000 Greenock folk were homeless. Hundreds and hundreds simply packed what they could and walked out of the town, making for Largs and the Ayrshire coast in one direction or Glasgow in the other. And everyone waited fearfully for the Germans once more to fly in with force.

But the Luftwaffe never again launched mass attack on Clydeside. Just when Londoners and Liverpudlians, Bankies and Greenockians and folk the length of Britain felt themselves on the brink of emotional collapse, an eerie lull set in. Bombers no longer flew in any number over Scotland or (with the curious exception of Hull, attacked through June into July as the Blitz otherwise petered out) anywhere else. The last truly appalling air raid of the war, on

London, was on 10 May, just two days after Greenock's ordeal: 550 bombers descended on the British capital and inflicted her worst night of all. Some 1,400 people died, including the mayors of Bermondsey and Westminster. Every mainline railway terminus was hit; many nationally important buildings, from Westminster Abbey to Scotland Yard and St Thomas's Hospital, were damaged. There were over 2,000 fires. Every bridge in London was blocked. A total of 5,000 homes were destroyed and 30 factories were wrecked. And the House of Commons took a direct hit; virtually all we see of the chamber today, painstakingly restored, is of post-war build. For the rest of the conflict, MPs would meet and debate across the lobby in the House of Lords.

Londoners wept openly in the streets; men and women began to whisper they could take no more. But that was it. The bombers of the Luftwaffe were, in fact, now stealthily transferred east, to occupied Poland and other fronts for Hitler's next move. Weeks later, Nazi Germany launched the wholesale invasion of the Soviet Union.

For the rest of 1941, there were but rare intrusions into Scottish skies by Junkers and Dorniers and Heinkels, all in daylight and starring lone aircraft; most of the targets, according to Andrew Jeffrey, were maritime. There was only one more serious air raid on the west of Scotland, on 25 April 1943 and to widespread surprise after such protracted inactivity. Incendiaries fell in Dumfriesshire, some on Kirkpatrick and Annan but more, rather pointlessly, on Ben Vorlich and in Loch Sloy. Later, another shower landed on Neilston and Barrhead as the aircraft flew in over Glasgow, and still more incendiaries were dropped at Crosshill, Strathbungo, Govan and elsewhere. Most of the fires launched did little damage and there was no loss of life: the most notable casualty was the beautiful Queens Park Church on Langside Road, an Alexander 'Greek' Thomson masterpiece, consumed in a spectacular blaze.

There were but final, lethal moments in Clydebank in 1941. On 22 May, two Bomb Disposal officers – Lieutenant Gerhold and Corporal Marshall – were called to deal with a 250-kg UXB which had been uncovered at John Brown's. As Marshall was defusing it, the bomb went off, blowing him to bits.

On 15 September 1941, as tugs manoeuvred in the old Beardmore's basin at Dalmuir, a sunken parachute-mine – undetected and unknown – detonated with extraordinary force. It blew off the stern of one squat little tug, the *Atlantic Cock*; she ended up on the other side of the Clyde, and the body of one of her crew was blasted 'to a terrific height' in the air, according to Iain MacPhail – 70 feet, according to a shaken witness. Nine, including the tug's skipper, were killed in this final snarl of the Clydebank Blitz.

On 9 May 1941, at the Campsie cemetery in Lennoxtown, a quiet little funeral was held – though not without some ill-feeling locally – before a very large but generally respectful crowd. With every decency observed – and Sergeant Johnstone, the local bobby who had arranged most of it, had even managed to secure the appropriate flag – the remains of Hauptmann Hansmann and Oberleutnant Coenen were laid reverently to rest, by the normal rites of Christian burial. The graves were marked with small, plain wooden crosses. A week later, a local Roman Catholic priest sounded off in the *Kirkintilloch Herald*, angry at the use of the Swastika in such a context. 'Why recognize a heathen cross? The Pope denounced it. The use of the Swastika at a Christian burial is a contradiction of the Christian spirit. Patriotism is all very well, but I don't see why we should recognize a pagan emblem as a patriotic emblem . . .'

For the rest of the war, in their season, fresh wild flowers were laid regularly on both lonely little graves by Lennoxtown children, who thought much and said very little.

10

ORPHANS OF THE STORM

HMS *Hood*, as Colin Castle details in his fine little book of notable ships constructed in Clydebank and district, was 'one of four battle-cruisers laid down in 1916 and the only one to be completed'. Launched at John Brown's in August 1918 and of course too late for service in the Great War, she had finally been commissioned in March 1920 and seen extensive but peacable service in the Home and Atlantic fleets. Her weaponry was once and twice updated and, at the last important refit in the winter of 1939–40, she acquired anti-aircraft guns, 20-barrelled rocket-launchers and the new feature of 'gunnery', radar. She was a huge vessel – over 860 feet long, 104 feet broad and drawing a weighty 32 feet at her deepest – and, considering her bulk and her weight of armaments, she was fast, capable of over 32 knots. HMS *Hood*, emphatically, was a ship of Empire.

'The Mighty *Hood*', as she was popularly known, was between the terrible global conflicts the largest warship in the world. Alone of her kind, and to those unaware of her faults – which was almost everyone – she had a majestic, purposeful profile. Only the *Queen Mary* eclipsed her as the locally crafted ship in which the people of Clydebank took the keenest pride. Not that the *Hood* was having so notable a war: to date, this spring of 1941, her most significant achievement (and a distasteful one at that) was her part in the destruction of the surrendered French fleet at Oran in July 1940, before it passed into the full control of the Third Reich. She had but one weakness, a cause of concern as early as the autumn of 1919: the adequacy of her armour against the best guns of the day, especially at the middle-belting about her vitals and anything that came straight down, in force from on high, to blast her maindeck. Experts were especially worried about the latest technology in munitions, armour-piercing delayed-action shells. Someone even suggested before her launch that, advanced as the ship was, it might be most prudent to scrap her. Extra plating was added and this and that was adjusted – but, as events would prove, not enough. In critical respects, the *Hood* was obsolete even before her stern kissed the Clyde.

Late in May 1941, the *Hood* had hopes of more substantive glory, and on the 24th and in the company of still another product of John Brown's yard, the *Prince of Wales*, she made contact with the lion of the Kriegsmarine, the battleship *Bismarck* and her consort *Prinz Eugen* in the Battle of the Denmark Strait, the chill wild waters which in fact lie between Greenland and Iceland. The running battle that ensued was confused, some of the facts are disputed, and controversy continues about various decisions of her commander, Vice-Admiral Lancelot Holland. What is certain is that at 06:00 hours, London time, with the *Hood* already hit and battered and with a fire out of control, another salvo of shells from the *Bismarck* caught her amidships. Almost in an instant a vast jet of flame screamed from about the mainmast of HMS *Hood*, followed by a huge explosion, destroying her aft-section. Her stern rose precipitously, then rapidly foundered; then her bow section sank no less rapidly, doomed gunners managing one last salvo at – or at least regarding – the *Bismarck* from a forward turret. The *Hood* had sunk less than three minutes after the fatal blow and only eleven after firing her first rounds; she sank so quickly that, of the 1,418 men aboard, only three survived, rescued by the destroyer HMS *Electra* about two hours after the loss of their vessel. The last, Ted Briggs, died in 2008.

Many old enough to remember those years of struggle still recall news of the sinking of HMS *Hood* as the most shocking of the war, eclipsing even the fall of Singapore. With only three surviving witnesses and – until it was located in 2001 – no sunken wreck to photograph or examine, there is little agreement as to the essence of her end, save that by one means or another her magazine exploded. The impact on British morale was profound, and greatly disturbed the government. The Royal Navy was now ordered, not least for its own reputation, to concentrate all resources on locating and destroying the *Bismarck*.

Days later, on the night of 26–27 May, while serving with the 4th Destroyer Flotilla and in company with four other vessels, the ORP *Piorun* – the Polish-crewed, Free Polish Navy hero of the Clydebank Blitz and another John Brown product – sighted the hounded, harried *Bismarck*. For hours they scurried after her, watching, dodging, shooting, harassing, their low profile and manoeuvrability of much help in evading her guns, and had soon radioed the German behemoth's position to lurking battleships *King George V* and *Rodney*. On 27 May 1941, within hours of safety, caught and disabled by Fleet Air Arm Swordfish biplanes and with her rudder hopelessly jammed, the *Bismarck*, grievously wounded and without power or steering and with no effective armaments still operable, foundered in the Atlantic, some 650 miles west of the French port of Brest. Of her 2,200 crew, only 205 were rescued. Among much and understandable British satisfaction, there was widespread praise for the *Piorun* and her youthful crew, who had taken on the pride of the German Fleet, helped encompass her destruction and lived to tell to the tale.

Many other Clydebank-built ships would distinguish themselves in the war. The *Queen Mary* and the *Queen Elizabeth* – which never quite attained the popularity or cachet of her sister, probably because of the dreich start to her career – were hugely valued as troop transports, being the only ships afloat able to carry an entire division, though the older sister's record was badly blotted when she accidentally ran down her escort, HMS *Curacoa*, off Northern Ireland in February 1942, with the loss of 364 lives. At the other extreme, the wee 1910 paddler *Eagle III*, renamed HMS *Oriole* for what was her second stretch of war service, put in nearly four years as a North Sea minesweeper and took part in the evacuation of Dunkirk, narrowly surviving a 12-hour grounding. The paddler *Duchess of Rothesay* (1895) likewise served in both world wars, performed heroically at Dunkirk and did her bit in minesweeping (for which, with their shallow draft and broad sponsons, paddle-steamers were well suited).

The 1905 *Gatwa* was yet another Dunkirk heroine from Clydebank. The battleship HMS *Ramillies*, turned out by William Beardmore & Co. in 1917, provided artillery cover for the Normandy landings in June 1944. The loss of HMS *Repulse* – with the *Prince of Wales* – to Japanese torpedoes, off Malaya, in 1942 was another hard stroke for British morale in the war; but the *Duke of York* (saved by the *Piorun* in March 1941) finally entered service in November 1942, and proved an invaluable escort for many Arctic convoys. In December 1943 she engaged the German battleship *Scharnhorst*, with fire of such lethal accuracy that the vessel was sufficiently crippled for other Royal Navy ships to finish her off with torpedoes. The *Duke of York* crowned her war with her presence in Tokyo Bay in August 1945, as the Japanese formally surrendered. In all, some 35 ships built at Clydebank, Bowling and Dumbarton served in the Second World War; 20 were sunk, or so battered by service as to be beyond economic repair.

One of the most depressing aspects of the Clydebank Blitz – considering the enormous loss of life, the wounds that throb to this day and the destruction of so much of the town – is how pointless it proved militarily. The Luftwaffe visited Clydebank with terror, but failed to destroy any important war production; some yards and facilities were hampered, and in most instances but for days or weeks.

The German lack of true strategic bombing capacity – her bombers being designed, really, for battlefield use, in support of troops; the impossibility of precision bombing by the scant technology of the day, and an undoubted degree of disorientation between lochs and fjords, the Clyde itself and Forth and Clyde Canal and the Great Western Road, were all factors. But Les Taylor is right to stress that 'unlike the Allied attack on Dresden, the first night of the Clydebank attack was intended as a strategic attack on key industrial facilities and not undertaken purely as a terror raid on civilians alone, regardless of having achieved this very effect.'

Taylor's excellent technical analysis of German tactics in the raid is too detailed to repeat here; but he does highlight the phenomenon of 'creep-back'; the tendency of bomber crews (on both sides) – especially if under attack – to drop their cargo prematurely and fly quickly away from danger. This explains why, in the first wave of the Luftwaffe from the east on 13 March, many bombs were dropped rather pointlessly over residential parts of western Glasgow and indeed as far east as Cumbernauld; the second (western) and the third wave (from the south) were far more devastatingly focused on Clydebank because, by that point, the Pathfinders of KG-100 had started those fortuitous, unmissable blazes at Dalnottar, Yoker and Singer.

In fact, Singer's – by no means the most important work of production in town – was the worst hit; hardly surprising, even before its mountain of lumber was set on roaring flame, once one considers its acreage and the relatively high, exposed position of the Kilbowie site. All that vast and precious stock of timber was lost, and several departments (including the rather stately office accommodation) destroyed or substantially damaged. Yet – and many Bankies found the sight both inspiring and comforting – the great Singer's clock and its tower had miraculously survived, chipped and smoked, but rising above the rubble of factory and town as a spirit undaunted and a talisman of survival.

Early in the attack, the Royal Ordnance Factory at Dalmuir had been bombed (killing three War Department police officers) and production was hampered for a while thereafter by burst water mains. The Turner's Asbestos Works – a product with its own connotations today, but which was then considered essential for insulation in ships and around other machinery – were ravaged by fire. Probably most serious, in terms of the war effort, was all the damage to the Admiralty's oil tanks at Dalnottar and Old Kilpatrick, to say nothing of the loss of much precious fuel – every drop borne to Britain at huge peril to the Merchant Navy, through seas infested with mines and slithering with U-boats. A Whitecrook firm, Aitchison's, which manufactured small marine engines, was besides hit hard and could not resume production for several months; not that national survival was likely to hinge on motorboats. But only one industrial concern – the Strathclyde Hosiery Company – was absolutely flattened; and all it made was stockings.

There were also transport difficulties, as Iain MacPhail further details. Two of the three railway lines that ran exuberantly through the town – the LMS track, at assorted points between Dumbarton and Scotstoun, and the LNER one, between Dalmuir and Clydebank Central – were hit by bombs, or had bomb-made craters rather too near the tracks for comfort, or badly shaken bridges that had to be inspected for safety. There were besides assorted UXBs and some blast to signal-huts and station buildings. Clydebank Central Station itself had been severely damaged and would not open again for months. (There is a good story of railway-related heroism from the March 1941 attack, when a senior ARP warden, John S. Steele, saw a passenger train ahead of him, cantering blithely towards the bomb crater Steele had just hastened past. Steele ran like fury towards the locomotive, gesticulating frantically and blowing his whistle, until the engineer pulled up in the nick of time.)

Yet Rothesay Dock, which had absorbed one blast or explosion and one bomb or Luftmine after another, and still surrounded by the charred remains of warehouses and the sprawled rubble of ruined buildings, was back in action within days; and Clyde river traffic generally in the vicinity within the week. Considering not just the considerable (if in many instances largely cosmetic or inconvenient) damage to yards and factories, the rapid recovery of Clydebank industry in the circumstances should still impress us.

Scarcely a fortnight after the raid, on 1 April 1941, a report from the Glasgow Emergency Reconstruction Panel is remarkably upbeat, and there is no reason to doubt the honesty of this confidential document. At John Brown's – the most important war-related Clydebank enterprise of all – the state of production was 'Normal in shipyard and machine shops; almost normal elsewhere.' Yet the damage report is sobering: '2 timber stores and pattern store destroyed. Experiment tank, funnel shed and shafting shop badly damaged. Roofs of brass finishing shop, tool room and pattern store damaged.' At Clyde Blowers Ltd – who made boiler equipment – it was normal, *simpliciter*. Arnott Young and Co. Ltd were 'normal' too. At Brockhouse & Co. Ltd, where parts for cars and trucks were turned out, it was likewise normal, despite 'severe blast damage' to roof and walls. Beardmore's (Diesel) Ltd in Dalmuir had nine furnaces in normal operation already and expected normal production by mid April. Yet two-thirds of the main shop had been wrecked, two furnaces destroyed by high-explosive bombs and all furnaces stopped for a period.

Dawson & Downie Ltd – marine pumps – reported 'almost normal' production, as did Steedman & McAllister (lifebelts) and Turner's Asbestos Cement works. D. & J. Tullis Ltd (they made heavy machine tools) had sustained considerable damage, including a high-explosive bomb devastating the workshop; two weeks later, though, they were at '70% normal production'. The Royal Ordnance Factory at Dalmuir reported a little limply, after a less than detailed admission of 'severe damage to roofs of factory' and 'offices damaged', that they were 'returning to normal production'.

The report of Singer's Manufacturing Co. Ltd – armaments and sewing machines – oozed majestic honesty. 'Timber yard, sawmill, wood preparing dept., small electric motors department with stock, maintenance dept. with stock, counting house, shipping shed with contents all destroyed. Foundry, forge, gas producers, locomotive shed, main offices, canteen all partly damaged.' The consequences? '50% of war production restored; sewing machine production – nil.' But the defence of the realm did not hinge on plackets and hems.

The measures of relief, the schemes of welfare quickly unleashed on Clydebank in the days after the raids were of motives as much military as humanitarian. The priority was to encourage as many as possible back to work as soon as possible, that the wheels of war production might rumble again. So, as MacPhail details and as we have seen, workers 'were given their meals at the Town Hall until the firms arranged their own canteens; travel vouchers were supplied free at first but after the middle of April a maximum fee of 3s. was required. Whitecrook Primary School was converted by the Scottish Special Housing Association to accommodate up to 250 homeless workers.' The strike of so-called apprentices in the Clydebank shipyards – most were time-served journeymen still cheated of a full tradesman's wages – was, as we saw besides, fast and willingly abandoned. 'On Friday 14th March, after the first raid, the secretary of the apprentice engineers, John Moore,

offered the services of the strikers to assist in clearing debris, acting as
messengers, etc.,' notes MacPhail. 'A Ministry of Labour Tribunal gave the
boys a promise that if they resumed work their claims would be considered;
and the two-week-old strike came to an end on Thursday March 20th,
national negotiations on wages starting the following day and an award in
favour of the apprentices' claims being made in due course.'

As for those without homes and of no essential trade or employment, and
those who could not work and the thousands of children as yet not of an age to
work, the authorities made other plans. That old pre-war, pre-Blitz Clydebank
so many mourn to this day had been substantially destroyed by the bombs of
the Luftwaffe. So many, too, had been killed, to the point where every
Clydebank resident had in one way or another been slashed by bereavement:
practically everyone had lost someone in their family or a cherished friend, to
say nothing of wider acquaintance. But what really sank that Clydebank
community – which would never return and could not, in human terms, be
rebuilt – was the scattering of so many survivors, by the thousand and across
the breadth of Scotland, and most of these for years. Many would never come
back. The children of the town, especially, were cast far and wide, as orphans
of the storm.

The thousands of Clydebank evacuees could not long be accommodated in
public facilities or other makeshift quarters, some of which had been resorted
to of desperate expediency: even a venerable Loch Lomond paddle-steamer,
the *Prince George*, at rest by Balloch pier, had been commandeered as
emergency lodging for homeless families. So for some time were her active
consorts, the *Princess May* and the *Prince Edward*. But the craft had soon to
ply for the summer: the authorities had sensibly let Loch Lomond excursions
continue throughout the war, as the anti-submarine boom over the Firth and
other security concerns had ended Clyde cruising for the duration; and these
were hugely popular weekend outings for war workers and their families.
Assorted schools in the Vale of Leven had besides to reopen for classes;
guesthouses throughout the Clyde resorts started noisily to fret about summer
trade. Those in authority now, by appeal and wheedling and by emotional if
public blackmail, sought to arrange private billets by the thousand. Officials
were alerted all over the country, and anyone with a spacious private home –
outwith the official evacuation areas – came under duress to put up those
bereft or dispossessed by the Luftwaffe. There was besides a financial induce-
ment: 5 shillings, per evacuee, per week, from the government to mine host.

The suffering of families, and especially of traumatised children, at this
time was considerable; all too often, as MacPhail rightly asserts, they were
'regarded as a burden or an imposition, and the result was ill feeling on both
sides'. Even those who received them with conspicuous graciousness were not
always averse to underlining at every opportunity the great charity involved.
Clydebank evacuees and orphans came under pressure to serve as farm
labourers, unpaid help in the shop or toiling domestic skivvies in arrangements

that were never well supervised. It is likely that not a few, besides, both girls and boys, attracted the sweaty attention of paedophiles, at a time when few children had the vocabulary to describe sexual acts and in an age when – should they even think of confiding to an adult – it was improbable they would be believed.

It is easy to forget, too, there had been awful publicity – in both local and national newspapers – after the wholesale evacuation of women and children in 1939: mothers who were illiterate, tipsy, pub-daft drabs; filthy ill-disciplined children with mange, worms and head-lice, relieving themselves on carpets and with no idea how to conduct themselves in self-consciously polite society. Many children, scared and homesick and even of most respectable background, wet beds continuously from stress and disorientation – and that was still more true of traumatised little Bankies who had come through so terrifying an experience.

There are, inevitably, horror stories, and Meg Henderson might here be allowed her head – though she is rather cruel to the receiving town – in narrating what remains one of the most notorious, not least from the future eminence of a child at the centre of it.

> Meanwhile the evacuated searched for homes, and the Laird family, a mother with two little boys, a baby girl in a pram and their red setter, Crumpet, had been evacuated to Kirkintilloch, a douce settlement of wealth and respectability outside Glasgow. Kirkintilloch, where . . . the citizens would not permit a pub within their community, for fear that the riffraff on the outside would enter their boundaries and bring drunkenness and debauchery to mar their genteel sensibilities. Instead the riffraff of Kirkintilloch took their own drunkenness and debauchery outside to the surrounding areas, where it so obviously belonged. That Mrs Laird had no idea of what had become of her husband was bad enough, but she and her children were taken around Kirkintilloch's grand villas, and bungalows with villa aspirations, in an attempt to find someone who would offer them a roof over their heads. But the God-fearing residents who obviously had room to spare didn't even offer a stable, at least not to the mother and her children. The red setter dog was something else, though; they were prepared to offer Crumpet a home. Eventually a miner and his wife, living in a council house with three children of their own, welcomed the Lairds into their home without a second thought and cared for them, Crumpet too.

The irony of all this went deep into the soul of wee Gavin, then eight years old. It also radicalised him: Gavin Laird became an active trades unionist and Labour supporter, becoming eventually General Secretary of the Amalgamated Engineering and Electrical Union, and has had a long and distinguished part in public life.

Little Sarah Hughes, her older brothers and her mother had endured a protracted and terrifying search for shelter – any shelter – as the bombs rained down.

My mother, who was expecting a baby, had no shoes, and she held me by the hair so I wouldn't get lost. Eventually we did get into a shelter in Montrose Street and stayed there until morning. Then we found my father and my brothers and went to my aunt's house. Later we went up on to the Boulevard to lie flat in the fields.

We were taken first to Helensburgh. As we travelled, shrapnel was hitting the bus and my mother was hysterical. When we got there, we were directed to St Joseph's Hall where we were given a camp bed and some clothes. Afterwards, we were evacuated to Craigendoran. It was difficult because nobody wanted a baby and three other children. But eventually we were placed in a house called Dunvegan, on Campbell Street . . .

It was easier for those who had, for instance, relatives or close friends in safe countryside locations, and could make private arrangements. The luckiest had got out of town just in time. 'My dear mother had been ill for six months before the Blitz and Dr Allan had ordered her to leave Clydebank,' Mary Brockway – née Armstrong – would write, from New Brunswick in Canada, in 1999. 'So she and my Dad went to Newmilns in Ayrshire and were there that night. Mother told me afterwards she had prayed for the people of Clydebank and her family. She read the 91st Psalm and was comforted by those wonderful promises of our God.' The family home was destroyed in the first raid, and those besides of Mary's brothers.

David Dyer's experience, related in the same splendid anthology of Clydebank stories, is perhaps average: no great kindness, no notable cruelty, just bewilderment, adaptation, acceptance and in time, for him, at least return. The Dyer family lived in Bowling, in a Windsor Street tenement, and their flat was all the more crowded that fateful 13 March as an Italian family, the Utinis, was staying with them:

The building was bombed and it collapsed, and my mother and myself were buried for thirty-six hours. My brother John, who was ten years old, was killed. Granny Utini was also killed. The reason, I believe, that my brother was killed was that he was sitting beside the fire with Granny Utini. And I and another child were under the table. I've been told that an incendiary bomb came down the chimney. And that was the blast that blew the house apart and killed my brother.

I sustained multiple bruising and shock, and my mother had severely damaged her leg. We subsequently ended up in Robroyston Hospital and one of the first mental pictures is of me playing in a ward and seeing the head doctor walking about the ward followed by two dachshund dogs.

The next picture I have in my mind is standing on a table in Bank Street in Alexandria wearing a wee pair of woolly knickers and a woolly semmit and being dressed in navy blue shorts, a navy blue jumper with a blue stripe, a tie with horizontal bars, socks, boots, a trench coat, a skull cap, a small suitcase with one or two belongings, and a Mickey Mouse gas mask. And a label tied round my neck, stamped, 'Evacuee'. We were then taken over to the station and I was evacuated to Ardrishaig.

I have only one or two pictures of Ardrishaig in my mind. There were four children in the house where we lived. We were looked after by what I thought was an old lady, she could have been anything between forty and sixty. I just don't remember. I remember the oldest boy was about twelve and he, very sadly, was drowned in Ardrishaig, in the harbour.

I spent eighteen months in Ardrishaig, till the time I was ready to go back to school. I was then sent back to . . . Renton because I had an aunt who lived there, and my mother was being discharged from Robroyston.

When I started in the Renton Public School I was the only child who got Red Cross parcels from America. I have a very strong mental picture of opening a box in the school. There was a toy Santa full of jelly babies, and a box of soap powder. And they both had burst. And all the jelly babies were mixed up with the soap powder.

After my father was discharged from the army, we were sent back to Bowling to live in temporary accommodation, because that's where we had come from. I lived there till I started High School in Clydebank. Then, after my first year in Clydebank High, I returned to Dumbarton, and that's where I've been ever since.

The United States, of course, had joined the Second World War in December 1941, and her citizenry generously supported assorted measures of comfort for young British evacuees. There is an eerie sense through Dyer's account as of a tape that has been wiped; of particularly distressing or painful memories that have been quietly deleted.

But the experience of Betty Smart – now Mrs Moore – was still more chaotic, no less frightening and at its lowest practically Dickensian. Hers is a detailed account, at once intimate and sorted and with abiding anger. Her opening description of the blast on her Dalmuir Home – 7 Beardmore Street – that killed her 48-year-old mother, Susan, her 11-year-old brother David and her baby brother Robert, and left her and her father James the only survivors, is written, as if to gain vital emotional distance, in the third person.

Just then there was an almighty bang, and all the lights were blown out, doors were crashing, windows smashing. Nobody could see what was happening. The children by this time were crying for the parents they could no longer see because of the darkness. Betty grabbed hold of somebody's hand, hoping it might be David's. Another loud bang and a terrible rumbling sound, screaming – and then SILENCE.

How long Betty had been lying there she did not know. All she was aware of was she could not move, she was jammed under something very heavy. She tried calling out, but nothing happened . . . [*Five and a half hours passed, she would later learn, and then:*] 'Just lie still, hen. We'll get you out.' Then more shouting. 'Teddy-bear coat did the man say? Aye, that's what it is.' More clanging, then there was a hint of daylight . . . The next thing she saw was the grief-stricken face of her father as he was handled the bundle in the teddy-bear coat. 'I've got you, Betty, you'll be just fine.'

Betty was duly extricated, without significant injury. That night, she and her father repaired to her grandparents' flat at Anniesland, and there endured still another night of bombing 'as the all too familiar wail of the siren once again filled me with a terrible fear. This time I was carried off to an air-raid shelter where I was comforted by my grandparents. How long this lasted I have no idea. My memory has been completely wiped out.'

She could remember very briefly attending school at Anniesland. Then she was sent with her grandparents to Port Bannatyne, by Rothesay on Bute, where two aunts had guesthouses. Betty Smart went to school here too – her fourth, and she was still a primary pupil. Eventually – once the German raids had ceased – they all went back to Anniesland, but her grandmother 'was not at all well. She never really recovered from the shock resulting from the Blitz. My father meanwhile was trying to arrange a more permanent home for me away from Clydeside. He had a distant relative in Blantyre and it was arranged I go there. How this came about I don't know, but this started the unhappiest time of my life.'

She had been sent, in all innocence, away to an environment of exploitation and abuse.

These people were complete strangers to me. There was a husband and wife and their son, his two boys and a bachelor son. Attendance at school number five was soon arranged, as were my daily duties in the house, these being I would set the table for all the meals, clear up after meals, wash and dry the dishes, keep the furniture dusted and, when required, get any shopping. Only then could I do my school homework. I never protested at bed-time. I was so tired I was grateful for the break.

Although I was doing quite well at school, nobody showed any interest, and even when my name was put forward to represent the school in a writing competition, nobody wanted to know. This competition covered the whole of Lanarkshire, and I was over the moon when I won. I was to be presented with my prize on prize-giving day. I asked if anybody would be coming that day, but was told nobody had any time and, anyway, anyone could write a composition. I consoled myself by thinking the school hall would be so busy no one would notice. But I knew I was alone.

After the summer holidays I was to start secondary school which was some distance away. I stayed in High Blantyre and the school was in Low Blantyre. It would take me a good twenty minutes to briskly walk there. I could do either Languages or Commercial. I opted for the latter, and for the first time I felt I was doing something for my future. I fell in love with Mr Pitman's Shorthand, and vowed I'd show them. Here was something they knew nothing about; it was a complete mystery to them.

One Saturday, when I went to bring the coal upstairs from the cellar in the backcourt, I discovered to my dismay the coalman had delivered that day, and the coal was all in big lumps, much too big for the fire, even if I had managed to fit it into the pail. I had to break it up. No hammer of course, so I thought if I dropped it on the ground it would break and I could lift the pieces onto the shovel – no waste. It was all working well, the coal breaking nicely with very little mess. Just then, I caught sight of Jenny, the woman looking after me. She had come down to the bin and, seeing my method of breaking the coal, nearly went berserk. She was carrying a brush and this she took over my back with such fury. How I got away from her flailing hands I don't know, but I rushed up the stairs and threw myself weeping sorely in to the bed, every bone aching.

I heard her come in the house carrying the pail. She banged the door closed, completely ignoring me. Later on I heard her setting the table. The family came home for tea and carried on with their meal. What excuse she gave for my absence I'll never know . . .

With quiet resolve, and no little guile, Betty Smart organised herself and, later that Saturday evening, as her ghastly hosts relaxed as usual with a play on the radio, she very quietly ran away, carrying a small but heavy suitcase and taking an elaborate succession of buses to Glasgow and Yoker – where she knew her father was lodged with her uncle. With convincing poise she talked herself deftly past suspicious conductresses and drivers. She was received warmly by her menfolk, if in great surprise, and – as she related her experiences – to mounting anger. What reprisals fell out in Blantyre she never knew, but Betty was allowed for the meanwhile to stay and – after the agreement of terms – permanently.

Not that the deal sounds so generous on any feminist reading. 'I realised if I were to stay, I would have to do my own laundry and share some of the household duties, and this would have to be fitted in with schoolwork. . . . After a few months, the lady who came to do the stair-washing had to give it up and, wishing to keep things running well, I volunteered to take this duty on. One Friday after school, I decided to start early before the stairs got too busy with workers arriving home for the evening. I was a bit shy of being seen by anyone. However, I had not bargained for children. Coming across this stranger, they wondered where I had come from. I had to laugh when one child said, "Who's she?" "Oh, she's the girl with two daddies." . . . Life for me was a bit hectic, but I was a much happier person and felt I could cope with whatever life in future held for me. After all, wasn't I the girl with two daddies?'

Inevitably, the fraught details and pressures of billeting became heated – between the desperation of families to find reasonably permanent lodging and the pressure officials piled on anyone with abundant room to spare – and, inevitably, it grew politicised. David Kirkwood, yet Labour MP for Dumbarton Burghs, was now nearly seventy years old, still suffused with the class-war vehemence of better, sharper days, and still stung in his humiliated pacificism. On 4 April there was a huge public meeting about the accommodation crisis – he had of necessity to be present. Eight hundred people turned up to hear – and question – Sir Steven Bilsland and the Under-Secretary of State for Scotland, Joseph Westwood. Westwood was pressed hardest; by this stage, Sir Steven was practically family. One local, speaking from the floor, demanded to know why Clydebank people were sleeping in the garages of pleasant, prosperous Milgavie, even as large houses in that little town stood empty. There was uproar. Kirkwood, playing to the gallery instinctively, declared righteously that if there were indeed big houses available, they should be taken over. Inevitably, someone then heckled, 'What about your house?'

Their Member of Parliament was able – with some spirit – to reply he had, at present, three families lodged in his home. His young tormentor interrupted this announcement, and the old tribune of the people lost his temper. 'It's nothing but ignorance on your part. Your kind all need a mob to support you,' snarled Kirkwood. But he had to endure for the rest of the meeting – even through his long-winded speech for the vote of thanks – murmurs and sniping and cat-calls. Professional politicians were not, in 1941, held in much more respect than they are now – especially after they had led Britain into this national disaster – and, apart from the high emotion around billeting, there was local anger against Kirkwood himself, who publicly supported the government's refusal to recognise shop stewards at the Royal Ordnance works in Dalmuir: a position, many reasonably felt, quite at odds with his own record during the Great War.

On 29 May 1941, as Iain MacPhail narrates, Kirkwood 'raised in the House of Commons . . . the conditions in which evacuees were billeted and declared that some had been treated as though they were criminals, citing as an example the case of a family of a father and mother with thirteen children living in a hut. Major Lloyd, MP for East Renfrewshire, the constituency in which the hut was situated, took the matter up as many of his constituents were angered by Kirkwood's language.'

But the aging Red Clydesider had goofed this time. Lloyd was shortly able to produce in the Commons – and read – 'a letter from the mother of the family expressing her gratitude and appreciation of the way she had been treated. Actually, a small committee had been formed locally to look after evacuees and had done their best for the family of fifteen, who refused to be separated. The hut was substantially built, 40 ft. by 20 ft., with a new floor of Oregon pine covered with linoleum, formerly in regular use by Girl Guides and well supplied with water, electric light, gas radiators and sanitary arrangements . . .'

For anyone familiar with typical workers' housing in Clydebank, this would have been for most families a signal improvement. The Glasgow, Dunbarton-shire and Renfrewshire papers soon fizzed with replies to Kirkwood's wild accusations. Meanwhile, the harried town clerks of Clydebank had for many months to field letter upon letter – hundreds of letters – from bombed-out locals begging for a house, any habitable house, in Clydebank.

In two instances detailed by Iain MacPhail, the inconveniences and ongoing instability endured by families in this position certainly fuelled their yearning. One little clan, from Buchanan Street in Dalmuir, had spent a chaotic fortnight more or less camped out in a Masonic hall in the Vale of Leven – shared, no doubt, with not a few other families – before being sent to the Vale of Leven Academy for three more exciting weeks, sleeping on the floor of the school hall (and, no doubt, with dozens of others.) The family was then shuffled to Cove, on the Loch Long side of the Rosneath peninsula and a lengthy journey from Clydebank, and divided by implacable authority when they arrived. The missus and their three youngest children were given a tiny hut; the father and the four oldest left to make what shift they could. They did not endure this for long, and made their way back towards Clydebank and a sister-in-law in Duntocher, 'where they were staying at the time of writing, nine of one family and nine of the other, sleeping on the floor for lack of beds'.

It was little better even for the heroes of the two frightful nights of bombing. Janet Hyslop might well have been head warden of E Group and a veritable rock of the First Aid Post at Radnor Park, but it had not saved her own home: 7 Third Terrace had been bombed to land-fill, and while Mr and Mrs Hyslop were squeezed into the house of the very Provost their two daughters were evacuated to Milnathort, in Kinross on the other side of Scotland. They won no provision as a family in the first allocation of repaired houses; meanwhile, the furious Mrs Hyslop had reports of this councillor and that remarking acidly just how comfortable she and other apparently privileged refugees had been made at Drumry Road. When the second allotting of homes neared, she wrote the Town Council in icy terms of these local baillies:

They seemed to be under the impression that because we were in ex-Provost Smart's house we had the comfort he had. On the contrary, we have one room in which three adults eat, sleep and live. No furniture except what we salvaged from the Warden's Post, ie. forms [benches] from the Church Hall with palliasses for beds, a table and three chairs. The house is occupied by Wardens and members of the First Aid – 15 in all . . . All the windows except part of one are boarded up and none of them open, with the result that the place gets stuffy and is not conducive to good health.

The memories of some forced out of Clydebank at the time include the comic. Bessie Bannister lived with her family in Parkhall, and on 14 March – because she was still recovering from flu – the family elected, when the alarm was raised, to stay in the house rather than brave the dank chill of the Anderson shelter in the garden. It saved their lives. In the morning, the house was still standing, but 'the shelter was devoid of all the sandbags and all the protection and sitting, full of boulders, on the edge of a huge crater. . . .'

'On the Friday evening, twenty-six of us went to Callander in a coal lorry,'

Bessie would write in 1999. 'I had an aunt in Callander who was on the home farm of an estate and she put everyone up, all twenty-six from that coal lorry. When I think back, it's something quite funny I remember. I had received a fur coat for my twenty-first birthday and the one thing I wanted to retrieve out of this Blitz was my fur coat. So I went to Callander with a face as black as coal, hands as black as coal and a fur coat . . .'

Children would cling through decades, as for some anchor to a past normality in a town that by dawn on 15 March 1941 had effectively ceased to exist, to the most intimate detail in memory. 'It was a beautiful, dry, moonlight night,' Isa Cameron – later Mrs MacKenzie – would recall of Thursday the 13th, 'and my brothers and I were all ready to go to bed. The sirens blew, so we had to get dressed again, finishing with the Sunday coat which is what we always did. I'll never forget that coat. It was a dusky pink material, with brown fur around the neck and down to the waist. It was fastened by a button at the waist and a toggle-shaped cloth strap at the neck. I always thought, and still do, it was one of the loveliest things I ever had . . .'

Other girls and boys tried to find some place in their mind – or were forced, by the overwhelming experience, into one – where they could impose an order on things, stick to a plan or routine. In the middle of the raid that killed her mother and her brothers, Betty Smart started to fret about baby Robert's pram; in the last words she and her mother would exchange, the child even suggested that 'as she was not very big, perhaps she could crawl out into the backcourt and rescue the pram' (obviously not thinking how it would get into this crowded place). As, hours later, her grieving parent carried her away, Betty 'caught hold of her father's sleeve. "The pram, Daddy," she said. "Did you get the pram?"'

Anne MacDonald – by 1999, Mrs Fielding – lived at 5 Hill Street in hapless Radnor Park and had returned there after three weeks' evacuation to Arrochar. The home was most strained, for her father was weak and ill. Decades later, though then only nine years old, she recalled the terror of that first raid, and her less than rational thoughts after survival, as they and other families descended progressively to the ground-floor flat for safety:

> Once settled again, someone opened the bathroom door. Everyone gasped as we watched the Terraces, Second and Third, crumpling like a pack of cards. Next, the windows of the flat were blown out by the blast from a nearby bomb. The glass of the fanlight above the main door shattered, showering slivers of glass down on us, many embedding themselves in my mother's neck. The younger children screamed in terror; for some reason I was mute.
>
> With the morning came the all-clear. We trooped upstairs. My father was fine, but oh! my poor mother's scrupulously clean house was a shambles. Soot and glass were everywhere. In the street outside, the scene was one of devastation. The houses on the opposite side of the street were ablaze and the glass was ankle-deep. I remember bargaining with God. 'Please, God, don't send me to Hell. Don't let us die. I'll be good. I'll go for the messages and help polish the

brasses, if You will save us.' The incongruity of these promises did not occur to me. I had never polished the brasses and went only on a rare errand, because my mother had to budget very carefully every week. In any case, would the brasses ever require polishing again and which shop would be open? The child in me was simply endeavouring to bring normality where there was none.

The MacDonalds, too, would have to trek; and then trek some more. Mr MacDonald, ailing as he was, ordered his wife and only child to head to the school premises at Janetta Street for evacuation before the Germans returned. But all went wrong, with the pair trapped overnight – after the little girl's frightened glimpse of the smoking ruin that had been Boquhanran School – and Anne's first encounter besides with Roman Catholic devotions. There 'would be no transport. Someone had blundered. Into the school basement we trailed, to face an interminable night. Women all around were praying aloud, strange frightening incantations such as we never prayed in Boquhanran Church. These were simply set prayers, but the fervour and intensity of the women scared me. . . .'

Meanwhile, oddly neglected by her mother – Mrs MacDonald was trying for word of her husband and his provision in hospital – the child wandered about this centre of crisis more than was good for her. 'As I strolled around looking in the school windows, I remember freezing inside. I saw my first dead body – no, I saw many dead bodies, and parts of dead bodies. No child should ever witness such a spectacle. I became confused. Was it too late to be good in the future? Was God angry with me? I racked my brains to think why. Gradually I reasoned that it was nobody's fault – it was the war.'

Anne and her mother were eventually conveyed to Milngavie, sleeping at first in the church hall. They had completely lost touch with her father and Mrs MacDonald was frantic with worry. They were eventually billeted with a local family and, weeks later, tracked down her father in the Vale of Leven Hospital, who could confirm that most of the extended family was safe, but for one widowed aunt. Mr MacDonald, sick as he was, had besides helped to fight fires when incendiary bombs threatened the hospital on the second night of raiding.

The family were then shifted to Lochgilphead in Argyll, after an aborted bombing raid over Milngavie. Anne made the best of it, thriving in a domestic atmosphere of worry and anguish: 'in the mainstream of community life – school, Sunday school and Brownies. Evacuees we were, but we were good ambassadors for Clydebank. We won practically all the prizes at the local school, no mean feat considering our fractured education since the outbreak of hostilities. I became a sixer in the Brownies and life was sweet again.'

Every so often, though, 'especially in church, I felt an overwhelming sadness and I wondered where my original classmates had gone. My mind grappled with one piercing truth: life was ephemeral and it was not only old people who died.' Negotiations now began, though, to secure a council house in Dalmuir, so a berth closer to home had to be found: the MacDonalds, after two years in

Lochgilphead and as the tide of the war emphatically turned in favour of the Allies, now settled in Cumbernauld for 15 months. In 1944 they settled in Dalmuir; 11 years later, Anne's parents won a home still better in Beech Drive, Parkhall. It was only at her father's death in 1957, from a long-term heart condition, that Anne learned that – just before the Clydebank Blitz – doctors had pronounced he had only a week to live, and could understand her mother's near hysteria at the time much better.

Anne MacDonald would spend some years as a teacher, and her reflections, in closing, show the depth of her own wounds in 1941. 'My pupils . . . thankfully did not possess all the extended vocabulary of our war-torn childhood. They did not use words like "direct hit", "landmine", "incendiary bomb", nor even "Blitzkrieg." . . . It seems fitting to ask a few questions at this point. From where did "ordinary" hard-working people find the steely, inward strength, the indomitable spirit and sheer raw courage to overcome such appalling hardships? Did it come from pride? From a sense of community? One thing is certain, the trendiest word of today never crossed their lips: "counselling" '.

There is no doubt that the fortitude, the self-discipline, the endurance and – for the most part, fraying only when there was abundant cause – the extraordinary patience of the people of Clydebank was remarkable.

But adults could come through such events with the ballast of years through the many little jolts and inequities of life. The laconic manner in which some adult experience of the Clydebank attack is narrated – often of the most ghastly sight or encounter – only reinforces this. Ruby Stewart, in 1941, was 27, three years married. She was returning from the Town Hall ARP training night when the bombing began on Thursday 13th. She later joined an advised exodus from her Radnor Park home on Second Avenue – it proved a well-founded warning – to the open acres of the High Park. 'On the way there I met a woman carrying a child, about three, on her back, and she also had a young infant in her arms. The child could not walk as she had hurt her foot. I took the baby – it was just three days old, the woman told me. It was one of twins, and the other twin had died. The mother said that this baby was now dying. I wrapped my Harris Tweed coat round it, but I felt it stiffen and die in my arms . . .'

There had been awful warnings, pre-war, by this and that expert as to untold outbreaks of psychiatric disturbance, and even predictions that mental casualties might well outnumber the physically injured by two or three to one. 'So, if the expected casualty figures had obtained,' Angus Calder sarcastically observes, 'everyone in London would very soon have been either mad or dead. But the war led to no great increase in neurotic illness in Britain, none, at least, which could be measured in the usual ways. There was no indication of any increase in insanity, and the number of suicides fell, while drunkenness statistics dropped by more than a half between 1939 and 1945.'

But children – especially small children – could react very differently, and boys especially seem often to have struggled to make sense of their Blitz experience: the sights and sounds they had come through, the felt terror of adults and the entire disorientation as streets were felled and whole localities were demolished. Lack of emotional maturity apart, we often forget the senses of a child – sight, hearing, sound – are of a range and acuity beyond that even of young adults. Sounds inaudible to their parents terrified them; mangled bodies on a town street were seared on the mind in high-definition intensity. Many grew up with dangerous emotional wounds. One five-year-old boy, of island parentage, bunkered down in the shelter for the night with his family. They arose to find practically every house on the street had been flattened. Many neighbours – including some of his own little pals – were dead. He, his mother and siblings were evacuated to the Hebrides to live in rural poverty. Sometimes he was sent to the rocks to fish: if he could catch no fish, they would that night not eat.

This man grew up to be a highly regarded minister, serving for over 30 years in assorted charges. Yet he has been haunted lifelong by nightmares, flash-backs and stress-related illness. His grown son, decades after the Blitz, can mimic the sound of Junkers and Heinkels – that ominous coming-and-going throb – so accurately, as he has heard from his father, and so eerily, that even at two removes from the event it raises the hairs on the back of your neck, as if remote and abiding terror were infectious.

Many of the children of Clydebank and district, in late-life accounts, hint at abiding trauma. Elizabeth Bailey has never been able to forget her schoolfriend Esther, and the innocence of their merry parting hours before Esther Anderson was killed. Irene Doherty – later Mrs McDonnell – was only eight years old; she and her family survived a direct hit, but she had caught flying glass in one eye; it was so badly damaged that surgeons had no option, the following day, but to remove it: she honestly admits it 'took me many years to come to terms with having an eye removed. I used to feel very angry about it. I'm sure that many of the personal hang-ups I suffered from during these early years could have been avoided or certainly lessened had I . . . been offered some form of counselling, either during or following hospitalisation. But nobody in author-ity seemed knowledgeable enough to identify and treat the thousands of war-time victims who suffered from post-traumatic stress and other psychological problems. . . .'

Yet even in Germany – which was repaid tenfold in bombs, over several years and on a prodigious scale – there were very few 'psychiatric air raid casualties', Calder confirms. Folk who had survived 'a "near miss", who had been buried alive or who had suffered directly from blast commonly showed marked neurotic symptoms and many others seem to have suffered from apathy, lethargy and general despondency as a side-effect of the raids and the weariness they brought with them. But certain types of mentally sick people actually felt better.' Clydebank and Scotland as a whole were in any event spared the sort of attritional bombing, over weeks and months, inflicted on, say, Liverpool and Hull, and most of all endured by the people of London.

Children, though, were very vulnerable indeed.

Take one instance from the 1999 account of another Clydebank survivor, naming herself only as 'VM': then 18 years old, she was bombed out with her family from Canberra Avenue. They counted themselves thankful, for across the road 'a house was demolished and a wee boy of three was buried under the rubble. He never really recovered from it. It left him mentally impaired.' Anne Newcombe – née Reekie – retreated quickly, with her mother and father, to the grandmother's house in Dumbarton, to find it bulging at the seams with almost all her Clydebank cousins, from small to grown, whose homes were demolished and who had no more than their stained, grubby garb. There was one lad 'who was so shocked that he was in a complete daze, being unable to speak or respond to anyone. My father kitted him out with a complete set of clothes but still there was no response. He then folded a handkerchief and put it into the breast pocket of his suit, at which point his cousin came to life and ran about, laughing, crying and shouting, "He's even given me a handkerchief." . . .'

That is the behaviour of trauma. There are stories of small boys who for months afterwards would start to tremble if someone so much as walked on the floor on the room above them, and who would scream at the sound of an aeroplane – any aeroplane. Indeed, for decades afterwards, many Clydebank Blitz survivors – into middle age and beyond – would involuntarily stiffen if an aircraft passed overhead, as Meg Henderson, brought up in Drumchapel in the late 1950s, has related. 'When I was a child shopping in Clydebank with my mother I used to laugh at the reactions of people in the streets to planes overhead. I couldn't understand why everyone looked up, why the noise made them look at each other and then look quickly away again . . .'

Father Sheary would tell Billy Kay, in 1981, 'It took me three years to get over the nervous reaction that set in . . . Every time I'd hear a plane, even in peace-time, when it came I used to go to pieces for long enough because of the effect that the bombers and the bombs had on me on that occasion, the 13th and 14th of March.' Writing in June 2010, Joan Baird – a survivor of the Blitz on Dumbarton – confides, 'After the war, the mark it left on me was that on my way home from Dumbarton Academy, roughly about a mile from my home, the first civil plane I heard, I ran like the wind in fear. It took me a long time to overcome – I could not stand the drone of a plane or the sound of works sirens.'

In fact, Irene Doherty did medical professionals some injustice: they were fully aware, not least from abundant and documented Great War evidence, of mental trauma after violence, catastrophe and fright. There were simply not the resources, the personnel or the time to do very much about it in 1941 – not least in the immediate context of an air attack that had left hundreds of people severely injured and maimed, amidst a grim fight for national survival. And there is chilling contemporary medical evidence as to the consequences of all this bombing and mayhem and upheaval for those who were not of an age to process it, as Angus Calder relays.

The effects of the Blitz on the children who lived through it, direct or indirect, are incalculable. One psychiatrist claimed from teachers' reports on eight thousand children evacuated from Bristol that there were about eight times as many cases of psychological disturbance among those who had remained in the city each night as among those who had gone to the tunnels on the outskirts. A nurse in a London children's hospital has described the behaviour of patients whose nerves had cracked. 'When they heard distant gunfire, they would sit up in bed and whimper like puppies. One little girl had gone completely dumb through terror, and another small child I knew went as stiff as a ramrod every time she heard the sirens. Her face turned scarlet, and she opened her mouth to scream, but no sound came.'

And some children of the Clydebank Blitz scream in silence to this day.

Not all experience of evacuation was negative. Rena Fleming – by 1999 Mrs Nimmo – returned with her family to Burns Street, Dalmuir, to find that nothing but smoke, wrecked houses and dead bodies remained. Her grandparents' house in Mountblow had been destroyed too. The Flemings were put up in Bearsden, then in Rutherglen, in most cramped conditions. Rena and her grandmother, it was decided, would move out to stay with relatives at Gateside in Fife. But, soon after their arrival, the old lady's health broke: Rena could not stay in the house without her (presumably there was no other woman resident). And so she ended up 'a true evacuee with label and small case', taken in by a shepherd and his wife, Bob and Peggy Millar, in a very isolated farm, Easter Gospetry, in Kinross. The childless couple had little choice in the matter: 'they had to take either two boys or one girl, because they had the accommodation. Luckily they chose me.' It could have been a disaster: ageing folk with no experience of children, in a cottage with neither gas nor electricity and a little girl from town who had never seen a cow. The learning curve on both sides was steep.

But it proved idyllic. Rena took to the Millars, and to the country life, and they to her. There was an abundance of good, home-grown food. She did well in the Gateside school, despite an involved daily journey, and the headmistress grew such regard for her that, on her death many years later, she bequeathed Rena some silver spoons. The Millars – who would gladly have adopted her – were heartbroken when, three years later, she went home to Clydebank with her mother. But Rena kept in touch with them for the rest of her life, till the death of Mrs Millar in 1991.

Denis Kearns was only four when, with his mother and four other siblings – there were eight Kearns in all, but were three were grown – he was evacuated to Helensburgh in 1941, where they ended up with the Blackie family in the now rather famous Hill House. This famous property at 8 Upper Colquhoun Street was designed by Charles Rennie Mackintosh himself early in the century for Walter Blackie, scion of a great publishing dynasty. Most regard this lovely home – now in the care of the National Trust for Scotland – as Mackintosh's greatest achievement after the Glasgow School of Art. After initial wariness – the old man had not wanted a 'mixed family' of both boys and girls – he and his daughter (and their servants) proved generous, unassuming hosts, and a happy bond was forged. The Kearns returned to Clydebank, like so many others, early in 1940: after the Blitz, though, they returned post-haste to Hill House where

> we were surprised to see that Mr Blackie had had a luxury air-raid shelter built in our absence. I certainly couldn't think of a more apt word to describe it. Having been designed and constructed to his own specifications, it was situated a couple of feet from the rear of the house and almost flush with the west gable end. Built from four courses of brick with a baffle wall protecting its heavy steel door, its reinforced concrete roof was sandbagged as was the outside of the baffle wall. Inside it had a WC and wash-hand basin, an electric cooker, a wood-burning stove and electric lighting. Finished with a course of roughcast and painted to match the house I've no doubt that even Rennie Mackintosh would have been tempted to give it his seal of approval . . .

'VM' had a stickier time Helensburgh of it with the Johnstones, a very grand couple who also lived in a very grand house. The girl and her mother had to share one little bedroom; her brother Peter was awarded one of his own. The house boasted a vast driveway, a housemaid, Margaret, and a cook of such character 'VM''s mother wickedly nicknamed her 'Clara Cluck'. Early in their stay – before she tuned into the Johnstone mores – 'VM' had a roaring row from Mrs Johnstone when she was sighted skipping up the front drive. In future, the lass was told in no uncertain terms, she was to come in by the servants' entrance. Only when this battle-axe was out did Margaret the maid once, fearfully, let them see into the dining room: 'beautiful, with a big, oval glass table'.

But, even in this most difficult, servile and impecunious position, 'VM' was a Clydebank girl who remembered, with conscious contempt, something one night that betrayed the arrogant gentlewoman's entire lack of moral imagination. 'We were still in Helensburgh in May, at the time of the Greenock Blitz, when the Germans bombed the ships and Lyle's Sugar.' Yet one witness only cooed, even as tracts of Greenock burned and men and women and children were dying. 'Everything was blazing,' 'VM' wrote nearly six decades later, 'and could be seen from Mrs Johnstone's house high above Helensburgh. She invited us up to Master Ivor's room for a better view. "It's a lovely view over Greenock, just like Fairyland," she said.'

11

THE BOMBING OF ETHICS

By 24 July 1943, as a vast armada of Allied bombers – there were 791 in the first wave of attack alone – rose from English soil to converge on the North Sea port of Hamburg, it was evident that Germany could no longer win the Second World War. Late in 1942, in what remains the largest land battle ever fought, Montgomery and the Eighth Army had finally trounced the Afrikakorps at El Alamein, and soon rolled up what remained of the Third Reich effort in North Africa and the Middle East, putting paid to any German hopes of subverting a signal strategic weakness: her lack of an oil supply since turning on Soviet Russia. She was now confined to what could be synthesised from coal, and production of an indifferent, dirty fuel had peaked that same year at 1.5 million gallons.

Late in January 1943, starved and wretched, encircled German forces at Stalingrad – reduced to gnawing the bones of dead horses – had finally to surrender to the Russians. Nothing in all the wiles and terror of Nazi propaganda could present this as anything but a catastrophe. It was a particular humiliation for Göring and his hopelessly directed Luftwaffe, who had proved wholly unable, despite the Reichsmarshall's boasts, to maintain an effective airlift of desperately needed supplies. Had even half of what the Reichsmarshall had assured the Führer been dropped, the Germans would have probably prevailed at Stalingrad.

'For the German public there was no disguise for the disaster,' observes Richard Overy. 'Too many were killed or captured to pretend that Stalingrad had not happened.' Göring's failure to plan and build a proper strategic bombing force before 1939 had still more dramatic consequence besides than the failure of the Blitz to knock out British war production; it meant that Germany had aircraft neither of the range nor the capacity to attack Soviet war production. It simply decamped wholesale behind the Urals, where no German plane could touch the factories soon churning out tanks and trucks and aircraft by the thousand, with the glad supply of plans, parts and material from the USA by fraught Royal Navy convoys through chill Arctic waters.

Hitler, enraged and increasingly delusional, insisted on another big push in the east, 'Operation Citadel' – on the Kursk salient of the Soviet line – but repeatedly postponed it and attempted to micro-manage at every level, taking obsessive interest in the detail of a new generation of very complicated tanks: the Third Reich war machine was increasingly encumbered by over-design. When he finally authorised the attack for July, British code-breakers had by now so compromised German communications that Stalin learned of the imminent assault before Hitler's own generals. On 4 July, 50 Wehrmacht divisions – some 900,000 men, with 2,700 tanks and 10,000 guns and backed by 2,000 aircraft – were pounded by a surprise Soviet barrage. The Germans moved the following day, and within hours it became plain both that (in stark contrast to 1941) Soviet commanders were trained and battle-hardened and that their cheap, reliable little tanks (most of the American T-34 design) could run rings round the ponderous new Tigers and Panthers of the Third Reich, heavily armoured and clever-clever as they were. By the evening of 12 July, after days fought with fantastic firepower and little or no quarter, the Russians had the field, after a battle that, as Overy puts it, 'tore the heart out of the German army' and which Heinz Guderian himself described as a 'decisive defeat'. Kursk was the single most important victory on land of the Second World War, and Stalin's Russia had wrested – and would retain – overwhelming advantage in armoured vehicles against Nazi Germany.

That spring, RAF's Bomber Command had resumed mass attacks on Germany's industrial heartland, the Ruhr valley, in what was really the only effective, non-defensive contribution the British could make to the Allied campaign: the effort of American bombers from English airfields for much of 1942 had been marked by appalling losses, largely from the characteristic American carelessness with *materiel* and the characteristic American insouciance by which, in the face of all advice, they mounted missions in daylight.

But a new man was now in command: Air-Chief-Marshal Arthur 'Bomber' Harris, Britain's most eager exponent of the Douhet theory – that modern war was won by the terror-bombing of civilians. Harris, who won command of offensive bombing in 1942, is not an appealing figure to modern taste. He had neither illusions nor any sentimental agonies as to his strategy (which, in fact, he had inherited, not invented; and which had first been essayed by the Germans on Guernica, Warsaw and Rotterdam). He spoke openly of 'dehousing' German workers. Stopped in his car for speeding one night by a policeman, who warned the Air-Chief-Marshal he might kill someone, Harris replied tartly, 'Young man, I kill thousands of people every night.' Once, infuriated by sententious homily from Sir Stafford Cripps – one of the prissiest members of the wartime Coalition – on the theme that 'God is my co-pilot', Harris gave a robust lecture on 'The Ethics of Bombing' at Bomber Command headquarters in Buckingham. There was appalled silence afterwards, before the HQ chaplain stood up and declared Harris should really have called his talk, 'The Bombing of Ethics'.

Nevertheless, Harris was now become death, the destroyer of worlds, and by every means equipped himself for the purpose. Though he never won the 5,000 strategic bombers he wanted, he soon had a great fleet of mighty four-engined aircraft, of capacity far beyond the Heinkels and Junkers which had waged the Blitz and able to carry bombs of a weight and explosive terror beyond anything dropped by the Luftwaffe. No bomb bigger than 1,000 kilograms fell on Clydebank (and, in fact, by German records they dropped just four of that weight). The new British planes, like the famous Avro Lancaster, 'could carry up to ten tons of bombs at a time,' relates Les Taylor, 'including huge 4,000-pounder "Cookies", 8,000-pounders and even ten-ton (22,000 lb) earthquake bombs, and they could carry them all the way across the Third Reich.'

Bomber Command also had two new important aids in navigation: the 'Oboe' target-finding device, ripped off from the Germans and using two fixed radio beams to direct special, flare-bearing Pathfinder planes to the chosen target; and an airborne radar system known as H2S, which allowed bombers, independently of any ground control, to fly blind through cloud and smog.

This night of 24 July 1943, even as ravaged German forces retreated from Kursk and as the darkly dubbed 'Operation Gomorrah' droned towards Hamburg, the RAF now rolled the dice with a third innovation, 'Window'. The idea was fiendishly simple: this first vast flight of aircraft dropped not bombs and incendiaries but – at one-minute intervals, and in enormous quantities – little pieces of aluminium foil. 'A few hundred strips stimulated the radar image of a Lancaster bomber,' records Overy. 'Thousands of strips rendered radar unusable.' Thrown into hopeless confusion, German ground defences and the increasingly piecemeal effort of inadequate Luftwaffe fighters brought down only 12 Allied bombers. Bomber Command returned, in still more lethal strength, on successive nights to the skies over Hamburg, pounded besides by day by the 8th US Air Force. They poured down incendiaries by the tens of thousands; bombs of a size, weight and number beyond anything in Luftwaffe capability, and inflicting below a horror quite eclipsing Coventry or Clydebank.

The emergency services of Hamburg disintegrated within hours as death rained down on the city. Fires raged, unchallenged and unchecked, for two days, gradually converging, in a heat increasingly incandescent, and the more so as the summer was unusually hot and city conditions unusually dry. First slowly, then in a mounting rush, air was sucked into the inferno as one great set of bellows. According to RAF airmen, wrote Michael Burleigh in 2000, 'it was "like putting another shovelful of coal into a furnace." This was a "firestorm", – one vast city-sized chimney of flame,' as Taylor vividly defines it, 'sucking in air (and people) at hurricane-force speeds for miles around and consuming everything and everyone in it'. There were only a handful of firestorms in the Second World War, and the Luftwaffe could never have wrought one.

Tonight, in Hamburg, as Burleigh flatly describes, 'freak air currents spread a storm of fire across a four-square-mile area. People on the streets flashed into flame, while those huddled in shelters died asleep as the fresh air was replaced by lethal gases and smoke. Others were transformed into fine ash. By the time the raids ceased, 45,000 people had been killed, and a further 37,000 injured. 900,000 had lost their homes – up to two-thirds of the population of Hamburg fled the city between the raids, spreading despondency and panic into the countryside.' The glow from the fires of Hamburg – which destroyed nearly three-quarters of the city – could be seen 120 miles away, and left, by the thousand, the corpses of even adults burned to such a crisp they could be stowed and carried in a suitcase. (Some were.)

On top of sustained and huge military reverses, great panic now spread among the German people. Hamburg's fate shook such leaders of the Third Reich as remained in touch with reality: it 'put the fear of God in me', Albert Speer, Hitler's pet architect and now armaments minister, would later confess in his memoirs. Hans Jeschonnek, Luftwaffe chief of staff, was shaken to his core, saying that besides the Hamburg immolation 'Stalingrad was trifling'. Two weeks later, after Bomber Command readily levelled Germany's rocket research facilities at Peenemunde in Norway, Jeschonnek followed Udet's example and shot himself.

The Luftwaffe was not quite out of the game. The spring of 1943 brought the hesitant 'Baedecker' raids over prettier English cities, like Bath and Norwich; and 21 April had seen a brief but determined attack on Aberdeen: 129 bombs were dropped, killing 98 civilians and 37 servicemen, just two weeks before that last attack in the west of Scotland. (Aberdeen was actually – in terms of frequency of attack – almost the most bombed place in Scotland: 24 raids are recorded, though the figure of 34 is often quoted. Its fishing-port neighbour Peterhead wins the prize with 28; and Fraserburgh was hit almost as many times: the jutting geography of the Buchan coast made it an easy option for German raiders, and it won the irreverent Scottish title of 'Hellfire Corner.')

With the secrecy of 'Window' now blown, for a time there was signal improvement in Germany's anti-aircraft and fighter defences. But, by year's end, it had been more than negated once the Allies had successfully adapted the sturdy Mustang – rolling out of American factories by the thousand – into a long-range escort fighter. Even yet the Luftwaffe could have turned the tide, for – not least by Albert Speer's direction – the Germans now had the world's very first operational jet-fighter, the Messerschmitt 262. It could outpace every other warplane on earth. It could have cut the near-nightly bomber fleets to ribbons. But, Hitler insisted, absurdly – he cared about killing the enemy, not protecting Germans – that it be adapted for civilian bombing; and his meddling delayed Me 262 production, and delayed it again. It was never available in sufficient numbers, despite superb results in battle from April 1944; and many clutches of Me 262s as could be subsequently built – the only plane the Luftwaffe could now safely operate against such overwhelming Allied superiority – were attacked on the ground, or bombed in their hangars, or before they ever flew. Hitler's enslaved subjects were finally defenceless under an Allied bombing force of such proportion it all but blotted out the sun.

On 12 June 1944, the first V1 – a pilotless flying bomb, with 1,870 lb of high explosive – hit London; and had even at this late hour the Germans put all their aerospace resources into producing this prototype Cruise missile by the tens of thousand (the 'doodlebug' was impossible to shoot down, though defending airmen did eventually learn how to tip them into crashing uselessly in the English Channel), the tide of events might have been held, if not turned. But Hitler instead insisted that untold time be diverted into his V2 rocket programme: still deadlier (it carried a full ton of explosive) but far more expensive, complicated and unreliable. In one of many instructive examples as to the self-defeating nature of total despotism, the V2 was largely built by slave labour: many of these helots were Jewish, and not a few would surreptitiously urinate on the weapon's internal circuitry when no one was looking, with spectacular consequence at launch.

The first V2 rocket landed – at Chiswick – on 8 September 1944, at supersonic speed and without a moment of warning, and some 518 would blast Greater London, killing 2,700 people, till the last bases were overrun by Allied troops in March 1945: between the 'buzz-bomb' and the rocket, some 1.5 million houses were destroyed or substantially damaged.

By July 1944 – after the success of the D-Day landings and, really still more significant, the collapse of Army Group Centre on the eastern front – there was no longer any doubt: Germany, perhaps as early as year's end, was going to lose the war. In the end, between Allied fiasco in the Netherlands, Hitler's last gamble of the Ardennes offensive and the indefatigable efforts of Albert Speer to maintain industrial production, and the hardiness of German soldiers, she held out a little longer, even as night upon night and day upon day, now enjoying near-entire freedom of the skies, Allied bombers pounded her cities to smouldering bricks.

On 13 February 1945, as the Third Reich continued to disintegrate and Allied soldiers now fought, from two fronts, through Germany herself, perhaps the most controversial air raid of the entire war – 'Operation Thunderclap' – was launched against Dresden, the seventh-largest city in Germany, famous for its china and the baroque beauty of its centre, hitherto all but unscathed. Bomber Command briefing notes described her now as 'an industrial city of first-class importance and . . . of major value for controlling the defence of that part of the front now threatened by Marshall Konev's breakthrough . . .' Rather more honestly, the notes declared besides that the mission would 'show the Russians when they arrive just what Bomber Command can do'. There was loose talk of 'transportation centres' and 'marshalling areas' supposedly of vital importance in the defence of Germany and of Berlin herself and by which, routing this division and that, the Nazis might be able to prolong the war by weeks.

Dresden was packed not with German troops, but refugees. The city's population, swollen by host upon host of frightened country people fleeing the Soviet advance, had ballooned from 630,000 to 1.6 million. Dresden's last air defences had been dismantled only in January, the guns going to the eastern front or in the increasingly hopeless effort at the Ruhr. Precautions against a raid – trenching in public parks; the erection of static water tanks; perfunctory advice to the public – fell well short of Clydebank's readiness in March 1941. In the whole city there was only one underground concrete bunker fit for service as a bomb shelter, and only Dresden's Gauleiter – Martin Mutschmann – was allowed to use it. Not one to take chances, as Robin Cross dryly notes, Mutschmann was besides building two more shelters – at public expense – for the exclusive use of him and his family.

It has been for so long fashionable to vilify Bomber Command and Air-Chief-Marshal Harris for what befell Dresden that we should remember it was expressly ordered by politicians. Churchill and Sir Archibald Sinclair both demanded it, and the Cabinet as a whole unhesitatingly decreed a terror-bombing policy throughout the war (though, in the Commons, ministers always denied this). Churchill was eager to demonstrate, to Stalin and the Soviet Union, just how British air power could mightily augment their efforts on the Eastern Front. Even he, though, would finally recoil, aghast, from its fruits in Dresden.

It was Shrove Tuesday, this 13 February 1945, and despite the last weeks of a desperate war very many Dresden children, as in happier days, had donned fancy dress and carnival clothes, and were readying now for bed as the first wave of Lancaster bombers – 244 of them – swept upon their city and the alarm was raised. Eerie green markers soon floated in the sky, augmenting the red blazes of weighty 'target indicator' incendiary bombs. It soon dawned on the leaders of the RAF assault that Dresden was wholly undefended. The 'Main Force' of Lancasters was ordered to still lower altitude, the better to concentrate their attack on all those troops and locomotives and stations and lengths of rail track below, as thousands upon thousands of townsfolk and evacuees fled for what shelter they could, piling into cellars or clambering into the tunnels and passageways of the main Dresden station. Soon, pilots and air-crew could see below the myriad flashes of lesser high-explosive bombs; and the slow creepy ripples of destruction as far bigger brothers detonated to frightful effect – and everywhere, across the breadth of Dresden, the glitter of thousands of incendiaries. On the ground, as Cross details, it was a very different experience:

> The 4,000-pound and 8,000-pound bombs smashed roofs and blew in windows while the incendiaries set individual buildings ablaze. Floors collapsed and huge tongues of flame burst through the shattered roofs, turning houses and apart-ment blocks into giant Roman candles. As the last Lancasters . . . flew away from the stricken city, the fires were coalescing, heating the air above and setting up a violent updraught, which in turn sucked in air from all sides into the centre of the fire area. As the firestorm took hold, this colossal suction created hurricane-force winds. During the worst night of the Blitz in London, 29th December 1940, the fires had spread as fast as a man could walk. In Dresden they were eating their way through the city as fast as a man could run . . .

And those bombers had been but the first attack, 'Plate-rack'; now, around 1.30 a.m., 529 Lancasters arrived in the righteous duties of 'Press-on', over a city whose telephone system was already down and whose civil defence officials had not yet grasped the catastrophe unfolding. The log book aboard one Lancaster would record laconically, 'Dresden. Clear over target, practically the whole town in flames.' But they began bombing, nevertheless, and three-quarters of all these new bombs were incendiaries.

The firestorm fed, and fattened. Temperatures rose to 1,000°C: thick jets of flame – many 50 feet high – hissed across streets and squares as a fury of baking, artificial winds began to tear through the burning city. Families had earlier hauled onto the street precious pieces of furniture, but this now 'burst into flames and was then tossed, blazing, through the streets by howling winds. Trees were uprooted or snapped like matchsticks. People caught in the open crawled on hands and knees gulping the air near the ground, but unaware whether their agonising progress was carrying them away from the flames or further into the firestorm. Others clung to railings, only to be seized by the suction and whirled, in a maelstrom of debris, into the inferno. Dead and dying lay where they fell in the melting, glutinous asphalt of the streets, their clothes burnt away, their bodies shrivelled like mummies. The corpses of children lay like fried eels on Dresden pavements. In the Altmarkt Square hundreds tried to escape the heat in the water tanks, but drowned in eight feet of water as fires raged all around them . . .'

Incendiaries by the hundred shattered the glass roof of the Hauptbahnhof railway station; soon smoke and toxic gases piled down the thick-crowded tunnels, suffocating men and women, boys and girls by the thousand. And still the bombs fell; and Dresden burned so bright that night became day. Two terrified Jewish refugees, Victor and Eva Klemperer, dashed about searching frantically for escape and survival and Victor's account remains one of the most detailed of the holocaust that was Dresden.

> After a while Eisenmann said: We must get down to the Elbe, we'll get through. He ran down the slope with the child on his shoulders; after five steps I was out of breath, I was unable to follow. A group of people were clambering up through the public gardens to the Bruehl Terrace; the route went close to fires, but it had to be cooler at the top and easier to breathe.
>
> Then I was standing at the top in the storm wind and the showers of sparks. To the right and left, buildings were ablaze, the Belvedere and probably the Art Academy. Whenever the showers of sparks became too much for me on one side, I dodged to the other. Within a wider radius nothing but fires. Standing out like a torch on this side of the Elbe, the tall building at Pirnaischer Platz, glowing white; as bright as day on the other side, the roof of the Finance Ministry.

Separated for some hours from her husband, Eva scurried desperately about the streets. At one point, she paused to light a snatched cigarette; she had no matches, and stooped to something blazing on the ground. It was a corpse.

The sights awaiting those who eventually tried to impose order, over the next few days, on what was left of Dresden scarcely bear reading about: everywhere the frazzled bodies of tormented children; the slightly larger biscuits that had been in life their parents. In one basement – where some 300 people had been sheltering when a high-explosive bomb came through the ceiling – there was but a soup of blood, flesh and bone a foot deep.

The SS took ruthless charge, and so chaotically that no one has ever been able to establish the Dresden death toll: it was probably close to 135,000. Soldiers who refused to carry out the most unpleasant recovery duties – even when generously rewarded with cigarettes and hard liquor – were shot on the spot. Looters were gunned down on sight. Slave-labourers from the Ukraine and even Allied prisoners-of-war were marshalled for the most repugnant jobs of all. Great pyres of blocks and girders were finally built, layer upon layer of corpses sandwiched together and trodden to compaction by nauseated troops, before fires were lit below with timber soaked in fuel – rites of Nazi disposal that sound frankly occult.

Thousands more were shovelled into mass graves. In one grotesque measure at subsequent identification, wedding rings – or, more often, the fingers to which they were attached – were snipped off by the hundred with bolt-cutters; eventually, 15,000 were collated. Hans Voigt, the schoolmaster in miserable charge of the Abteilung Tote – 'Dead Persons' Department' – wrote later of his task:

> Never would I have thought death would come to so many people in so many different ways . . . Never had I expected to see people interred in that state: burnt, cremated, torn and crushed to death; sometimes the victims looked like ordinary people apparently peacefully sleeping; the faces of others were racked with pain, the bodies stripped almost naked by the tornado; there were wretched refugees from the East clad only in rags, and people from the opera in all their finery; here the victim was a shapeless slab, there a layer of ashes shoveled into a zinc tub.

It had become a habit of bomber-crews – borrowed, like other vulgarities, from the Americans – to scrawl some name or jibe on each bomb as it was loaded; and there were many Scots in Bomber Command and among ground-crew besides. Not a few of the monsters that hurtled down on Hamburg and Dresden – and many other parts of Germany – bore one chalked word, CLYDEBANK.

On the afternoon of 30 April 1945, Adolf Hitler killed himself in his Berlin bunker. At 2.40 a.m. on 7 May, in Eisenhower's war room at Reims, Colonel-General Alfred Jodl signed the instrument of unconditional German surrender, whereby German High Command – and, indeed, everyone in the country, military and civilian – undertook 'to carry out at once, without argument or comment, all further orders that will be issued by the Allied Commanders on any subject'. Jodl laid down his pen, and asked permission to say a few words. It was granted. 'With this signature,' croaked the Colonel-General, 'the German people and the German Armed Forces are, for better or worse, delivered into the hands of the victors . . . In this hour, I can only express the hope that the victor will treat them with generosity.' Silence hung in the air. No one responded. In October 1946, after most dubious conviction for alleged war crimes, Jodl – an able, honourable man – would hang at Nuremberg.

In March 1941, Bessie Bannister had fled Clydebank for Callander, making grimy passage in the back of a coal lorry in her treasured fur coat. A year or two after the war, she travelled to Germany with Glasgow's celebrated Orpheus Choir, enlisted belatedly in the service and uniform of the Entertainment National Service Association for the morale of occupying British troops. It was a trip tinted by irony: as a lifelong socialist, and avowed pacifist and a vocal member of the Peace Pledge Union, Sir Hugh Roberton – and his Orpheus Choir – had in 1941 been banned from BBC broadcast for the duration of the war.

The wretchedness of German civilians Bessie witnessed was sobering:

> The train was going very slowly because everything was just a mass of rubble and the train was more or less picking its way through. And running alongside the train were all these displaced people. We had all been given rations, a kind of packed meal, for the journey, and I remember the boss [*Sir Hugh*] coming round all the compartments and telling us that not one of us was to eat that food. We were to throw it out to these people.
>
> As we came to Hamburg, it was springtime and the place was covered in lilac trees growing among all this sheer devastation. But the smell of Hamburg could never be forgotten, because the dead were still there underneath the rubble.
>
> The big railway station was still there, very badly battered, and just across from it in a building that had once been a hotel there was the ENSA headquarters and an officers' transit camp with a NAAFI restaurant alongside it. We stayed there for ten days while we were doing our performances . . . and every day, while we were there, people came with bunches of lilac because they were so pleased. The concerts weren't supposed to be for German civilians, but, once they heard about the choir, they couldn't be kept out.
>
> I remember one incident, when I had left my dirty uniform and I had gone back expecting to wash it myself, but found it wasn't there. When I went back in the evening, there it was laundered and my shoes were brushed. So when we found the girl who had done this, we asked her what we could do for her and she asked us just to give us a wee slice of our soap. So, of course, we gave her cakes of soap. But we found they were wonderful girls and they would have done anything for us.

Bessie Bannister's most treasured experience, though, as Europe returned to normality and the Germans of the West, at least, to older paths of decency, had fallen earlier, at an officers' transit camp in Cuxhaven. 'Sir Hugh, the boss as we called him, always asked us to sing to the waiters and waitresses wherever we went. So, when we went into this dining room (it was all German civilian population who were attending to us) he just stood up and said, "We'll sing the

Brahms." And [*then*] we sang *Silent Night*. Immediately these people all just
stopped and tears were streaming down their faces. One of our wags in the choir
said, "Surely we're not as bad as all that!" But it was because they hadn't been
allowed to listen to music like that during the war years. They were so moved by
it, and it was a moment that endeared them to us . . .'

The history of post-war Clydebank is of a new town. Of the thousands and
thousands who left in March 1941, a high proportion never returned; and
many more only came back after months or years. The absence of so many on
war service, and the need in the national emergency to give war production
workers priority in the allocation of scant housing, were other factors. But
through it all ran a sorrow unique in Scotland.
   Fitfully, over the years, as Billy Kay observed in his transcription of that
1981 Radio Scotland broadcast, Clydebank 'was eventually rebuilt, but the
communal culture of the tenements with its closely knit family groups could
never return. Instead, people were scattered into ill-planned housing schemes
where the impersonality of the environment produced in many a sense of
isolation. The same could be said of many other towns. In Clydebank,
however, the possibly nostalgic memory the people have of the pre-war
community is overwrought with the terrible personal tragedies most families
were touched by.'
   Everyone, it seemed, had lost someone; many, besides, had been bereft of
relatives, and the winds of war removed still more menfolk from the family
circle. And, inevitably, between protracted school attendances in this or that
nook of a far country, and by jobs taken on and friendships built and roots put
down, many Clydebank people – as families and as individuals – ended up
settling in the localities where, in the fraught spring and summer of 1941, they
had been hastily billeted. Many would nevertheless have returned if they
could, but little could be built while the war endured, and the pain of this time
– and, for many, that would endure for years to come – is deftly caught by Meg
Henderson's novel.

> There had been some rebuilding after the war, but not enough, despite letters
> constantly arriving at the council offices from exiled Bankies asking when they
> could come home. Inevitably many never did. They had boarded whatever
> transport was available on the Friday and Saturday after the bombings and
> made their lives wherever they were taken to. They all left with the firm intention
> of 'going home' as soon as new houses were built, but those who wanted to return
> far outnumbered the rebuilding programme, and as their families grew up
> elsewhere, their ties loosened. There were gaps all over Clydebank where those
> who remembered the layout of the old town could still identify what had stood
> and who had lived where. It wasn't uncommon even in the Fifties to come across
> some returned exile standing before a gap in tears, seeing in their memory the
> home they once lived in, recalling friends and relatives they had lost. It was hard to
> pick up the pieces when so many of the fallen pieces were still visible.

There was a darker complication besides; the allocation of council houses inevitably bestowed enormous power in the hands of local government officials, and still more, those of a well-connected councillor. The vast majority, of course, in Scotland's civic history have been honourable and upright men. But there have always been the bent and, even in recent decades, councillors have been disgraced and local by-elections forced by embarrassing scandal. In one documented instance, ironically – the Clydebank Blitz memories, in 1998, of Charles Clunas – it actually steered a family back to the town.

The Clunas clan were actually from Johnstone in Renfrewshire, but Charles's father, a committed union man and Labour supporter and an able toolfitter, had been long blacklisted by local employers. Unable to secure another job in Johnstone, he kept his union membership quiet and secured a situation at Singer's in Clydebank. Until the war, the family had lived for a decade at 398 Dumbarton Road, but on the outbreak of hostilities Mrs Clunas and the children returned to Johnstone: they all survived the war (though endured the agonising night of 13 March 1941, when Mr Clunas walked all the way down to Johnstone not knowing if his wife or children or indeed the town had survived; and they in their turn waited hour upon hour for him, not knowing if he were alive or dead). The couple had, it seemed, long hoped to return one day to their native airt, as Charles relates,

. . . and this looked like a good time to do something to change the situation. As I was as cocooned as ever I was on the outer periphery of the affair, but I know they sought an interview with either the Provost or the Housing Convener, anyway the Big Man in Johnstone Council housing. I thought this was a big deal, but of course both my parents were well-known left-wingers and the Johnstone Town Council, like virtually all those in the west of Scotland, was Labour-controlled, so the man they went to see had been known to them for twenty years or more. When they came back, my father's face was like thunder and my mother was a lot less cheery in front of us than her usual self. It had apparently been put to them that if they were not prepared to produce some 'key money' (a contemporary euphemism for a bribe) there was nothing doing. I remember the quotation still. 'Lots of folk would like a council house, you know. Some would give fifty, aye, a hundred pounds for a council house.' Whoever he was he had tried it on with the wrong man; my father had an utter disgust for corruption of any kind, no matter how trivial. So I didn't grow up a Johnstonian, for we all went home to Clydebank in the summer of 1943.

The government, early in the war, had promised material compensation for all who had lost homes and possessions to bombing; and – by tortured bureaucracy and complex claim process – Clydebank families over months and years finally won modest grants of cash. Inevitably there was dissatisfaction, murmuring and dark local humour. 'There were people that were saying that they had this in their house and the next thing and it got blitzed,' Mary

Rodgers chuckled in 1981. 'They done away with rubbish and they got new stuff. And they'd lost a fur coat in the Blitz and never had a fur coat in their life. It made you laugh at the time.'

A student for the Free Presbyterian ministry, Donald MacLean – Gorbals-reared of Coigach and Raasay parentage, and who had served for the duration as a Royal Navy officer – found himself appointed as the Church's representative to an official committee 'that was going to divide up the cake; the compensation for the churches which had lost property in Clydebank'. In his ninety-sixth year, in June 2010, Mr MacLean was one of the last living to remember Free Presbyterian worship in the town, which was latterly a station of the main St Jude's congregation in Glasgow. 'There was a prayer meeting on Thursday night, and you would go down – Mr MacKenzie our minister would go down, and a few of us would come from Glasgow. We had no office-bearers there, but there was a professing man. And the church was right beside the station – the main Clydebank station, and that was why it was bombed.'

The board of recompense was chaired by no less than the Reverend John White, at the time still the most eminent minister of the Kirk, a former Moderator, architect of the Great Union of 1929 and best remembered today for his unsettling invective after the Great War against Irish immigration and the death of 'Protestant Scotland'. He was not to be trifled with, Mr MacLean recalls. 'Well, our case was up first – the Free Presbyterian Church of Scotland – and it was declared we would get 100 per cent compensation. Then, I think, it was the Roman Catholic Church, and – well, they got a lot, but it wasn't 100 per cent of their claim. And this priest got up – there were laymen there, a lot of Roman Catholic people, backing him – and he was most dissatisfied, and he announced, "We will take this to a higher authority." And Dr White looked at him, and said – in a *very* grand voice – "Than this committee there is *no* higher authority."' Mr MacLean chuckled, 'And I rather enjoyed that, as you might imagine.' But the Free Presbyterian Church was never rebuilt, nor services resumed, for such people as there had been were scattered, most towards or in Dumbarton. The money was sensibly applied to their cause and property in that town, where Free Presbyterian services would be held until 2004. Ordained in 1948, Mr MacLean retired in February 2000, after a notable 40-year pastorate in Glasgow. He died a few weeks after we spoke.

When peace at last came with the surrender of Japan in August 1945, Britain was all but bankrupt – with, besides, in shifting geopolitics, a new military menace already evident by the end of 1946 and the stand-off of the Berlin airlift. Even by the formation of an abashed, free West Germany by decade's end, the Cold War with Soviet Russia had set in. It would endure for over 40 years – so long that what was effectively the peace treaty finally ending the Second World War only emerged in 1990, in the final terms of German reunification – and the Russian menace entailed a heavy military commitment from Britain and much spending on men, weapons and hardware.

Crippled by war loan repayments to America and obsessed with the need to maximise exports, the new Labour government under Clement Attlee managed nevertheless to nationalise key industries, erect the National Health Service, complete the apparatus of a welfare state. But it presided over a bleak 'austerity Britain', making momentous decisions – such as an independent atomic-weapons capability – with scant reflection and pursuing an unimaginative, Unionist line in Scotland, quite abandoning the historic Labour commitment to home rule and electoral reform. Nor did it build more than a fraction of the desperately-needed new homes, in Clydebank or anywhere else. Of course, the country was broke; there were still thousands of troops of necessity stationed overseas; and (as is often forgotten) most of the senior Labour ministers had been in power since 1940, in Churchill's Coalition, and were ageing and increasingly exhausted.

These were grey, hard years, remembered through decades for the terrible winter of 1946–47: on 23 January, heavy snow began. Blizzards continued to mid-March, and everywhere the links of road and rail, of industry and of transport seized up or closed. Electric poles and cables tumbled everywhere: soon, households were forbidden to cook between nine and twelve in the morning or between two and four in the afternoon. The Thames froze solid, as did most lakes and rivers. Sheep and cattle died by the tens of thousand and, among the elderly especially, the mortality rate rocketed.

Most, still, relied on coal for heating and hot food; but – and, as Minister of Fuel and Power, Manny Shinwell's standing was permanently dented – stocks of coal, despite his assurances, proved inadequate, and in any event the post-war stuff was of dire quality, soft and sulphurous and stony. Meanwhile – and this had not happened even at the lowest point of the war – the Labour government had been rationing bread since July 1946. This was a panicked and ineffectual decision by John Strachey, the Food Minister, whom we first met as a thoughtful ARP volunteer in London. Bread-rationing still further clotted bureaucracy and maddened the country's housewives, while doing little or nothing to reduce consumption. In an inspired moment, the Conservatives – reinventing themselves rapidly after their 1945 rout – came up with the slogan, 'Starve with Strachey and Shiver with Shinwell.'

In the last weeks of March 1947, the thaw set in – with devastating floods. It snowed again, heavily, in April. It snowed again even on 1 May. Confidence in the Attlee government had by this point on many sides collapsed, though the abiding belief it was at last hounded from office is a myth. Its standing did recover: Labour narrowly won the 1950 election and, when Attlee foolishly called another in 1951, Labour actually won more votes than the Tories – and indeed what remains an all-time Labour record – 48.8 per cent of the poll. Unfortunately, much of it was piled high in the groaning majorities of very safe divisions. The Tories won more seats and took office with a thin but adequate majority.

Winston Churchill was 76 years old and already a walking pharmacy, entrusted with a second term in office largely, as John Mackintosh later joked, as a reward for his first. Some say this swansong oversaw the worst administration of any post-war prime minister. Churchill was dozy, scatter-brained and

indulgent, preoccupied with books and pets (a dog, a cat and a budgerigar) and –
though he clung to office till 1955 – never fully recovered from a 1953 stroke.

But his party had regained power largely on the promise of building homes
for a homeless country – 300,000 a year; a task taken up with suave poise by
the new Minister of Housing, Harold Macmillan. Macmillan, a very interesting man and with strong Scottish roots – he was the great-grandson of a
Gaelic-speaking Arran crofter, whose son had founded the family publishing
empire – oozed laid-back calm. He proved himself a better prime minister than
he is often credited, calmly directing Britain's retreat from Empire and fixing
her sights permanently on a new European role. Meanwhile, the MP for
Bromsgrove never lost an opportunity to remind the public how ardently he
was fulfilling an explicit electoral commitment. 'Lovely day, Minister,' reporters would call to him on Downing Street. 'Yes,' Macmillan drawled,
through yellowed teeth, 'a lovely day for building 300,000 houses . . .'

Many thought the commitment impossible; in Aneurin Bevan's last year in
the same department, fewer than 200,000 had gone up. The economic climate,
too, proved worse than anyone had expected: bricks and cement, steel and
timber, were simply not available in sufficient quantity and had to be imported
– in exchange for precious American dollars. To make more bricks, Macmillan
actually imported more labour – from war-ravaged Italy. He built his houses:
301,000 between 1 November 1952 and 31 October 1953; 318,000 in the
1953 calendar year; a prodigious 350,000 in 1954. But he achieved it by
cutting corners: cut-price designs, poor materials, rushed and inadequate
workmanship. The public housing built in this period, and for years to come,
was indifferent and – where they have not been improved or demolished – their
tenants curse them yet for damp, condensation and chill. Thousands of
Scottish children cough and wheeze of a winter in some of the worst examples
to this day.

Clydebank, like everywhere else, slowly clotted with new ticky-tacky dwellings. But there was little effective planning, local vision or far-sighted leadership. For most of the last 80 years, in one form or another, she has been ruled
by a Labour-dominated one-party state, generally complacent and on occasion
corrupt. (There was a brief, uncertain Scottish National Party interregnum
in the late 1970s.) She has not, until very recent years, enjoyed effective
Parliamentary representation; and her devastation in 1941 never really im-
printed itself – in any duration – on the wider public consciousness.

There was little special help from central government for places like
Clydebank: in the corridors of local power, councillors lacked generally the
discernment to think of infrastructure, a truly attractive built environment or
any sort of coherent townscape. In any event, reconstruction was fitful, even
patchy; and, by the time the standard of Labour representation began to
improve, it was under a Conservative administration that hated local councils
and especially those of what it was pleased to dub the 'loony Left'. Through
my own boyhood, there were gaps everywhere in Clydebank; and weed-thick
35-year-old tumbled ruins. By the late 1970s, especially along Glasgow Road,

much of the place seemed simply derelict. One or two bombed sites in Dalmuir were only at last built on in the present century. 'Clydebank never got the chance to rebuild,' Janet Hyslop would lament to Billy Kay. 'And where Coventry and lots of towns in England, which were badly bombed, were given the money to rebuild, Clydebank wasn't . . .'

Kathleen McConnell, in the 1960s, saw still more cause for bitterness, in a city Allied bombers had not 20 years before hammered to gravel. 'Later on in years I went to Italy via Germany and we stopped off at Essen. Really and truly I nearly lost my eyesight. It was built beautifully. The shops were full of goods – jewellery, leather goods – and everyone seemed to be so well off, and that stayed in my mind because when I came back to Clydebank after my holiday, there we were, b'God, still sitting in the rubble.'

She was by no means the first to reel at the contrast between British prosperity and comfort, 20 and even 30 years after Jodl surrendered at Reims, and the standard of living in nations we had allegedly beaten. Yet the 'economic miracle' of West Germany – already the talk of nations as early as 1963 – was, if anything, a dividend of defeat.

Under terms much more sensible, if in some respects more ferocious, than after the Great War, West Germany was forbidden to maintain more than token armed forces: troops in what been the proud Wehrmacht tradition were formed in wholly new regiments, forced into slovenly and ill-fitting uniforms and forbidden to wear the decorations or carry the battle-honours of past, contentious triumph. Besides, with her industries and plant bombed to scrap, she had to rebuild factories and yards, with new technology and with all the skill and pride and biddability of the German people. They are an obedient folk, as Frederick Forsyth has observed: it is their greatest strength and their greatest weakness.

West Germany besides benefited heavily from American aid, most notably under the Marshall Plan: most aid to Britain, such as it was, was vested in armaments for continued world-power delusions, and Clyde shipyards were still building riveted ships with the plate-yard thump of Victorian steam hammers – though shifted rapidly, and with fraught union negotiation, to welded construction from the early 1950s. Victory, it seemed, brought its own punishment.

For years after the war – not least with the scant supply of housing – Clydebank practically boomed, with a real shortage of labour and shipyards toiling to replace all the vessels lost to the U-boat, the mine and the Luftwaffe, or refurbish, for a renewed civilian role, assorted merchantmen soiled and battered by protracted service in the Crown. Nor had jet travel yet dethroned the passenger liner. Indeed, John Brown's would launch two famous ships in the decades ahead: a new Royal Yacht, the *Britannia*, in 1953, and another eminent Cunarder, the *Queen Elizabeth 2*, in 1968. Yet she, with a realistic eye on the times, was designed for cruising rather than a fast Atlantic commute; and the 'QE2' would be the last great Clyde-built ship. Fittingly, she had a Blitz connection: Cunard's chief naval architect – head of a team of six in charge of her design – was Dan Wallace; as a boy, Dan and his family had been bombed out of Bannerman Street.

Nor – especially in these years of austerity – was there much diminution in demand for the town's immaculately-crafted sewing machines. Yet even in that regard, as Meg Henderson details, there was a most unwelcome peace dividend: Singer's might have been the emperor of its manufacture, but

> The rest of the world had quickly cottoned on, and there was a build-up of strong competition from within Europe. Somewhat ironically Japan entered the industry upon the direct order of US General Douglas McArthur. After the defeat of Japan in 1945, McArthur decided that instead of producing munitions Japan should manufacture sewing-machines, and Singer's would henceforth be banned from exporting to Japan. To make sure the seal had really been set on Singer's, American investment in Japan was to include the company's plans and patents to build up the industry, so that by the late Fifties three hundred Japanese companies were making over 2 million machines. It was little wonder, given the effects of the emerging competitors and their nationalities, that an oft-heard quip in Clydebank was, 'Jist who *did* win the war, then?' But even so there was a stubborn belief that things would improve. This was *Clydebank*, a town that had survived, a town that *would* survive, because the rest of the world knew they produced quality goods, and the rest of the world would stay loyal to them. It was only *right* after all . . .

It is unlikely the shrewd people of the Risingest Burgh – long hardened in the ways of a given economic order and its ruling classes – were quite as naïve as Henderson suggests. Nor, while the reasons she lists for the inexorable decline of Clyde shipbuilding in the latter half of the twentieth century are valid, are they quite complete. Certainly, governments elsewhere – in South Korea and West Germany, for example – invested heavily in the industry, as the British government did not. Certainly they embraced – and even searched for – yet better designs and technology, as the complacent old firms of the Clyde did not; so that in time there was an exasperating waiting list before an order was even begun, and then the vessel's construction took, by the new standards of the world, inordinately long.

And, certainly, markets vanished. By the launch of the *Queen Elizabeth 2*, the day of the fast transatlantic liner was gone. (The majestic *Queen Mary* retired in 1967 and the *Queen Elizabeth* in December 1968.) The appetite for leisurely tropical cruising rather dwindled too; nor did the Royal Navy now order much Clyde tonnage, or – especially in a service which, by the late 1980s, had more admirals than ships – vessels of notable size. The Suez crisis of 1956 – and the canal's protracted closure, forcing tankers to take the long way round from the sands of Araby – led inevitably, as Henderson points out, to demand for the much bigger 'VLCC' (very large crude carrier) and, in time, to the super large crude carrier; neither John Brown's nor any other Clyde yard was big enough, or had the capital to rebuild and expand its facilities.

But it is not to wink at the well-documented rapacities of yard owners or the petty despotism of foremen, nor to forget decade upon decade of exploitation, to point out the part played in the industry's decline – and indeed the sclerotic problems of the private Scottish economy generally – on irresponsible trades unionism and the worst little games of power-crazed shop stewards, to the point that by the 1970s it was one of the most fraught aspects to the general sense of British decline. Paul Johnson was by no means entirely unjust, in 1972 – and when he was still a Labour partisan – to observe that many

> . . . of these unions were already ancient. Some could trace misty origins back to the seventeenth century. They reflected the chaotic structure of British industry, in their multiplicity and anomalies, in their fear of change, and in their complex and irrational methods of business, using procedures for calculating wage-rates and defining occupations that went back to the eighteenth century, sometimes beyond. The trade union movement was already the House of Lords of the British working-class, waving historic banners, defensive in outlook, resisting innovation on principle . . . they still tended to regard new machines as a potential threat; their unions were organized to conserve, not to elevate. . . . In a society which is politically free but socially unjust, the workers will naturally combine together to influence events. The kind of influence they exert will depend very large on the kind of education they receive. If British trade unions are traditionally minded, obscurantist, incompetent, anti-progressive, even reactionary – and of course they are – the fault lies with society as a whole. The English [sic] have chosen to provide the minimum of education for the mass of the people: and they have therefore produced a blind and obstinate giant, with a marked tendency to delinquency. Seen in the long perspective of the last hundred years, the influence of the British trade union movement has been almost wholly destructive.

Johnson's thoughts were no doubt coloured by the notorious 'Spanish practices' of the print and allied trades unions in his own newspaper industry, which would endure till the mid 1980s and fell leadenly even in Scotland: the old *Scottish Daily Express*, the greatest newspaper we have ever had north of the border, was largely destroyed by the antics of one man, an NUJ shop-steward, Danny McGhee, who would call the whole printing floor out on strike (and so prevent morning publication, a financial disaster no newspaper can frequently endure) should editors dare to run an article or even a cartoon he did not like. But anyone who attained political awareness around 1979 and the notorious 'Winter of Discontent' – which destroyed a fundamentally sensible Labour government, and put the party out of power for 18 years – can shudder sympathetically. By the 1970s, even Clydeside trades unionism could do little more than posture: with one famous exception, it was still capable of tactical success, but of no wider vision or long-term strategy.

The Clyde herself was dying, a trend that would only accelerate from the late 1980s. From the mid 1950s, a fleet of stately river steamers – all operated, in varied incarnations of state ownership, by what is now Caledonian Mac-Brayne – grew rapidly obsolete, as city crowds deserted the coasts of Clyde for the new, affordable attractions of package holidays to the likes of the Costa del Sol, and a network of assorted Firth commutes from this or that island or Cowal and Rosneath hamlet was rapidly reduced to a handful of routes operated, by the mid 1970s, almost wholly by car ferries.

By the advent of the Scottish Transport Group in 1969, only five traditional steamers survived; within the decade all were gone, save for the paddle-steamer *Waverley* (who owes her own survival to determined enthusiasts, and whose future for several years after her rescue hung by gossamer). One of the most bitterly regretted casualties was the famous, Dumbarton-built *King George V*, an innovative 1926 twin-screw turbine steamer, the first with a largely enclosed promenade deck and, as originally fitted, with daringly high-pressure machinery. She flew like a gull and was a first-class sea-boat, and was for most of her long career a MacBraynes ship. The *King George V* donned the colours of war as a Clyde tender; she made six runs as a troop transport from Dunkirk; and on one occasion she carried Winston Churchill himself – out to a battleship for a critical transatlantic voyage to meet President Roosevelt. After the war – with occasional diversions – she became thirled to Oban, with highly popular cruises to Iona and Staffa, Fort William, and the Morvern coast. Her sailings were profitable to the very end; nevertheless, in September 1974 she was meanly withdrawn. She then spent seven years languishing in a Cardiff dry dock. She had just been sold on – and largely refitted for use as a floating restaurant on the Thames – when a dozing tramp set her on fire in the autumn of 1981. Repairs were deemed uneconomic; the gorgeous *King George V* was at last casually dumped in a bleak Welsh estuary for the sea to break her up.

Meanwhile, the general craze to placate the motor car had seen swathes of Glasgow demolished for new motorway links and the 'Clydeside Expressway', with a new road bridge and a Clyde Tunnel in turn encompassing the loss, by 1981, of all but one of the traditional cross-river ferries. Even as this book was being written, the very last – from Yoker to Renfrew – in the spring of 2010 escaped closure by a whisper, though the sturdy craft supplied by the Strathclyde Passenger Transport Executive have been retired and the brief crossing is maintained by something uncomfortably similar to a powered wheelbarrow.

With the move to containerisation of ocean cargo – handled readily by new facilities at Greenock – from the late Sixties fewer and fewer ocean-going vessels troubled to venture upriver. Between 1970 and 1980 alone, as memory attests and any juxtaposition of photographs from, say, the same vantage near the Clydeside Expressway will prove, Glasgow docklands became a ghostly townscape of deserted transit-sheds, empty quaysides and rusty cranes. Through the Seventies, the ships vanished. Through the 1980s and to this day, docks themselves started to disappear, filled in and asphalted over.

By 2000, upriver dredging was now so infrequent that the *Waverley* – the only substantial vessel now sailing to the city centre – occasionally bumped the bottom; by the end of 2006, a new road bridge at Pacific Quay prevented her passage east of Govan. The riverside was prettified, with new railings and granite coping and a Clydeside Walkway. A crane was conserved as an industrial monument; one of the domes of the old passenger tunnel as a casino. Where once had been industry and bustle, and all the banter and energy of those 'who go to sea in ships and in great waters trading be', all was but theme park and playground: clubs and restaurants and brightly lit night-scape, concert halls and entertainment venues, and copse upon copse of innovatively designed and very expensive 'low-density' housing for urban professionals. The Clyde was no longer an artery. It was Vanity Fair.

In 1968, the five major shipyards left standing – Fairfields at Govan, Alexander Stephens and Sons at Linthouse, Yarrow Shipbuilders Ltd and Charles Connel and Company at Scotstoun, and John Brown's at Clydebank – were welded into one faintly desperate amalgamation, a new consortium called Upper Clyde Shipbuilders, and with much lubricating government cash (which owed more than a little to a new threat emerging against local Labour hegemony: the Scottish National Party, months earlier, had won a sensational by-election at Hamilton, and has had continuous Parliamentary representation ever since). But still the problems, the mounting drought of orders, the walk-outs and wildcat strikes and almost fantastically inept management continued. By 1971, only Yarrow's, already largely dependent on defence contracts, still turned a profit; and at a critical moment – when Upper Clyde Shipbuilders hit serious cash flow difficulties – the Conservative government of Edward Heath refused it a £6 million loan.

Heath, with less conviction and emphatically less success than his Tory successor, was still thirled to the new economic free-market doctrines of his 'Selsdon Man' declaration in 1970; and chief among its tenets was a flat denial of any government help for lame ducks. This was neither as ruthless nor as stupid as it sounds. Since 1945, the general Tom Johnston approach to the governance of Scotland – subsidy, quangos and government by the divine right of experts and the official testament of fat reports – had been maintained complacently by Secretaries of State of both major parties, and would gen-erally obtain (for all the mythology of Scotland's Thatcherite night) to the advent of devolution itself. Great, monumental industrial schemes – the Ravenscraig steelworks, the Corpach pulp mill, the Invergordon smelter – were established, with much new infrastructure and ongoing public subsidy, but with little regard for economic viability or the convenience to market. Scotland was still thirled, practically by government diktat, to obsolete, heavy and in most instances dirty industries that employed thousands and thousands of men to make things or hew out resources a changing world wanted less by the year. Even by 1971, it was obvious that British government had no business 'backing winners'; it was such a duffer at it.

Yet now, on the upper reaches of the Clyde, Heath met his first and wounding political reverse – and not at the hands of either Labour or the SNP (the Liberals did not count) but at those of three determined young

Communists, Jimmy Reid, Jimmy Airlie and Sammy Barr, who quickly
persuaded the union leadership and members to a robust new sort of protest.
There would be no strike at Upper Clyde Shipbuilders. Instead, and with spirit,
they organised a 'work-in'. Even unpaid, the yards would complete the ships
they were constructing. They would prove – whatever the hysterics of the
cheap Tory press – that the men of Clydeside were neither indolent nor work-
shy. Reid, handsome and ebullient, and Communist councillor to Faifley,
Clydebank toured the yards to insist on discipline; on the importance of
workers presenting the best image to the British public that they could.
Surviving television footage of one Reid address – with evident humour
and his emphatic fist – still moves one today. 'We are not going to strike.
We are not even having a sit-in strike. Nobody and nothing will come in and
nothing will go out without our permission. And there will be no hooliganism
– there will be no vandalism – there will be no' – pause; chuckle – '*bevvying*,
because the world is watching us.'

There was huge public sympathy throughout Clydebank, Glasgow and
beyond: one demonstration in the city was attended by 80,000 people. Two
former shipyard workers, Matt McGinn and Billy Connolly – already making
their mark as entertainers – diverted the crowds at one with banter and song,
and Tony Benn made a rumbustious speech. Donations poured in, and Reid
made sure the funds were honestly counted and appropriately handled. At one
meeting, he proudly announced they had just received a £5,000 cheque (and
flowers) from John Lennon. One doughty old Marxist stared in entire
confusion. 'But Lenin's deid,' he whispered.

The UCS sit-in caught the global imagination and, across Britain, much
interest and support. Heath, beleaguered by now on several fronts, wilted
rapidly, and in February 1972 the government announced that two of the
yards – Fairfield's and Yarrow's – would be spared, and a third, John Brown's,
would be sold. It was the first in a succession of U-turns that progressively
weakened his authority and finally his administration. And, indeed, these
Glasgow slips – now operated by BAE Systems Surface Ships – remain in
business to this day, a market leader in the construction of cutting-edge
warships for everyone from the Royal Navy to the Sultan of Brunei.

But John Brown's does not. It would build no more ships, completing its last
– the *Alisa*, a bulk grain carrier, in 1972 – and then enjoyed reasonable success,
under a variety of owners, as John Brown Engineering, concentrating on the
production of industrial gas turbines and pipeline, and latterly under the name
Kvaerner Energy; the link with Clydebank finally ended in 2000, when gas
turbine fabrication ceased and 200 workers – the days when thousands had
poured out on the whistle to Glasgow Road had long gone – were made
redundant. The old shipyard, and its huge shed, were given over in 1972 – first
to Marathon Oil and then UiE Scotland – to the building of oil platforms for
the North Sea, despite its awkward west coast location. It shut its gates, for the
last time, in 2001.

Jimmy Reid had become, and despite ill-health, remained till his death in

August 2010, a Scottish institution. In February 1974 he stood for Clyde-bank's new Parliamentary division, Dunbartonshire Central, and won nearly 6,000 votes – 14.6 per cent of the poll and the best Communist performance in any Westminster seat, to this day, since 1959. He might even have won, had the archdiocese of Glasgow not expressly (and outrageously) ordered the children of Mother Church not to vote for him. Thereafter, Reid's political star mysteriously waned. By 1979, he had unbent sufficiently to become Labour candidate in Dundee East, but – even as SNP MPs were routed across Scotland, amidst the ruins of the first government scheme for devolution, and though practically anyone else that year would have beaten Gordon Wilson, the douce folk of Broughty Ferry and likeminded suburbs were not inclined to oust a Scottish Nationalist for a man straight out of the Communist Party. Nor, envious of his intellect, his charisma and his high public profile, did the wider Labour movement ever warm to him. Reid would never, in fact, enter Parliament: he built a reputation as a thinker, writer and broadcaster, and by the new century was himself a supporter of the SNP.

By the 1960s, Singer's belatedly grasped the seriousness of their plight in the global sewing-machine market, having failed since the war to make any real investment in new plant and new ideas. Unfortunately, management in distant America only came up with half the answer, and with consequences that would appal the local survivors of the Blitz. They failed entirely to modernise their industrial sewing-machine division – the commercial blunder which finally sank their British operation – but moved nevertheless to build an entire new Clydebank factory, with new equipment, to turn out a bright new generation of domestic sewing machines. The decision was announced in 1961; it entailed the demolition of the sprawling Edwardian complex – and, to horrified towns-folk, it entailed the destruction of the Singer's Tower and Clock.

It is unlikely, even a decade later – by which time folk were far more conservation-minded, and Clydebank's local government rather less supine – that such an outrage could have been accomplished, still less of a building which, by its sheer, majestic survival in March 1941, was more than just a landmark to Clydebank people: it was an assurance, a talisman, one of their few enduring links to another town and what had, in certain respects, been a sweeter and surer yesterday and to loved ones lost to fire and blast.

But, far away in America, those who ran Singer's were remote, pleasant, uncomprehending – and implacable, 'and in 1963,' Meg Henderson justly rages, 'horrified Bankies watched their clock disappear in front of them. The final insult was that the hands of the clock were made into ashtrays, an insult the Bankies would never forgive or forget. To the local people it was a precious link with the past, but to the Americans it was just a clock in the way of their new building, and they turned a deaf ear to the pleas of the townspeople. There was investment to try to rescue the factory, but not enough, and not in the right areas. Without investment there would be no improvement, and without improvement there would be no investment. . . .'

'I cried when they pulled down Singer's Clock,' one townswoman later told Tom McKendrick. 'You could see it from anywhere in Clydebank. . . . it was the only thing left. It came through the Blitz untouched – it was a symbol of survival and meant so much to the people of Clydebank . . . I hate them for that.' Anger, bitterness and a mounting sense of insecurity slowly corroded Singer's industrial relations, never those of unalloyed sunshine even in better times. In the first six months of 1965, alone, according to Henderson, there were 75 separate work stoppages.

It was too late, as events would prove, for Singer's, fast approaching a world where more and more women quit the life of the full-time wife and mother for one form or another of paid employment, and towards our own day of a globalised economy. Far Eastern sweatshops today furnish our more ruthless supermarkets and chain stores – capable, in 2010, of selling T-shirts for a pound, a complete school uniform for a fiver and a machine-washable gentleman's suit for less than £30. Why bother to make your own? From 1970, the market for household sewing machines – essentially generational – declined remorselessly in Europe. In 1980, beleaguered and strike-torn, Singer's finally gave up the ghost. Its manufacturing at Kilbowie ceased for ever. The site was acquired by the authorities, rapidly levelled of its indifferent Sixties construction, and – in what might have been a joke, had one any confidence in the wit of Margaret Thatcher and her Scottish viceroy – was soon occupied by the gleaming headquarters of a new quango, the Scottish Development Agency.

The 1963 vandalism at Singer's was but part of a wider planning failure that has left the new Clydebank wallowing as, in many ways, a failed townscape, without coherence or character. The wrecker's ball continued gaily to swing till 1980: in 1978, for instance, just about the oldest property standing – 'Thomson's Buildings', the original tenement accommodation for J. & G. Thomson employees on Clydebank Terrace – was demolished.

Their indifferent construction apart, many new council-house developments, such as the Faifley estate, were badly planned and oddly sited. 'Fifely', as it was quickly dubbed, sits on hilly ground, and is thick with flights of stairs; in some instances, two just to advance from pavement level to your own front door and, as Henderson observes, scarcely ideal for the old and infirm, or young mothers struggling with weans, shopping and pushchair. Such buildings could only have been designed by a man. Faifley besides is at the edge of Clydebank, a protracted trip by bus from its amenities and its employers, and its residents – as in other peripheral developments locally – felt uncomfortably estranged from Clydebank proper.

Such moves were of a piece – common generally in the development of post-war Scotland, and seen most infamously in modern Edinburgh – with what, subconsciously or otherwise, seems to have been a positive desire to remove the poorest, unluckiest and most vulnerable from the centre of our towns and cities to their margins, 'from the sight of the rich,' as T.C. Smout snaps, 'to peripheral estates . . . that became in turn notorious centres for crime and social problems . . . abnormal spatial segregation of the social classes'.

Even in Glasgow, and with Labour dominant since 1933, the system perpetuated that Victorian, and embarrassingly Scottish, distinction between the 'respectable' and the 'undeserving' poor. By the whim of officials, and no doubt often by mere bleak spite, families and individuals who passed subjective muster might well win admission to what remain Scotland's best achievements in social housing, the 'Ordinary' homes in Knightswood or Mosspark; others, classed as feckless (and, presumably, verminous) were, with life-changing consequence, classed as 'Rehousing' cases and, as Smout darkly concludes, folk consigned even in the Sixties or Seventies to the likes of Blackhill were 'condemned as certainly, and as irretrievably, as a family sent to a Victorian poorhouse'.

The result of all this has been rightly described by Smout as a '"new feudalism" that gave immense power to the officials of corporation housing departments, deprived the working class of the chance to own their own homes ("the greatest of anti-inflationary nest-eggs") and often tied people to one spot in a dying local economy'. When the Thatcher government took power in 1979, it forced through Parliament the absolute right of council-house tenants to buy their home, on the most generous terms; but the detail of this legislation (which, for instance, forbade local authorities to invest the proceeds of sale in building more social housing) was a signal factor in the modern curse of homelessness and vagrancy.

It has, admittedly, been inflamed by social change, family breakdown, widespread drug abuse and so on; but, whatever one might think of the 1974–79 Labour government and its destruction at the hands of the union barons, these were not days when families had to live in a single room, Britain had the highest rate of unmarried teenage pregnancy in Europe and beggars beset you on our city streets. Inevitably, over the last 30 years, council-house sales removed the best housing stock from the public sector and deprived the most fragile estates of their natural, sensible leaders.

The Thatcher administration cannot be blamed for the collapse of our old manufacturing industries – which had been living on borrowed time, in a fast-changing world, since the 1950s – but it showed the most cynical regard for its human consequence, which trapped acres of central Scotland, to this day, in ennui and ugliness and multigenerational unemployment. And deindustrialisation was only accelerated by the ideology of monetarism and, ironically, the strength early under that long Conservative government of North Sea oil, which effectively made the pound a petro-currency, kept it unnaturally strong and seriously hampered the export of goods from Scotland and everywhere else.

As if to opiate the disowned masses, North Sea oil revenues were spent not in vital investment or infrastructure but on a new serfdom of welfare-state bounty (most notably, the notorious 'incapacity benefit', keeping the work-averse and the unemployable out of unemployment statistics, their calculation re-jigged some 18 times by the 1987 general election) and, from 1988, generous tax cuts for the rich, fuelling a reckless consumer boom that, in the end, did much in inevitable recession to bring down Thatcher herself. Two decades on – as highlighted embarrassingly in the Glasgow East by-election of July 2008 – one could indeed speak, as Nairn-raised London commentator Fraser Nelson did, of a 'Third Scotland': hundreds of thousands effectively exiled from modern society, its enterprise and duties and rewards, and all but voiceless in national life.

This includes, inevitably, many Clydebank residents and, in wider Scottish awareness, Clydebank herself, with her sprawling and largely charmless lay-out, her old central streets now shorn of stores and amenities, her vandalised and deserted margins by the river (especially towards Yoker) and such forlorn bids for achievement as the Clyde Shopping Centre. Bright and futuristic – with its nicely landscaped slice of the Forth and Clyde Canal – when built, it seems today distinctly tired, with no obvious relationship to the wider town and not readily accessed on foot. The Clyde Centre amounts to an enclosed, indoor and somewhat down-market mall, in a town that otherwise seems dominated by derelict churches, dodgy-looking pubs and an inordinate number of betting shops.

Clydebank, as Gerry Hassan and Peter Lynch summarised its character in their study of our political geography, 'is working class, with a high propor-tion of council houses and above-average unemployment,' abounding in 'social inequalities'. To the casual visitor, as an eminent local politician (who would not thank us for attribution) remarked despairingly some months ago, the built environment of today's Clydebank 'simply doesn't make sense'.

Clydebank acquired its own football club, joining the Scottish League in 1965, but it was destroyed at last by incomprehensible boardroom decisions, selling off its old Kilbowie Park ground and failing to acquire another. It was declared bankrupt in 2002, leaving the town without a major football team and the first to crash out of the League – since Third Lanark in 1937 – in 35 years.

The town had hosted notable triumphs: Clydebank was from its start, and remains, the base of Radio Clyde, launched in 1976 and perhaps the most successful local commercial radio station in the United Kingdom, of enduring, intelligent character and with proven ability to identify and foster broad-casting talent. But, from 1996, she has no longer even controlled her own affairs. Clydebank District Council, under an inept and manifestly gerryman-dering endeavour by the Major administration, was dissolved into a new single-tier system of Scottish local government, herself under the aegis of a new West Dunbartonshire Council – with the moneyed, rural quarters of what historically had been West Dunbartonshire hacked improbably into Argyll and Bute, from Roseneath and Helensburgh to the prettier villages on the eastern shores of Loch Lomond.

This was probably part of a scheme (so far unsuccessful) to improve Conservative prospects in the Westminster division of Argyll and Bute; and there were undoubtedly Leftist romantics in what remained of the new authority happy to pronounce it a 'nuclear-free zone', now that Faslane and Trident submarines were beyond Dunbartonshire bounds. For most of its brief history, though – stalked by ineptitude and on occasion tainted by corruption – West Dunbartonshire Council, in incessant trouble with the national auditor, has been all but a national joke; and, though Clydebank is by a good margin its largest community, it is administered dourly from Dumbarton itself. Since 2007 – after a new voting system denied Labour a majority of seats, and a minority Labour administration could not survive for more than a matter of months – it has been run by the SNP with the support of assorted Independents, though with little sign so far of sustained success against perhaps intractable problems.

By 1990, one dreadful legacy of the past eclipsed even the Blitz in local awareness: Clydebank, it emerged, had the highest percentage of asbestos-related disease of any community in Britain, and probably in all Europe. Though the dangers of blue asbestos fibres had been recognised as early as 1930 – they are, for instance, highly carcinogenic – powerful vested interests, and a general contempt for the welfare of working people, had all but blocked wider public awareness or any meaningful protection of workers. Asbestos, highly resistant to fire and heat and chemicals, usefully tensile and with strong insulating properties, had been an important Scottish product as early as 1884, primarily for lagging or boarding engines, burners, boilers and so on. In that year, six of Britain's largest asbestos manufacturers – 19 in all were listed in one British trade directory – were in Glasgow. By the twentieth century, there were no fewer than 50 in Glasgow's Post Office Directory. From 1938, Turner's Asbestos Factory was pumping out the stuff at Dalmuir: at its peak, in the 1950s, they employed some 320 people, and would only close in 1970.

Asbestos was used, as we have seen, in enormous quantities, in shipbuilding – and packed or filed or hewn, aboard vessels under construction, by the 'white mice', men daily saturated in its insidious powder. Its use only increased as the century matured and there was yet more pressure for measures of fire-prevention aboard ship and in public buildings. As recently as 1980, 13-year-old classmates and I, awaiting lessons in biology at the huts that served as an annexe to Jordanhill College School, could (and did) pull woolly asbestos, by the handful, from holes kicked in the external timber cladding, with no idea of what it was or what it might do. It was used even in classroom panelling: pulling out a single drawing pin, as Joan Baird – lynchpin of the Clydebank Asbestos Group, established in 1992 – has observed starkly on film, released hundreds of microscopic asbestos fibres into the air children were breathing. Even today, it is a hidden hazard in many Scottish public buildings.

'The extent of the exposure,' Clydebank Asbestos Group material declares, 'can be gauged from the fact that there were forty-two shipbuilding and ship-repairing yards in Scotland in 1960 – *thirty-two of which were located on Clydeside*. The *Queen Elizabeth 2*, built at John Brown's in Clydebank between 1965 and 1967, provides a prime example of the extensive use of asbestos in ship construction at this time, and at peak more than 3,000 workers were employed . . . Many of these, across a whole range of trades

including laggers, joiners, plumbers, french-polishers, plasterers and electri-
cians were exposed to asbestos dust.'

A number of serious diseases have been long linked to asbestos exposure,
most respiratory, and several – lung cancer, asbestosis and the particularly
nasty mesothelioma – insidious and deadly. Asbestosis, a scarring of the lungs
caused by breathing in fibres over many years of exposure, is irreversible: the
first case in Britain was diagnosed as long ago as 1924. Lung cancer, though
primarily linked to cigarette-smoking – a factor long wielded, with other
bourgeois assumptions about working-class lifestyles, to belittle claims for
compensation generally over asbestos-related illness – needs no introduction;
mesothelioma is a cancer of the lung lining and, in a especially nasty
complication, can also attack the internal wall of the stomach. A probable
link has been drawn besides between asbestos and assorted malignancies of the
gastrointestinal tract, but not yet proven to scientific certainty.

Asbestos was not just a hazard for Clydebank workers. Women and
children who had to scrub clothing thick with the stuff were at like peril
through decades. Those who lived close to the Turner's plant at Dalmuir were
casually exposed to it in the atmosphere; the bombing and fire of March 1941
no doubt released great quantities of the stuff over a still wider environment.
Asbestos besides was used in the construction of houses and public buildings
into the 1980s, and for brake-liners and the like as recently as 2005, when its
production or use was finally banned throughout the European Union. The
import of asbestos to Britain was only prohibited in 1999, and it is being
stripped painfully – under strict conditions and, of course, with protective
clothing – from British structures to this day. Meanwhile, Clydebank continues to lead the United Kingdom in asbestos-related disease and death.

William Baird – Joan is his spirited, campaigning widow – was 75 when
diagnosed with mesothelioma in March 1996, after exposure decades earlier
and over a number of years, as a welder engaged in projects at home and
abroad. Youthful for his years, handsome and spry and with a beautiful
singing voice, he took six lingering, painful months to die. Claims for
compensation, on his behalf and those of many others, have been waged
over the years: all have been resisted strenuously and – until December 2006 –
their families were denied any claim after their deaths, even if the sufferer had
won a settlement in his lifetime.

As the past of Clydebank is the dignity of manual labour and skilled trades
and strong women, so it is one besides of bombs and fire and asbestos, of
injustice and grief. There are increasing endeavours for thoughtful celebration
– and remembrance – of that past, while quietly dismantling its uglier scars.

From early in the present century, West Dunbartonshire Council and
Scottish Enterprise have worked jointly for the 'regeneration' of the town's
waterfront, laying utilities and carving yet more miles of walkway, removing
most of the industrial archaeology while conserving others, such as the great
Titan Crane by what once – now filled – was the Rothesay Dock. Clydebank
College, too, has opened on a new and elegant campus. And even what

appeared a colossal slap in the face – the construction of a magnificent (and very private) hospital on the town's waterfront, by Health Care International, with substantial funding by the Major administration and in the hope of lucrative trade in sick sheikhs – turned to public advantage. The palace of privilege never proved viable and in 2002, soon after Jack McConnell's elevation as First Minister, it was bought out by the Scottish Executive for £37.5 million and put to effective use as an NHS facility to cut waiting times. Today the Golden Jubilee Hospital treats patients from Galloway to the Outer Hebrides.

And, for all her difficulties and a sustained and most unfair hand from remote centres of power, Clydebank yet fosters those who can raise beauty from ashes, such as the noted and highly original artist Tom McKendrick, born there in 1948: his shimmering work, in various media, is rooted firmly in the town's industry and craftsmanship. And the present century has seen the emergence of a gifted young film-maker, Iain McGuinness, who has to date produced two luminous documentaries about his Clydebank hometown, and is a talent to watch.

The one shining glory Clydebank cannot secure is just one of her great, surviving ships. She was swatted aside, in 1998, by Leith for the decommissioned *Britannia;* and, in 2007, lost out in the bidding for the retiring *Queen Elizabeth II*, which has been sold for static use to Dubai. There are the most forlorn hopes – some day, somehow – for the *Queen Mary* entombed at Long Beach, Los Angeles, in concrete these 40 years, and at present with an uncertain future.

What Clydebank's brief, doughty history reflects shamefully, in T.C. Smout's words, is the mystery, since the dawn of the Industrial Revolution, of 'how little one of the top two or three richest countries in the world did for its citizens until well on into the twentieth century'. In a new century, and under a new Scottish political order, she remains a firmly marginalised corner of a little land where, under ongoing genuflection to experts and the conventional wisdom of any given time, those in power – of all parties, Labour and Nationalist, Conservative and Liberal Democrat – continue to order Scottish affairs in enduring sub-Thatcherite values and to the general disadvantage of those denied a voice, a platform or significant capital, not because they are less deserving or less articulate or less aspiring, of weaker character or meaner capacity, but merely because they are less lucky.

12

THE FLOWERS OF THE FOREST

They lie yet at the Old Dalnottar Cemetery, amidst the stirrings of new spring this Saturday morning, 13 March 2010; though today – I am early – matting has been laid on the ground before the Clydebank Blitz Memorial, against damp and mud and soft sod, and for the convenience of those who will come. In fact it has been a dry, cold spring; last night saw hard frost, and today is beautiful, with a crisp light breeze and blue skies and scudding little clouds and soft timid sun, and it crosses my mind that it was just such a day 69 years ago, before the bombers came.

A funeral has just concluded – the hearse and cars and mourners in retreat, from a distant corner of this large and tree-gridded graveyard; but there is a young family by the far end of this mass grave, laying flowers by one of the scant monuments rising from it: grandchildren, I think, and great-grand-children. I do not intrude on them.

There is a stone 'in loving memory of the Rocks Family, killed by enemy action, 13–14 March 1941' and here with them all Patrick Rocks himself, who fled to Ireland in his grief, was laid to his own rest in March 1954. Set in the ground – almost illegible – is the humble, concrete plaque for Albert Bowman, one of the ARP wardens who died. Near him, Henry Aird was buried in 1979, almost 40 years after his wife Marion and their teenage daughters Isabella and Tomina were slain by the Luftwaffe at Church Street, Clydebank.

Still another stone commemorates Christine Cameron McNair, the 37-year-old wife of James MacDonald – and their daughters, Jessie (16) and Brenda (5), and besides their son, James, who was 10. To her, and to them, James MacDonald raised this stone; but, though he now lies here too, it does not bear his name, for no one was left to undertake it.

So many have gone, including most of the witnesses we have met in this story. There is the stone over the spot where, in 2001, Kathleen McConnell joined the rest of her sundered family. James Hastings had a distinguished career in local government – crowned as town clerk of Elgin – and even in the 1980s gave a quiet, thoughtful interview about March 1941. David Kirkwood retired from Parliament, after a single-year term for a new division of East Dunbartonshire, in 1951, and sank onto plush red benches as Baron Kirkwood, and wrote his memoirs, and died in 1955. Manny Shinwell endured – a sparkling presence to the last – until his death in 1986 at the age of 102. Father Sheary, priest at Dalmuir in 1941, served subsequently in Toryglen and Glasgow – by which settlement, in 1976, he was Canon Sheary; he died in

January 1982, soon after his radio testimony the previous year. And, in March 1987, 46 years after the Clydebank Blitz, Ellen MacKinven was finally laid to rest – at the age of 90 – beside her late husband and her only son in a lovely Kintyre graveyard. Few today can now recall the Clydebank Blitz as adult experience.

In another cemetery, the Campsie graveyard by Lennoxtown, a drably dressed war widow, with but scant English, came about 1950. Frau Hansmann had come to mourn in person her husband, Stafellkapitan Hauptmann Hansmann, and to make the arrangements – as was general practice – for the exhumation and return of his remains for final rest in the Fatherland. But she met not with anguish in Lennoxtown, nor felt any hostility. The grave had been respectfully tended. There was a peace and a beauty to the place, and she felt a great calm. She gave her decision; her Hauptmann would remain in this quiet spot. And, though she eventually remarried, by her arrangement a simple memorial stone was erected, and flowers were laid regularly on the anniversary of his death, and every year – and for many years to come – she flew in from Germany to visit that Campsie cemetery and be by her first man's grave. That beside him, of Oberleutnant Coenen, remains unmarked to this day.

But they are coming now, in Clydebank, others who remember, coming to the Old Dalnottar Cemetery – cars pulling up, doors slamming, morning coughs, quiet words of greeting, and they step in off the main drive, through yews and cypresses, and from another angle and from the trickle that remains of that funeral clergy have detached themselves, and as the little congregation of remembrance forms on and around the matting and before the Clydebank Blitz Memorial it builds very quickly – suddenly 40, then 60, then more. Most, though not all – there are some teenagers, a couple of mothers younger than I – are late in years, and most, though not all, are appropriately dressed: black ties, dark suits, few flames of colour save navy and grey. But there is a flash of gold civic links draped on shoulders, and there is Provost Denis Agnew; and there are fine old men in black blazers and black berets and a blaze of scarlet sash, exotic, and as I hear their voices I realise that they are Polish, and that these are brave boys of the *Piorun*, yet as erect as they were seven decades ago, and almost as strong.

Father Gerard Tartaglia, parish priest at St Margaret's in Whitecrook, Clydebank, assured and genial, introduces himself briefly to me, as an order of service is handed to all, and when all are ready – on the dot of eleven – he assumes his place, and we begin. He gives out the 23rd Psalm, and presents it unaccompanied, as majestically and deft of pitch and pace as any Presbyterian, and the notes of 'Crimond' rise in this grove, and the singing is strong, and to my great surprise in the day we are in almost everyone sings, and heartily, and without the aid of strings or keyboard.

There are readings, there are prayers, both from the priest and from the Reverend Margaret Yule, of Radnor Park Parish Church, and another bidding prayer besides, beautifully worded, from a spry old gentleman called John

McNeill, who is a Justice of the Peace and whose wife, Helen, has done so much to make sure the Clydebank Blitz is not forgotten.

Her mother lost all her family that night, and no identifiable remains were ever found: over decades, regularly visiting this spot whenever she felt defeated or sad, the old woman besides never missed the annual service of commemoration. And when, after the fiftieth, in 1991, Clydebank District Council declared it would not be continued, she was distraught. She would not submit to that, nor would her daughter and son-in-law. Clergy were rallied; support was exhorted. The little ceremony has continued, every Saturday morning nearest to the anniversary, be it brightest sun or raining in rods, ever since. Nor did the McNeills and their friends stop there. The dedicated Clydebank Blitz chapel at Kilbowie St Andrew's Church, and that 1998 volume of memories – *Untold Stories* – and much else besides is largely the sacrificial achievement of Helen McNeill.

There are two minutes of silence, with but the wind in the evergreens, the purr of traffic on the Boulevard and, dimmer and distant, over the Erskine Bridge.

Wreaths are laid – by the Provost, by the Polish Consul-General, by the survivors of the *Piorun*, by councillors, by representatives of the emergency services, and sprays and posies besides by orphans and grandchildren and great-grandchildren and white-haired friends and neighbours of the lost. Then Father Tartaglia leads us in 'Abide With Me' – again, most hearty and earnest – and then a piper plays the closing lament, and the air is ancient, most Scottish, recognised in moments.

It is so easy to focus on the mechanics of what happened – aircraft and bomb tonnage – or the grim realities of death and destruction, and yet lose sight of the sorrow endured through decades since by those bereaved in March 1941, and whose homes and kindred were torn asunder.

'I was twelve at the time,' Patrick Donnelly – whose widowed mother and all his siblings were killed on Pattison Street – nearly 30 years ago told Billy Kay. 'Always remember carrying my young sister up to school, Margaret, that was my favourite. We were a pretty close family, you know, up to the Blitz, and that was it. It was terrible. I would say that, for the next three years, that I could see myself walking down the streets of Helensburgh on my own, and I'd burst out crying – it really took me years to get over it. To think I actually had four sisters and a brother, my mother, and that was me completely on my own.'

'When I think of the 13th of March 1941,' said Kathleen McConnell, 'I often say to myself – that one night changed our whole life. The family, you would say, never ever got together again as a family should be, and when it did we were all changed. I would love to have known my sister and my brother and my mother as a grown-up. In my family, my mother was killed, she was thirty-one; my eldest sister, she was killed – she was about twenty-two, and my eldest brother was killed – he was just coming up for twenty-one. And I always thought of the old song, "The Flowers o' the Forest are A' Wede Away . . ."'

I've seen the smiling of fortune beguiling,
I've felt all its favours and found its decay –
Sweet was its blessing, and kind its caressing,
But now 'tis fled, 'tis fled far away;
I've seen the forest adorned the foremost
With flowers of the fairest, most pleasant and gay;
Sae bonnie was their blooming, their scent the air perfuming,
But now they are withered and a' wede away.

I've seen the morning with gold the hills adorning,
And the dread tempest roaring before parting day –
I've seen Tweed's silver streams glitt'ring in the sunny beams,
Grow drumlie and dark as they roll'd on their way –
O fickle fortune, why this cruel sporting?
O why thus perplex us, poor sons of a day?
Thy frowns cannot fear me, thy smiles cannot cheer me –
For the flowers of the forest are a' wede away.

As we hover for a minute or two afterwards, a trim, alert old gentleman – in his eightieth year, it emerges – engages me in conversation. He is Hector Cairns, and he lives nearby at Drums in Old Kilpatrick; a child of Clydebank and a survivor of the Blitz. This yearly service is important to Hector; and when I comment on the lack of any military representative – one is used at such affairs to some member of the Forces turning up, resplendent in uniform, replete with wreath and a clockwork salute – Hector says that is entirely as it should be. And it is how they want it kept, for this was a civilian tragedy and not one of soldiering, though on occasion the Forces have tried to muscle in. And I realise Hector Cairns is right.

There is another service to follow now – in honour of the Poles, by the Town Hall – and Hector insists that I come, and that he will drive me. As we bowl out along the Boulevard, and in by Old Kilpatrick, it dawns on me I have been practically adopted for the afternoon; and that Hector Cairns is taking me into Clydebank, by the long way round, for a reason.

He drives with pace and skill, after many years of experience, and of course he points things out, like the access road and slip for the old Erskine ferry; but mostly he is identifying where things were; where this and that had stood until mid-March 1941, and as we go through Dalmuir and Hector indicates one replacement or reinstatement or gap after another the intensity of the German assault is driven home; and – though he does not articulate it – the burden of remembering the community he knew, in every shop and tenement and detail. It lives now only in his head and those of his generation, and with each passing year fewer survive who bear it, and the weight on Hector Cairns and his contemporaries, as that Clydebank continues inexorably to retreat from us, is all the more.

Solidarity Plaza, on Glasgow Road across from the magnificent Clydebank

Town Hall, was dedicated in April 2005 and, in its silky granite and plaques on plinthed boulders and a dominating obelisk, is at once in honour of the people of Clydebank themselves and of the men of ORP *Piorun*, 'Defenders of Clydebank'. The service here is brief; there is no singing. We are then pressed to step over the road for refreshments; and Hector is going, so I go.

Clydebank Town Hall is no longer a citadel of local government. But it is an atmospheric Victorian building, redolent with municipal pride, all balustrades and panelling. Portraits of past provosts line the feature staircase. In the chamber upstairs hang portraits still more interesting, of great Clydebank ships. Dozens and dozens of folk have come in. I had anticipated tea and biscuits: what follows, homely and delicious, is a feast. There are indeed hot beverages and soft drinks (and a nip of something stronger for those who want it) but there are besides bowls of broth, and fat filled rolls, and plates to come of macaroni and cheese and after that of rhubarb crumble and custard, and biscuits, and baking; we queue for all this in an anteroom dominated by a painting of the *Queen Mary*, and it is served in generous portions by cheerful ladies. There is no ceremony here, no pomposity; it is as the plain and welcome fare served, these days, in a village hall after an island funeral.

Hector ensures I neither starve nor perish of thirst. Politicians of one stripe and another introduce themselves – councillors, MSPs, Provost Agnew. 'This is a big giveaway, isn't it?' he beams, fingering his weighty chain of office. Another local minister – by whose endeavour I came in the first place – now introduces herself. Revd Peggy Roberts, warm and sensible, is minister of Kilbowie St Andrew's, and so fluent that you might well not spot the trace of an accent. In fact, her given name is Annegret; and Mrs Roberts is by birth and upbringing German, who married a Scot and raised a family in Perthshire. (Months later, by chance, I will learn the folk-singer Alastair Roberts is her son.) She has been in Scotland for over 30 years and tells me flatly that, even in Clydebank, she has at no time ever had an unpleasant encounter, or a word of bitterness, on account of her origins. 'I have to admit,' she confided in a recent e-mail, 'I had never heard of the bombing of Clydebank, or many of the other places, when I was growing up in Germany. Sometimes it feels that, wherever I turn, my ancestors have been there and caused death and destruction. History lessons kept things pretty general . . .'

The welcome generally is such – this is a warm-hearted place of kindly people – that it is well over an hour before Hector and I briefly resume our tour. He pauses, looking up and down the Glasgow Road, and tells me how this was – and still should be – the true main street, a bustle of life and commerce, but that was smashed by the bombs and withered through decades since. He drives me then into the eastern parts of Clydebank, till we are almost over the border and in Yoker and Glasgow, and in a clutch of solid and largely pre-war council houses he parks at a certain corner.

This is Whitecrook – they call it Old Whitecrook now – and we are sitting in Hector's car by the junction of North Elgin Street and East Barns Street. 'This,' says Hector, 'right where we're parked, is where the very first parachute-mine fell, on the first night. They were dreadful things. They didn't go deep, you know, make a crater. They detonated immediately, on the surface, and the blast went over a huge field . . .'

His home was 2 McDonald Crescent, perhaps 60 yards away, 'though there were only eight of us; my older brother was away in the RAF. The blast blew in the windows. We were in the Anderson shelter, and the second night, you know, there was much more anxiety, and neighbours and their friends – Mr and Mrs Middleton, and some folk they brought, they piled in with us. It was an Anderson shelter, in the back-garden, and it was meant for ten people, but there were fourteen or fifteen of us.'

'That must have been very uncomfortable,' I say.

'Well, what mattered was that you were safe. It was a lot better being in a shelter than not being one. And my father had done a good job – dug it in deep, and covered with earth, and turf, and grass growing thick. And after the second night, we found this paving-stone on it – driven deep – one of those cobbles, or sets, heavy, maybe eighteen inches by twenty. And it had gone almost through the sod and was maybe half an inch from the zinc. So if we hadn't had so well covered a shelter – well, that would have blown right in and I don't know what it could have done to us.'

As it was, there was a casualty. 'Well, a second land-mine came down, that night, the 14th – the McDonald Crescent corner with East Barns Street – and there was this elderly lady in with us, in her eighties, and we had reinforced the shelter with timber spars, with nuts and bolts, and the blast blew in the door, and a bolt smashed straight into her nose. She died later – I don't know if it was days or weeks or how much later. I don't think I knew her name. There was a lot of older folk like that, who just died of shock, really – delayed reaction – and I don't believe they're counted in the statistics, and of course we were out and away by then . . .'

Hector sighs, 'It was just the window-panes of our house damaged the first night, and the ceiling down, the plaster; but the second night, that land-mine blew out the gable-end, and the staircase, and the casements of the windows too, and took a section of the roof off, and we had to go then. Now MacPhail's book just says that was a 500-lb bomb, but it was the full thing – a big land-mine; I saw the parachute silk, and the ropes, the next day, just on the ground there. They used those houses later, you know, with all the fronts blown out, for house-to-house training – combat-training, the Commandos, and later Americans, shooting and so on, so the war seemed just to go on . . . North Elgin Street, there was nothing left as far as you could see from here, after 14th March, the Saturday. And the other side of McDonald Crescent, the fronts were off all the houses, like dolls houses, you could see right in . . .'

These houses were all duly repaired, he says, or the worst hit replaced all together. 'It might have been better if they had replaced most of them, but it was wartime. Materials were short. They just salvaged stuff and piled it in John Brown's recreation ground, and they would go and get you a door and stick that door in, and never mind if it quite fitted or not, but of course we couldn't stay for a while anyway.'

The Cairns had to leave. 'There was this awful, long, 24-hour journey to Inveraray, on Saturday, and then we got to Ireland, and we were there for six months. And, you know, there was folk I never saw again, people I was in school with, neighbours. You just lost touch. I don't know when that old lady died. People I knew, they went to the Vale of Leven, they went all over Scotland, and they never came back – Clydebank didn't come back.'

And, again, there is that distance of remembering in the keen features of Hector Cairns, the weight of decades, and there is no more to be said.

Then, by my request, we head still further east, till we are out of West Dunbartonshire and on Dumbarton Road and in Yoker, through what even in my boyhood had been unassuming, sorrowful tenements and where now there is nothing very much.

We turn right, and park, and walk down a great cobbled slipway to look over to Renfrew and watch the ferry ply her trade, and I tell him of Donald, trim and frail and in his mid-sixties, and who first took me here in the autumn of 1976. From Cross in Lewis, Donald laboured from an early age – polishing coffins, breaking rocks on the new Glencoe road; and then he trained for joinering, and settled in Glasgow, and married a girl, Alice, from two villages along, and they made home in Govan. On Sabbath, they went to Gaelic sermon in Partick, but for the rest of the week Donald went daily by tram and this ferry and another tram to Clydebank, where he worked at John Brown's and on 'Hull 552': and there he stood, watching with thousands of others, when the *Queen Elizabeth* was launched on 27 September 1938. But, like many island contemporaries, he was in the Royal Naval Reserve, and was duly called for war, and Alice had to go home to Lewis with their little girl. That child did not survive; but, in November 1940, Alice was delivered of a little boy, another Donald MacLeod, my father. And that, I explain to Hector, is one emotional anchor I have with his community, and the Singer sewing machines prized by both my grandmother and – to this day – my mother, as immaculate and as reliable as they were when bought.

We walk down till the Clyde itself – still and silky, for the tide is in flood – laps at our shoes. I am struck by the clarity of the water – my boyhood memory is of something distinctly green, scummy – and I dip my hand, and dare to sip. It is at once salt and sweet. This is no longer an artery or highway; but salmon swim it again, and it is cleaner today than for over 200 years. The area around us, though – neat if tired in the 1970s – is now vandalised, half-demolished and singularly ugly. What was once a characterful restaurant, overlooking the Yoker slipway, is now a burnt-out shell. There is no longer any sense of daily commute by proud working men; just a coarse, graffiti-thick bleakness suggesting they are all dead and gone.

The last rite is a service at Kilbowie St Andrew's, well up Kilbowie Road, and to the side of the auditorium is the quiet corner, on a raised floor, that is the Clydebank Blitz Memorial Chapel. There is a stained-glass commemorative pane – electrically backlit – and, in tapestry, the arms of the old Clydebank Burgh Council: this is another Helen McNeill accomplishment, which she worked on in 1997 over weeks at the Clydebank Museum, and made known that anyone wanting to commemorate a loved one lost in the Blitz could come and insert a stitch. Many indeed did. No one was rejected if their bereavement fell outwith Clydebank, Liam Stewart has noted: if 'they found the context appropriate, they added their stitch.'

But there is something else, and an immaculately dressed elder, hovering in attendance, is happy to show it to me. It is a great book, beautifully bound, every word inside handwritten and in immaculate calligraphy, and so precious that before Nathaniel Lees – a very youthful 85 – will even touch it, he dons pristine, white cotton gloves. Inside, first, are signed statements of benediction, in 1997, by Thomas, Cardinal Winning, and the Moderator of the General Assembly of the Church of Scotland; I cannot resist a smile at the order, but it is wiped in moments as, wordlessly, Mr Lees turns page upon page, and the record of street upon street, the men and women of this burgh and their children and their children's children who were slain, and the homes and families obliterated. On Crown Avenue alone, there are dozens of dead recorded: at Second Avenue, nearby, there were 80 fatalities. Mr Lees, brought up on Crown Avenue and a lad of 16, was bombed out with his family, escaping with nothing at all but the school uniform he wore; he knew practically everyone whose name is here scripted. As if by instinct, or reverence, I do not touch these pages, nor ask if I might.

Many more come for the act of worship and remembrance than the chapel can accommodate; they sit in the main kirk beside us. Another priest is in charge – Father Joe Mills, of St Mary's, Duntocher. He was born only a few months after the Clydebank Blitz though, as he reminds us (perhaps a little pointedly, eying the assorted politicians of the Left), 'I was already in existence, in my mother's womb.' We sing weightier and, frankly, indifferent hymns; we recite the Lord's Prayer; there are prayers for the dead (again) and a reading from the Apocrypha.

The service closes with the clergy by an altar, and a lighting of candles. This is not in my own faith tradition, and I do not participate, nor is anything more said. Father Mills and the Reverend Peggy stand wordlessly by, as they file from pew after pew – most old, grey-headed, determined, some in tears – and file in dignity, and take a candle, and light it, and place it; there are but the muted notes of an organ, and the steady shuffle of Clydebank feet; and the tea-lights build up in a pyramid, a cataract of fire.

Downstairs, afterwards, in a simple and welcoming hall, we sit informally around tables: there is much tea and prodigious quantities of home baking. Many more make themselves known: the mother of a boy, Iain Simpson, who was in my class in school, and John and Helen McNeill, and – when I am quietly escorted to her – a quiet little woman, not far from tears, who talks softly of that night when she clambered disobediently onto the draining-board by the sink and watched wide-eyed as bombs started to fall on Jellicoe Street, and the eerie brightness of that night, and the river of fire. She is Anne Holmes, granddaughter of Patrick Rocks.

As the end of a grim century neared – one in which new learning and technology had so greatly extended the reach of human evil – a little party worked quietly one day in the tower that alone still stands of the old Cardross Parish Church; the rest cleared, levelled to sill height and lawned over in 1954 to serve as an abiding memorial to the Blitz on Clydeside.

After weeks of work to clean, repair and secure, and in thought of an imminent new millennium, they sealed their labours with a simple stone plaque. It reads

> *To the glory of God*
> *The tower of this church*
> *was restored as a witness*
> *to past faith and future hope*
> *Summer 1999*
> *'Look Forward in Faith'.*

THOSE LOST IN THE
CLYDEBANK BLITZ

MARCH 1941

Not without regret, concluding a book that has generally covered the devastation and loss of life by enemy action in Clydeside and Greater Glasgow during the Second World War, I am constrained by space to listing here only those who died or were fatally injured within the bounds of Clydebank Burgh Council in March 1941. My apologies to the people of Alexandria, Cardross, Dumbarton, Greenock, Port Glasgow, Glasgow, Paisley and every other Scottish parish where hearts were broken by the Luftwaffe.

I have listed everyone alphabetically within the generally accepted, distinct communities in the former local authority – Bowling; Clydebank and Dalmuir – as one unit: the shared, sweeping streets make that impossible to avoid; Duntocher; Hardgate; and Old Kilpatrick – and, in the final section, those who died or were fatally injured in the Clydebank Blitz but did not live in the burgh, being visitors or emergency-workers on duty on the lethal nights of that spring. Where the locale of their end is known, they are besides mentioned *passim* under that street.

The complications in drawing up such a list are rapidly evident. Many people were not killed in their homes and, in not a few instances, nowhere near them – out visiting friends and relatives when the siren wailed, or caught on the street and running for cover or a communal shelter as they could. On such happenstance and by such decisions, by individuals, amidst an experience particularly terrifying in its utter helplessness, lives and family fortunes duly turned – or perished. Such a roll of honour can never be complete, or incontestably accurate in every detail, and the work of research, clarification and debate will continue for a long time.

It was evidently the habit of the officials responsible for compiling the earliest lists to standardise all Scottish patronymic surnames as 'Mc', capitalising the paternity. Practice in this varied from parish to parish and registrar to registrar; in four generations, my own surname has been variously recorded – in the same district of Lewis – as 'MacLeod', 'McLeod', 'Macleod' and 'MacLeod' again. I have taken the liberty, where the cognomen is obviously Highland, of adjusting to 'Mac', while retaining the paternal capital in every instance. In what must remain a work in progress, and for a future edition of this book, anyone with family or private information on such a detail or anyone else named (or missing from, or inaccurately placed) in this list is most welcome to contact me.

I am indebted immeasurably to Mr Tom McKendrick – the pre-eminent scholar in this grim area – for gladly sharing the data he has collated and logged so far, and from which all these names are drawn. The research here is emphatically that of Mr McKendrick, over many years, though I have cross-referenced with Iain MacPhail's 1974 list for middle-names and other detail, and where they disagree on an individual's age, I have gone with Mr McKendrick's on the basis of his recent and exhaustive research. Typing out every single name – manually, over days, in a format more accessible to the general public and organised by locality and street – has brought home to me the scale of tragedy and loss as nothing else: at points, recording yet another infant or, yet again, an entire family, it has been so harrowing I have had to abandon my desk for some minutes.

As will be apparent, not everyone finally died in Clydebank; and in all too many instances of those names we now here record and reverence, bodies were never recovered or never identified. It is besides probable in war-time conditions that others besides died, in March 1941, who were never found, never missed, never recorded, and whose names cannot now be known save unto God.

John MacLeod
jm.macleod@btinternet.com

BOWLING

COLUMBIA COTTAGE
Donald MacIntosh
Age: 36
At First Aid Post, Old Kilpatrick, 14 March 1941. Fireman (Auxiliary Fire Service)

3 SOMMERVILLE TERRACE
Janet Richardson MacPherson
Age: 38
At Pattison Street, 13 March 1941

WINDSOR PLACE
Jane Adair
Age: 40
At Windsor Place, 13 March 1941

John Adair
Age: 10
At Windsor Place, 13 March 1941

William Adair
Age: 40
At Windsor Place, 13 March 1941

John Dyer
Age: 11
At Windsor Place, Bowling, 13 March 1931

60 WINDSOR PLACE
Rosina Brown
Age: 60
At Windsor Place, 13 March 1941

CLYDEBANK AND DALMUIR

21 ABERCONWAY STREET
Annie Jamieson Walker
Age: 45
At 59 Whitecrook Street, 14 March 1941

57 ABBOTT CRESCENT
Jean Kidd
Age: 13
At 425 Glasgow Road, 13 March 1941

Jeanie Black McKain
Age: 56
At 425 Glasgow Road, 13 March 1931

14 ALDER ROAD
Winifred McQuillan
Age: 18
At Emergency Hospital, Lennox Castle, 15
March 1941; injured at 14 Alder Road, 15
March 1941

16 ALDER ROAD
Helen King
Age: 67
At 16 Alder Road, 13 March 1941

Robert King
Age: 26
At Emergency Hospital, Lennox Castle, 14
March 1941; injured at 16 Alder Road, 13
March 1941

21 BANNERMAN STREET
Jane McKain
Age: 39
At 425 Glasgow Road, 13 March 1941

7 BEARDMORE STREET
Ellen Nixon Bainbridge
Age: 13
At 7 Beardmore Street, 14 March 1941

Thomas Bainbridge
Age: 16
At 7 Beardmore Street, 14 March 1941

Josephine MacAulay
Age: 9

At 7 Beardmore Street, 14 March 1941

Annie McClory
Age: 9
At 7 Beardmore Street, 14 March 1941

James McClory
Age: 7
At 7 Beardmore Street, 14 March 1941

John McClory
Age: 5
At 7 Beardmore Street, 14 March 1941

Mary McClory
Age: 3
At 7 Beardmore Street, March 14 1941

Matthew McClory
Age: 10
At 7 Beardmore Street, 14 March 1941

Sarah McClory
Age: 36
At 7 Beardmore Street, 14 March 1941

David Smart
Age: 11
At 7 Beardmore Street, 14 March 1941

Robert Smart
Age: 1
At 7 Beardmore Street, 14 March 1941

Susan Smart
Age: 36
At 7 Beardmore Street, 14 March 1941.

BEARDMORE'S WORKS, DALMUIR
See **James Bowles, Minnie Cooper** and **Andrew
Shaw** under NON-RESIDENTS.

8 BEATTY STREET
Frederick Massey
Age: 69
At Emergency Hospital, Lennox Castle, 14
March 1941; injured at Clydebank, locale
unknown, 13 March 1941

12 BEATTY STREET
Samuel Evans Currie
Age: 37
At 12 Beatty Street, 13 March 1941

Thomas Lockhead Currie
Age: 65
At 12 Beatty Street, 13 March 1941

Johanna Dobbie Marshall
Age: 72
At 12 Beatty Street, 13 March 1941

Peter Marshall
Age: 78
At 12 Beatty Street, 13 March 1941

Agnes Lochhead Kilpatrick
Age: 31
At 12 Beatty Street, 13 March 1941

Andrew David Kilpatrick
Age: 31
At 12 Beatty Street, 13 March 1941

Ian McGregor Russell
Age: 9
At 12 Beatty Street, 13 March 1941

Margaret Brown Russell
Age: 43
At 12 Beatty Street, 13 March 1941

14 BEATTY STREET
Samuel Pillar
Age: 52
At 14 Beatty Street, 13 March 1941. ARP
Warden

19 BEECH DRIVE
Mary Aston Hunter
Age: 16
At 19 Beech Drive, 13 March 1941

Sarah Aston Hunter
Age: 43
At 19 Beech Drive, 13 March 1941

BENBOW HOTEL
James Dunleavy
Age: 54
At Janetta Street, 13 March 1941

Alexander Blair MacLennan
Age: 63
At Benbow Hotel, Dalmuir, 14 March 1941

Bessie McNair
Age: 60
At Blawarthill Hospital, 14 March 1941;
injured on 13 March 1941 at Benbow Hotel,
Dalmuir

David McNamarra
Age: Unknown
At Benbow Hotel, Dalmuir, 13 March 1941

Agnes Mealyea
Age: 50
At Blawarthill Hospital, 15 March 1941;
injured on 13 March 1941 at Benbow Hotel,
Dalmuir

George Morrison
Age: 83
At Benbow Hotel, Dalmuir, 13 March 1941

9 BIRCH ROAD
Joseph Struthers
Age: 37
At 9 Birch Road, 14 March 1941

56 BOQUHANRAN ROAD
Samuel Douglas Ramage
Age: 31
At 76 Second Avenue, 13 March 1941. Fire
Watcher.

35 BRIAR DRIVE
John Stewart
At Royal Infirmary, Glasgow, on 16 March
1941; injured at Briar Drive, 14 March 194.

10 BROOM DRIVE
Elizabeth Scott Peden
Age: 47
At 10 Broom Drive, 13 March 1941

Elizabeth Peden
Age: 16
At 10 Broom Drive, 13 March 1941

Robert Peden
Age: 52
At 10 Broom Drive, 13 March 1941

14 BROOM DRIVE
Agnes Campbell
Age: 22
At 14 Broom Drive, 13 March 1941. First Aid
Post member

Annie Campbell
Age: 16
At 14 Broom Drive, 13 March 1941.

Ellen Campbell
Age: 23
At 14 Broom Drive, 13 March 1941. Auxiliary
nurse

Martha Campbell
Age: 21
At 14 Broom Drive, 13 March 1941. First Aid
Post member

Mary Jane Chambers Campbell
Age: 52.
At 14 Broom Drive, 13 March 1941.

18 BROOM DRIVE
Charles Hughes
Age: 61
At 18 Broom Drive, 13 March 1941

11 BRUCE STREET
Allan MacKechnie
Age: 46
At Blawarthill Hospital, 14 March 1941;
injured 13 March 1941, locale unknown

6 BUCHANAN STREET
Elizabeth Couch Baxter
Age: 53
At 78 Second Avenue, 13 March 1941.

10 BUCHANAN STREET
Archibald Walker
Age: Unknown
At Clydebank, locale unknown, 15 March
1941

10 BURNS STREET
Margaret Malaugh
Age: 18
At 10 Burns Street, 14 March 1941.

11 BURNS STREET
Isabella Moore
Age: 56
At Emergency Hospital, Lennox Castle, 14
March 1941; injured on 13 March 1941 at
Royal Ordnance Factory, Dalmuir

12 BURNS STREET
Euphemia Burns
Age: 80
At Royal Infirmary, Glasgow, 17 March 1941.
Injured on 14 March at 97 Canberra Avenue

104 CANBERRA AVENUE
Kathleen Semple
Age: 11
At Base Hospital, Larbert, 17 March 1941;
injured at Burns Street Shelter, 14 March 1941

Sheila Semple
Age: 7
At Burns Street Shelter, 14 March 1941

2 CASTLE STREET
Wallace Cochrane
Age: 1 year 5 months
At 2 Castle Street, 14 March 1941

Duncan Dinning
Age: 3
At 2 Castle Street, 14 March 1941

Jane McPherson Dinning
Age: 41
At 2 Castle Street, 14 March 1941

Janet Mitchell Hopkirk Dinning
Age: 15
At 2 Castle Street, 14 March 1941

Annie Harris Johnston
Age: 54
At 2 Castle Street, 14 March 1941

Nathaniel Scott – see NON-RESIDENTS

Alfred Westbury
Age: 22
At 2 Castle Street, 14 March 1941

Alfred Westbury
Age: 54
At 2 Castle Street, 14 March 1941

Elizabeth McInnes Westbury
Age: 56
At 2 Castle Street, 14 March 1941

Samuel Alfred Westbury
Age: 27
At 2 Castle Street, 14 March 1941

Walter Westbury
Age: 12
At 2 Castle Street, 14 March 1941

4 CHERRY CRESCENT
Jeanie Elliott MacLean
Age: 47
At Wardens' Post, Janetta Street, 13 March
1941

Margaret MacLean
Age: 18
At Wardens' Post, Janetta Street, 13 March
1941

6 CHERRY CRESCENT
John Toland
Age: 53
At Trades Hotel, Miller Street, 13 March 1941

12 CHERRY CRESCENT
Peter Graham
Age: 52
At Wardens' Post, Janetta Street, 13 March
1941

10 CHURCH STREET
Albert Bowman
Age: 18
At Royal Infirmary, Glasgow, 14 March 1941:
place of injury unknown. ARP warden

Archibald Bowman
Age: 16
At 10 Church Street, 13 March 1941

Hannah Bowman
Age: 19
At 10 Church Street, 13 March 1941

Lillian May Bowman
Age: 46
At 10 Church Street, 13 March 1941

78 CLARENCE STREET
Christina Wright
Age: 26
At 78 Clarence Street, 15 March 1941

Dougald Wright
Age: 53
At 78 Clarence Street, 15 March 1941

Maria Wright
Age: 55
At 78 Clarence Street, 15 March 1941

Martha Wright
Age: 31
At 78 Clarence Street, 15 March 1941

53 CLYDE STREET
Margaret Clarkson
Age: 32
At Benbow Hotel, Dalmuir, 13 March 1941

31 CORNOCK STREET
John MacDonald
Age: 65
At Janetta Street, 13 March 1941

1 THE CRESCENT
Elizabeth Hunter Millar
Age: 62
At 1 The Crescent, 14 March 1941

2A THE CRESCENT
Ian Prentice Dick
Age: 34
At 2A The Crescent, 14 March 1941. ARP
ambulance driver

William Dick
Age: 26
At 2A The Crescent, 14 March 1941

48 CROWN AVENUE
Robert White
Age: 18
At La Scala Picture House, 13 March 1941

55 CROWN AVENUE
Isabella Scotland Shaw
Age: 20
At Church Street, 13 March 1941

64 CROWN AVENUE
William White Duncan
Age: 37
At 64 Crown Avenue, 14 March 1941

Margaret MacKenzie
Age: 16
At 64 Crown Avenue, 21 March 1941

Annie Wilson Robertson
Age: 10
At 64 Crown Avenue, 14 March 1941

David Robertson
Age: 15
At 64 Crown Avenue, 14 March 1941

Margaret McCole Robertson
Age: 46
At 64 Crown Avenue, 14 March 1941

Mary McAllister Robertson
Age: 12
At 64 Crown Avenue, 14 March 1941

Elizabeth Skinner
Age: 9
At 64 Crown Avenue, 14 March 1941

Joan Skinner
Age: 43
At 64 Crown Avenue, 14 March 1941

Joan Roberta Skinner
Age: 4
At 64 Crown Avenue, 14 March 1941

Margaret Jane Skinner
Age: 12
At 64 Crown Avenue, 14 March 1941

Robert Skinner
Age: 40
At 64 Crown Avenue, 14 March 1941

Robert Skinner
Age: 2
At 64 Crown Avenue, 14 March 1941

66 CROWN AVENUE
Esther Anderson
Age: 13
At 66 Crown Avenue, 14 March 1941

Thomas Anderson
Age: 33
At 66 Crown Avenue, 14 March 1941

Mary Dolan
Age: 15.
At 66 Crown Avenue, 14 March 1941

Thomas Dolan
Age: 49
At 66 Crown Avenue, 14 March 1941

Thomas Paul Dolan
Age: Unknown [MacPhail – see Glasgow list]
At Royal Infirmary, Glasgow, 15 March 1941;
injured at 66 Crown Avenue, 14 March 1941

Elizabeth Heggie
Age: 35
At 66 Crown Avenue, 14 March 1941

Charlotte 'Lottie' Heggie
Age: 11
At 66 Crown Avenue, 14 March 1941

40 DRUMRY ROAD
Thomas Hamilton
Age:75
At Emergency Hospital, Lennox Castle, 14
March 1941; injured at Clydebank, locale
unknown

60 DUMBARTON ROAD
Patrick Duffy
Age: 42
At 60 Dumbarton Road, 14 March 1941

89 DUMBARTON ROAD
Alexander Howie
Age: 19
At The Crescent, 14 March 1941

Jane Gillian Howie
Age: 24
At The Crescent, 14 March 1941

131 DUMBARTON ROAD
Daniel Busby
Age: 48
At 131 Dumbarton Road, 14 March 1941

Andrew Dunn
Age: 62
At 131 Dumbarton Road, 14 March 1941

John Dunn
Age: 24
At 131 Dumbarton Road, 14 March 1941

Mary Martin Dunn
Age: 38
At 131 Dumbarton Road, 14 March 1941

433 DUMBARTON ROAD
James Boyd
Age: 41
At 433 Dumbarton Road, 14 March 1941

470 DUMBARTON ROAD
John Walker
Age: 71
At Western Infirmary, Glasgow, 15 March
1941; injured at 535 Dumbarton Road, 14
March 1941

543 DUMBARTON ROAD
Peter Crombie
Age: 73
At 9 Pattison Street, 13 March 1941

672 DUMBARTON ROAD
George Alexander Hislop
Age: 65
At 672 Dumbarton Road, 14 March 1941

Martha Maria Hislop
Age: 66
At 672 Dumbarton Road, 14 March 1941

745 DUMBARTON ROAD
Agnes Barbour Paterson Reid
Age: 41
At Dumbarton Road, 14 March 1941

752 DUMBARTON ROAD
Charles Campbell
Age: 38
Place of injury unknown; 14 March 1941.
Sergeant, Home Guard

775 DUMBARTON ROAD
Christina Fotheringham
Age: 72
At 775 Dumbarton Road, 14 March 1941

Annie Reid
Age: 46
At 775 Dumbarton Road, 14 March 1941

781 DUMBARTON ROAD
John Anthony McGeehan
Age: 13
At 781 Dumbarton Road, 14 March 1941

Elizabeth McIntosh Quigg
Age: 18
At 781 Dumbarton Road, 14 March 1941

Robert Wark
Age: 27
At 781 Dumbarton Road, 14 March 1941

79 DUNTOCHER ROAD
Isabella McLean Cooper
Age: 20
At 12 Beatty Street, 13 March 1941

8 EAST BARNS STREET
Margaret Teresa Donaghue Gallagher
Age: 30
At 2 Napier Street, 13 March 1941

1 ELM ROAD
William MacKechnie
Age: 39
At 425 Glasgow Road, 13 March 1941

45 ERSKINE VIEW
Mary Loughlin
Age: 19
At Jellicoe Street, 13 March 1941

3 FIRST STREET
Mary Adams
Age: 55
At 3 First Street, 14 March 1941

14 FIRST TERRACE
Hugh Wood
Age: 36
At Wardens' Post, Janetta Street, 13 March 1941

John Wood
Age: 15
At Wardens' Post, Janetta Street, 13 March 1941

Margaret Wood
Age: 5
At Wardens' Post, Janetta Street, 13 March 1941

21 GLASGOW ROAD
Trevor Parry Roberts
Age: 39
At 3 Brown's Buildings, 14 March 1941

398 GLASGOW ROAD
Duncan Gardner
Age: 33
At Emergency Hospital, Lennox Castle, 22 March 1941; injured at Masonic Hall, 13 March 1941

425 GLASGOW ROAD
Robert James Haggerty
Age: 7
At 425 Glasgow Road, 13 March 1941

Angus MacKenzie
Age: 32
At 425 Glasgow Road, 13 March 1941

Martha MacKenzie
Age: 36
At 425 Glasgow Road, 13 March 1941

Robert McEwan MacKenzie
Age: 4
At 425 Glasgow Road, 13 March 1941

John MacKinlay
Age: 30
At 425 Glasgow Road. ARP Warden

Marion McKain MacKinlay
Age: 27
At 425 Glasgow Road, 13 March 1941

William MacKinlay
Age: 6
At 425 Glasgow Road, 13 March 1941

431 GLASGOW ROAD
Mary Bicker
Age: 73
At 431 Glasgow Road, 13 March 1941. Listed as 'Maria' in Scottish National War Memorial

Isabella Black
Age: 63
At 431 Glasgow Road, 13 March 1941

James Black
Age: 71
At 431 Glasgow Road, 13 March 1941

Caroline Blyth
Age: 19
At 431 Glasgow Road, 13 March 1941

Robert Blyth
Age: 54
At 431 Glasgow Road, 13 March 1941

Sarah Blyth
Age: 54
At 431 Glasgow Road, 13 March 1941

Adam Divers
Age: 11
At 431 Glasgow Road, 13 March 1941

James Divers
Age: 54
At 431 Glasgow Road, 13 March 1941

James Divers
Age: 17
At 431 Glasgow Road, 13 March 1941

Margaret Anderson Divers
Age: 42
At 431 Glasgow Road, 13 March 1941

Joseph McBride
Age: 38
At 431 Glasgow Road, 13 March 1941

Marion McClelland
Age: 4
At 431 Glasgow Road, 13 March 1941. MacPhail gives Christian name as 'Marina'.

Marion McClelland
Age: 32
At 431 Glasgow Road, 13 March 1941

Agnes MacLean Graham MacIntyre
Age: 59
At 431 Glasgow Road, 13 March 1941

Grace Mulhern
Age: 59
At 431 Glasgow Road, 13 March 1941

Jessie Annie Williams
Age: 74
At 2 Napier Street, 13 March 1941

9 GOLFVIEW DRIVE
Peter Hunter Johnstone
Age: 44
At Royal Ordnance Factory, Dalmuir, 13 March 1941. Police Sergeant (War Department)

13 GORDON STREET
Alexander Lochhead
Age: 17
At 62 Radnor Street, 14 March 1941. Firewatcher

19 GORDON STREET
Helen Parke
Age: 1 year 7 months
At 19 Gordon Street, 13 March 1941

25 GRAHAM AVENUE
James Harvey
Age: 13
At 25 Graham Avenue, 13 March 1941

27 GRAHAM AVENUE
Thomas Duncan
Age: 90
At 27 Graham Avenue, 13 March 1941

Helen Morrison
Age: 38
At 27 Graham Avenue, 13 March 1941

Helen Morrison
Age: 10
At 27 Graham Avenue, 13 March 1941

Margaret Ruleu Morrison
Age: 1
At 27 Graham Avenue, 13 March 1941

William Kane Jeffreys Morrison
Age: 9
At 27 Graham Avenue, 13 March 1941

Christina Wilson Thomson
Age: 19
At 27 Graham Avenue, 13 March 1941

Margaret Thomson
Age: 42
At 27 Graham Avenue, 13 March 1941

Margaret Thomson
Age: 20
At 27 Graham Avenue, 13 March 1941

Williamina Thomson
Age: 24
At 27 Graham Avenue, 13 March 1941

31 GRAHAM AVENUE
Charles Finnen
Age: 1 year 4 months
At Second Avenue, 13 March 1941

35 GRAHAM AVENUE
Agnes MacKay
Age: 22
At 161 Second Avenue, 13 March 1941

39 GRAHAM AVENUE
Henry Robertson
Age: 49
At Diesel Works, Dalmuir, 13 March 1941

16 GRAHAM STREET
Neil Dougall
Age: 32
At Yarrow's Shipyard, 14 March 1941. ARP Warden

34 GRANVILLE STREET
Alexander Campbell
Age: 39
At 62 Radnor Street, 14 March 1941

James Leckie
Age: 73
At Granville Street, 14 March 1941

4 GREER QUADRANT
See Rosemary Thomas and Russell Thomas in NON-RESIDENTS section

14 GREER QUADRANT
Catherine MacLachlan Hughes
Age: 59
At 14 Greer Quadrant, 13 March 1941

6 HAWTHORN STREET
Alistair John MacKenzie Reid
Age: 3 months
At 6 Hawthorn Street, 14 March 1941

9 HILL STREET
Robert Melone Macfarlane
Age: 18
At Broom Drive, 13 March 1941. ARP
Messenger

5 HORNBEAM DRIVE
James Taylor
Age: 17
At 5 Hornbeam Drive, 13 March 1941

6 HORNBEAM DRIVE
George Mack
Age: 18
At 6 Hornbeam Drive, 14 March 1941

James Mack
Age: 35:
At 6 Hornbeam Drive, 14 March 1941

John Mack
Age: 64
At 6 Hornbeam Drive, 14 March 1941

24 JELLICOE STREET
Ellen Kennedy
Age: 20
At 9 Pattison Street, 13 March 1941

Hugh Alexander Kennedy
Age: 23
At 9 Pattison Street, 13 March 1941

54 JELLICOE STREET
James MacCormack
Age: 19
At Jellicoe Street, 13 March 1941

72 JELLICOE STREET
Malcolm George H. MacDougall
Age: 70
At 72 Jellicoe Street, 13 March 1941

78 JELLICOE STREET
Mary Boyle
Age: 84
At 78 Jellicoe Street, 13 March 1941

Margaret Cameron
Age: 16
At 78 Jellicoe Street, 13 March 1941

Jean Dennis
Age: 59
At 78 Jellicoe Street, 13 March 1941

Samuel Dennis
Age: 65
At 78 Jellicoe Street, 13 March 1941

Samuel Dennis
Age: 19
At 78 Jellicoe Street, 13 March 1941. Home
Guard

Annie Kernachan
Age: 8
At 78 Jellicoe Street, 13 March 1941

Janet Kernachan
Age: 41
At 78 Jellicoe Street, 13 March 1941

Richard Kernachan
Age: 45
At Castle Square, 14 March 1941

David McCourt MacLean
Age: 17
At 78 Jellicoe Street, 13 March 1941

Edith Mark MacLean
Age: 47
At 78 Jellicoe Street, 13 March 1941

James Given Spence MacLean
Age: 13
At 78 Jellicoe Street, 13 March 1941

John MacLean
Age: 56
At 78 Jellicoe Street, 13 March 1941

Ann Rocks
Age: 1
At 78 Jellicoe Street, 13 March 1941

Annie Rocks
Age: 54
At 78 Jellicoe Street, 13 March 1941

Elizabeth Rocks
Age: 28
At 78 Jellicoe Street, 13 March 1941

Francis Rocks
Age: 21
At 78 Jellicoe Street, 13 March 1941

James Rocks
Age: 4
At 78 Jellicoe Street, 13 March 1941

James Rocks
Age: 32
At 78 Jellicoe Street, 13 March 1941

John Rocks
Age: 19
At 78 Jellicoe Street, 13 March 1941

Joseph Rocks
Age: 17
At 78 Jellicoe Street, 13 March 1941

Margaret Rocks
Age: 2
At 78 Jellicoe Street, 13 March 1941

Patrick Rocks
Age: 6
At 78 Jellicoe Street, 13 March 1941

Patrick Rocks
Age: 28
At 78 Jellicoe Street, 13 March 1941. Honour –
Royal Humane Society for Lifesaving.

Theresa Rocks
Age: 25
At 78 Jellicoe Street, 13 March 1941

Thomas Rocks
Age: 13
At 78 Jellicoe Street, 13 March 1941

Thomas Rocks
Age: 5 months
At 78 Jellicoe Street, 13 March 1941

George Watson
Age: 72
At 78 Jellicoe Street, 13 March 1941

George Logan Watson
Age: 38
At 78 Jellicoe Street, 13 March 1941

Isabella Watson
Age: 66
At 78 Jellicoe Street, 13 March 1941

James Watson
Age: 36
At 78 Jellicoe Street, 13 March 1941

Lillian Watson
Age: 19
At 78 Jellicoe Street, 13 March 1941

39 JOHN KNOX STREET
John Gray
Age: 69
At 39 John Knox Street, 14 March 1941

74 JOHN KNOX STREET
Thomas Gallagher
Age: 12
At 2 Napier Street, 13 March 1941.

KENILWORTH ALBERT ROAD
William Somerville Hunter
Age: 49
At 76 Second Avenue, 13 March 1941

104 KILBOWIE ROAD
George Sutherland
Age: 59
At Yarrow's Shipyard, 14 March 1941

3 KITCHENER STREET
William MacKinlay
Age: 64
At 76 Second Avenue, 13 March 1941

14 KITCHENER STREET
Patrick Graham
Age: 31
At Killearn Hospital, 22 March 1941; injured
at Clydebank – date unknown, March 1941.
ARP Warden

11 LIMETREE DRIVE
Mary Bennett
Age: 52
At 18 Limetree Drive, 13 March 1941

15 LIVINGSTONE STREET
John McLafferty
Age: 47
At La Scala Picture House, 13 March 1941

28 LIVINGSTONE STREET
Adam Busby
Age: Unknown
At Blawarthill Hospital, 14 March 1941. Place
of injury unknown. ARP Warden – decoration,
BICMMS

30 LIVINGSTONE STREET
Charles Gilland
Age: 17
At Robroyston Hospital, 14 March 1941;
injured at Livingstone Street, 13 March 1941.
Home Guard

31 LIVINGSTONE STREET
George Coghill
Age: 65
At 31 Livingstone Street, 13 March 1941

Edward William Mowat Donaldson
Age: 47
At 31 Livingstone Street, 13 March 1941. ARP
Warden

32 LIVINGSTONE STREET
William Aird
Age: Unknown
At Blawarthill Hospital, 15 March 1941;
injured 13 March 1941, locale unknown

William McCrindle
Age: 25
At Blawarthill Hospital, 14 March 1941;
injured at Clydebank, locale unknown, 14
March 1941

69 LIVINGSTONE STREET
Jessie Haslie Borland
Age: 1 year, 9 months.
At 69 Livingstone Street, 13 March 1941

Thomas McLaughlin Hamilton
Age: 37
At 69 Livingstone Street, 13 March 1941

David Stewart
Age: 13
At Blawarthill Hospital, 15 March 1941;
injured on 13 March 1941, locale unknown, 69
Livingstone Street assumed

18 MILLER STREET
Patrick McGeady
Age: 65
At 11 Second Avenue, 13 March 1941.

NAPIER STREET – see also **George Anderson,
David Campbell** and **Jonina Commiskie** in
NON-RESIDENTS section

2 NAPIER STREET
Evelyn Doherty
Age: 6
At 2 Napier Street, 13 March 1941

Francis Joseph Doherty
Age: 43
At 2 Napier Street, 13 March 1941

Francis Doherty
Age: 15
At 2 Napier Street, 13 March 1941

John Anthony Doherty
Age: 13
At First Aid Post, Elgin Street School;
presumably injured at 2 Napier Street; 13
March 1941

Margaret Doherty
Age: 9

At 2 Napier Street, 13 March 1941. Listed as
'Rita' in Scottish National War Memorial

Mary Doherty
Age: 19
At 2 Napier Street, 13 March 1941

John Green Henderson
Age: 20
At Canniesburn Auxiliary Hospital, 15 March
1941; injured on 13 March 1941, locale
unknown

Mary Henderson
Age: 41
At 2 Napier Street, 13 March 1941

Michael Hughes
Age: 74
At 2 Napier Street, 13 March 1941

Sarah Jane Hughes
Age: 69
At 2 Napier Street, 13 March 1941

Hugh MacConnell
Age: 20
At 2 Napier Street, 13 March 1941

Mary Kate MacConnell
Age: 39
At 2 Napier Street, 13 March 1941

Mary Francis MacConnell
Age: 21
At 2 Napier Street, 13 March 1941

Margaret McFadden
Age: 31
At 2 Napier Street, 13 March 1941

Michael McFadden
Age: 50
At 2 Napier Street, 13 March 1941

Thomas John McFadden
Age: 52
At Robroyston Hospital, 15 March 1941; local
and date of injury uncertain, 2 Napier Street
assumed

Angelina Ventilla
Age: 48
At 4 Napier Street, 13 March 1941

4 NAPIER STREET
Mary Hope Cook
Age: 54
At Spencer Street, 13 March 1941

Rose Docherty
Age: 15
At 4 Napier Street, 13 March 1941

Kathleen McGuigan
Age: 15
At 4 Napier Street, 13 March 1941

Theresa McGuigan
Age: 44
At 4 Napier Street, 13 March 1941

Margaret McKendrick
Age: 6
At 4 Napier Street, 13 March 1941

Robert McKendrick
Age: 4
At 4 Napier Street, 13 March 1941

Thomas McKendrick
Age: 8
At 4 Napier Street, 13 March 1941

Louis Ventilla
Age: 5
At 4 Napier Street, 13 March 1941

Michael Ventilla
Age: 64
At 4 Napier Street, 13 March 1941

8 NAPIER STREET
Helen Ventilla
Age: 21
At 8 Napier Street, 13 March 1941

32 PARK ROAD
Alexander MacRae
Age: 83
At 32 Park Road, 14 March 1941. Listed as
'McRae' in Scottish National War Memorial

7 PATTISON STREET
Hugh Donnelly
Age: 11
At 7 Pattison Street, 13 March 1941

Margaret Donnelly
Age: 3
At 7 Pattison Street, 13 March 1941.

Mary Catherine Donnelly
Age: 42
At 7 Pattison Street, 13 March 1941

Maureen Donnelly
Age: 7
At 7 Pattison Street, 13 March 1941

Rosaline Donelly
Age: 13
At 7 Pattison Street, 13 March 1941. Listed as
'Roseleen' in Scottish National War Memorial

Theresa Donnelly
Age: 3
At 7 Pattison Street, 13 March 1941

Brenda MacDonald
Age: 5
At 7 Pattison Street, 13 March 1941

Christina MacDonald
Age: 36
At 7 Pattison Street, 13 March 1941

Donald MacDonald
Age: 10
At 7 Pattison Street, 13 March 1941

Jessie Gribbon MacDonald
Age: 16
At 7 Pattison Street, 13 March 1941

Violet MacKay
Age: 36
At Blawarthill Hospital, 14 March 1941;
injured at Dalmuir West Shelter, died same day

Edward MacMillan
Age: 15
At Pattison Street, 13 March 1941

8 PATTISON STREET
James Kelly
Age: 2
At 9 Pattison Street, 13 March 1941

Mary Kelly
Age: 31
At 9 Pattison Street, 13 March 1941

9 PATTISON STREET
James Simpson Brimer
Age: 72
At 9 Pattison Street, 13 March 1941

Jane Cryan
Age: 74
At 9 Pattison Street, 13 March 1941

Agnes Hunter MacGregor
Age: 55
At 9 Pattison Street, 14 March 1941; listed as
'MacGregor' in Scottish National War
Memorial

Norman MacLennan
Age: 7
At 9 Pattison Street, 13 March 1941

Archibald James Miller
Age: 61
At 9 Pattison Street, 13 March 1941

Eileen Theresa Miller
Age: 7
At 9 Pattison Street, 13 March 1941

Mary Miller
Age: 53
At 9 Pattison Street, 13 March 1941

Sheila Miller
Age: 10
At 9 Pattison Street, 13 March 1941

Elizabeth Scott
Age: 43
At 9 Pattison Street, 13 March 1941

Morag Scott
Age: 12
At 9 Pattison Street, 13 March 1941

Nathaniel Scott see NON-RESIDENTS

Walter Scott
Age: 7
At 9 Pattison Street, 13 March 1941

Elizabeth Stewart
Age: 10
At 9 Pattison Street, 13 March 1941

Jane Strachan
Age: 73
At 9 Pattison Street, 13 March 1941

Margaret Thom – see NON-RESIDENTS

10 PATTISON STREET
Archibald Smith Canning
Age: 3
At 9 Pattison Street, 13 March 1941

Daniel Canning
Age: 2 months
At 9 Pattison Street, 13 March 1941

Delia Gallagher
Age: 15
At 10 Pattison Street, 13 March 1941

12 PATTISON STREET
Isabella Gillespie Boyle
Age: 10
At 12 Pattison Street, 13 March 1941

Margaret Gow Boyle
Age: 36
At 12 Pattison Street, 13 March 1941

William Boyle
Age: 40
At 12 Pattison Street, 13 March 1941

Ralph Andrew Drummond
Age: 40
At 12 Pattison Street, 13 March 1941

Gladys Drummond
Age: 38
At 12 Pattison Street, 13 March 1941

James Carrigan Drummond
Age: 7
At 12 Pattison Street, 13 March 1941

Ralph Andrew Drummond
Age: 10
At 12 Pattison Street, 13 March 1941

Margaret Fraser
Age: 42

At 12 Pattison Street, 13 March 1941

Agnes MacKechnie
Age: 34
At 12 Pattison Street, 13 March 1941

Emma Sheila MacKechnie
Age: 9
At 12 Pattison Street, 13 March 1941

Michael John Sidney MacKechnie
Age: 34
At 12 Pattison Street, 13 March 1941

Patrick McMorrow
Age: 65
At 12 Pattison Street, 13 March 1941

Sarah McMorrow
Age: 56
At 12 Pattison Street, 13 March 1941

George Porter
Age: 56
At 12 Pattison Street, 13 March 1941

Samuel Porter
Age: 63
At 12 Pattison Street, 13 March 1941

23 PLANETREE ROAD
Isobel Aird
Age: 18
At 10 Church Street, 13 March 1941

Marion Aird
Age: 44
At 10 Church Street, 13 March 1941

Tomina Aird
Age: 15
At 10 Church Street, 13 March 1941

44 RADNOR STREET
Mary Ann Murphy
Age: 67
At Blawarthill Hospital, 15 March 1941;
injured at 44 Radnor Street, 14 March 1941

57 RADNOR STREET
Hugh Hart
Age: 60
At 60 Radnor Street, 14 March 1941

60 RADNOR STREET
Thomas Dean
Age: 29
Unknown; 60 Radnor Street assumed, 14
March 1941; Chief Engine Room Artificer –
service no. D/MX 49919

Euphemia Dempster
Age: 54
At 60 Radnor Street, 14 March 1941

Gilbert Dempster
Age: 54
At 60 Radnor Street, 14 March 1941

Mary Best Bradley Dempster
Age: 57
At 60 Radnor Street, 14 March 1941

Mary Dempster
Age: 29
At 60 Radnor Street, 14 March 1941

Doris Kelly
Age: 16
At 60 Radnor Street, 14 March 1941

Hugh Kelly
Age: 49
At 60 Radnor Street, 14 March 1941

Sarah Kelly
Age: 47
At 60 Radnor Street, 14 March 1941

Elizabeth Lockwood
Age: 14
At 60 Radnor Street, 14 March 1941; listed
as 'Lockhead' in Scottish National War
Memorial

Frederick Lockwood
Age: 10
At 60 Radnor Street, 14 March 1941; listed
as 'Lockhead' in Scottish National War
Memorial

Margaret Sanders Lockwood
Age: 38
At 60 Radnor Street, 14 March 1941

Margaret Lockwood
Age: 5
At 60 Radnor Street, 14 March 1941; listed as
'Lockhead' in Scottish National War Memorial

Joseph Martin
Age: 40
Locale unknown, 60 Radnor Street probable.
Service No. D/K 60165; home address is listed
as Dumfries, but Radnor Street resident in
March 1941

Catherine Richmond
Age: 43
At 60 Radnor Street, 14 March 1941

Catherine Richmond
Age: 5
At 60 Radnor Street, 14 March 1941

Christina Richmond
Age: 17
At 60 Radnor Street, 14 March 1941

Douglas Richmond
Age: 10
At 60 Radnor Street, 14 March 1941

Elizabeth Richmond
Age: 7
At 60 Radnor Street, 14 March 1941

Janet Richmond
Age: 3
At 60 Radnor Street, 14 March 1941

John Richmond
Age: 41
At 60 Radnor Street, 14 March 1941

John Richmond
Age: 15
At 60 Radnor Street, 14 March 1941

Margaret Richmond
Age: 13
At 60 Radnor Street, 14 March 1941

Peter Russell – see NON-RESIDENTS

Archibald Wilson – see NON-RESIDENTS

26 ROBERTSON STREET
John Moore
Age: 66
At Yarrow's Shipyard, 14 March 1941

4 ROSEBERY PLACE
Archibald Adamson
Age: 19
At Church Street shelter, 13 March 1941.
Home Guard

Andrew Graham
Age: 67
At Glasgow Road, 13 March 1941

8 ROWAN DRIVE
George Henderson
Age: 48
At 8 Rowan Drive, 13 March 1941

ROYAL ORDNANCE FACTORY,
DALMUIR
For details of **William Lyons**, **Thomas Marlin**
or **Martin**, and **Murdoch MacKenzie** see NON-
RESIDENTS

SECOND AVENUE
Annie Beaton
Age: 10
At Second Avenue shelter, 13 March 1941

6 SECOND AVENUE
Madge Guiney
Age: 16
At 78 Clarence Street, 15 March 1941

Sarah Guiney
Age: 45
At 78 Clarence Street, 15 March 1941

Mary Stevenson
Age: 66
At 78 Clarence Street, 15 March 1941

48 SECOND AVENUE
Janet Sharp Findlay Slater
Age: 16
At Spencer Street, 13 March 1941

72 SECOND AVENUE
Anna Cahill
Age: 11
At 72 Second Avenue, 13 March 1941

Elizabeth Cahill
Age: 10
At 72 Second Avenue, 13 March 1941

Wilhelmina Cahill
Age: 47
At 72 Second Avenue, 13 March 1941

Wilhelmina Cahill
Age: 4
At 72 Second Avenue, 13 March 1941

Grace Dunn
Age: 43
At 59 Whitecrook Street, 13 March 1941

Grace Dunn
Age: 20
At 74 Second Avenue, 13 March 1941

Mary Dunn
Age: 42
At 74 Second Avenue, 13 March 1941

Samuel Harris
Age: 69
At 72 Second Avenue, 13 March 1941

Rebecca Mullinger
Age: 50
At 72 Second Avenue, 13 March 1941

William Mullinger
Age: 17
At 72 Second Avenue, 13 March 1941

74 SECOND AVENUE
Nora Cullen
Age: 32
At 74 Second Avenue, 13 March 1941

Patrick Cullen
Age: 27
At 74 Second Avenue, 13 March 1941

Charles Doran
Age: 62
At 74 Second Avenue, 13 March 1941

Isabella Doran
Age: 25
At 74 Second Avenue, 13 March 1941

Mary Doran
Age: 65
At 74 Second Avenue, 13 March 1941

Elizabeth Jane Duffy
Age: 64
At 74 Second Avenue, 13 March 1941

Daniel Jobling
Age: 9
At 74 Second Avenue, 13 March 1941

James Jobling
Age: 11
At 74 Second Avenue, 13 March 1941

John Jobling
Age: 16
At 74 Second Avenue, 13 March 1941

Mary Jobling
Age: 39
At 74 Second Avenue, 13 March 1941

William Jobling
Age: 17
At 74 Second Avenue, 13 March 1941

John Lindsay
Age: 10
At 74 Second Avenue, 13 March 1941

Margaret Lindsay
Age: 7
At 74 Second Avenue, 13 March 1941

Violet Lindsay
Age: 40
At 74 Second Avenue, 13 March 1941

James Stevens
Age: 77
At 74 Second Avenue, 13 March 1941

Annie Williamson
Age: 5
At 74 Second Avenue, 13 March 1941

Catherine Williamson
Age: 37
At 74 Second Avenue, 13 March 1941

James Williamson
Age: 7
At 74 Second Avenue, 13 March 1941

Janette Williamson
Age: 6
At 74 Second Avenue, 13 March 1941

76 SECOND AVENUE
James Coutts – see NON-RESIDENTS

Edward Diver
Age: 76
At 76 Second Avenue, 13 March 1941

Edward Diver (son)
Age: 50
At 76 Second Avenue, 13 March 1941

Edward Diver (grandson)
Age: 8
At 76 Second Avenue, 13 March 1941

Edward Diver (grandson)
Age: 13
At 76 Second Avenue, 13 March 1941

Hugh Diver
Age: 81
At 76 Second Avenue, 13 March 1941

John Francis Diver
Age: 44
At 76 Second Avenue, 13 March 1941

Margaret Diver
Age: 11
At 76 Second Avenue, 13 March 1941

Mary Diver
Age: 76
At 76 Second Avenue, 13 March 1941

Mary McDermott Diver
Age: 44
At 76 Second Avenue, 13 March 1941

Annie Gillies
Age: 62
At 76 Second Avenue, 13 March 1941

Margaret McLaren Gillies
Age: 23
At 76 Second Avenue, 13 March 1941

John McGill
Age: 10
At 76 Second Avenue, 13 March 1941

Mary McGill
Age: 47
At 76 Second Avenue, 13 March 1941

John MacKenzie
Age: 56
At 76 Second Avenue, 13 March 1941

Mary MacKenzie
Age: 59
At 76 Second Avenue, 13 March 1941

James Peoples
Age: 37
At 76 Second Avenue, 13 March 1941

James Peoples
Age: 1
At 76 Second Avenue, 13 March 1941

Janet Turpie Gardiner Peoples
Age: 28
At 76 Second Avenue, 13 March 1941

78 SECOND AVENUE
Alexander MacKenzie
Age: 70
At 78 Second Avenue, 13 March 1941

Margaret Boomer Rankin
Age: 6
At 78 Second Avenue, 13 March 1941

80 SECOND AVENUE
Rachel Reid
Age: 70
At 80 Second Avenue, 13 March 1941

128 SECOND AVENUE
Emma Scrimshire
Age: 16
At Spencer Street, 13 March 1941

158A SECOND AVENUE
John Chisholm Anderson
Age: 69
At 158 Second Avenue, 14 March 1941

159 SECOND AVENUE
James Summers Findlay
Age: 1
At Second Avenue, 13 March 1941

John Duthie Findlay
Age: 26
At Second Avenue, 13 March 1941

Andrew Patterson
Age: 58
At 159 Second Avenue, 13 March 1941

Cecil Stevens
Age: 41
At 159 Second Avenue, 13 March 1941

James Woods
Age: 10
At Second Avenue, 13 March 1941

161 SECOND AVENUE
Archibald Graham
Age: 41
At 161 Second Avenue, 13 March 1941. ARP
Rescue Service

William Malcolm
Age: 6
At 161 Second Avenue, 13 March 1941

Edward McSherry
Age: 12
At 161 Second Avenue, 13 March 1941

James McAndrew McSherry
Age: 10 months
At 161 Second Avenue, 13 March 1941

Lucy McSherry
Age: 2
At 161 Second Avenue, 13 March 1941

Margaret McSherry
Age: 3
At 161 Second Avenue, 13 March 1941

Mary Jane McSherry
Age: 40
At 161 Second Avenue, 13 March 1941

Mary McSherry
Age: 14
At 161 Second Avenue, 13 March 1941

Matthew McSherry
Age: 16
At 161 Second Avenue, 13 March 1941

Sheila McSherry
Age: 5
At 161 Second Avenue, 13 March 1941

Annie Nisbet
Age: 45
At 161 Second Avenue, 13 March 1941

James Nisbet
Age: 50
At 161 Second Avenue, 13 March 1941

James Nisbet
Age: 16
At 161 Second Avenue, 13 March 1941

John Nisbet
Age: 13
At 161 Second Avenue, 13 March 1941

163 SECOND AVENUE
Hannah Ahern
Age: 80
At Killearn Hospital, 31 March 1941; injured
on 13 March at 150 Second Avenue

Charles Henry
Age: 74
At 163 Second Avenue, 13 March 1941

Elizabeth Henry
Age: 65
At 163 Second Avenue, 13 March 1941

Evelyn Lee
Age: 7
At Wardens' Post, Janetta Street, 13 March
1941

James Lee
Age: 5
At Wardens' Post, Janetta Street, 13 March
1941

Kathleen Lee
Age: 9
At Wardens' Post, Janetta Street, 13 March
1941

Margaret Mary Lee
Age: 32
At Wardens' Post, Janetta Street, 13 March
1941

Margaret Lee
Age: 11
At Wardens' Post, Janetta Street, 13 March
1941

SECOND TERRACE
For details of **Martin Brown** and **William
Shuter**, see NON-RESIDENTS.

1 SECOND TERRACE
Catherine Walsh
Age: 5 weeks
At Janetta Street, 13 March 1941

Mary Wood
Age: 63
At Royal Infirmary, Glasgow, 14 March 1941;
date and Clydebank locale of injury unknown

2 SECOND TERRACE
Ethel Gillespie
Age: 25
At 2 Forrest Street, Blantyre, 16 March 1941;
injured on 14 March 1941

3 SECOND TERRACE
Mary Cairns
Age: 50
At 3 Second Terrace, 13 March 1941

4 SECOND TERRACE
Rosetta Bell
Age: 31
At 4 Second Terrace, 13 March 1941

13 SECOND TERRACE
Eric Betty
Age: 16
At Clydebank, 15 March 1941. Formerly
Middlemiss

2 SINGER STREET
Bridget Boyle
Age: 36
At 74 Second Avenue, 13 March 1941

Elizabeth Ann Boyle
Age: 5
At 74 Second Avenue, 13 March 1941

William Boyle
Age: 38
At 74 Second Avenue, 13 March 1941

William Boyle
Age: 3
At 74 Second Avenue, 13 March 1941

2 SOMERVILLE STREET
Rose Anne Campbell
Age: Unknown.
At Blawarthill Hospital, 15 March 1941;
injured 13 March

1 SPENCER STREET
John Forrester
Age: 57
At 1 Spencer Street, 13 March 1941

Margaret Forrester
Age: 48
At 1 Spencer Street, 13 March 1941

Marie Young
Age: 6
At 1 Spencer Street, 13 March 1941

7 SPENCER STREET
Agnes Clason
Age: 5
At 7 Spencer Street, 13 March 1941

Elizabeth Clason
Age: 8
At 7 Spencer Street, 13 March 1941

Nellie Clason
Age: 31
At 7 Spencer Street, 13 March 1941

9 SPENCER STREET
John Morgan
Age: 62
At Robroyston Hospital, 17 March 1941;
injured at 9 Spencer Street, 13 March 1941

10 SPENCER STREET
Patrick Curran
Age: 77
At 10 Spencer Street, 13 March 1941. Also
listed as 'Peter' in Scottish National War
Memorial

4 THIRN AVENUE
John Jolly
Age: 67
At Royal Infirmary, Glasgow, 14 March 1941;
injured at Clydebank. Formerly known as
'Jollie'

8 WALLACE STREET
Joseph Logan
Age: 24
At 76B Second Avenue, 13 March 1941

4 WHIN STREET
John Colquhoun Spence
Age: 58
At 4 Whin Street, 13 March 1941

6 WHIN STREET
John Young Gibson
Age: 54
At Whin Street, 13 March 1941

41 WHIN STREET
John Fleming
Age: 24
At 41 Whin Street, 13 March 1941. MacPhail
spells surname as 'Flemming'.

43 WHIN STREET
William Daniels
Age: 44
At 43 Whin Street, 13 March 1941

51 WHITECROOK STREET
Jessie Chalmers Wade
Age: 13
At 57 Whitecrook Street, 14 March 1941

57 WHITECROOK STREET
Georgina Borland
Age: 43
At 57 Whitecrook Street, 14 March 1941

John Peebles Borland
Age: 44
At 57 Whitecrook Street, 14 March 1941

Catherine Haggert Bradley
Age: 24
At 57 Whitecrook Street, 14 March 1941

Janet France
Age: 54
At 57 Whitecrook Street, 14 March 1941

John Frumage – see NON-RESIDENTS

Martha Thomson Galloway
Age: 55
At Blawarthill Hospital, 15 March 1941;
injured at 57 Whitecrook Street, 14 March
1941

Thomas Thomson Galloway
Age: 22
At 57 Whitecrook Street, 14 March 1941

William Geddes
Age: 15
At 57 Whitecrook Street, 14 March 1941. Also
known as William Thomson. Brother of Jessie
Chalmers Wade, killed in the same incident.

Elizabeth Given
Age: 30
At 57 Whitecrook Street, 14 March 1941

James Lawrie
Age: 26
At 57 Whitecrook Street, 14 March 1941

Susanna Peddie
Age: 74
At 57 Whitecrook Street, 14 March 1941

Charles Edward Waite
Age: 34
At 57 Whitecrook Street, 14 March 1941

59 WHITECROOK STREET
Charlotte Reavey
Age: 46
At 59 Whitecrook Street, 14 March 1941

Jeanie Munro Sharp
Age: 48
At 59 Whitecrook Street, 14 March 1941

61 WHITECROOK STREET
Peter Marks
Age: 61
At 61 Whitecrook Street, 14 March 1941

DUNTOCHER

13 CARLEITH TERRACE
Joseph Allan
Age: 10
At 13 Carleith Terrace, 14 March 1941

WAULKMILL
Elizabeth Manuel
Age: 90
At Killearn Hospital, 18 March 1941; injured
on 14 March 1941 at Waulkmill, Duntocher

HARDGATE

BLACK'S LAND
John Morton
Age: 76
At Clyde Hosiery Mill, Hardgate, 14 March
1941

29 COLBREGGAN GARDENS
Elizabeth Deans
Age: 28
At 46 Colbreggan Gardens, Hardgate, 13
March 1941

Thomas Deans
Age: 37
At 46 Colbreggan Gardens, Hardgate, 13
March 1941; ARP Warden – decoration
AMINA

Thomas Deans junior
Age: 2
At 46 Colbreggan Gardens, Hardgate, 13
March 1941

45 COLBREGGAN GARDENS
Elizabeth Lyons
Age: 67
At 45 Colbreggan Gardens, Hardgate, 13
March 1941

46 COLBREGGAN GARDENS
James Hunter
Age: 55
At 46 Colbreggan Gardens, Hardgate, 13
March 1941

Margaret Hunter
Age: 55
At 46 Colbreggan Gardens, Hardgate, 13
March 1941

OLD KILPATRICK

196 DUMBARTON ROAD

Isabella Colquhoun
Age: 59
At 196 Dumbarton Road, 14 March 1941

56 DUMBARTON ROAD
John Barclay
Age: 60
At Old Kilpatrick, 14 March 1941. ARP
warden

See also **Walter Bilsland**, **William MacGregor**
and **George McLaren** under NON-
RESIDENTS

NON-RESIDENT BUT KILLED OR
FATALLY INJURED AT CLYDEBANK

George Anderson
Age: 50
At Napier Street, 13 March 1941; firewatcher
of 20 Kelvingrove Street, Glasgow

Walter Bilsland
Age: 31
At Old Kilpatrick, 14 March 1941; AFS
fireman of 12 Park Crescent, Dumbarton

James Bowles
Age: 41
At Emergency Hospital, Lennox Castle, 17
March 1941 – injured at Beardmore's Works,
Dalmuir; of 34 Woddrop Street, Dalmarnock,
Glasgow

Martin Brown
Age: 46
At Cottage Hospital, 14 March 1941; injured
at Second Terrace, 13 March 1941; address not
known

David Campbell
Age: 31
At Galbraith's store, Napier Street, 13 March
1941; of 9 Richard Street, Anderston

Jonina Commiskie
Age: 62
At 4 Napier Street, 13 March 1941; of
Ardmore House, Cardross

Minnie Cooper
Age: 65
At Beardmore's Works, Dalmuir, 13 March
1941; of 8 Burn Terrace, Cambuslang

James Smith Coutts
Age: 37
At 76 Second Avenue, 13 March 1941; of 256
Rigby Street, Glasgow

Michael Crerand
Age: 39
At Killearn Hospital, 14 March 1941; injured
at Dalmuir West, 13 March 1941; of 129
Thistle Street, Glasgow

John Furmage
Age: 33
At 57 Whitecrook Street, 14 March 1941; of
16A Bute Street, Falkirk.

Matthew Girvan
Age: 36
At Canniesburn Auxiliary Hospital, 14 March
1941; injured at Clydebank, locale unknown,
14 March 1941; of 29 Salamanca Street,
Parkhead

William Robert Lyons
Age: 50
At Royal Ordnance Factory, Dalmuir; of 33
Belltrees Crescent, Paisley. Sergeant, Police
War Reserve. MacPhail gives his Paisley
address as 17 Blythswood Drive.

Thomas Marlin
Age: 37
At Royal Ordnance Factory, Dalmuir, 13
March 1941; of 176 Edgefauld Road,
Glasgow; also listed as 'Martin' in Scottish
National War Memorial. Constable, War
Department

Murdoch MacKenzie
Age: 56
At Royal Ordnance Factory, Dalmuir, 13
March 1941; of 39 Old Dumbarton Road,
Glasgow

William McGregor
Age: 34
At Electric Lamp Factory, Old Kilpatrick; 13
March 1941; of 28 Wilson Street, Alexandria;
Patrol Officer (Auxiliary Fire Service)

George McLaren
Age: 28
At Old Kilpatrick, 14 March 1941; of 88
Dumbuck Road, Dumbarton; Leading Fireman
(Auxiliary Fire Service)

Peter Russell
Age: 38
At 60 Radnor Street, 14 March 1941; of 6
Stewart Place, Catrine, Mauchline, Ayrshire

Nathaniel Scott
Age: 29
At 2 Castle Street, 14 March 1941; 43
Stevenston Street, Glasgow. Home Guard
MacPhail gives his Clydebank address as 9
Pattison Street, Dalmuir.

Andrew Shaw
Age: 29
At Beardmore's Works, Dalmuir, 13 March
1941; of 10 Elvan Street, Glasgow

William Shuter
Age: 31
At Second Terrace, 13 March 1941; of 196
High Street, Dumbarton

Margaret Thom
Age: 71
At 9 Pattison Street, 13 March 1941; of 154
Glenburn, Prestwick, Ayrshire

Rosemary Russell Thomas
Age: 9
At 4 Greer Quadrant, 13 March 1941; of 170
Hope Street, Glasgow

Russell Llewellyn Thomas
Age: 37
At 4 Greer Quadrant, 13 March 1941; of 170
Hope Street, Glasgow. ARP Warden

Thomas West
Age: Unknown
At Robroyston Hospital, 17 March 1941;
injured on 13 March 1941 at West Thomson
Street; of 26 Sinclair Street, Milngavie

Archibald Wilson
Age: 31
At 60 Radnor Street, 14 March 1941; of 42
Millbrix Avenue, Glasgow

David Wilson
Age: 29
At 76 Second Avenue, 13 March 1941; of 342
Nuneaton Street, Glasgow

THE *ATLANTIC COCK* EXPLOSION, CLYDEBANK
15 September 1941

Nine men, including the skipper of the tug,
were killed by the detonation, underwater, of
an unexploded parachute mine at Dalmuir six
months after the Clydebank Blitz, of whom Iain
MacPhail identified three and I, to date, a
fourth. The others appear to have been
members of HM Forces; in such instances, in
times of war, details of registry of death are
closed to the general public. These are the last
deaths, by direct if delayed enemy action, from
the Clydebank Blitz of 13–15 March 1941.

Andrew Lawson Anderson
Age: 53
6 Stanley Street
15 September 1941, at Beardmore's Basin,
Dalmuir

Archibald Brownlie Marshall
Age: 43
57 Moodiesburn Street, Glasgow
15 September 1941, at Beardmore's Basin,
Dalmuir

John Morrison
Age; 39
3 Inchlea Street, Glasgow; of 30 Lionel, Port of
Ness, Isle of Lewis
15 September 1941, at Beardmore's Basin,
Dalmuir

Alexander Stewart
Age: 57
Greenock: address unknown; master of the
Atlantic Cock

TWO POEMS FOR JIM MACKINVEN

You came on summer evenings
with your head in a cloud,
your eyes mazy with staring
at sheep or tree or mountain:
that was the way you'd be caring
for what lies behind the look,
not to be said aloud,
nor fully brought to words,
with your blue exercise book
and filled pages of writing
in a boy's pencilled hand.
You would be looking to me
to read and understand,
catching the thing below it,
the thought you had almost said.
I told you to write as you could,
with the Scots words in your head,
and you would grow to a poet.
Still those calm evenings remain,
forever untouched by pain.
Nothing can kill the past:
what was, is still good.

There have been boys like you,
brave and handsome and gay,
or sad with the old sadness
of high hills at break of day
when the heather is drenched with dew
and the birds scarcely wakened:
sadness that is sweet too,
that lies in the wild mouth of singing,
that is part of being a Scot.
These boys have died or been killed

by the English, by poverty, by drowning at sea,
and some were good and some not,
but all had lain on a mother's knee
and for all a mother's long mourning
and a place not to be filled,
and a sore pain to the last.
Yet they had lived and been happy,
they had become part of the river
of folks' lives which is Scotland.
Nothing could change the past.

So for you, part of that river,
ah, part of Scotland forever,
for you too, no forgetting,
but remembering, rather with joy,
with no resenting or regretting,
the careless grace of a boy
with his young eyes fixed far,
beyond parents, beyond friends,
to the moon glens where dreams are
and the known world ends.
And remembrance with delight,
that will some day not be pain,
of the child's body stretched gently at night,
under the father's roof and the fierce rain,
when the storm went where it would;
and the child's smile at the hearth-side.
What was, is still good.
And remembrance, with right pride,
of growth and strength and the mind forming
and shapes beginning to show
as the words drifted past
through the head of the young poet.
Ah good and sure to know,
however cruel the present,
nothing can hurt the past.

                                    Naomi Mitchison (1897–1999)

I saw him once,
a look of learning on his face,
clear, respectful eyes
bright with reading and listening,
dazzled with songs in the air
and beauty beside him.
a boy sickening

for writing books and for love,
his hands asleep on the kilt
bright and shadowy as his young cheek.

I saw him twice,
this time behind a piano
giving the dancers music to dance to.

I saw a poem of his,
a cup of clear water
placed in the tomb for the dead to drink.
And a bride perfectly chosen.

I heard of him later,
killed on Clydebank,
he has a poem
he could not write.
Before he had loved
he died for man's hate.

Joan Adeney Easdale (1913–1998)

Naomi Mitchison – radical, practical, a little fierce – scarcely needs introduction; she is one of the great Scotswomen of twentieth century literature, with whom only such as Muriel Spark could be equated. Mitchison spent most of her very long life in Carradale, raising a brood of lively children and hosting, over many years, memorable house-parties in that lively and at times chaotic home.

A frequent visitor in the late 1930s was Joan Adeney Easdale, a talented young poet 'discovered' by Virginia Woolf and whose first collection was published when she was only seventeen. Adeney's abilities are undoubted but her life was comprehensively derailed by the Second World War, an unhappy marriage, some singularly incompetent doctors and wretched, irreversible descent into psychotic illness. Under stern medical advice to wilt into the role of a good wife and mother, Mrs Joan Rendell gave up writing entirely and destroyed every scrap of her work – and grew ever more miserable and crazy. She spent her final decades as little more than a derelict in Nottingham, calling herself 'Sophie Curly', well known to the local police, shunned by her terrified family and frequently attacked and raped. Her life in 2008 was the subject of a moving book, *Who Was Sophie?*, by her granddaughter, the actress Celia Robertson.

These poems have not before been published and, but for transcription by Ellen MacKinven and, later, their careful preservation by Jim's cousin, Mrs April Simpson, they would not have survived.

SOURCES

BOOKS ABOUT THE CLYDEBANK BLITZ

Untold Stories: Remembering Clydebank in War Time, Clydebank Life Story Group, Clydebank College, Clydebank, 1999 (three printings), 2003. This rich paperback collection of memoirs and reflections on March 1941 began as a project for a Clydebank College writing class, and is a powerful anthology of accounts let down only by its awful 'perfect' binding: my copy fell apart in a few days.

This Time of Crisis – Glasgow, the West of Scotland and the North Western Approaches in the Second World War, Andrew Jeffrey, Mainstream Publishing, Edinburgh and London, 1993. This fluent and generously-illustrated book details all the impact of the conflict on the west of Scotland and makes the important point that, in so maritime a nation, talk of the 'Phoney War' is absurd – the Battle of the Atlantic and some minor aerial assault had immediate impact. The Clydebank material in Jeffrey's chapter on Scottish experience of the Blitz, 'With the Greatest Fortitude', is almost all lifted (with acknowledgement) from MacPhail, but Andrew Jeffrey's highly detailed description of the various bombings of Glasgow and elsewhere is authoritative.

Clydebank Blitz, Tom McKendrick, no publisher, Clydebank 1986. A copy of this booklet has quite eluded my determined search, but most of the material can cautiously be assumed now to be on the artist's website.

The Clydebank Blitz, I.M.M. MacPhail, Clydebank Town Council, Clydebank, 1974; reprinted 1991, 1995 (Clydebank District Council); 2000 (West Dunbartonshire Libraries and Museums). A study of remarkable detail, authority and concision – the book, with a number of appendices, is only 105 pages long – by a distinguished Dunbartonshire school teacher and scholar.

Luftwaffe Over Scotland, Les Taylor, Whittles Publishing, Dunbeath, 2010. Describing itself as 'the first complete history of the dramatic and often brutal air attacks that took place in almost every village, town and city in Scotland during The Second World War', Taylor's generously-illustrated volume has a discipline and credibility rare in this genre of upstairs-bedroom private studies of the Second World War. His focus is very much on the tactical and strategic aspects of the air campaign and the technology of the day.

'The Clydebank Blitz', Billy Kay, *Odyssey: Voices from Scotland's Recent Past – The Second Collection*, ed. Billy Kay, Polygon Books, Edinburgh University Student Publications Board, Edinburgh, 1982. The but lightly edited transcript of a superb Radio Scotland documentary broadcast in February 1981, a virtual tone-poem of Clydebank voices free of any intrusive narration and which did much to revive wider awareness of the German assault on Clydebank. Almost 30 years on, the recording has not lost its power to move and no better programme on the Clydebank Blitz will ever be aired. One or two survivors asked for the cover of pseudonym when this book was published: Kathleen McConnell, for instance, is described as 'Miss Docherty'.

BOOKS ABOUT CLYDEBANK

Changing Identities – Ancient Roots: The history of West Dunbartonshire from earliest times, ed. Ian Brown, Edinburgh University Press, 2006. Commissioned by the Cultural Services arm of West Dunbartonshire Council, this anthology of essays covers a variety of themes. The paper 'Enlightenment, Arts and Literature in West Dunbartonshire', by Alan Riach, has some interesting reflections on the Clydebank Blitz in modern Scottish fiction.

Rent Strike! – The Clydebank Rent Struggles of the 1920s, Sean Damer, Clydebank, 1982. A 'Clydebank People's History Pamphlet', of relentlessly Marxist analysis and vocabulary. A more sober account, 'The Clydebank Rent Strike', by Iain Russell, can be found in

The History of Clydebank, John Hood, Clydebank District Council/Parthenon Publishing, Carnforth, 1988. A lavishly-illustrated and substantial coffee-table book, with many worthwhile if very earnest essays by a range of academics and commentators, inevitably constrained by its municipal-socialist sponsorship and with unduly rosy accounts of post-war development. The chapter on the Blitz, by John Hood himself, is oddly perfunctory.

Clydebank in Old Picture Postcards, John Hood, Zaltbommel, European Library, 1985. A collection, self-evidently, of old postcards.

Bygone Clydebank, John Hood, Stenlake Publishing Ltd, Ayrshire, 2005. A 50-page booklet of old photographs of the town, its infrastructure, shops and commerce.

Old Clydebank, Sheila Struthers, Stenlake Publishing, Ayrshire, 1984. A 58-page booklet of old photographs in identical format to the Hood volume a year later, but with more emphasis on Clydebank people and their social and leisure activities.

CLYDEBANK IN FICTION

The River Flows On, Maggie Craig, Hodder Headline Book Publishing, London, 1998. A romantic novel set in Clydebank and in the Catherine Cookson genre, though Craig's story of Kate Cameron and her much-twanged heartstrings is not nearly as sharp or well executed and the punches in the book's closing pages are soon seen coming. It has since slid from obscurity into oblivion.

The Holy City, Meg Henderson, Flamingo Press, London, 1996. A hugely ambitious book attempting to combine biting social history with the life and trials of a young Clydebank woman, Marion MacLeod. Henderson has to negotiate a variety of rapids and self-made obstacles, from the combination of fiction and agitprop through the unfortunate choice to use regional dialect to her occasionally paranoid politics, a hatred for Christianity and churchmen that is unfaltering and at times intrusive, and the odd inaccuracy or anachronism. She nevertheless pulls it off in a story whose pace and passion make *The Holy City* at once angry and unputdownable.

Fergus Lamont, Robin Jenkins, Canongate Ltd, Edinburgh, 1979; paperback editions 1990, 2001. Even before the bombs start falling, the parallels between the anti-hero's hometown of 'Gantock' and Clydebank are evident; even in what has become a crowded genre – dark examination of the Scottish male psyche and the Scottish human condition – the book is a universally acknowledged classic.

BOOKS ABOUT THE BLITZ AND THE BRITISH HOME FRONT

The People's War: Britain 1939–1945, Angus Calder, Jonathan Cape Ltd, London, 1969; Pimlico edition 1992. Rightly described by one reviewer as a '*tour de force* of historical reconstruction', Calder's prodigiously researched and coldly objective account of life in Britain during the Second World War has often been emulated, but will never be equalled.

The Myth of the Blitz, Angus Calder, Jonathan Cape Ltd, London, 1991; Pimlico edition 1992. A much briefer, demanding and distinctly cynical 'deconstruction' of the Blitz and its abiding place in cherished national legend, with much cultural reference. The general sneering tone and what are now most dated references to the politics of Britain in the Thatcher era greatly diminish his thesis.

Wartime: Britain 1939–1945, Juliet Gardiner, Headline Book Publishing, London, 2004. An attempt, a generation on, to repeat Angus Calder's 1969 feat – and which inevitably suffers by comparison. There are but a few lines of reference to Clydebank.

Greenock Revisited, Stewart Gemmill, Greenock, 2000. An early and modestly priced e-book, available for download at http://www.greenockrevisited.-co.uk, with a full account of the Greenock Blitz and many sobering and evocative photographs of the devastation – taken by the late James Hall, under the usual wartime restraints – as well of the same streetscapes in our own day. Gemmill's moving and highly detailed book, suffused by deep knowledge of and love for his community, is the best account to date of Greenock's ordeal in May 1941 and includes some striking material – such as the notes of a German pilot who took part in the attack – as well as very many photographs, both in 1941 and barely a decade ago, that bring the experience of civilian bombing lurchingly home.

Living Through The Blitz, Tom Harrisson, William Collins Sons & Co. Ltd, London, 1976. Professor Harrisson, a larger-than-life personality with an impressive collection of personal enemies, was a noted anthropologist and, in 1936, founder of Mass Observation, which bade 'to supply accurate observations of everyday life and *real* (not just published) public moods', and this book – drawing on all its material for the first time – was the first to give a realistic impression of general sentiment and emotion under German bombing with a particularly good section on Clydeside (though he seemed disconcertingly to think Kintyre an island in the Hebrides). Harrisson was killed in a 1975 road accident in Bangkok as he was travelling home to correct the proofs, which may account for the subsequent and unjust neglect of this very important book.

Forgotten Voices of the Blitz and the Battle for Britain: A New History in the Words of the Men and Women on Both Sides, Joshua Levine, Ebury Press, London, 2006. Levine's fat oral history was produced in association with the Imperial War Museum. There is virtually no Scottish material.

How We Lived Then: A History of Everyday Life during the Second World War, Norman Longmate, Hutchinson & Co. Ltd, 1971; Pimlico edition 2002. Rather than seeking head-on challenge to the Calder tome, Longmate wisely narrowed his focus to the austerities, hardships and amusements of civilian life. There is occasional 'Clydeside' detail, and the book is still respected and in print.

A People's War, Peter Lewis, Channel 4 Books, London, 1986. A 'TV tie-in', accompanying the eponymous series produced by Thames Television for the Channel 4 station, Lewis's book is an exceptional instance of the genre, drawing on much original research for the programme and with a sharp, majestically-written new look at Britain's Second World War experience as it began rapidly to edge from popular memory. There is excellent, original Clydebank material.

Backs to the Wall: London Under Fire 1940–1945, Leonard Mosley, Weidenfeld and Nicolson Ltd, London, 1971. Still the best account of the 'Battle of London' ever written.

The First Day of the Blitz – September 7, 1940, Peter Stansky, Yale University Press, Newhaven and London, 2007. A highly detailed account, expertly executed and – as one reviewer observed – 'up there with the best' in the wallow of books about the Blitz.

Children of the Blitz – Memories of Wartime Childhood, ed. Robert Westall, Viking, London, 1985; Penguin edition, 1987. There is a chapter on what Westall – author of the 1975 children's novel *The Machine Gunners*, set in wartime Tyneside and later dramatised in 1983 by the BBC – is pleased to describe as the 'provincial Blitz', including unattributed memories of an Edinburgh boy about the home front in that city; but there is no Clydebank material.

BOOKS ABOUT THE SECOND WORLD WAR AND NAZI GERMANY

Berlin – The Downfall 1945, Anthony Beevor, Viking Ltd, London, 2002; Penguin Books edition, 2003. The definitive account of the Third Reich in her death throes.

The Third Reich – A New History, Michael Burleigh, Macmillan Publishers Ltd, London, 2000. The best one-volume account of Hitler, Nazi Germany, her crimes and the German experience of the Second World War ever likely to be written. Burleigh focuses – rightly – on Nazism as effectively a religion with all the trappings of religion and all the delusional danger of a false one.

Blood, Sweat and Arrogance and the Myths of Churchill's War, Gordon Corrigan, Weidenfeld and Nicolson, London, 2006; Phoenix edition, 2007. While instructive, corrective and on occasion salutary, Corrigan's effort is not quite so successful as his earlier deconstruction of abiding myths about the First World War, *Mud, Blood and Poppycock*. His evident admiration for the German generals and their army seems oddly shorn of moral context and, even allowing for the strength of many strictures on Winston Churchill, it is difficult not to feel Corrigan demeans himself in undue vehemence against an incontestably great man.

Fallen Eagle – The Last Days of the Third Reich, Robin Cross, Michael O'Mara Books Ltd, London, 1995; Caxton Editions, 2000. Though much shorter than the great Beevor account to come, it is concise and masterful with appalling detail of the bombing of Dresden.

Blood, Tears and Folly – An Objective Look at World War II, Len Deighton, Jonathan Cape Ltd, London, 1993; Pimlico edition, 2005. Though best known as a thriller writer of scrupulous research, Deighton is no slouch as a historian and this account of the first two years of the war is of impeccable authority, with unusually even examination of the German war machine and important detail of the available military technology on all sides.

The Face of the Third Reich, Joachim C. Fest, trans. Michael Bullock, Weidenfeld and Nicolson Ltd, London, 1970; Pelican edition 1972; first published as *Das Gesicht des Dritten Reiches: Profile einer totalitären Herrschaft*, R. Piper, Munich, 1963. One of the earliest, sober German accounts as to how his nation fell victim 'to a group of psychopaths', Fest's profile of Hermann Göring is especially good. Fest himself served in the war and was taken prisoner by the Allies.

The Second World War, John Keegan, Century Hutchinson Ltd, London, 1989. For many years a senior lecturer at Sandhurst military college, Keegan's sober, scholarly and accessible book remains one of the best one-volume histories of the war available.

Why the Allies Won, Richard Overy, Jonathan Cape Ltd, London, 1995; second Pimlico edition (fully revised and with epilogue), 2006. The definitive and most readable analysis of how the Allies achieved in 1945 a victory, which 'though comprehensive – was far from inevitable'. Overy explores the tactical, strategic, technological, industrial and even the moral reasons why Nazi Germany and militarist Japan finally crashed to defeat, from a very strong position, in the Second World War.

On the Natural History of Destruction, W.G. Sebald, trans. Anthea Bell, Penguin Books Ltd (Hamish Hamilton imprint), London, 2003; first published as *Luftkrieg und Literatur*, Carl Hanser Verlag, 1999. Sebald's dark book was the first serious German exploration of their experience of Allied bombing during the Second World War as reflected in literary fiction; and how so many German 'writers allowed themselves to write it out of their experience and avoid articulating the horror'. It is not comfortable reading, though one does wonder if Sebald – who died in 2001 – entirely grasped the lack of moral equivalence between terror-bombing by an aggressive, criminal state under totalitarian dictatorship and terror-bombing in defence by the Western civilisation it threatened to destroy.

The Rise and Fall of the Third Reich – A History of Nazi Germany, William L. Shirer, Secker and Warburg Ltd, New York, 1959. Righteous, American and occasionally strident; but a modern classic by a distinguished American correspondent who – as CBS radio correspondent in pre-Pearl Harbour Berlin – personally knew many of the Nazi leaders and who invented the world news round-up style of broadcast used in all outlets to this day. Shirer was in 1955 granted full access to all the archive material of Nazi Germany captured intact by the Allies and, while now in some respects rather dated, his book is a world-renowned text never since out of print.

BOOKS ABOUT BRITISH HISTORY AND POLITICS

Harold Macmillan – A Biography, Nigel Fisher, Weidenfeld and Nicolson Ltd, London, 1982. An early and affectionate portrait of an enduring statesman and early foe of the National Government's appeasement policy, since rather eclipsed by Alastair Horne's two-volume life and other recent studies.

A Spirit Undaunted – The Political Role of George VI, Robert Rhodes-James; Little, Brown and Company, London, 1998; Abacus edition 1999. Rhodes-James has a particularly sharp chapter on the domestic difficulties of the post-war Labour government and the frightful winter of 1946–47.

A History of the English People, Paul Johnson, revised edition, Weidenfeld Paperbacks, London, 1985; originally published as *The Offshore Islanders*, Weidenfeld and Nicolson Ltd, London, 1972. Described by one reviewer as a 'wild, eccentric, highly prejudiced, polemical and most readable whirl through our island story,' Johnson's analysis of British trades unionism is especially interesting as, in 1972, he was still outspokenly allied with the Left, moving to the Thatcherite Right at decade's end.

A History of the Modern World – From 1917 to the 1990s, Paul Johnson, revised edition Weidenfeld Paperbacks, London, 1991 – first edition, 1984. A stimulating and at times very original account of the planet between the world wars, and subsequently.

The Birth of the Modern – World Society 1815–1830, Paul Johnson, Weidenfeld and Nicolson Ltd, 1991; Orion Books Ltd paperback, 1992. Useful material especially on the technology of the Industrial Revolution and the impact of the 'Age of Steam'.

The Life and Times of George V, Denis Judd, Weidenfeld and Nicolson Ltd, London, 1973. A neat account of a man rightly described as our 'first great constitutional monarch', in a series of informed biographical essays on the English and British monarchy which should not be despised for its remorseless marketing as a book-club option through the 1970s and early 1980s.

King George V, Kenneth Rose, Weidenfeld and Nicolson Ltd, London, 1983, Phoenix Press edition, 2000. The definitive life of our present Queen's grand-father and one of the truly great biographies in the last 30 years.

British Prime Ministers and Other Essays, A.J.P. Taylor, Allen Lane/The Penguin Press, London, 1999; Penguin Books edition, 2000. A posthumous collection of articles and lectures by a remarkable Left-leaning historian, an early star of British television (famous for his immaculate, unscripted lectures) and with not the least aversion to controversy.

A Prime Minister on Prime Ministers, Harold Wilson, David Paradine Histories Ltd/Weidenfeld and Nicolson Ltd/Michael Joseph Ltd, London, 1977. While no doubt the recently retired premier had the aid of researchers and some ghost-writing, his voice is nevertheless evident in eminently sensible essays on, for instance, Lloyd George, Baldwin, MacDonald, Chamberlain, Churchill and Attlee. Wilson rightly declined to compromise the book with reflections on holders of the office after 1963.

BOOKS ABOUT SCOTTISH HISTORY AND POLITICS

Without Quarter – A Biography of Tom Johnston, Russell Galbraith, Mainstream Publishing, Edinburgh and London, 1995. Though at times very loose and colloquial in tone, it is a fair assessment of the man universally held as the greatest-ever occupant of the Scottish Office.

Restless Nation, Alan Clements, Kenny Farquharson and Kirsty Wark, Mainstream Publishing, Edinburgh and London, 1996. Another TV tie-in – with a BBC Scotland series – and an illustrated, very accessible account of post-war Scottish politics and the devolution debate.

Above Scotland – The National Collection of Aerial Photography, David Cowley and James Crawford, Royal Commission on the Ancient and Historical Monuments of Scotland, Edinburgh, 2009. There are some majestic images of old industrial Clydebank.

Shinwell Talking – A Conversational Biography to Celebrate His Hundredth Birthday, John Doxat, Quiller Press Ltd, London, 1984. A delightful selection of warm, waspish and often very funny Shinwell table-talk.

Among Friends, Alastair Dunnett, Century Publishing Co. Ltd, London, 1984. Even by the standards of self-regarding late-life memoir, Dunnett's autobiography is at times rather hard to take. It is best on his generally successful period as the editor of two Scottish national newspapers, the *Daily Record* and *The Scotsman*.

The Scottish Church 1688–1843, Andrew L. Drummond and James Bulloch, The Saint Andrew Press, Edinburgh, 1973. The first in a succession of sparkling, immaculately researched volumes in Scottish church history by two distinguished parish ministers, with much social and cultural insight, especially on the Industrial Revolution.

The Church in Late Victorian Scotland 1874–1900, Andrew L. Drummond and James Bulloch, Edinburgh, 1978. This proved the final volume in a trilogy – Bulloch's death in 1981 precluded a fourth – with much important and at times damning social comment on the conditions in which most ordinary Scots lived and the fumbling efforts of assorted churches to do nothing very much about it.

The Road to Home Rule – Images of Scotland's Cause, Christopher Harvie and Peter Jones, Polygon at Edinburgh/Edinburgh University Press Ltd, Edinburgh, 2000. A heavily illustrated but intelligent look at modern Scotland with a particularly good chapter on the early Labour movement.

The Political Guide to Modern Scotland, Gerry Hassan and Douglas Fraser, Politico's Publishing, London, 2004. An updating of an earlier, 2000 Hassan volume – with Fraser taking the place of Peter Lynch – the book's emphasis is as a profile of the Scottish Parliament and Westminster constituencies, with much additional reference material besides. The study of the Clydebank and Milngavie division is especially good.

Katharine Atholl 1874–1960 – Against the Tide, S.J. Hetherington, Aberdeen University Press, Aberdeen, 1989. A solid if at times rather leaden study of this colourful politician, who destroyed her own political career in passionate opposition to appeasement and the Chamberlain administration's settlement of the Munich crisis. A new biography is understood to be in preparation by Elizabeth Quigley.

Our Scots Noble Families, Thomas Johnston, with preface by J. Ramsay MacDonald MP, 'Forward' Publishing Co. Ltd, Glasgow, 1999; modern paperback edition, Argyll Publishing, Glendaruel, 1999, with an introduction by Brian D. Osborne. Tom Johnston's pitiless, scrupulously researched account of the intrigue, robbery and rapine by which our eminent so-called aristocratic houses won lands, power and fortune caused a mild furore at the time and has still the power to shock. Osborne's essay in the new edition is informative and astute. He points out, inter alia, that until after the Great War Johnston's native county was always referred to as Dumbartonshire – 'Dunbartonshire' is a modern affectation, though probably ineradicable.

The Diary of Kenneth A. MacRae – A Record of Fifty Years in the Christian Ministry, ed. Iain H Murray, The Banner of Truth Trust, Edinburgh, 1980.

A History of the Scottish People 1560–1830, T.C. Smout, William Collins and Sons Ltd, London, 1969. An important social history of Scotland, acclaimed at the time and still regarded as a standard work.

A Century of the Scottish People 1830–1950, T.C. Smout, Collins, London, 1986. A 'detailed exploration of a complex world of deprivation and social division', with an angry if disciplined moral core that lends it momentum and integrity.

The Scottish Secretaries, David Torrance, Birlinn Ltd, Edinburgh, 2006. With a sparkling foreword by James Naughtie, this splendidly researched and written book by a young and respected journalist – who, unusually for our day, combines that trade with serious scholarship – deserves to be more widely read. The profile of Tom Johnston is just one of many astute, often faintly feline assessments. Torrance has since written a widely praised life of George Younger and an assessment of the Thatcher years in Scotland, and at the time of writing was completing an eagerly-awaited biography of Alex Salmond.

BOOKS ABOUT GLASGOW, THE CLYDE AND CLYDE STEAMERS

Clydebank 100 – Ships from Clydebank and District, Colin Castle, West Dunbartonshire Libraries and Museums, Dumbarton, 1996. A reverential but fact-packed volume profiling 100 notable vessels, from the early transatlantic liner *Bothnia* (1874) to the *Queen Elizabeth 2* of 1967.

Clyde River and Other Steamers, C.L.D. Duckworth and G.E. Langmuir; Brown, Son and Ferguson Ltd, Glasgow, 1990 (4th edition; earlier editions in 1937, 1946 and 1972, with a third edition supplement in 1982). This partnership of two Glasgow shipping enthusiasts – though Langmuir survived Duckworth by over 40 years – invented, before the Second World War, what has since become an entire genre of books on British coastal shipping.

West Highland Steamers, C.L.D. Duckworth and G.E. Langmuir; Brown, Son and Ferguson Ltd, Glasgow, 1987 (4th edition; earlier editions in 1935, 1950 and 1967) – another much-loved work, with particular emphasis on David MacBrayne Ltd and its successors.

Up Oor Close – Memories of Domestic Life in Glasgow Tenements 1910–1945, Jean Faley, White Cockade Publishing, Oxford, 1990 (in association with the Springburn Museum Trust.) A warm, anecdotal account of pre-war Scottish working-class life.

Glasgow from the Air – 75 Years of Aerial Photography, Carol Foreman, Birlinn Ltd (in association with the Royal Commission on the Ancient and

Historical Monuments of Scotland), Edinburgh, 2006. Foreman's judicious text links many spectacular plates, including some of Clydebank and others emphasising the changes in the upper Clyde environs and economy even since the late 1960s.

Down the Clyde, Jack House, W. and R. Chambers Ltd, Edinburgh and London, 1959. A delightful little book by 'Mr Glasgow' himself; Jack House (1906–91) was a much-loved city journalist and broadcaster and a light, popular writer on all things Scottish, of abundant common sense and entire lack of pretension. A cheerful 'aristologist' – he assured young reporters this was an expert in the art of dining – he maintained that a 'real steak pie' was the one reliable test of a good restaurant; and that the very best steak pie in the country was to be found at the Boulevard Hotel, Clydebank. *Down the Clyde* is a book evidently written for sale to excursion-steamer passengers heading all the way 'doon the wa'er' from the city centre at Bridge Wharf, identifying every shipyard and chain-ferry and resort and stately house and Highland promontory one might sea, with the odd tasty murder thrown in: an evocative and gentle account of a river much changed and a Scotland largely gone, complete with contemporary advertisements for cigarettes, magazines, hotels and car-hire.

Portrait of the Clyde, Jack House, Robert Hale Ltd, London, 1969. A larger but somehow more subdued description including, this time, the upper Lanarkshire reaches of the river.

Cardross – The Village in Days Gone By – An Illustrated Historical Walk, Arthur F. Jones, Dumbarton District Libraries, 1985. A gentle, illustrated booklet with original and detailed material on the Cardross Blitz.

Echoes of Old Clyde Paddle Wheels – The First Sixty Years from the Comet of 1812, Andrew McQueen, Glasgow, 1923 – modern paperback edition by Strong Oak Press, Stevenage, 2001. A warm account of the pioneering years of timber hulls and steeple-engines, in facsimile of the original type.

The Victorian Summer of the Clyde Steamers – 1864–1888, Alan J.S. Paterson, David and Charles Ltd, Newton Abbot, 1972; modern paperback by John Donald, an imprint of Birlinn Ltd, Edinburgh, 2001.

The Golden Years of the Clyde Steamers – 1889–1914, Alan J.S. Paterson, David and Charles Ltd, Newton Abbot, 1972; modern paperback by John Donald, an imprint of Birlinn Ltd, Edinburgh, 2001. Two classic studies, affectionate and detailed, of great days on the Firth of Clyde.

A MacBrayne Memoir, Brian Patton, Martins the Printers Ltd, Berwick-upon-Tweed, 2009. A splendid volume fat with photographs and with a very good chapter on the 1878 *Columba*.

The Kingdom of MacBrayne, Nick S. Robins and Donald E. Meek, Birlinn Ltd, Edinburgh, 2006; updated paperback edition, 2008. A magnificently produced and lavishly-illustrated book.

Along Great Western Road – An Illustrated History of Glasgow's West End, Gordon R. Urquhart, Stenlake Publishing, Ayrshire, 2000; revised edition, 2002. An elegant coffee-table volume which, though containing only evocative black-and-white images, was a critical and commercial success.

The Clyde Passenger Steamer – Its Rise and Progress During the Nineteenth Century from the 'Comet' of 1812 to the 'King Edward' of 1901. Captain James Williamson, James MacLehose and Sons, Glasgow, 1904. An important and lively, beautifully written text that can be readily viewed or downloaded online. It is also offered in paperback by various print-on-demand companies, either side of the Atlantic, though a first-edition can now be found without undue difficulty for less than £40.

ARCHIVE MATERIAL

Contemporary newspaper reports of the Clydebank Blitz – and many other aspects of the Home Front in 1941 – are all but useless to the historian; the British press was, for the duration of the Second World War, under heavy censorship by the Ministry of Information.

An extensive 'Clydebank Blitz' collection of papers, press-cuttings and photographs is held by West Dunbartonshire Council and may readily be viewed.

Various, dry, statistic-laden and cautious reports on the Scottish experience of German bombing were prepared during the war for assorted departments of government local and national. The most important are the *Return on Analysis of Casualties of raids on Clydeside on 13/14 and 14/15 March 1941*, published by Glasgow City Corporation in 1947 and which may be consulted in the City Archives and Special Collections, Records of the Town Clerk, at the Mitchell Library, 210 North Street, Glasgow. They also hold *Raids on Clydeside – Office of the Regional Commissioner, Scotland*, in the Report of the Office of Public Works 1938–1948. *Scotland Under Fire – Note on Enemy Air Attacks from October 1939 to February 29 1944* was published by the Press Office, St Andrew's House, Edinburgh, on 13 October 1944.

WEBSITES

There are many helpful websites and discussion boards on the Clydebank Blitz and the wider bombing raids in west-central Scotland during the Second World War. However, today's glowing page on the worldwide web is tomorrow's vacant, yawning URL: one promising site, 'theclydebankstory.com', simply disappeared as I was writing this book; and while there are some useful pages on Wikipedia the reality of 'Wikivandalism' and its openness to subversion by every sort of prankster or anorak mean it must be used with great caution.

The BBC website contains a wealth of oral testimony and photographs on 'Home Front Britain', of which this Clydebank example – http://www.bbc.co.uk/ww2peopleswar/stories/53/a1112653.shtml – is typical.

The Clydebank Blitz page of local sage and artist Tom McKendrick – http://www.tommckendrick.com/code/blitzintro_alt.htm – is well worth a visit, not least for his powerful paintings and images.

Glasgow City Council maintain a site, 'The Blitz on Clydeside' – http://www.glasgow.gov.uk/en/Residents/Libraries/Collections/Blitz/Clydebank/

More detailed still is 'The Clydebank Blitz in Words and Pictures', laid on by West Dunbartonshire Council: http://www.west-dunbarton.gov.uk/arts-culture-and-libraries/cultural-services/heritage/clydebank-blitz/

There are two very useful message boards, with a wealth of anecdote, including this one in the 'Glasgow Guide' network – http://discuss.glasgow-guide.co.uk/index.php?showtopic=5396 – and a splendid 'Hidden Glasgow' page, 'Bombs over Glasgow in WW2' – http://www.hiddenglasgow.com/forums/viewtopic.php?f=15&t=2878&sid=044182fbc031e0f7390-c6af0862e41d7

I am greatly indebted to this fine website for much interesting detail on the *Queen Mary* – http://www.thecunarders.co.uk/Queen%20Mary.htm. And evocative Pathé footage of her naming and launch can be viewed at http://www.youtube.com/watch?v=VfuhUzkSdI8.

FILM

Iain McGuinness, a rising Clydebank talent, has produced two very worthwhile documentaries about his community, readily available on DVD or download. His very first film, *Post-Blitz Clydebank*, was born as a student project and made for only £3,000, with an extended 28-minute 'director's cut' made available in March 2008: it can be bought online at http://www.post-blitzclydebank.co.uk/index.php

Clydebank Through A Lens is a worthwhile study of the town from the 1960s to the 1980s, with evocative archive footage and deftly shot, sensitive interviews; the film was released in December 2009, and can be ordered from this website: http://www.clydebankthroughalens.co.uk/m@ilshot/clydebank_through_a_lens.html.

INDEX

Inveraray 268
Invergordon 253
Inverness 38
Iona, isle of 252
Iona (1864), PS 39
Iraq 200
Ireland 13, 19, 60, 63, 66, 268
Irish Free State 66, 88
Irish Guards 89
IRA (Provisional Irish Republican Army) 13
Irish immigration to Scotland 46–47, 52;
     prejudice against, 46, 53–54, 56; from Keir
     Hardie, 56; 246
Irish Famine 46
Irish Land League 54
iron industry 29, 36
'Isolationist' policy in America 17
Italy 14

J & G Thomson Ltd 21, 22; bought out by
     John Brown's, 22–23, 24; 25, 36;
     construction of PS *Columba*, 38
Jacobite movement 50
Jamaica Street, Glasgow 27
James Gray Street 204
James MacCulloch, tobacconist and
     newsagent 81
James Young & Co., soap factory, Glasgow
     204
Janetta Street 129, 169, 229
Janetta Street School (new Clydebank High
     School campus) 130–131, 161, 169, 189,
     190, 194, 229
Japan, surrender of 246; post-war industry,
     250
Jeffrey, Andrew 106, 108, 119, 128, 129,
     131, 132, 143–144, 145, 147, 149, 158,
     161, 162, 165, 171, 176, 178, 179, 190,
     191, 203, 209, 210, 212, 213
Jellicoe Street 112, 124–127, 143, 269
Jericho Street 140
Jeschonnek, Hans, Luftwaffe Chief of Staff
     238
jet flight, pre-war German disinterest in 91
Jewish slave-labour sabotage of V2 rockets
     239
Jews, Nazi persecution of 12, 18
Jodl, Alfred 12, 242–243, 249
John Brown & Co. Ltd 24, 57, 68 *et seq*;

80, 103, 104, 107, 118, 136–137, 138,
     143, 176–177, 210, 215, 216, 219–220,
     249; inadequacy for modern oil tanker
     production, 250; merger into Upper Clyde
     Shipbuilders, 253; sale of and final
     disappearance, 254; asbestos risk, 259–260
John Brown Engineering 254
John Brown's Recreation Ground 267
John Knox Street 79, 80, 81, 102
John McChleary's shoe shop 81
John Wood & Co., Port Glasgow 34
Johnson, Paul 251
Johnston, Tom 56–57, 59, 62, 66, 67; mixed
     political legacy, 76; and Clydebank
     concerns, 102; and Clydebank Blitz, 121;
     at mass-funeral in Dalnottar, 193; and
     official casualty figures, 195; worries over
     Scottish nationalism, 196; legacy of, 253
Johnstone, Renfrewshire 245
Johnstones of Helensburgh 234
Johnstone, Sergeant 213–214
Jones, Arthur F. 207, 208, 209
Jones, Peter 57
Jordanhill, Glasgow 8, 22, 26
Jordanhill College School 9, 259
Judd, Denis 73
Junkers 88 bomber 6, 92, 108, 112, 115,
     137, 168, 196, 210, 211, 213, 231, 236
'Jupiter Complex' 86
Jura, Isle of 204

Kampfgruppe 100, German 'Pathfinder'
     bomber-force 94, 106, 111, 113, 217
Kampfgeschwader 100, elite 'Pathfinder'
     force 111, 217
Katharine, Duchess of Atholl 84
Kay, Billy 79, 100, 131, 136, 140, 144, 152,
     160, 170, 175, 184, 232, 246, 264
Kaystone Road, Knightswood 162
Kearns, Denis 233–234
Kearns family 233–234
Keil School 109
Keir Hardie Hall 15
Keitel, Wilhelm 12
Kelburn Street, Barrhead 165
Kelly, Henry, Town Clerk and Civil Defence
     Controller of Clydebank 99–100; 106,
     107, 142, 145, 146, 151, 160; destruction
     of home on second raid, 162; 170